hali • Mario M. Cuomo

Covey • R. J. Goldstone • Mairead Corrigan

orman Vincent Peale • Dr. Homer A. Jack •

n • Asghar Ali Engineer • Rabbi Phillip S.

imer • Raiman Panikkar • Bishop James K.

Richard Deats • Ann & John Rush • Sir

a Majid) • Robert L. Holmes • Rev. Jose

vid Dellinger • Pamela S. Meidell • Dr.

hi • Alvin F. Poussaint • William Lucy

rdaro • Michael Boover • Edward M. Eissey

n • Fredrick Franck • Ien van den Heuvel

lly E. Hanson • John M. Richardson, jr.

on C. Zahn • Mubarak Awad • Laura M.

rnie S. Siegel • Andrey E. Serikov • Glen

ite • Martin E. Hellman • Brent Jonsson

ddick • Walter Wink • Kate Lebow • Terry

ers • Bill McKibben • Milan Opocensky

n Willson • Patricia McCarthy • Michael

• Father Niall O'Brien • Michael True

McAleer • Sister Falaka Fattah • Marilou

Kerr Peirce • Lou Torok • L. W. T. Wolcott

Maxine Hong Kingstone • Arun Gandhi

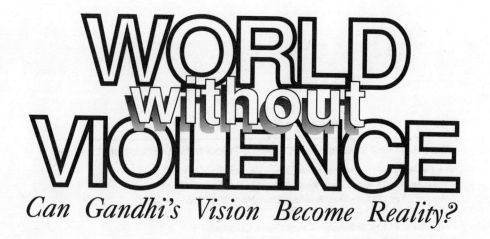

WORLD without VIOLENCE

Can Gandhi's Vision Become Reality?

NONSECTARIAN
NONPROFIT ORGANISATION

M. K. Gandhi Institute For Nonviolence

Christian Brothers University,
650 East Parkway South,
Memphis, TN 38104.
U.S.A.
Tel. (901)725 0815
Fax. (901)725 0846

WILEY EASTERN LIMITED
NEW AGE INTERNATIONAL LIMITED
New Delhi ● Bangalore ● Bombay ● Calcutta ● Guwahati
Hyderabad ● Lucknow ● Madras ● Pune ● London (U.K.)

WILEY EASTERN LIMITED · NEW AGE INTERNATIONAL PUBLISHERS LIMITED

NEW DELHI   : 4835/24 Ansari Road, Daryaganj, New Delhi 110 002
BANGALORE : 27, Bull Temple Road, Basavangudi, Bangalore 560 004
BOMBAY   : 128A, Noorani Building, Block No. 3, First Floor, L.J. Road,
              Mahim, Bombay 400 016
CALCUTTA   : 40/8, Ballygunge Circular Road, Calcutta 700 019
GUWAHATI   : Pan Bazar, Rani Bari, Guwahati 781 001
HYDERABAD : 1-2-412/9, Gaganmahal, Near A V College, Domalguda, Hyderabad 500 029
LUCKNOW   : 18, Pandit Madan Mohan Malviya Marg, Lucknow 226 001
MADRAS   : 20, 2nd Main Road, Kasthuribai Nagar, Adyar, Madras 600 020
PUNE   : Flat No. 2, Building No. 7, Indira Co-op. Housing Society Ltd.
              Indira Heights, Paud Fatta, Erandawane, Karve Road, Pune 411 038
LONDON   : Wishwa Prakashan Ltd., Spantech House, Lagham Road, South Godstone,
              Surrey, RH9 8HB, U.K.

ISBN: 81-224-0674-2

Published by H.S. Poplai for Wiley Eastern Limited, 4835/24, Ansari Road, Daryaganj,
New Delhi 110 002. Typeset by Types & Graphics, 5; Shraddhanjali, Sir Vithaldas
Nagar, Sarojini Naidu Road, Santacruz West, Bombay 400 054 and printed at Baba
Barkha Nath Printers, Kirti Nagar, New Delhi

                                                        Printed in India.

Production: M.I. Thomas

Arun Gandhi
Aug. 2, 1995
P.S.U.

*This book is dedicated to my nephew, **Kush**,*
who, like millions before him around the world,
*was brutally murdered on **December 14, 1993,** in **South Africa**.*

Acknowledgments

There are so many people I need to thank for the birth of this Institute and this volume, both of which are inter-related, that I am afraid I may overlook someone. So, at the very outset I offer my sincerest apologies for any oversight or lapse.

I would like to thank the many people who readily responded to my invitation to write and the few who wrote but we could not accommodate in this volume for one reason or another. Very special thanks are due to Rita and Gary Manson for the design of the jacket of the book.

Sincere thanks also need to go to Bro. Theodore Drahmann, the former President of Christian Brothers University in Memphis, without whose vision and verve the Institute would not have started in Memphis. Others who made the process of birthing easy were James Gilliland, Harry Moore, Gerard Vanderhaar, Carol Chumney and William Zaccola. The Board of Directors of the Institute, past and present, the well-wishers, volunteers, donors and the warm and hospitable community in Memphis added to the sustenance and growth of the Institute.

Thanks are also due to : Ms. Mertie Buckman for donating $5,000 to make this book possible, to all the members of the Board for coming up with names and addresses; to Tom Yellin and his secretary at ABC News in New York for finding addresses, to my daughter, Archana Prasad, for pouring through volumes of Who's Who at her library in Henrietta, New York; to Life Magazine for sharing their celebrity list, to Carol Lynn Yellin for her expert advice, to my son, Tushar, in Bombay, India, for doing the Typesetting at short notice, to Mr. Malay Mishra at the Indian Embassy in Washington for helping find a publisher, to the publishers for accepting the challenge of bringing out this book in time for the October 2, 1994, commemoration and above all, many, many thanks are due to my wife, Sunanda, who shouldered the burden of typing and retyping manuscripts and letters with some assistance from Gabrielle Songe and Dee Colwell.

This volume is the result of the combined efforts and dedication of many.

Message from President Robinson

During my State Visit to India in 1993 I had the great privilege to visit the Sabarmati Ashram on the anniversary of the birth of Mahatma Gandhi. He inspired me as a young person, then as a lawyer involved in human rights and in the status of women. Now as President of Ireland I find that the values of Gandhi continue to be relevant, inspiring and vital to our world.

We in Ireland esteem and value the enormous contributions of Mahatma Gandhi, Gandhiji, to the whole world through the values he advocated and lived, the values of truth, non-violence and co-operative working together.

I am delighted to have this opportunity to be associated with the further study and appreciation of Mahatma Gandhi, for the future of our planet and its development along the principles laid down by this great son of India.

MARY ROBINSON
PRESIDENT OF IRELAND

CONTENTS

Foreword
Arun Gandhi   *13*

M. K. Gandhi On Nonviolence
M. K. Gandhi   *18*

Rumblings Of Discontent
Hillary Rodham Clinton   *22*

Beyond Peace : Towards A World Without Violence
Boutros Boutros Ghali   *29*

Eye For An Eye - Injustice
Mario M. Cuomo   *31*

A Crisis Of Meaning
Bill Bradley   *33*

The Dilemma Of The Absolute Pacifist
Linus Pauling & Daisaku Ikeda   *36*

The Way To A Valueless Society
Stephen R. Covey   *39*

Can South Africa Achieve A Peaceful Non-Racial Democracy
R. J. Goldstone   *45*

Politics With Principles?
Mairead Corrigan Maguire   *47*

A Birthday Letter To Gandhi
Pam McAllister   *55*

Melting The Heart Of Stone
Carl Sagan   *57*

Spiritual Awakening
Norman Vincent Peale   *64*

Religious Intolerance India's Greatest Tragedy
Since Gandhi's Assassination
Dr. Homer A. Jack   *66*

Science Without Humanity
Alan Lightman   *74*

When God Takes Care Of You
Andrew Young   *76*

The Power Of Greed
Harry Schwarz   85

Islam And Nonviolence
Asghar Ali Engineer   88

Caught In A Web Of Negativity
Rabbi Phillip S. Berg   91

Gandhi The Tactician
John Kenneth Galbraith   95

Gandhi In South Africa
Nadine Gordimer   97

The Nine Sutras Of Peace
Raimon Panikkar   98

Give Nonviolence A Chance
Bishop James K. Mathews   106

Violation Of Gender Rights
Ellen Goodman   112

A World Without Violence?
Richard Ernst   115

The Kingdom Of God
Richard Deats   116

The Pilgrims Of Peace
Ann & John Rush   118

The Eighth Blunder
Sir Ranulph Fiennes   122

A Vision Quest
Rev. Lila C. Forest (Rabiya Majid)   123

From Lenin To Gandhi
Robert L. Holmes   125

The Power Of Love
Rev. Jose "Chencho" Alas   127

When, When, O God Shall Men Be Brother To Man
Swami Nirmalananda   129

The Degradation Of The Masters
David Dellinger   131

Experiments With Nonviolence In The Nuclear Age
Pamela S. Meidell   134

Gandhi The Political Moralist
Dr. Raghavan Iyer   *138*

Would You Ever Kill?
Bruce Kent   *146*

Human Rights In China
Fang Li-Zhi   *148*

Violent Means = Violent Ends
Alvin F. Poussaint   *150*

Guns Are As American As Appelpie
William Lucy   *152*

What Did Gandhi Mean By Satyagraha?
Sissela Bok   *155*

Transforming Relationships In The Balkans
Margaréta Inglestam   *159*

A Call For A Resistance Church
Frank Cordaro   *165*

The Things That Make For Peace
Michael Boover   *171*

The Kingdom Of God Is Within Us
Michael Boover   *172*

Song For The Cleansing The Cleanser & The Cleansed
Michael Boover   *173*

Light Of Love
Edward M. Eissey   *175*

Peace Starts With Me
Jean Bethke Elshtain   *177*

Great Contemporary Tragedy
Dr. Eknath Easwaran   *179*

The Dove Of Peace
Fredrick Frank   *187*

Dilemma Of A Politician
Ien van den Heuvel   *188*

Reflections On Gandhi And Democracy
Benjamin R. Barber   *191*

Reflections On Violence In Northern Ireland
Richard R. Fleck   *196*

The Power Of Personal Example In Overcoming Racism
  Holly E. Hanson   *198*

Lessons From Sri Lanka : Politics Without Principles
  John M. Richardson, Jr.   *203*

Anger, Retribution And Violence
  Raymond M. Smullyan   *210*

Religious Intolerance Leads To Violence
  Udo Schafer   *212*

Is Fearlessness Possible?
  Gordon C. Zahn   *215*

Nonviolence In The Context Of Palastinian Independence
  Mubarak Awad, Laura M. Bain, David T. Richie   *218*

In Search Of A Definition
  Paul Lansu   *223*

Reverence For Life
  Bernie S. Siegel   *226*

Nonviolence A New Way For Russia
  Andrey E. Serikov   *228*

Pursuit Of True Knowledge
  Glen Lockhart   *231*

Ten Fringe Benefits In A World Without Violence
  Steve O'Donnel   *234*

Morality And Politics : The Lessons Of Gandhi
  Grazina Miniotaite   *235*

Resist Not Evil
  Martin E. Hellman   *237*

Get Rid Of The Prophets
  Bernt Johnsson   *240*

The Causes Of War
  John M. Swomley   *242*

Commitment To A Culture Of Nonviolence
  Hans Kung   *244*

The Recipe For Violence
  Anita Roddick   *246*

Nonviolence Does Work
  Walter Wink   *248*

"Whom To Be Blamed"
  Kate Lebow — 250

World Without Violence
  Terry Michael Tracy — 256

Peace Through Religion
  Zena Sorabjee — 257

The Face Of Greed
  Barry Sanders — 260

Where Happiness Hangs Like A Fog
  Bill McKibben — 268

Christian Perspective Of Nonviolence
  Milan Opocensky — 270

The Oneness of Humankind
  Nathan Rutstein — 273

Tolstoy, Nonviolence And Russia
  T. A. Pavlova — 275

The Imperative Of Revolutionary Nonviolence
  S. Brian Willson — 280

Worship : Surrender, Sacrifice, Freedom
  Patricia McCarthy — 279

Peacemaking Through Nonviolence
  Michael Nagler — 289

Nonviolence Begins With Breakfast
  Ingrid Newkirk — 300

Satyagraha And Liberation Of Russia In 1905
  Yelena Demidova — 304

The Philippines : Its Time To Listen To Gandhi
  Father Niall O'Brien — 307

Knowledge Without Character : Power, The University And The Violence Of The Status Quo
  Michael True — 313

The Power Of Suffering Love
  James McGinnis — 319

A Mother's Anguish
  Dorothy Walpole — 325

Knowledge With Character
    John McAleer   *326*

Poems

A New World Order
    Sister Falaka Fattah   *329*
Out Of Ashes Peace Will Rise
    Marilou Awiakta   *330*
When Earth Becomes An "It"
    Marilou Awiakta   *331*
Dying Back
    Marilou Awiakta   *332*
Jewel Of The Universe
    Don Mullan   *333*
Gandhi Of Porbundar
    Don Mullan   *335*
A Lofty Diadem
    John Jeffs   *336*
Hank The Drummer
    Maggi Kerr Peirce   *337*
Enough
    Maggi Kerr Peirce   *339*
A New World Prayer
    Lou Torok   *341*
Beyond Violence
    L. W. T. Wolcott   *344*
A Sleep Of Prisoners
    Christopher Fry   *347*

Photographs (Central Insert)

King's Inspiration
    Bishop James K. Mathews   *I*
Balance Of Power
    Dewa Nyoman Batuan   *II & III*
Peace Flag
    Maxine Hong Kingston   *IV*

Foreword

Among the many silly questions we asked Grandfather (Mohandas K. Gandhi) was one that always evoked a toothless, throaty, guffaw. As a 12 year old grandson privileged to live with him during the most historic period in his life (1946-47), I often asked him this question simply to hear him laugh. It was so infectious and hearty. The silly question we kept asking was : How long would you like to live ?

Each time Grandfather responded with a twinkle in his eyes : "Well, about 125 years." Sometimes he would go on to explain : "There is so much I want to do that I need at least 125 years to accomplish it."

October 2, 1994, marks the 125th anniversary of his birth. If he had had his wish would the world be a better place than it is today? We could debate this question for the next 125 years and not reach an answer. Does that mean a debate is futile? No. I believe debate and dialogue are cornerstones of the philosophy of nonviolence and can never be futile. If approached intelligently, and with an open mind willing to learn, dialogue is the wisdom that enlightens human minds.

A lesson that I learned from Grandfather in 1946 is one that needs to be learned by all human beings especially now when our minds shrink in direct proportion to our expanding purses. Grandfather said : "Remember always that your mind should be like a room with many open windows. Let the breeze flow in from all the windows but refuse to be blown away by any one." Closed minds, like closed rooms, become intolerable and unlivable. There was another related lesson that he taught me.

"A good education is a combination of book experience and life experience. Book experience gives you knowledge and a career. Life experience gives you understanding and the ability to build human relationships." The best career in the world can only bring material benefits which would be of little consequence if one did not have the ability to understand, accept and, most importantly, appreciate different cultures, customs, creed and races. Historians and philosophers will disagree with the contention that human relations are today worse than they ever were in human history. History has been moving in circles not because this is natural but because we refuse to learn lessons from history to avoid previous mistakes and move forward. The question we must ask is : Should we be going round in circles or should human progress be measured vertically moving upwards.

Grandfather believed in Plato's theory that human beings are basically good and that they succumb to evil circumstances in life. Can we begin to change those evil circumstances or must generations of human beings wallow in the corrupting filth of modern life? The answer to this question lies in our perceptions and priorities.

So, what has this got to do with the 125th birth anniversary of Gandhi's birth? A great deal. The title of this book says it all. Can his vision become reality or is it futile to even try? There are two traits that I inherited from my parents and grandparents. To act on an impulse and to consider nothing impossible. So, in the true Gandhian spirit I woke one morning in June, 1993, fired with an impulse. Can I put the question : **World Without Violence — Can Gandhi's Vision Become Reality?**, to important people around the world and ask them to write their honest opinions? The first important person I asked was my wife, Sunanda, who has been an equal partner in life. She said : "Go for it." I went.

The Institute invited a cross section of men and women from around the world ranging from President George Bush to the Dalai Lama and hundreds of others in between. That both President Bush and the Venerable Dalai Lama declined our invitation is unfortunate. We wanted to incorporate all points of view. That we couldn't get people to disagree was not because we did not try. On reflection, it seems obvious that not even President Bush, Gen. Schwarzkopf or Gen. Colin Powel would want to say in writing that a World Without Violence is an unrealistic Utopian ideal.

This book is not a commemorative volume but, hopefully, an inspirational volume. Grandfather never did enjoy birthday celebrations nor did he like commemorative books. "My life is my message," he said and I think that sums up the purpose of this book. He showed us how to live nonviolently and resolve conflicts peacefully. He also said : "My life is an experiment with Truth" and hoped that generations to come would continue that experiment. Just as a CEO of a large corporation would drive his executives to bring out the best in them Gandhi drove his followers to achieve perfection. He did not expect to create a generation of *"Mahatmas"* any more than CEOs except to create generations of Presidents. He challenged people to strive for high ideals in the manner of a teacher urging students to try harder. One would be a lamentable teacher if that person advised students to wallow in moral turpitude.

As we approach a new century and a new millennia, we are swept by a tidal wave of mind-blowing hate. The 20th Century must go down in history as the period when humanity reached the upmost depths of barbarism. After the atom bombs were dropped over Hiroshima and Nagasaki in 1945 Grandfather was asked : "What do you think the future of humanity will be?" His reply was as full of pathos as it was prophetic. He said humankind has narrowed its options. The question is no longer confined to the merits or demerits of violence or nonviolence. The focus is now on Nonviolence or Non-existence. Two decades later Dr. Martin Luther King Jr. made the same prediction. The prophecy is now becoming a reality.

Violence, like cancer in the human body, is eating up human society but we are lulled into believing it will not happen to us. We express concern but are unwilling to make changes in our attitudes. We memorialize hate and erect monuments to the follies of humankind. We claim that these monuments serve as historic reminders of the blunders we committed. The reality is these monuments only serve to keep old wounds festering. The plight of Bosnia is an example of hate being stoked and revenge being sought after centuries of co-existence. History is simply a record of violence and hate and the baser deeds of human beings.

At the root of all the violence in our personal and public lives are the "Seven Blunders" that Grandfather gave me as a talisman in 1947. The eminent teacher writer Stephen Covey has expanded what he calls the "Seven Sins" and allowed us to reproduce it in this book. The question that we need to ask ourselves is : Are we going to continue to live with the "Seven Blunders" as inevitable or, as Grandfather desired, can we work to change them to "Seven Wonders"?

The seven blunders as described by Grandfather are :

Wealth Without Work
Pleasure Without Conscience
Knowledge Without Character
Commerce Without Morality
Science Without Sacrifice
Politics Without Principles

I added the eighth to the list which is *Rights Without Responsibilities*. We agitate for more rights but not many of us talk about our responsibilities in a democracy. A nation or a society cannot be cohesive or strong if citizens refuse to shoulder their responsibilities.

At the root of all the violence that humanity has experienced over several centuries, and still continues to do so, is the life style that makes individuals more self-centred and selfish. Materialism and morality, Grandfather said, have an inverse relationship. Life today has become so materialistic that morality is all but flushed down the drain. The question we need to ask ourselves today is : Can we afford to live in an immoral society? The answer is, obviously, no. By the same token, can we live in a materially impoverished society? The answer still is no. We need to find an equitable balance between materialism and morality in order to create harmony.

"The world has enough for everyone's need, but not for everyone's greed," Grandfather admonished us when we indulged in waste. He once made me look for a three inch but of a pencil that I had thoughtlessly discarded for several hours to illustrate his point. I was just 12 years old then and like most children my age I decided I deserved a new, longer pencil. Little did I know that a simple request for a new pencil would lead to protracted interrogation by Grandfather. It still had not dawned on me that Grandfather was a unique personality or that he would make me go out and look for the pencil butt.

I searched diligently, much of the time with the aid of a flashlight since it was late evening. This was my first exposure to his philosophy of nonviolence.

Nothing is worthless or expendable. People have spent time, money and energy in the manufacture of a pencil, he said. Not to speak of the natural resources used for the purpose. Wasting it is violence against nature and violence against people. Waste also encourages us to consume more than we actually need. This, in turn, means we are depriving someone, somewhere of something that could make a big difference in their lives. It is this careless and reckless consumption that is at the root of much of the violence, Grandfather said. Surely, we can change this if we try.

The "Evil Empire" of Communism, not unexpectedly, destroyed itself. This, However, does not mean socialist philosophy is evil. Grandfather believed we are all, at heart, socialists because we are concerned about others, we go out of our way to help people who are in distress, we share things with others and so on. Communism or socialism failed because the State tried to impose it by law and by force. Grandfather believed the best form of socialism is that which comes from the heart. He called it Trusteeship. He explained that each of us are trustees of the talents we possess. It is not ours to use and exploit selfishly, but use it socially, for the good of as many people as you can reach. He said this is an awareness that should come from within, it cannot be imposed by any government.

Capitalism too can be destructive in so far as it makes one selfish, self-centered and greedy. The success of a few capitalists is built on the failure of many. This success and failure is not a measure of the abilities or disabilities, nor a measure of the brain-power or the brawn-power of individuals and societies. It is a measure of the extent to which we are willing to exploit people for personal gains. Materialism requires that we know the price of everything but the value of nothing.

Gandhi believed when making profits supersedes welfare of the people then humanity is in trouble because life is not about making profits at the expense of people it is about making profits with people. He had the same objections to the inventions of machines that replace people. He called that "Science Without Humanity" and, therefore, unethical. If machines made life easier for people and helped achieve a degree of efficiency without creating massive unemployment he accepted it. We now know the value of what Gandhi was trying to tell us. The cut-backs, the lay-offs, the transfer of more and more low-technology jobs to developing nations are signs of corrosion in a capitalist society. Life is about people and when people become redundant life becomes precarious. One would have to be blind as a bat not to recognize symptoms of cancer. For some materialism is an ideal measure of progress. After all any technology that can make more profits is progress for some but it is not for many others who cannot enjoy it. Technological revolution is mercilessly destroying human society and is responsible for much of the greed, selfishness, self-centredness and distress that is the cause of wars and violence. We can achieve a World Without Violence if, to paraphrase Grandfather, If we stop trying to remake the world and start remaking ourselves.

— *Arun Gandhi*

M. K. Gandhi On Nonviolence

If we have truth in us, it is bound to have its effect, and truth is love, but without love there can be no truth. *Satya* - truth and *Ahimsa* - nonviolence are so intertwined that it is practically impossible to disentangle and separate them.

They are like two sides of a coin, or rather of a smooth unstamped metallic disc. Who can say, which is the obverse and which is reverse? Nevertheless *Ahimsa* is the means; truth is the end. Means to be means must always be within our reach, and so *Ahimsa* is our supreme duty. If we take care of the means, we are bound to reach the end sooner or later. When once we have grasped this point, final victory is beyond question.

As I proceed in my search for truth it grows upon me that truth comprehends everything. It is not in *Ahimsa*, but *Ahimsa* is in it. What is perceived by a pure heart and intellect is truth for that moment. Cling to it, and it enables me to reach pure truth. There is question there of divided duty. But often enough it is difficult to decide what is *Ahimsa*. For instance, the use of disinfectants is *Himsa* - violence, and yet we cannot do without it. We have to live a life of *Ahimsa* in the midst of a world of *Himsa*, and that is possible only if we cling to truth. That is how I deduce *Ahimsa* from truth. Out of truth emanate love, tenderness, humility. A votary of truth has to be humble as the dust. His humility increases with his observance of truth.

It appears that the impossibility of full realization of truth in this mortal body led an ancient seeker after truth to the appreciation of *Ahimsa*. The question which confronted him was: " Shall I bear with those who created difficulties for me, or shall I destroy them? " The seeker realized that he who went on destroying others did not make headway, but simply stayed where he was, while the man who suffered those who created difficulties marched ahead, and at times even took the others with him... The more he took to violence, the more he receded from truth. For in fighting the imagined enemy without, he neglected the enemy within.

Without truth there is no love, without truth it may be affection, as for one's country to the injury of others; or infatuation, as of a young man for a girl or love may be unreasoning and blind, as of ignorant parents for their children. Love transcends all animality and is never partial. True love is boundless like the ocean and swelling with one, spreads itself out and crossing all boundaries and frontiers, envelopes the whole world.

I cannot practise *Ahimsa* without the religion of service and I cannot find the truth without practising the religion of *Ahimsa*.... I am striving for the kingdom of heaven, which is spiritual deliverance. For me the road to salvation lies through incessant toil in the service of my country and of my humanity. I want to identify myself with everything that lives. In the language of the *Gita*, I want to live at peace with both friend and foe. My patriotism is for me a stage on my journey to the land of eternal freedom and peace. Thus it will be seen that for me there is no politics devoid of religion. They subserve religion. Politics bereft of religion is a death-trap because it kills the soul.

Truth is absolute, knowledge relative. Truth, in itself one and entire is reflected diversely in a myriad of facets in the reasons of men... Pride then stops the process of search and discovery, of distinguishing the true from the false, by which knowledge grows, while we go about extirpating not error, which is always with us, but our opponents, who may be wiser than we.

On each occasion one should honour another's sect, for by doing so one increases the influence of one's own sect and benefits that of the other man . . . . again, whosoever honours his own sect or disparages that of another man, wholly out of devotion to his own, with a view to showing it in a favourable light, harms his own sect even more seriously. Therefore, concord is to be commended, so that men may hear one another's principles and obey them.

The golden rule of conduct . . . . is mutual toleration, seeing that we will never all think alike and we shall always see Truth in fragment and from different angles of vision. Conscience is not the same thing for all . . . . Even amongst the most conscientious persons, there will be room enough for honest differences of opinion. The only possible rule of conduct in any civilised society is, therefore, mutual tolerance.

Everybody is right from his own standpoint, but it is not impossible that everybody is wrong. Hence the necessity for tolerance, which does not mean indifference to one's own faith, but more intelligent and purer love for it. Tolerance gives us spiritual insight, which is far from fanaticism as the north pole from the south.

It has been my experience that I am always true from my point of view and often wrong from the point of view of my honest critic. I know that we are both right from our respective points of view. And this knowledge saves me from attributing motives to my opponents or critics . . . . I very much like the doctrine of the manyness of reality. It is this doctrine that has taught me to judge a *Mussulman* (Moslem) from his own standpoint and a Christian from his.... My *Anekantvada* (*Jain* doctrine of the many aspects "not one" - of reality) is the result of the two doctrines of *Satya* and *Ahimsa*.

It is this law of love which, silently but surely, governs the family for the most part throughout the civilized world. I feel that nations cannot be one in reality, nor can their activities be conducive to the common good of the whole humanity, unless there is this definition and acceptance of the law of the family in national and international affairs, in other words, on the political platform. Nations can be called civilized only to the extent that they obey this law.

In short, a *Satyagraha* struggle is impossible without capital in the shape of character. It is the test of our sincerity. It requires solid and silent self sacrifice. It challenges our honesty and our capacity of national work. It is a movement that aims at translating ideas into action. And the more we do, the more we find that much more must be done than we had expected. And this thought of our imperfection must make us humble.

A body of civil resisters is, therefore, like an army subject to all the discipline of a soldier, only harder because of want of excitement of an ordinary soldier's life. And as a civil resistance army is, or ought to be, free from passion and free from the spirit of retaliation, it requires the fewest number of soldiers. Indeed one PERFECT civil resister is enough to win the battle of right against wrong.

In a *Satyagraha* campaign the mode of fight and the choice of tactics, e.g. whether to advance or retreat, offer civil resistance or organized nonviolent strength through constructive work and purely selfless humanitarian service are determined according to the exigencies of the situation. A *Satyagrahi* must carry out whatever plan is laid out for him with a cool determination giving way to neither excitement nor depression.

My experience has taught me that a law of progression applies to every righteous struggle. But, in the case of *Satyagraha* the law amounts to an axiom. As the *Ganga* (river Ganges) advances, other streams flow into it, and hence at the mouth it grows so wide that neither bank is to be seen and a person sailing upon the river cannot make out where the river ends and the sea begins. So also as a *Satyagraha* struggle progresses onward, many another element helps to swell its current, and there is a constant growth in the results to which it leads. This is really inevitable, and is bound up with the first principle of *Satyagraha*. For in *Satyagraha*, the minimum is also the maximum, and as it is the irreducible minimum, there is no question of retreat, and the only movement possible is an advance. In other struggles, even when they are righteous, the demand is first pitched a little higher so as to admit of future reduction, and hence the law of progression does not apply to all of them without exception... The *Ganga* does not leave its course in search of tributaries. Even so does the *Satyagrahi* not leave his path which is sharp as the sword's edge. But as the tributaries spontaneously join the *Ganga* as it advances, so it is with the river that is *Satyagraha*.

What one regards as true *Satyagraha* may well be otherwise. *Satyagraha*... cannot be resorted to for personal gain, but only for the good of others. A *Satyagrahi* should always be ready to undergo suffering and pecuniary loss.... The triumph of *Satyagraha* is always unattached to the attainment of the object of *Satyagraha*.... fasting for the sake of personal gain is nothing short of intimidation and the result of ignorance.

Satyagraha is gentle, it never wounds. It must not be the result of anger or malice. it is never fussy, never impatient, never vociferous. It is the direct opposite of compulsion. It was conceived as a complete substitute for violence. The reformer must have consciousness of the truth of his cause. He will not then be impatient with the opponent, he will be impatient with himself; Even fasts may take the form of coercion. But there is nothing in the world that in human hands does not lend itself to abuse. The human being is a mixture of good and evil, Jekyll and Hyde. But there is least likelihood of abuse when it is a matter of self suffering.

Rumblings Of Discontent

— Hillary Rodham Clinton

. . . . We are at a stage in history, I would suggest, in which remolding society certainly in the West is one of the great challenges facing all of us as individuals and as citizens. We have to begin realistically to take stock of where we are, stripping perhaps away the romanticism, to be able to understand where we are in history at this point and what our real challenges happen to be.

And I say that it is not just an American problem because if one looks around the emerging democracies, at Asia, if one looks certainly here in North America, you can see the rumblings of discontent, almost regardless of political systems, as we come face to face with the problems that the modern age has dealt us.

And if we take a step back and ask ourselves, why is it in a country as economically wealthy as we are despite our economic problems, in a country that is the longest surviving democracy, there is this undercurrent of discontent — this sense that somehow economic growth and prosperity, political democracy and freedom are not enough — that we lack at some core level meaning in our lives individual lives and meaning collectively — that sense that our lives are part of some greater effort, that we are connected to one another, that community means that we have a place where we belong no matter who we are. And it isn't very far below the surface because we can see popping through the surface the signs of alienation and despair and hopelessness that are all too common and cannot be ignored. They're in our living rooms at night on the news, they're on the front pages; they are in all our neighborhoods.

On the plane coming down I read a phrase in an article in the newspaper this morning talking about how desperate conditions are in so many of our cities that are filled with hopeless girls with babies and angry boys with guns. And yet, it is not just the most violent and the most alienated that we look to. The discontent of which I speak is broader than that, deeper than that. We are, I think, in a crisis of meaning. What do our governmental institutions mean? What do our lives in today's world mean? What does this economic global event that Texas Governor Ann Richards spoke mean? What do all of our institutions mean? What does it mean to be educated? What does it mean to be a journalist? What does it mean in today's world to pursue not only vocations, to be part of institutions, but to be human?

And, certainly, coming off the last year when the ethos of selfishness and greed were given places of honor never before accorded, it is certainly timely to ask ourselves these questions.

One of the clearest and most poignant posings of this question that I have run across was the one provided by Lee Atwater as he lay dying. For those of you who may not know Lee Atwater was credited with being the architect of the Republican victories of the '70s and the 80's. The vaunted campaign manager of Reagan and Bush. The man who knew how to fight bare-knuckled in the political arena, who was willing to engage in any tactics so long as it worked and he wasn't caught at it.

And yet, when Lee Atwater was struck down with cancer, he said something which was reprinted in Life Magazine, which I cut out and carry with me in a little book I have of sayings and Scriptures that I find important and that replenish me from time to time that I want to share with you.

He said the following : "Long before I was struck with cancer, I felt something stirring in American society. It was a sense among the people of the country, Republicans and Democrats alike, that something was missing from their lives, something crucial. I was trying to position the Republican Party to take advantage of it. But I wasn't exactly sure what it was. My illness helped me to see that what was missing in society is what was missing in me,. A little heart, a lot of brotherhood.

The '80s were about acquiring — acquiring wealth, power, prestige. I know. I acquired more wealth, power and prestige than most. But you can acquire all you want and still feel empty. What power wouldn't I trade for little more time with my family? What price wouldn't I pay for an evening with my friends? It took a deadly illness to put me eye-to-eye with that truth, but it is a truth that the country, caught up in its ruthless ambitions and moral decay, can learn on my dime.

I don't know who will lead us through the '90s, but they must be made to speak to this spiritual vacuum at the heart of American society, this tumor of the soul."

That to me will be Lee Atwater's real lasting legacy, not the elections that he helped to win.

But I think the answer to his questions — " who will lead us out of this spiritual vacuum" — The answer is all of us. Because remoulding society does not depend on just changing government, on just reinventing our institutions to be more in tune with present realities. It requires each of us to play our part in redefining what our lives are and what they should be.

We are caught between two great political forces. On the one hand we have our economy — the market economy — which knows the price of everything, but the value of nothing. That is not its job. And then the state or government which attempts to use its means of acquiring tax money, of making decisions to assist us in becoming a better, more equitable society as it defines it. That is what all societies are currently caught between — forces that are more complex and bigger than any of us can understand. And missing in that equation, as we have political and ideological struggles between those who think market economics are the answer to everything, those who think government programs are the answers to everything, is the recognition among all of us that neither of those is an adequate explanation for the challenges confronting us.

And what we each must do is to break through the old thinking that has for too long captured us politically and institutionally, so that we can begin to devise new ways of thinking about not only what it means to have governments that work again, not only what it means to have economies that don't discard people like they were excess baggage that we no longer need, but to define our institutional and personal responsibilities in ways that answer this lack of meaning.

We need a new politics of meaning. We need a new ethos of individual responsibility and caring. We need a new definition of civil society which answer the unanswerable questions posed by both the market forces and the governmental ones, as to how we can have a society that fills us up again and makes us feel that we are part of something bigger than ourselves.

Now, will it be easy to do that? Of course not. Because we are breaking new ground. This is a trend that has been developing over hundreds of years. It is not something that just happened to us in the last decade or two. And so it is not going to be easy to redefine who we are as human beings in this post-modern age. Nor will it be easy to figure out how to make our institutions more responsive to the kind of human beings we wish to be.

But part of the great challenge of living is defining yourself in your moment, of seizing the opportunities that you are given, and of making the very best choices you can. That is what this administration, this President, and those of us who are hoping for these changes are attempting to do.

I used to wonder during the election when my husband would attempt to explain how so many of the problems that we were confronting were not easy Democratic — Republican — liberal — conservative problems. They were problems that shared different characteristics, that we had not only defined clearly, but search for new ways of confronting.

Then some one would say, well, you know, he can't make up his mind, or he doesn't know what he wants to say about that. When instead what I was hearing and what we had been struggling with for years is how does one define these new issues. How do we begin to inject some meaning? How do we take old values and apply them to these new — for many of us — undreamed of problems that we now confront? And that is what all of us must be engaged in our own lives, at every level, in every institution with which we interact.

Let me just give you some examples. If we believe that the reconstruction of civil society with its institutions of family, friendship networks, communities, voluntary organizations, are really the glue that holds us together; if we go back and read deTorqueville and notice how he talked over and over again about the unique characteristics that he found among Americans and rooted so many of those in that kind of intermediary institution of civil society that I just mentioned, then we know we have to better understand how they have changed over time, and to try to find meaning in them as they currently are.

That's why the debate over family values over the past year, which was devised for political purposes, seemed so off-point. There is no debate that our family structure is in trouble. There should be no debate that children need the stability, the predictability of a family. But there should be debate over how we best make sure that children and families flourish. And once that debate is carried out on honest terms, then we have to recognize that either the old values matter, or the nearly as old idea that only state programmatic intervention matters are both equally fallicious.

Instead we ought to recognize what should be a common sense truth — that children are the result of both the values of their parents and the values of the society in which they live. (We have) to make sure parental values are the ones that will help children grow and be strengthened, and how social values equally must be recognized for the role they play in how children feel about themselves and act in the world. And then we can begin to have what should be a sensible conversation about how to strengthen both. That's the kind of approach that has to get beyond the dogma of right or left, conservative or liberal. Those views are inadequate to the problems we see.

Any of you who have ever been in an inner city, working with young people as I have over the years, will know as I do the heroic stories of parents and grandparents who, against overwhelming odds, fight to keep their children safe — just physically safe, and who hold high expectations for those children, whose values I would put up against any other person in the country, but who has no control over the day-to-day violence and influence that comes flooding in the doors of that housing project apartment, and who need a society that is more supportive of their value than the one they currently have.

Equally all of us know the contrary story of families with enough economic means, affluent enough to live in neighborhoods that are as safe as they can be in our country today, so they have the social value structure of what we would hope that each child in America could have in terms of just basic kinds of fundamental safety and physical well-being, but whose parental values are not ones to promote a childhood that is a positive one, giving children the chance to grow up to achieve their own God-given potential. So that the presence of values of society are not enough, either.

There are so many examples of how we have to think differently and how we have to go beyond not only the traditions of the past, but unfortunately for many of us, well-held and cherished views of the past, and how we have to break out of the kind of gridlock mentality which exists not just in the Congress from time to time, but exists as well in all of us as we struggle to see the world differently and cope with the challenges it has given us.

Yet I am very hopeful about where we stand in this last decade of the 20th century, because for all of the problems that we see around us, both abroad and at home, there is a growing body of people who want to deal with them, who want to be part of people who want to deal with them, who want to be part of this conversation about how we break through old views and deal with new problems. And we will need millions more of those conversations.

Those conversations need to take place in every family, every workplace, every political institution in our country. They need to take place in our schools, where we have to be honest about what we are and are not able to convey to our children; where we have to be honest about the conditions which are confronting so many of our teachers and our students day in and day out; where we have to be honest that we do have to set high expectations for all children and we should not discard any because of who they are or where they come from.

We need to hold accountable every member of the educational enterprise -- parents, teachers and students. Each should be held accountable for the opportunity they have been given to participate in one of the greatest efforts of humankind, passing on knowledge to children. We have to expect more than we are currently getting.

We also need to take a hard look at other institutions. We are in the midst of an intensive effort of trying to determine how we can provide decent, affordable health care to every American. In that process we have had to ask hard questions about every aspect of our health care system. Why do doctors do what they do? Why are nurses not permitted to do more than they do? Why are patients put in the position they're in?

We have with us today Bill Moyers, who helped to enlighten all of us about how what we currently have is a system for promoting health. What we need to do is recognize how each of us, whether we are a care giver or a care receiver — and that role may change from time to time as we go through life — we will have to think differently about health care. We will have to come up with a system that promotes wellness, promotes health and provides care for us when we are sick that we can afford.

But to give you just one example about how this ties in with what I have said before about how these problems we are confronting now in many ways are the result of our progress as we have moved toward being modern men and women. Our ancestors did not have to think about many of the issues we are now confronted with. When does life start; when does life end? Who makes these decisions? How do we dare to impinge upon these areas of such delicate, difficult questions? And, yet, every day in hospitals and homes and hospices all over this country, people are struggling with those very profound issues.

These are not issues that we have guidebooks about. They are issues that we have to summon up what we believe is morally and ethically and spiritually correct and do the best we can with God's guidance. How do we create a system that gets rid of the micromanagement, the regulation and the bureaucracy, and substitutes instead of human caring, concern and love? That is our real challenge in redesigning a health care system.

I want to say a word about another institution and that is the media, because it is the filter through which we see ourselves and one another. In many ways the challenge confronting it is just as difficult as those confronting any other institution we can imagine. How does one keep up with the extraordinary pace of information now available? How do we make sense of that information? How do we make values about it even if we think we have made sense? How we rid ourselves of the lowest common denominator that is the easiest way of conveying information? How do we have a media that understands how difficult these issues are and looks at itself honestly because the role it must play is so critical to our success in making decisions about how we will proceed as a society?

I remember in the beginning of the campaign being asked a question at an editorial meeting in South Carolina that my husband was at to meet a lot of the editors and reporters from a lot of the small-town papers. These are not folks who you'll see on a TV station anywhere; these are people who got up every day and did the best they could to put out the paper that covered their community or their region. And one of the men, after hearing my husband speak, said, "Now, you've talked about how we have to change society. But as a journalist, how do I change to be able to understand and to report on all those changes?" My husband said,

"You know, I can't answer that. That's something you have to answer. But I'm really glad you asked that question, because every institution in our life has to ask those hard questions about who we are, what contribution we make to dealing with our problems and to injecting meaning again in the lives of us all."

So every one of our institution is under the same kind of mandate. Change will come whether we want it or not, and what we have to do is to try to make change our friend, not our enemy. But probably most profoundly and importantly, the changes that take place on the individual level as people reject cynicism, as they are willing to be hopeful again, as they are willing to take risks to meet the challenges they see around them, as they truly begin to try to see to be treated, to overcome all of the obstacles we have erected around ourselves that keep us apart from one another, fearful and afraid, not willing to build the bridges necessary, to fill that spiritual vacuum that Lee Atwater talked about.

You know, one of my other favorite quotes is from Albert Schweitzer. He talks about how you know the disease in Central Africa called sleeping sickness; there also exists a sleeping sickness of the soul. Let us be willing to help our institutions to change, to deal with the new challenges that confront them. Let us try to restore the importance of civil society by committing ourselves to our children, our families, our friends; and to reaching out beyond the circle of those of whom we know, to the many others on whom we are dependent in this complex society; and what we can do to help ease their burden.

Our greatest opportunities lie ahead, because so many of the struggles of the Depression and The World War and other challenges posed by the Cold War and communism are behind us. The new ones are equally threatening. But we should have learned a lot in the last few years that will prepare us to play our part in remolding a society that we are proud to be a part of.

*First Lady **Ms. Hillary Rodham Clinton** wears several hats, a renowned attorney from Arkansas, a Rhodes scholar, mother and capable wife of President of the United States. She is known for her concern for women and children and has been appointed by the President to head the Health Care Committee.*

Beyond Peace : Towards
A World Without Violence

— Boutros Boutros Ghali

In recent years, peace-making has become the most publicized feature of United Nations activity. And within the general topic of peace-keeping operations, the images most readily conjured up by the media are those of the Blue Helmets in the former Yugoslavia and Somalia. To a certain extent the media attention lavished on these two cases is justified. Somalia and the former Yugoslavia represent two of the most important UN operations in recent years, both in terms of size and in terms of importance for world peace.

Yet United Nations peace-keeping operations today go far beyond the activities where television crew are most often present. There are currently some fifteen peace-keeping missions of the United Nations and UN personnel serve elsewhere as military observers, or civilian negotiators. Whenever there is a conflict, the United Nations is present to convince the parties to the conflict to return to negotiations, to facilitate these negotiations and to help provide conditions where a recurrence of the conflict is impossible. In the many "hot points" across the globe, the United Nations operates along a continuum of peace operations from preventive diplomacy, to peace-keeping and peace-making, to post-conflict peace-building. From Afghanistan to Zaire, that is the reality of United Nations peace operations.

But there is more. Indeed the resources of the United Nations, and the daily work of UN staff and volunteers, go far beyond peace operations, and even in the expanded sense of the past few years. Most of the resources and efforts of the Organization go towards the other aspect of United Nations work : development.

Just as the word "peace-keeping" must be defined anew, so must the word "development". What was once a matter of economics is now seen to involve many dimensions. We are forced to this new perception by the realization that development, in its traditional meaning, has failed to transform poor countries and countries in post-conflict situations. Achieving a new vision of development may well be the most challenging intellectual task of our time. Just as peace-operations are situated along a continuum from preventive diplomacy to peace-keeping and peace-building, so is development.

Development must be redefined as a process, ranging from the provision of infrastructure and an enabling institutional environment, to fostering economic growth, to protection of the environment to special attention paid to the most vulnerable social groups and finally to political development.

Political development means helping societies develop along an institutional environment where political participation, the respect of human rights and the equality of all before the law are respected. In short, political development is democratization in the widest sense of the word.

In recent years, the United Nations have ventured into an entirely new field: long-term, nationwide monitoring of human rights. The first example was in El Salvador, in the context of the peace agreement which brought an end to armed conflict in that country. A second is under way, with the Organization of American States, in Haiti. Similar efforts were undertaken in the Baltic States, in the former Yugoslavia and in many other cases.

A new office has been created in New York to deal with requests for electoral assistance. Several elections and referenda have been monitored; the examples of Cambodia and Eritrea come most readily to mind. Others are in preparation — for instance in Western Sahara.

The search for peace is a laudable activity, yet it cannot be the ultimate goal of the United Nations. the pursuit of peace, while neglecting development can only produce a short-term halt in hostilities. Peace is a prerequisite for development; democracy is essential if development is to succeed over the long term.

The work of the United Nations is thus far more comprehensive than an exclusive focus on the former Yugoslavia and Somalia would seem to imply. There is hardly an area in the fields of peace and development in all their dimensions where the United Nations is not present. The spirit of Gandhi lives at the United Nations.

*Boutros Boutros-Ghali was appointed Secretary-General for a five-year term by the General Assembly on December 1991. Prior to that he had been the Deputy Prime Minister for Foreign Affairs of Egypt and held various high ranking posts in the Egyptian Parliament. The Secretary-General has had a long association with international affairs as deplomat, jurist, scholar and widely published author. **Mr. Butros-Ghali** has received numerous awards and honours internationally for his diplomatic and human rights work.*

Eye For An Eye – Injustice

— *Mario M. Cuomo*

This is a time of disorienting violence and moral disorder in America. For the victims — and the perpetrators — the damage is bitter, lasting. And to the millions who bear witness through their television screens, the consequence is a slow dissolution of our faith in one another — cumulative, although not irreversible.

But as faith dissolves, the crystal of an ugly thought begins to form.

When it appears to the people that crime is rampant, that the criminal seems immune from apprehension and adequate punishment, and that nothing else is working -- then no one should be surprised if they demand access to a savage remedy: execution at the hands of the state.

I have profound respect for the people who have raised their voices -- and occasionally their fists -- asking for the death penalty.

But after the sincerest effort, I have not been able to bring myself to agree with them. I have resisted, with the power of veto, every attempt to make the death penalty part of my state's criminal justice system. And I will continue.

I believe with all mind and heart that the death penalty would not help us; it would debase us. That it would not protect us; it would weaken us.

I have spoken of my opposition for more than thirty years. For all that time I have studied the question. I have debated it hundreds of times.

I have heard all the arguments, analyzed all the evidence I could find, measured public opinion — When it was opposed, when it was indifferent, when it was passionately in favor.

And always I have concluded that the death penalty is wrong. That it lowers us all; that it is surrender to the worst that is in us; that wielding the official power to kill by execution has never elevated a society, never made a single person safer, never brought back a life, never inspired anything but hate.

It is a question that has transcendent significance: one whose answer describes in fundamental ways what we are as a people; one that projects to ourselves, and to the whole world, our most fundamental values... one, even, that helps configure our souls.

I maintain that we should refuse to allow this time to be marked forever in the pages of our history as the time we were driven back to one of the vestiges of our primitive condition, because we were not strong enough, because we were not intelligent enough, because we were not civilized enough, to find a better answer to violence... than violence itself.

Governor Mario Cuomo has repeatedly opposed capital punishment in the state of New York. He condemns the death penalty as a particularly repugnant form of violence because it is imposed under the authority of the state.

A Crisis Of Meaning

— Bill Bradley

For the people of the United States, the 1990s are a time of uncertainty and division. As family businesses go bankrupt, AIDS spreads, kids have kids, and families hit with illness have no health insurance, Americans fear for the future of their children and the future of the nation.

At its core, what America faces is a crisis of meaning. Without meaning, there can be no hope; without hope, there can be no struggle; without struggle, there can be no personal betterment. Do we want our children to have an understanding of what it means to be a human being and how to care for others, or an understanding of what it takes to step on someone else for success and how to tell more effective lies? Individualism degenerates into greed without agreement on its limits. The microchip may be faster than the human brain, but it's not connected to a heart. A new drug might defeat a disease, but it won't eradicate hatred. Technology can't tell us what's right and what's wrong. Achieving personal excellence and extending a helping hand are indispensable element of an American future that is assuming responsibility for our country and our planet.

The challenge for American political leadership is to convert this crisis of meaning into the path to moral, economic, and social rejuvenation. As the memory of Mahatma Gandhi's life reminds us, there is a connection between our highest aspiration and our deepest anguish, and the right leadership will confront us truthfully with the circumstances of our lives, not just the choices for government.

For example, how can we expect our children to follow the rules if we continue to make excuses for those who break them?

How can we hold government bureaucrats accountable for results if we never take the time to learn what happens in the classrooms of our children, so we can hold our schools accountable for results?

How can we reinvigorate our democratic process if we sit at home, passively, in front of the TV?

How can we fail to see that individualism will degenerate into greed if there is no common agreement on its limits?

How can we fail to see that the market which gives the lowest prices, highest quality goods is also the market that makes no distinction between the music of Bach and the violence of the latest TV drug drama?

How can we fail to see beyond the clutter of hyped news and information overload to the simple imperatives of child-rearing and the simple pleasures of family life?

For 12 years morality in American politics has focused on such issues as school prayer, abortion, pornography. Each of these subjects has moral implications and deserves thoughtful discussion, but to define morality exclusively in those terms is to be absolutely blind to the injustices of our economic system and the violence in our social fabric. A Gandhian view today would force us to action. A Gandhian view would confront official abuse as well as human suffering, and it would ask each of us to look into ourselves for wisdom and strength.

How can we be moral and burden our children with the debts of our own excesses? How can we be moral and fail to shore up the economic circumstances of middle class American families? How can we be moral and turn our back on the poor?

Isn't it the obligation of parents to nurture their children?

Isn't it the obligation of the teacher to teach, nurses to give comfort?

Isn't it the obligation of each citizen to ask what you owe another human being simply because he or she is a human being?

Isn't it the obligation of government to refrain from taking money from taxpayers unless it's accounted for and produces results?

These ideas flow from citizens as individuals to me and to other public officials. But it starts with the people, not with me. Self-mastery, as Gandhi showed, comes from the inside, not the outside.

Idealism seems out of sync with the kind of spiritual erosion that public behavior has produced. Yet I can't help but think back to 1964 when the U.S. Senate passed the Civil Rights Act, which among other things desegregated hotels and restaurants. I was a young man then, and I was in the senate gallery that night. I remember thinking : America is a better, more just place because of this. To make America and the world a better place — that's the idealism that caused me to go into politics. And that's the idealism that gets me to work early every morning.

So even in these cynical times I've made a deal with the people of New Jersey and America. I work to deserve their trust; they keep their expectations high for my work. I try to be truthful and honest; they try to dream again of a better future for themselves and our country. And if we both do our job, we'll build a better America and a safer, more prosperous world.

Senator Bill Bradley is currently serving his third term in the U.S. Senate. His positions on the Senate Finance Committee, Energy and Natural Resources Committee and the Special Committee on Aging enable him to focus aggressively on his three major concerns : strengthening the nation's economy, addressing the crisis in our cities and defining the U.S. post cold-war role in the world.

The Dilemma Of The Absolute Pacifist

— Linus Pauling & Daisaku Ikeda

Pauling : I certainly would support a Buddhist drive for peace; but, as I have said, I support all peace movements, even those conducted by communists. But I have doubts about absolute pacifism. What are absolute pacifists to do in a world that is not populated by absolute pacifists? Would it be possible to pursue an absolutely pacifist course under another Adolph Hitler, who wanted to dominate the world and eliminate everyone except German Aryans?

During World War II, some of my students were pacifists. One of them, an idealist, a Jew, and a vegetarian, was imprisoned. Since the prison authorities refused to recognize his vegetarianism and insisted on serving him meat, he nearly starved. Once released from jail, he was almost imprisoned a second time for failing to register for the draft. At his second trial, the judge asked whether he believed in God. Although he may have believed in God, he confused the issue by arguing with the judge over the definition of the term. Still, on this occasion, he managed to stay out of jail.

With the exception of cases like his, the United States authorities were lenient with conscientious objectors and allowed them to work off their military obligations at various tasks. One of my students worked in a California lumber camp with other conscientious objectors. Two or three other workers worked with him on war projects, but I had to convince them that our tasks were too remote from fighting the enemy to trouble their consciences.

A German friend, a gifted violinist, physicist, and mathematician, was a pacifist who nonetheless was at first inducted into the German army. For a while, he operated an aircraft battery — he wrote me saying he thanked God he never hit anything — but later was taken out of the army and assigned to a factory where he applied his knowledge of mechanical process in improving operational efficiency.

In spite of his brilliance, he was not made a professor until he was sixty years old because the Nazis would not award professorships to anyone who was not a member of their party. Consequently, he had a hard time making a living. Nonetheless, unlike many much less fortunate individuals, he survived the war.

Ikeda : The problem of absolute pacifism is and always has been difficult. In both theory and practice, it is hard to draw a line clearly dividing right from wrong in connection with it. Although understandably a thoroughly confirmed, absolute pacifist might be willing to face death for his faith. As you say, what good would an absolute pacifist be able to do under a Hitler-like regime?

We have already mentioned Einstein's predicament in feeling impelled by the Nazi threat to recommend to President Roosevelt that the United States go ahead with research leading to the production of the atomic bomb. He was a pacifist in a world not inhabited completely by fellow pacifists:

I was well aware of the dreadful danger which would threaten mankind were the experiments to prove successful. Yet I felt impelled to take the step because it seemed probable that the Germans might be working on the same problem with every prospect of success. I saw no alternative but to act as I did, although I have been a convinced pacifist.

— Einstein on Peace

He was afraid of what might happen if the Nazis succeeded in the nuclear research, he knew they were conducting at the time. He called himself a convinced, not an absolute, pacifist. Nonetheless, the following quotation from an apologia he published in Japanese newspapers after World War II suggests that absolute pacifism was his ideal

Gandhi, the greatest political genius of our time, indicated the path to be taken. He gave proof of what sacrifices man is capable of once he has discovered the right path. His work on behalf of India's liberation is living testimony to the fact that man's will, sustained by an indomitable conviction, is more powerful than material forces that seem insurmountable.

— Einstein on Peace

In the past, international relations have generally been controlled exclusively by diplomats and politicians. Today, however, sophisticated developments in technology and transportation have greatly altered the traditional arrangement. On one level, it has become more common for supreme leaders of the national states to meet person to person. On another level, tourism and cultural and sports events greatly accelerate the pace at which ordinary peoples come to know and understand each other, thus putting a more generally human face on the way history is made. This is as it must be. Instead of allowing themselves to be led about by the noses at the beck and call of the national states, the ordinary citizens must assume the principal role in history.

Before concluding our dialogue, I should like to touch briefly on Japan's role in the contemporary world. Although the Japanese people themselves may not always enjoy the fruits of national affluence as fully as they would like, Japan has become a great economic power and as such is expected by other nations to make suitable contributions to the management of the world. As the only nation ever to have suffered an atomic bombing, Japan certainly has a mission of contributing to the peace of the whole planet. Since you have visited Japan often and understand our nation well, your advice in this connection would be most welcome.

Pauling : Japan must continue refusing to rely on a large military force and refrain from developing nuclear weapons. In this way, Japan can be a leader in the drive for world peace. As a consequence of her rapid technological growth, Japan has become one of the most important nations. The health of Japanese people has improved greatly in the last fifty years. For example, life expectancy has become much higher than it was in the Japan of the 1930s.

Japan has made a step in the direction of freeing the world of war by limiting its military establishment since the end of World War II. I realize that the steps are being taken toward expanding the armed forces. But the part of the prosperity of the nation in the past twenty-five years has been made possible by the absence of a great military drain (of the usual 10 to 20 percent of the gross national product) on the budget. I can see no reason for Japan to assume the burden of a large military force.

Dr. Linus Pauling, the world's only winner of two unshared Nobel Prizes (chemistry in 1954 and peace in 1962), celebrated his 93rd birthday on February 28, 1994. In 1963 he joined as a staff at the Centre for the Study of Democratic Institution where he largely developed himself to the study of the problems of peace and war. Dr. Pauling has received honorary degrees from over thirty U.S. and foreign universities. Currently, he is Research Professor, Linus Pauling Institute of Science and Medicine, Palo Alto, California.

Mr. Daisaku Ikeda studied philosophy, politics, literature, art, economics, law, chemistry, and other subjects under his mentor Josei Toda. He has been president of Soka Gakkai International (SGI), a lay Buddhist organization for the promotion of peace, culture, and education. Mr. Ikeda was named Poet Laureate of Japan in December, 1981, and received the United Nations Peace Award in August 1983. He has authored several books.

From A Lifelong Quest for Peace : A Dialogue Between Linus Pauling and Daisaku Ikeda. © 1992. Reprinted with permission of Jones and Bartlett Publishers, Inc. Boston. MA. This dialogue is translated by Richard L. Gage.

The Way To A Valueless Society

— Stephen R. Covey

Mahatma Gandhi said that seven things will destroy us. Notice that all of them have to do with social and political conditions. Note also that the antidote of each of these "deadly sins" is an explicit external standard or something that is based on natural principles and laws, not on social values.

Wealth Without Work. This refers to the practice of getting something for nothing–manipulating markets, and assets so you don't have to work or produce added value, just manipulate people and things. Today there are professions built around making wealth without working, making much money paying taxes, benefiting from free government programs without carrying a fair share of the financial burdens, and enjoying all the perks of citizenship of country and membership of corporation without assuming any of the risk or responsibility.

How many of the fraudulent schemes that went on in the 1980's, often called the decade of greed, were basically get-rich-quick schemes or speculations promising practitioners, "You don't even have to work for it?" That is why I would be very concerned if one of my children went into speculative enterprises or if they learned how to make a lot of money fast without having to pay the price by adding value on a day-to-day basis.

Some network marketing pyramidal organizations worry me because many people get rich quick by building a structure under them that feeds them without work. They are rationalized to the hilt; nevertheless the overwhelming emotional motive is often greed: "You can get rich without much work. You may have to work initially, but soon you can have wealth without work." New social mores and norms are cultivated that cause distortions in their judgment.

Justice and judgment are inevitably inseparable, suggesting that to the degree you move away from the laws of nature, your judgment will be adversely affected. You get distorted notions. You start telling rational lies to explain why things work or why they don't. You move away from the law of "the farm" into social/political environments.

When we read about organizations in trouble, we often hear the sad confessions of executives who tell of moving away from natural laws and principles for a period of time and begin overbuilding, overborrowing, and overspeculating, not really reading the stream or getting objective feedback, just hearing a lot of self-talk internally. Now they have a high debt to pay. They may have to work hard just to survive-without hope of being healthy for five years or more. It's back to the basics, hand to the plow. And many of these executives, in earlier days, were critical of conservative founders of the corporations who stayed close to the fundamentals and preferred to stay small and free of debt.

Pleasure Without Conscience. The chief query of the immature, greedy, selfish, and sensuous has always been, "What's in it for me? Will this please me? Will it ease me?" Lately many people seem to want these pleasures without conscience or sense of responsibility, even abandoning or utterly neglecting spouses and children in the name of doing their thing. But independence is not the most mature state of being–it's only the middle position on the way to interdepedence, the most advanced and mature state. To learn to give and take, to live selflessly, to be sensitive, to be considerate, is our challenge. Otherwise there is no sense of social responsibility or accountability in our pleasurable activities.

The ultimate costs of pleasures without conscience are high as measured in terms of time and money, in terms of reputation and in terms of wounding the hearts and minds of other people who are adversely affected by those who just want to indulge and gratify themselves in the short term. It's dangerous to be pulled or lulled away from natural law without conscience. Conscience is essentially the repository of timeless truths and principles — the internal monitor of natural law.

A prominent, widely published psychologist worked to align people with their moral conscience in what was called "integrity therapy." He once told me that he was a manic — depressive. "I knew I was getting suicidal," he said. "Therefore I committed myself to a mental institution. I tried to work out of it, neutralize it, until I reached the point where I could leave the hospital. I don't do clinical work now because it is too stressful. I mostly do research. And through my own struggle, I discovered that integrity therapy was the only way to go. I gave up my mistress, confessed to my wife, and had peace for the first time in my life."

Pleasure without conscience is one of the key temptations for today's executives. Sometimes on airplanes I'll scan the magazines directed at executives, noting the advertisements. Many of these ads, perhaps two-thirds of them, invite executives to indulge themselves without conscience because they "deserve it" or have "earned it" or "want it," and why not "give in" and "let it all hang out?" The seductive message is, "You've arrived. You are now a law unto yourself. You don't need a conscience to govern you anymore." And in some ads you see sixty-year-old men with attractive thirty-year-old women, the "significant others" who accompany some executives to conventions. Whatever happened to spouses? What happened to the social mores that make cheating spouses illegitimate behavior?

Knowledge Without Character. As dangerous as little knowledge is, even more dangerous is much knowledge without a strong, principled character. Purely intellectual development without commensurate internal character development makes as much sense as putting a high-powered sports car in the hands of a teenager who is high on drugs. Yet all too often in the academic world, that's exactly what we do by not focusing on the character development of young people.

One of the reasons I'm excited about taking the Seven Habits into the schools is that it is character education. Some people don't like character education because, they say, "that's *your* value system." But you can get a common set of values that everyone agrees on. It is not that difficult to decide, for example, that kindness, fairness, dignity, contribution, and integrity are worth keeping. No one will fight you on those. So let's start with values that are unarguable and infuse them in our education system and in our corporate training and development programs. Let's achieve a better balance between the development of character and intellect.

The people who are transforming education today are doing it by building consensus around a common set of principles, values and priorities and debunking the high degree of specialization, departmentalization, and partisan politics.

Commerce (business) Without Morality (ethics). In his book Moral Sentiments, which preceded Wealth of Nations, Adam Smith explained how foundational to the success of our system is the moral foundation: how we treat each other, the spirit of benevolence, of service, of contribution. If we ignore the moral foundation and allow economic systems to operate without moral foundation and without continued education, we will soon create an amoral, if not immoral, society and business. Economic and political systems are ultimately based on a normal foundation.

To Adam Smith, every business transaction is a moral challenge to see that both parties come out fairly. Fairness and benevolence in business are the underpinnings of the free enterprise system called capitalism. Our economic system comes out of a constitutional democracy where minority rights are to be attended to as well. The spirit of the Golden Rule of win-win is a spirit of morality, of mutual benefit, or fairness for all concerned. Paraphrasing one of the mottos of the Rotary Club, "Is it fair and does it serve the interests of all the stockholders?" That's just a moral sense of stewardship toward all of the stockholders.

I like that Smith says *every* economic transaction. People get in trouble when they say that *most* of their economic transactions are moral. That means there is something going on that is covert, hidden, secret. People keep a hidden agenda, a secret life, and they justify and rationalize their activities. They tell themselves rational lies so they don't have to adhere to natural laws. If you can get enough rationalization in a society, you can have social mores or political wills that are totally divorced from natural laws and principles.

I once met a man who for five years served as the "ethics director" for a major aerospace company. He finally resigned the post in protest and considered leaving the company, even though he would lose a big salary and benefit package. He said that the executive team had their own separate set of business ethics and that they were deep into rationalization and justification. Wealth and power were big on their agendas, and they made no excuse for it anymore. They were divorced from reality even inside their own organisation. They talked about serving the customers while absolutely mugging their own employees.

Science Without Humanity. If science becomes all technique and technology, it quickly degenerates into man against humanity. Technologies come from the paradigms of science. And if there's very little understanding of the higher human purposes that the technology is striving to serve, we become victims of our own technocracy. We see otherwise highly educated people climbing the scientific ladder of success, even though it's often missing the rung called humanity and leaning against the wrong wall.

The majority of the scientists who ever lived or are living today, have brought about a scientific and technological explosion in the world. But if all they do is superimpose technology on the same old problems, nothing basic changes. We may see an evolution, an occasional "revolution" in science, but without humanity we see precious little real human advancement. All the old inequities and injustices are still with us.

About the only thing that hasn't evolved are these natural laws and principles – the true north on the compass. Science and technology have changed the face of most everything else. But the fundamental things still apply as time goes by.

Religion (Worship) Without Sacrifice. Without sacrifice we may become active in a church but remain inactive in its gospel. In other words, we go for the social facade of religion and the piety of religious practices. There is no real walking with people or going the second mile or trying to deal with our social problems that may eventually undo our economic system. It takes sacrifice to serve the needs of other people – the sacrifice of our own pride and prejudice, among other things.

If a church or religion is seen as just another hierarchical system, its members won't have a sense of service or inner worship. Instead they will be into outward observances and all the visible accoutrements of religion. But they are neither God-centered nor principle-centered.

The principles of three of the Seven Habits pertain to how we deal with other people, how we serve them, how we sacrifice for them, how we contribute. Habits 4,5, and 6 – win-win interdependency, empathy, and synergy – require tremendous sacrifice. I've come to believe that they – require a broken heart and a contrite spirit – and that, for some, is the ultimate sacrifice. For example, I once observed a marriage where there were frequent arguments. One thought came to me: "These two people must have a broken heart and a contrite spirit toward each other or this union will never last." You can't have a oneness, a unity, without humility. Pride and selfishness will destroy the union between man and god, between man and woman, between man and man, between self and self.

The great servant leaders have that humility, the hallmark of inner religion. I know a few CEOs who are humble servant leaders – who sacrifice their pride and share their power – and I can say that their influence both inside and outside their companies is multiplied because of it. Sadly, many people want "religion," or at least the appearance of it, without any sacrifice. They want more spirituality but would never miss a meal in meaningful fasting or do one act of anonymous service to achieve it.

Politics Without Principles. If there is no principle there is no true north, nothing you can depend upon. The focus on the personality ethic is the instant creation of an image that sells well in the social and economic marketplace.

You see politicians spending millions of dollars to create an image, even though it's superficial, lacking substance, in order to get votes and gain office. And when it works, it leads to a political system operating independently of the natural laws that should govern – that are built into the Declaration of Independence: "We hold these Truths to be self-evident, that all Men are created equal, that they are endowed by their Creator with certain unalienable Rights, that among these are Life, Liberty, and the Pursuit of Happiness...."

In other words, they are describing self-evident laws: "We hold these Truths to be self-evident." The key to a healthy society is to get the social will, the value system, aligned with correct principles. You then have the compass needle pointing to true north – true north representing the external or the natural law – and the indicator says that it is what we are building our value system on: they are aligned.

But if you get a sick social will behind the political will that is independent of principle, you could have a very sick organization or society with distorted values.

For instance, the professed mission and shared values of criminals who rape, rob, and plunder might sound very much like many corporate mission statements, using such words as "teamwork," "cooperation," "loyalty," "profitability," "innovation," and "creativity." The problem is that their value system is not based on a natural law.

Figuratively, inside many corporations with lofty mission statements, many people are being mugged in broad daylight in front of witnesses. Or they are being robbed of self-esteem, money, or position without due process. And if there is no social will behind the principles of due process, and if you can't get due process, you have to go to the jury of your peers and engage in counterculture sabotage.

In the movie the Ten Commandments, Moses says to the pharaoh, "We are to be governed by God's law, not by you." In effect he's saying, "We will not be governed by a person unless that person embodies the law." In the best societies and organizations, natural laws and principles govern — that's the Constitution — and even the top people must bow to the principle. No one is above it.

The Seven Habits will help you avoid these Seven Deadly Sins. And if you don't buy into the Seven Habits, try the Ten Commandments.

*Dr. Stephen R. Covey has taught leadership principles and management skills for more than 25 years to leaders in business, government, and education. His portfolio includes more than 150 of the Fortune 500 companies, as well as thousands of mid-sized and smaller organisations. He is founder and chairman of Covey Leadership Center, a more than 300-member international firm whose mission is to empower people and organizations to significantly increase their performance capability in order to achieve worthwhile purposes through understanding and living Principle-Centered Leadership. He has written several books including **Seven Habits of Highly Effective People**, and many others.*

(Excerpted from "Principle-Centered Leadership" by Dr. Stephen R. Covey, permission to reprint granted by Dr. Covey.)

Can South Africa Achieve Peaceful Non-racial Democracy?

— R. J. Goldstone

It was probably in South Africa that the *Mahatma* had his first serious and personal experience of racial discrimination. For that reason in particular it is appropriate and a special privilege for a South African to contribute to World Without Violence.

For more than a century the white rulers of South Africa were guilty of three of the Seven Blunders - Pleasure without Conscience, Commerce without Morality and Politics without Principles. The stark issue now facing this country is whether those blunders preclude South Africa from becoming a peaceful non-racial democracy.

On the positive side there is the almost miraculous goodwill - an absence of hate - on the part of the great majority of black South Africans who suffered so much indignity and who were so seriously prejudiced and disadvantaged by reason of their race and colour. On the negative side is the belief of a majority of black and South Africans in racial exclusivity and ethnic government. They do not recognize that a commitment to ethnicity or racism necessarily deprecates and devalues the worth and dignity of other racial or ethnic groups.

There is only one peaceful way in which a multi-ethnic and multi-cultural society can exist in peace and security. That is by a democratic government fostering a common loyalty to all of its citizens in the recognition of their fundamental equality and dignity.

In short, South Africa will only defeat the violence presently threatening its very existence when it has a form of government and a constitution which preclude its rulers from committing any of the sins called by Gandhi the Seven Blunders of the World. If that can be achieved South Africa could provide an affirmation of Gandhi's faith in the capacity of human beings to find peaceful solutions for the conflicts plaguing our world.

Judge R. J. Goldstone is known for impartial and meticulous judgements as a Judge of Appeal in South Africa. As a senior judge heading a commission looking into the causes of the violence in which as many as 15,000 South Africans have died since late 1984, *Judge Goldstone* released a report in December 1993. The report said the commission had concrete evidence that hit squads aligned with the Inkatha Freedom Party had been working to sow fear, distrust and disillusionment in Black townships like Bhambayi and other settlements in Natal province.

The Goldstone Commission, as it is called, was created in 1991 by President F. W. de Klerk to look into the causes of black violence.

Politics With Principles?

— Mairead Corrigan Maguire

Sometime ago I was speaking to a professor of psychiatry about world peace. He told me he believed that scientists in the world community know the problems that humanity is faced with, such as environment, poverty, etc., and that in many cases, solutions to these problems already exist. He believed much of the intellectual analysis has been done on these problems, and what is needed now is to be able to touch people's hearts and create the confidence and collective will of the people of the world to change things.

I am convinced there is much more in what he says. There is a growing world recognition and consensus that war and militarism, environmental problems, poverty, social injustice, human rights violations, and lack of real democracy are urgent problems facing us all. We need international co-operation. The money can be made available if the will exist both in the people of the world and their governments. I believe that the will of ordinary people of the world and their governments. I believe that the will of ordinary people to do something to deal with these problems already exist, but it is not yet being reflected in the politics of their governments. Many of the world's governments have actually cut military budgets. Yet, we all know that if money was made available from each country's military budget and diverted into appropriate United Nations Institutions, millions of lives could be saved immediately, and the money could go a long way toward solving other problems.

There is nothing I have said so far that each of us does not know in our hearts to be true. So I have to ask myself, "Am I only wasting paper in saying all this?" If so, then I must take responsibility for every act I do, which in turn affects others and the planet.

Taking responsibility for our own actions may be the greatest contribution we can all make toward solving these problems, and is surely part of the process of beginning to create what Martin Luther King, Jr. called "the beloved community." Can you imagine how different things could have been in Hitler's Germany had people taken personal responsibility for their actions?

This thought came back to me very strongly a few years ago when I made a pilgrimage to Auschwitz Concentration Camp, in Poland. It was the most horrible place I have ever entered. I walked around weeping and all the while silently asking myself, "How could human beings do this to fellow human beings?"

In one of the gas chambers, a rabbi and a priest led our small group in prayer. During the prayer, local church bells rang out. I asked a companion about the bells. He explained that they were the bells of the local Catholic church for Sunday Mass. He went on to say that this torture camp could not have operated without the help of local Catholics, who presumably serviced and worked in the camps, and went to church on Sunday.

I left Auschwitz with the utter conviction that we must uphold human life and rights and each work passionately for justice. We must learn from the horrors of the past, we must not repeat them.

When we speak to people about my belief that we need to live out and teach active nonviolence at every level of society, people often ask, "Ah! But what about Hitler?" They are right to ask this question, but it is important to bear in mind that the death of Hitler did not mean the death of fascism. We must remember, too, that Hitler was only one man. It was thousands of people taking on the "spirit" of Hitler — hate, cruelty, etc. — that made Auschwitz possible. Had each person taken responsibility for his or her own actions, and not merely said. "It was for my country, I was only following orders, etc.," things would have been very different. Of course, some were afraid for themselves and their families, but we must strive to overcome fear with courage and to do what our hearts tell us to be right.

The personal need to inform our conscience, and to do what our conscience tells us to be right, is important for our spiritual and physical wholeness, and for the wholeness of others and of our planet. The making of weapons of destruction, even if one is only very slightly involved in the process, is participating in the death of fellow human beings and the destruction of the environment. These weapons are killing people without ever having been fired since the money involved to build them could be feeding the hungry.

The nuclear Trident submarines are polluting the seas and destroying the oceans which we need for our very lives, and putting the safety of all of us daily at risk. Everyone remembers Chernobyl, but it is not generally known that there have been many accidents involving nuclear material over America (i.e., airplane crashes or accidental dropping of bombs). Independent critics say there have been 125 fires and explosions at nuclear production sites. Between 1945 and 1980 there were 691 nuclear weapons tests in the United States. In 1963 nuclear tests went underground. However, underground tests still send fall out by releasing radioactive clouds. Colonel Raymond Brim (formerly in charge for 10 years of monitoring leaks) said, "Americans were exposed to dangerous levels of radiation from safe underground tests all through the 1960's and 1970's and remain in danger today. Just as the risk of fall out continues, so do the conscious government effort to cover up the situation."

For forty years there existed the illusion that nuclear weapons were a mutual deterrent and provided stability between the United States and the Soviet Union. With the ending of the Cold War, many people are lulled into thinking the nuclear danger is over. However, we are now faced with possibly even greater danger, due to lack of control in new republics of the former U.S.S.R., and the potential spread of nuclear weapons to smaller nations eager for nuclear technology. (There are four former Soviet republics with nuclear weapons and eleven republics with tactical short-range weapons.)

Smaller nations will sign the Non-proliferation Treaty in 1995 only if the big nuclear powers are willing to commit themselves to stop nuclear testing and begin nuclear disarmament. If the U.S. does not give a clear lead on this the Non-proliferation Treaty will not be renewed, and the nuclear arms race will escalate beyond control.

Some people will try to fool themselves that these nuclear weapons will not be used; but remember Hiroshima and Nagasaki. Remember also that it was not necessary to drop these nuclear bombs in order to end the war. The use of nuclear weapon was also threatened through the Vietnam war.

The late Father George Zabelka, who was a Catholic priest on Tinian Island in 1945, and blessed the crew going out to bomb the cities of Hiroshima and Nagasaki, spent his later life working for world peace. He took personal responsibility for his part in the terrible crime against the Japanese people, and returned to Hiroshima and Nagasaki to ask forgiveness of the *Hibakusha* (survivors). Several years ago during a visit to Japan, I asked the forgiveness of the Japanese for the bombing of Hiroshima and Nagasaki. I believe it is only by saying we are sorry for the wrong we have done that we can move forward in genuine reconciliation and healing.

Many of us were deeply inspired by the life of Father Zabelka as he walked around the world for peace, with the words "Hiroshima" and "Nagasaki" on each shoe. His message to all was "stop making war respectable." Father Zabelka followed in the footsteps of two other great prophets of nonviolence America has given the world — Martin Luther King Jr. and Dorothy Day. Their lives inspired millions, as I believe Father Zabelka's life will continue to do even after his death on April 11, 1992. Up until the last days of his life he continued to hand out peace buttons, saying, "Do something for peace." In his early life, his army friends nicknamed him "General George," but he will live on in our hearts as our friend who was a gentle prophet of nonviolence.

With his words, he reminded us that we must put people above our flags and nationalism, and stop glorifying war and violence. We honor those who, in the past, believing it was the only way to resist evil, went to war. But now the human family has a new way - the way of nonviolence. So, in the future, when a dictator or a country's government takes a country to war, it will be considered a sign of weakness, impatience, and an inability to solve human conflict with imagination and vision. We people of the world need to have international laws that protect us from murderous and barbaric wars often carried out in our names, but without our consent. International laws could be established so the political leaders are held accountable for their war crimes.

It would be nice to speculate that perhaps by the time such legislation comes into place at the United Nations, it will already be obsolete, since war itself will have become obsolete. But who could have believed that, following the end of the Cold War and so much progress brought about by the nonviolence of the peoples of the former Eastern Block countries, that our leaders could have again taken us backwards to the war in the Persian Gulf. The war left behind such suffering and tragedy. Words do not come to me to describe the barbarism of it all.

No one can be in any doubt today how the weapons of war have developed from tanks to the use of thermonuclear, chemical and bacteriological arms. In an article in the Vatican newspaper, in July, 1992, tracing the development of warfare from early Christian times (when Christians did not kill and refused to be soldiers, following Christ's commandment to love their enemy) up to present-day weapons of mass destruction, the writer ends by saying, "It is necessary to conclude that war is always immoral." This is a vitally important statement.

Down through history, many Christians have struggled in conscience with a choice between Jesus' nonviolent love of enemies and the allegedly "just war" theory. Father William Johnston, writing about "just war" theory in his book, *Letters to Contemplatives*, says, "It seems to me that we cannot have peace until we throw the old just war theology out of the window and search for something new based on the gospel."

It seems to me also time for military workers and those who participate in trafficking of death machines around the world to search their conscience regarding working on death machines. In August, 1981, Bishop Matthiensen said in Amarillo, "We urge individuals involved in the production and stockpiling of nuclear bombs to consider what they are doing to resign from such activities, and to seek employment in peaceful pursuits."

Hilter's Germany could have been very different had individuals taken responsibility for their actions. In his book, *Conjectures of a Guilty Bystander*, Thomas

A Birthday Letter To Gandhi

— *Pam McAllister*

Happy Birthday, Gandhiji! Who would have believed at your birth in the little town of Porbundar, India, that your first heartbeat would be celebrated and cherished 125 years later by a radical feminist living in New York City? Tonight I will turn on the TV news and hear, I'm sure, about children shooting each other in school, about other children caught in crossfire, about war and homelessness, hunger and hate. This is my world, Bapu. And still, you are here. Your spirit sustains me. Your photograph hangs on my wall.

As a feminist advocate of nonviolent action, I have encountered much resistance to your philosophy among my activist peers. This resistance is understandable : we are leery of anything that would appear to limit our range of options in challenging justice. We stumble over words and images. "Fight back" is a cry for strength for women tired of centuries of war, rape, battery, harassment, limited opportunities, broken dreams, crushed spirits. And "fight back" has the feel, if not the intent, of muscle, of clenched fist, of deft jabs and kicks. In the movies, romanticized "revolutionaries" chant heady slogans of death. In progressive newspapers, "freedom fighters" always carry guns. Jesus' admonition to "turn the other cheek" (revolutionary advice taken out of context and pitifully misinterpreted by most Bible-readers) is scorned as masochistic acceptance of oppression and an excuse for inaction. The word "pacifism" sounds too much like passivity, the word "nonviolence" sounds weak, and the word *"Satyagraha"* draws a complete blank. Still, I say to my sisters - Listen ! Gandhi said, "The first principle of nonviolent action is that of non-cooperation with everything humiliating". **Non-violent cooperation with every thing humiliating!** stand up! Act up! Fight back! — but do it without in turn humiliating another.

For the past decade it has been my passion to collect examples from around the world of women's creative use of nonviolent action and "noncooperation with everything humiliating". These stories are abundant, but buried. In 1705, English feminist Mary Astell observed, "Since the Men being the Historians, they seldom condescend to record the great and good Actions of Women". Sadly, this observation still holds true, and so I have set for myself the task of recording our stories, bringing them to life again that we might learn from our own resourceful legacy. Over centuries, women have experimented with and refined the tactics of nonviolence — vigil, marches, resistance, petitions, lysistrata actions, labor strikes, boycotts, sanctuary, hunger strikes, physical obstruction, civil disobedience. With these actions women have fought against slavery, organized for economic justice, raised our voices against censorship, worked for peace and justice. "If nonviolence is the law of our being," you proclaimed, "the future is with women." You were inspired by the courage of the women around you and with the sufferage activists in Europe. I am inspired by Women's courage too.

You also taught us, "Nonviolence is not a garment to be put off at will. Its seat is in the heart, and it must be an inseparable part of my very being". Though your *brahmacharya* experiments are a feminist's nightmare, in most other respects you demonstrated with your daily life that true nonviolence has to be a creed, not a policy, not a technique, not a tactic. You set an example in your attention to diet, to spinning, to silence and listening, and in your fearlessly wearing only a loincloth and shawl even in overdressed London. I say to my sisters — O Listen! It is time for us to grow beyond tactics and embrace nonviolence as "an inseparable part of our being". Nonviolence is about speaking the whole complicated truth, the truth of our rage, the truth of our longing, the truth of our tears and our laughter, the truth of our smallest fears and our grandest dreams.

As our fragile world creeps anxiously towards the year 2000, it is my sincere hope that women around the world will continue to be bold in our noncooperation with everything humiliating and will nurture all of humanity toward the day when no one will be the "Other" at the end of the gun. These are my musings on your 125th birthday — you who named yourself an "Untouchable" even while the world proclaimed you the *Mahatma*, the "Great Soul". Thank you for your experiments with Truth. Happy Birthday, Gandhi.

Love,
Pam McAllister

*In 1982, **Pam McAllister** edited the acclaimed anthology **Reweaving the Web of Life : Feminism and Nonviolence** (New Society Publishers, Philadelphia). Since then she has written two books **This River of Courage : Generations of Women Resistance and Action** (NSP, 1988). In 1992, Pam authored **Standing in the Need of Prayer**, a book of devotions for prisoners, published by the Presbyterian Criminal Justice Program. She is the Administrator of the Money for Women/Barbara Deming Memorial Fund, Inc. which gives grants to feminists in the arts. She is also a musician and has worked as a church organist and choir director for over twenty years.*

Melting The Heart Of Stone

— Carl Sagan

Our craving for heros is so ancient it predates our humanity. You can find it everywhere among the higher primates. We have a hereditary, built-in predisposition to follow and revere the dominant, or alpha, male. The young, and not just the young, long for role models. We need to be reassured that it is within our powers to behave more admirably than we ordinarily do. And so we manufacture heroes, most often out of perfectly ordinary people who have a particular skill for drama, music, sports, business, war, politics, or as — sometimes in the entertainment industry — just good looks. The hero is a focus of our thinking; the news media attend to him; children wish to be like him when they grow up; adults fantasize having him as a friend.

But primates have another predisposition, the episodic overthrow of the alpha male by a cabal of underlings. For us the existence of heroes is also a rebuke for not doing better. Bitter resentment of heroes is also easy to understand. Accordingly, we need reassurance that the hero is mortal and flawed. Since none among us is without flaws, heroes are toppled from their pedestals with satisfying frequency, especially — because information tends to flow more freely there — in democracies; especially — because of advances in communications technology — in our time.

When political and religious heroes rise, some of us are jealous and bitter, but many are buoyed by their success and made hopeful for the future; when their flaws are revealed, some of us take deep satisfaction, but many are disappointed and disillusioned. This recent acceleration of the process of exaltation and repudiation has helped to intensify cynicism, a yearning for an earlier heroic age, and pessimism about the future.

In some cases we are surely too severe in our debunkings. With the manifold constraints that society imposes on all those who grow up under its control, only the most submissive and unheroic characters will not have skirted the conventions or the law one way or another. Can't we bear heroes who also have flaws? Is it not childish to demand perfection from those we admire and hold dear?

Mohandas Karamchand Gandhi — widely called the *Mahatma*, the Great Soul

— was murdered on January 30, 1948. In a memorial service shortly after the assassination, Albert Einstein said,

Generations to come, it may be, will scarce believe that such a one as this ever in flesh and blood walked upon this earth ... He demonstrated that the allegiance of men can be won, not merely by the cunning game of political fraud and trickery, but through the living example of a morally exalted way of life.

In England, South Africa, and India, Gandhi had studied the European conquerors of indigenous peoples all over the world — their easy habit of command, their smug sense of superiority, their advanced weaponry, their casual ethnocentrism and xenophobia. What tool could a numerically superior, but technically inferior people use, without spilling rivers of blood, to secure their liberty against such an oppressor?

Martin Luther King, Jr. paid tributes to Gandhi for being the first person in history to apply the method of non-violent civil disobedience on a large political scale and with striking success. Gandhi counselled oppressed peoples not to repay violence with violence, but not to be compliant and obedient either. Instead, he advocated putting your body on the line, showing, by your willingness to be punished in defying an unjust law, the justice of your cause. Gandhi's restraint, his unwillingness to return evil for evil, aimed at transforming the opponent. "Real suffering bravely borne melts even a heart of stone", he said. Violence, even in the cause of justice, even in response to violence, is in the long term counterproductive : "There is no wall of separation between means and ends." Those who violently rebel — no matter how just their cause — teach that violence is the solution to our problems. What kind of leaders do violent revolutions let rise to the top? If we're not very careful, they and their successors become tyrants no better, and perhaps even worse, than those they replace.

In its ultimate use, Gandhi's method required bravery and valor at least at the level exercised by winners of the Victoria Cross or the Congressional Medal of Honor. "Wherein is courage required", he asked, "In blowing others to pieces from behind a cannon or with a smiling face to approach a cannon and to be blown to pieces?"

An astute assessment of Gandhi was made by the famous British classicist, Gilbert Murray :

Persons in power should be very careful how they deal with a man who cares nothing for sensual pleasure, nothing for riches, nothing for comfort or praise, or promotion, but is simply determined to do what he believes to be right. He is a dangerous and uncomfortable enemy, because his body which you can always conquer gives you so little purchase upon his soul.

"My ambition is much bigger than independence," Gandhi Said in 1928. "Through the deliverance of India I seek too deliver the so-called weaker races of the earth from the crushing heels of Western exploitation in which England is the greatest partner . . . . India's coming into her own will mean every nation doing likewise."

"If India becomes free," he told Franklin Roosevelt in the midst of the Second World War, "the rest will follow." India was the linchpin of the British Empire. The usurpation of territory through out Africa, the Mediterranean, and the Middle East was justified by imperial policy as essential to safeguard the links to India. Once India became independent in 1947, the ostensible justification for much of the British Empire collapsed. India's example inspired indigenous people in colonial nations all over the world. In this sense, Gandhi's militant non-violent non-cooperation freed a quarter of the world from imperialism.

On the other hand, global social, political and economic forces in the immediate post-war period were all working in the direction of decolonialization and inde-pendence. Had Gandhi never lived, had there been no early stirrings of independence in India, the Empire would almost certainly have dissolved anyway. Perhaps Gandhi accelerated the natural time-scale by a generation or to.

A few thousand imperial soldiers and bureaucrats had bullied the second most populous nation on Earth into subjugation. Gandhi had found a way to win freedom from that little island in the North Sea without a bloody revolution, without turning the victims of colonialism into mass murderers. He stripped imperialism of its romance and gold trim and revealed it to be simple theft. He made it much easier for other countries to win their freedom. It is no wonder he is venerated all over the planet.

Gandhi had no illusions about Utopia accompanying independence. Newly in-dependent nations will of course make mistakes, he said. But they would be their mistakes. Nor did he imagine that living standards would rapidly improved with independence. "Once India gains her independence, how long will it take her to reach Britain's standard of living?" he was once asked by a British official. His answer: "It took Britain half the globe's resources to reach its current standard of living. How many globes will it take India to reach Britain's standard of living?"

Perhaps his most daring proposal was to forestall the partition of India into two nations, one Hindu and one Muslim, by offering the Presidency of a newly free and united subcontinent to the head of the Muslim League, M.A. Jinnah. Gandhi's Hindu associates were appalled, the proposal was rejected, and it may have provided an additional reason for his assassination by radical Hindu nationalists. But I wonder whether a free India with such a beginning would not have been happier, more prosperous, less burdened by vendetta, and more deserving of the admiration of the world.

Where did Gandhi's brilliant insight into the power of nonviolent disobedience come from?

"Long before Gandhi," writes James MacGregor Burns in his book *Leadership*, "Christian thinkers were preaching nonviolence". But how long before Jesus were Indian thinkers preaching nonviolence? It goes back at least to Ashoka in the third century B.C. and Buddha in the sixth. A Zen Buddhist parable illustrates the tradition:

When a rebel army took over the Korean town, all fled the Zen temple except the Abbot. The rebel general burst into the temple, and was incensed to find that the master refused to greet him, let alone receive him as a conqueror.

"Don't you know," shouted the general, "that you are looking at one who can run you through without batting an eye?"

"And you," said the abbot, "are looking at one who can be run through without batting an eye!"

The general's scowl turned into a smile. He bowed low and left the temple.

In his childhood, Gandhi came upon a stanza in Gujarati, his native language, *"that gripped my mind and heart. Its percept — return good for evil — became my guiding principle."*

What the formulations of Burns and many others omits is that Gandhi's way is much more than non-violent resistance and disobedience to those unjustly in power. For this, there was another, more personal and more instructive, source of insight:

"I learnt the lesson of non-violence from my wife, when I tried to bend her to my will. Her determined resistance to my will on the one hand, and her quiet submission to the suffering my stupidity involved on the other, ultimately made me ashamed of myself and cured me of stupidity in thinking that I was born to rule over her."

As this paragraph makes clear, Gandhi had an ability, unusual in any of us, unprecedented among world leaders, and almost unknown among alpha males, for self-criticism. He has been taken to task for authoritarianism toward his wife and family and followers; for his struggle against the sexual impulse (without which this volume would have needed another editor); for his belief that a modern India could thrive as a decentralized federation of villages, subsisting on home handicraft technology; and, most unfairly, as Winston Churchill complained, for being a "half-naked fakir" with the temerity to negotiate on behalf of India with "the representative of the King Emperor" But no one criticized Gandhi more than Gandhi :

(the) path of self-purification is hard and steep. (one) has to become absolutely passion-free in thought, speech and action, to rise above the opposing currents of love and hatred. attachment and repulsion. I know that I have not in me as yet that triple purity inspite of constant ceaseless striving for it. That is why the world's praise fails to move me, indeed it often stings me. To conquer the subtle passions seems to me to be harder far than the physical conquest of the world by the force of arms....

I have not the qualifications for teaching my philosophy of life. I have barely qualifications for practicing the philosophy I believe. I am but poor struggling soul yearning to be ... wholly truthful and wholly non-violent in thought, word and deed, but ever failing to reach the ideal.

How could non-violent disobedience deter a modern army? Gandhi's only answer was by making them witness the courage of huge numbers of people unafraid of dying for their cause. "Behind the death-dealing bomb there is the human hand that releases it", he said, "and behind that still is the human heart that sets the hand in motion." But the heart is not engaged if the eyes and ears convey nothing of the horror. Aerial bombardment or naval gunnery — to say nothing of nuclear warfare — do not confront the slaughterers with the slaughtered. Indeed, this is one of the great efficiencies of modern warfare — arranging that only very thoughtful soldiers, possessed of vivid imaginations, need suffer any pangs of conscience.

When Kashmir was invaded in 1947, Gandhi did not object to the use of the Indian Army for defense. A month before his death, he was asked by General Cariappa how he could preach non-violence to the Army and simultaneously expect them to defend the country. He replied, "I am still groping in the dark for the answer. I will find it and give it to you some day".

Predictably, the Nazis did not think much of Gandhi's methods. In his The Myth of the Twentieth Century, published in 1930, the chief Nazi ideologist, Alfred Rosenberg, lamented that "the leader of Young India, Mahatma Gandhi, declares again and again that he does not think of a violent revolution against India."

Such a revolution is what Rosenberg knew about and hoped for. He consoled himself with the thought that "... an activist wing is at work .... under the direction of the National Bolshevist Pandit Nehru. The latter seems to be getting the upper hand."

Of course nothing of the sort happened. Jawaharlal Nehru's veneration of Gandhi, although not to the point of blind obedience, is evident, especially in his prison letters.

But this raises an interesting question : Was the effectiveness of Mohandas Gandhi much greater because the alternative was, or seemed to be, violence? Was the effectiveness of Martin Luther King Jr. in the United States enhanced by the presence of other brilliant and charismatic leaders willing to use "any means necessary"?

In South Africa, the African National Congress grew up in the Gandhian tradition. But by the 1950s it was clear that nonviolent non-cooperation was making no progress whatever with the ruling white Nationalist Party. So in 1961, Nelson Mandela and his colleagues formed a military wing of the ANC, the *Umkhonto we Sizwe*, the Spear of the Nation, on the grounds that the only thing whites understand is force. In light of recent history, were they right or wrong?

I have before me a letter by Gandhi to a British official, written in Bettiah and dated May 30,1917, shortly after his return to India from South Africa. He had taken up the grievances of the peasants of Gujarat and Bihar : "If Mr. Gandhi and his colleagues," he writes of himself in the third person, "are removed, it is expected that the leaders will one after another step into the breach ... the forcible removal of the mission is likely to lead to terrorism."

The letter closes, "Yours truly," but these two words, in a gesture I find reassuringly human, have been angrily struck in the same hand that signs the letter: "M. K. Gandhi". His civil disobedience was not yet fully devoid of the threat of violence.

Perhaps there are circumstances in which non-violent civil disobedience does not work, or not without an accompanying threat of a less principled alternative. But there are circumstances — probably many more than we realize — in which it does work, in which, despite what seems to be insurmountable obstacles, justice can be wrought by those who seem powerless. Gandhi's insight that almost all of us can be moved, that almost all of us have untapped reserves of compassion for our fellow humans, is a hypothesis that bears looking into by large-scale experiments.

The *Mahatma* awakened the global conscience about some of the great evils besetting our species, among them ethnocentricism, xenophobia, colonialism, and violence. In the seriousness of his objectives, and in his blending of theory, exhortation, and practice, he is one of the greatest heros — arguably the greatest — of the twentieth century.

But were Gandhi (who believed our inability to remember past lives was a kindness) somehow brought back to India today, I think he would be in anguish at the rampant, politically sanctioned, ethnocentrism and xenophobia; the still seething hostilities of Hindus, Moslems, Tamils, Sikhs, and indigenous peoples on the northeast frontier; the development of nuclear weapons on the subcontinent; police torture; rampant corruption and inefficiency; the continuing mistreatment of women, including immolation of wives for their dowries; and the pervasive abuse of the untouchables. He might wonder that he had left no successors, that there is no effective political force on the subcontinent employing his non-violent methods. India today is very nearly as it would have been had Gandhi never lived. A similar judgment applies, I think, to the rest of the planet as well.

We have very far to go. But I don't think Gandhi would have despaired. Instead, he would have selected the injustices most susceptible of being undone by non-violent action, and set to work. Because of the telecommunications revolution, each act of Gandhian courage — like the lone protestor who faced down a tank division outside Tiananmen Square — can awaken and inspire people worldwide.

Gandhi's way is very hard. But after all, one reason we have heroes is to inspire us to do more than we ever thought was possible.

Carl Sagan, who delivered the 1991 Nehru Memorial Lecture in New Delhi, teaches and does scientific research at Cornell University in Ithaca, NY. Our ambiguous relation with "alpha males" is described in his book (with Ann Druyan) **Shadows of Forgotten Ancestors : A Search for Who We Are** *(New York : Random House, 1992.)*

Spiritual Awakening

— *Norman Vincent Peale*

It is a mistaken notion that violence is a valid way to convey an opposed opinion. *Mahatma Gandhi* spent his whole life helping his fellow citizens achieve their independence. What it took George Washington seven years of bloody war to accomplish, Gandhi did over more than thirty years by the power of quiet, loving nonresistance.

Jesus made it clear that the most important thing in the world is our relationship to God and to others. When we achieve that, everything good will follow.

Unfortunately, there are hundreds of thousands of young people living today who have never known a genuine thrill. Lacking it, they fall back on synthetic substitutes — drugs and violence.

But they are entitled to know in their time what former generations knew in theirs : what it is to be part of something truly great — something that endows living with fascination and excitement. They simply cannot understand how spiritual commitment can supply this quality but when they really find it, they do go for it.

One time, while I was speaking in Calgery, Alberta, Canada, a fine looking man of about thirty-five came up to me with a beautiful wife and two children. He said, "Let me tell you something. Everything you said in this meeting is absolutely right and I will vouch for it. Take a look at me. I have been in and out of jail ever since I was a young boy. I never killed anybody, but I knifed a man once — and thank God he didn't die. I was bad, corruptible teenager, who resisted all goodness. I turned my back on my mother, my father, everything.

"One night a friend came to me and said, 'I want you to go with me, Jerry, to an entertainment.' Expecting some fun, I went along but stopped in front of a church.

"'What do you mean, entertainment?

My friend replied, 'You'll like this.'

"We went into the church where there was a big crowd singing songs. There was some music and entertainment, but then a young man got up and recounted a long story of the kind of life he had lived. I was fascinated, it was like my own life. Finally I heard him say, 'Jesus Christ came into my life and changed me.'

"This impressed me. Right there before my eyes was living proof that something could happen. So I gave my life to Christ. I was so bad that no kind of reasoning could help me, but in one instant I passed from crime to Christ. And life has been great ever since."

Changed people change situations. You can change things for sure — not through destructive force or an artificial substance — but through an individual spiritual experience.

*Norman Vincent Peale, Author of forty-three books, of which **Power of Positive Thinking**, one of the most successful books ever published, has been translated into forty-two languages, with a sale of over 20 million copies worldwide. Released in April 1991 is **This Incredible Century, Dr. Peale** comments on each decade since his birth, including personal remembrances interwoven with the history of the 20th Century. **Dr. Peale** has received several awards including Presidential Medal of Freedom, presented by President Reagan.*

This piece was probably the last one he wrote before he died.

Religious Intolerance
India's Greatest Tragedy
Since Gandhi's Assassination

— Dr. Homer A. Jack

The history of India is the history of centuries of conquest often by religion and often with much violence and killing. One exception was part of the era of the *Mughal* Emperor *Akbar* (1542-1605) when an effort was made to deal with all religions with unusual tolerance.

India is the mother of world religions and has welcomed another four. Buddhism, Hinduism, Jainism, and Sikhism originated in India. Christianity, Islam, Judaism and Zorastrianism were welcomed to India. Yet this birth of new religions and the absorption of outside ones has not been automatic. Hinduism has usually been less tolerant than its reputation in the West during the 20th century. An early nineteenth century *Hindu* who tried to "modernise" his religion was Ram Mohan Roy (1774-1833). He came to be considered to be "the father of modern India". He established the liberal *Hindu* sect, the *Brahmo Samaj*, with some connections with British Unitarianism. The Tagore family was identified with this tradition.

A later nineteenth century reformer of Hinduism was Swami Vivekananda (1863-1902). He became well known in the world, and India, by his stardom at the World's Parliament of Religions at Chicago in September 1893. Phrases from his speech at the closing of that first multireligious congress in modern times are still used to counter the proselytizing of all world religions, including his own :

"If anyone here hopes that (religious unity) will come by the triumph of any one of the religions and the destruction of the others, to him I say, 'Brother, yours is an impossible hope.' Do I wish that the Christian world become Hindu? God forbid. Do I wish that the Hindu or Buddhist world become Christian? God forbid . . . . The Christian is not to become a Hindu or a Buddhist, nor a Hindu or a Buddhist to become a Christian. But each must assimilate the spirit of the others and yet preserve his individuality and grow according to his own law of growth."
In this same address Vivekananda added : "The Parliament . . . has proved to

the world that holiness, purity, and charity are not the exclusive possession of any church in the world, and that every system has produced men and women of the most exalted character. In the face of this evidence if anybody dreams of the exclusive survival of his own and the destruction of the other, I pity him from the bottom of my heart, and point out to him that upon the banner of every religion would soon be written in spite of their resistance : 'Help, and not Fight'. . ."

Swami Vivekananda had much influence on the thinking of both Mohandas Gandhi and Jawaharlal Nehru (first Prime Minister of independent India), certainly more so than the World's Parliament of Religions had on these leaders. However, Nehru wrote briefly about the Parliament in his volume, *The Discovery of India*, which he wrote while in prison. In discussing Vivekananda generally, Nehru wrote, "passionately Vivekananda condemned the meaningless metaphysical discussions and arguments about ceremonies, and especially the touch-me-notism of the upper castes. 'Our religion is in the Kitchen. Our God is the cooking-pot and our religion says: "don't touch me, I am Holy".

Yet realism came from another Indian, Nirad Chaudhury in his Autobiography of an Unknown Indian. He wrote : "Hinduism has an uncanny sense of what threatens it. No plausible assurances, no euphemism, no disguise can put its ever-alert instincts of self-preservation off its guard."

Mohandas Gandhi was born a *Hindu* and died a *Hindu*. Yet his political work both in South Africa and India involved close working relationships with *Muslims* and members of other religions. He had to deal with religious pluralism and often spoke about it. Indeed, Gandhi frequently wrote about communalism.

"Hinduism . . . is the most tolerant creed because it is non-proselytizing and it is as capable of expansion today as it has been found to be in the past." (1916)

"Intolerance betrays want of faith in one's cause." (1921)

"I see no way of achieving anything in this afflicted country without a lasting heartfelt unity between Hindus and Mussalmans of India. I believe in the immediate possibility of achieving it because it is so natural, so necessary for both and because I believe in human nature." (1924)

"The Golden rule of conduct is mutual toleration, seeing that we will never all think alike and we shall see truth in fragments and from different angles of vision." (1926)

"If you cannot feel that the other faith is as true as yours, you should feel at least that the men are as true as you."(1927)

"To revile one another's religion, to make reckless statements, to utter untruth, to break the head of innocent men, to desecrate temples or mosques, is a denial of God." (1929)

"I do not like the word tolerance . . . Tolerance may imply a gratuitous assumption of the inferiority of other faiths to one's own, whereas Ahimsa (nonviolence) teaches us to entertain the same respect for the religious faith of others as we accord to our own, thus admitting the imperfections of the later." (1933)

"Even as a tree has a single trunk, but many branches and leaves, so there is one true and perfect religion, but it becomes many, as it passes through the human medium. Imperfect men put it into such languages as they can command, and their words are interpreted by other men equally imperfect. Whose interpretation is to be held to be the right one? Everybody is right from his own standpoint, but it is not possible that everybody is wrong. Hence the necessity of tolerance, which does not mean indifference to one's own faith, but more intelligent and purer love for it . . . True knowledge of religion breaks down the barriers between faith and faith. . ." (1935)

The fighters of Indian freedom long had the vision of an independent secular state. The All India Congress Committee of the Indian National Congress (founded in 1885) debated, adopted, and sent to the Karachi Congress of 1931 a resolution on Fundamentalist Rights and economic program. This declared that "any constitution which may be agreed to on its behalf should provide, among others, the following fundamental rights and duties : (i) Every citizen shall enjoy freedom of conscience and the right to freely profess and practice his religion, subject to public order and morality; (ii) All citizens are equal before the law, irrespective of religion, caste, creed or sex; (iii) no disability attaches to any citizen by reason of his or her employment, office of power or honour, and in the exercise of any trade or calling; (iv) All citizens have equal rights and duties in regard to wells, tanks, roads, schools and places of public resort, maintained out of state or local funds. . . "

In April 1948, after independence but before the Constitution of independent India was completed and adopted, Prime Minister Nehru delivered a speech to the Constituent Assembly endorsing a pending resolution against communalism. "Communalism should be eliminated from Indian life ... This Assembly is of opinion that no communal organisation which by its constitution or by the exercise of discretionary powers vested in any of its officers or organs, admits to or excludes from its membership persons on grounds of religion, race and caste, or any of them, should be permitted to engage in any activities other than those essential for the bona fide religious and cultural needs of the community, and that all steps, legislative and administrative, necessary to prevent such activities should be taken."

The Constitution of independent India was adopted by the Constituent Assembly in November 1949 and entered into force on 26th January, 1950. India, by its Constitution, is a "Sovereign Socialist Secular Democratic Republic with a parliamentary form of government elected on the basis of universal adult franchise." In article 14-18, all citizens, individually and collectively, are guaranteed the following basic freedoms : 1. The right to equality meaning equality before law; prohibition of discrimination on grounds of religion, race, caste, sex or place of birth; equality of opportunity in matters of employment; and abolition of titles." Articles 25-28 guarantee "the right to freedom of conscience and free profession, practice and propagation of religion."

The serious erosion of secularism in independent India did not begin at *Ayodhya* in 1986 or even 1992. Prime Ministers since Nehru, and other politicians, were easily influenced by religious and other minorities asking for special favours in return for political support - votes on the federal and state levels.

Prime Minister Rajiv Gandhi's government banned Salman Rushdie's "Satanic Verses", in what appeared at the time to be an easy way to pander to the *Muslim* minority. An attempt was made to give special status to *Aligarh Muslim University*. Also the initial treatment of *Sikhs* in the *Punjab* by Nehru's daughter (Mrs. Indira Gandhi) and grandson (Rajiv Gandhi) did not reflect pristine secularism.

The most publicised example of the erosion of secularism was the *Shah Bano* case and its implications.

Ahmed Khan of *Indore* in 1978 divorced his wife of 43 years, *Shah Bano*, and refused to pay maintenance (alimony) asserting that customary Muslim Law (*Shariat*) did not demand it. *Shah Bano* went to court, and in a series of judgements, the courts decided that according to the criminal code of India, she must be paid maintenance. The final ruling in 1986 caused some *Muslims* in parts of India to riot. This led Rajiv Gandhi's Congress Party to get a law through the federal parliament asserting that the criminal code did not apply to Muslim marriages and that a Muslim husband could act according to customary Muslim law and leave maintenance of divorced wife to her family or the Muslim community. This new Law - the Muslim Women's Bill - caused consternation if not rioting in the *Hindu* community and in some sections of the *Muslim* community, especially women.

The *Shah Bano* "case" helped worsen *Hindu-Muslim* relations for more than a decade and probably helped bring more India-wide focus on the *Ayodhya* situation after 1986.

Ayodhya - meaning "a place of no wars" - is a small city several hundred miles southeast of *Delhi*. It is also east of *Lucknow*, the capital of *Uttar Pradesh* state, the largest in India with 139 million population. Today *Ayodhya* has about 15,000 residents, about one-fifth being *Muslims*. It is said that it is a city of 8,000 shrines. At *Ayodhya* in 1528-29 the founder of the *Mogul* dynasty, the Timurid prince *Babr* or *Babur*, built a three-domed mosque - *Babri Masjid*. This was a century before the *Taj Mahal* was built (between 1632-54), outside *Agra*, 200 miles west of *Ayodhya*.

For several centuries the *Babri Masjid* was used, one of many in *Ayodhya*. Some *Hindus* in the meantime identifide the *Babri Masjid* as the exact location where the *Hindu* warrior-king, *Ram*, was born 5,000 years ago. In 1949, idols of *Rama* and his consort, *Sita*, appeared inside the *Babri Masjid*. There was a immediate controversy over whether they were placed there by humanbeings or by the gods! (Nehru and his Congress Party ruled in New Delhi and the *Uttar Pradesh* state at the time). There was no immediate outcry, although some *Muslims* took the case to court. There was no judicial ruling.

In the 1960s local *Hindus* were demanding that the *Babri Masjid* be "restored" as a temple. By 1970 *Hindus* appealed to the courts that they be allowed to worship in the *Babri Masjid*. A magistrate ordered that the *Masjid* be padlocked pending clarification on the facts - was it originally a *Hindu* temple ? In February 1986 *Hindus* again petitioned the court to allow them to restore the temple. Congress under Prime Minister Rajiv Gandhi was in power at the center and also ruled *Uttar Pradesh*. A judge allowed the locks on the *Babri Masjid* to be opened and the shrine was in effect converted into a *Hindu* Temple. This decision caused widespread rioting and deaths.

In 1990, the *Vishva Hindu Parishad* (VHP) sponsored a pilgrimage to *Ayodhya* to demolish the *Masjid*. This was led by L. K. Advani who rode across India in a chariot-cum-Toyota looking like a Bombay-film version of an ancient vehicle for warriors. The *Kar Sevaks* at *Ayodhya* were stopped from demolishing the *Masjid*, but not before some were killed during communal riots in several parts of India. This situation brought the downfall of the V.P. Singh Government in Delhi. The Congress Party resumed power, with the *Bharatiya Janta Party* (BJP) becoming the chief opposition in parliament.

In the autumn of 1992 several developments occurred. Professor B.B. Lal made a report on archaeological excavations at the *masjid*/temple. The VHP and the All-India *Babri Masjid* Action Committee (AIBMAC) held negotiations. Pressure was put on the Muslims to give up their claim to a 2.77 acre plot adjacent to the *Masjid*.

The Supreme Court of India on November 28th ruled that construction of a temple on the site of the *Babri Masjid* must not be allowed and agreed to rule on the ownership of the disputed land. However, it accepted a plea from the *Uttar*

Pradesh Government to allow the singing of hymns at the disputed site by *Kar Sevaks*. The Court ruled that this injunction was against any construction of a new temple. Also the Supreme Court appointed a special judge to maintain scrutiny on the spot and file daily reports.

The National Integration Council (NIC) met in late November, although boycotted by the BJP. The Council supported "any action" the Prime Minister would take to enforce the law on the *Ayodhya* issue.

The *Muslim* community of India agreed to forsake all claims to the *Babri Masjid* if it were declared by archaeologists to have been the site of a *Hindu* temple. The *Muslims* hoped, however, that the *Masjid* would not be demolished, but a *Hindu* temple built around it.

The Chief Minister of *Uttar Pradesh*, Kalyan Singh, (whose BJP government came to power in 1991) assured the Prime Minister that events would be controlled on December sixth.

Between July and December 1992, Prime Minister P.V.Narsimha Rao tried to negotiate a solution to the impasse. He declared, "I can fight the BJP, but I cannot, and no one else for that matter, can fight Lord *Ram*." Yet his actions at the time and certainly in retrospect can only be called weak and temporising, putting too much faith in promises of the fundamentalistic *Hindus* and not sufficiently appealing to the Indian Constitution and other law.

No solution to the impasse appeared possible as December began. The right-wing *Hindu* leaders appeared somewhat divided about whether to accept a face-saving symbolic *Kar Seva* on December sixth or to go beyond that compromise and begin constructing the temple.

The destruction of the *Babri Masjid* was not "spontaneous". Evidence points to an orchestrated, premeditated act by several *Hindu* organisations.

The violence at *Ayodhya* on December Sixth resulted in much tragedy and other actions. Only the briefest outline can be given here. Reactions occurred on several levels : by the Indian people often in religious groups, by the Indian government, and by those outside India itself.

As a result of the demolition of *Babri Masjid*, there were communal riots not only in *Ayodhya* on December sixth, but the next day and for weeks afterwards in an estimated 135 or more cities throughout India. A conservative estimate puts the deaths over 1,200 during the first month, with thousands more injured and much property destroyed. It was the worst violence in India since partition of the country. All reports indicated that the "majority" of deaths were *Muslims* "Killed by local (Hindu) police".

The demolition of the *Babri Masjid* at *Ayodhya* on December 6, 1992, is only the latest tragedy in *Hindu/Muslim* relations in post-independent India.

The Indian Government and all Indian Institutions and people must act with all deliberate speed to reverse the trend of India's becoming a *Hindu* state and losing its secular character.

Any march to *Ayodhya* to rebuild the *Babri Masjid* would be foolhardy and only encourage more violence which again could not be limited to *Ayodhya*. A plan is needed whereby both the *Babri Masjid* and a *Ram Mandir* could be built. If both were constructed side by side they could become a national place of prayer and pilgrimage. Delicate negotiations are necessary to reach this goal, validated by both the federal parliament and most *Hindu* and *Muslim* organisations and communities.

All political parties must forgo the use of religion for their own partisan ends. The leaders of Hinduism and *Islam* must not allow their religions to be politicised.

Educational programs for children, youth, and adults must be accelerated for national integration and against communalism.

Hindu/Muslim understanding remains much more of a *Hindu* problem than a *Muslim* one. The *Muslim* must be sensitive to *Hindu* feelings, yet *Hindus* and Hinduism as a vast majority control the agenda which could make India a whole nation again.

The Government of India and Indians at all levels must return to their principal task: to strengthen the economic and social life of the majority of the people - the rural and urban poor.

The continuing plight of Dalits and untouchables in India must be addressed. This problem is related to *Hindu/Muslim* relations.

The secular state in India and the separation of church and state in U.S.A. are not ends in themselves. Further exhilaration, beginning on an international level, are needed on enhancing the spiritual life of believers and indeed of all peoples in all nations without succumbing to continuing and often rising fundamentalism.

Religious fundamentalism is not monolithic. It can be exploited by politicians and clerics, yet it need not be violent or totalitarian. Fundamentalism can respect other religions and secular authorities must persevere in working with fundamentalists in all religions, but not pander to any of their intolerant or undemocratic demands.

One of the best observations about *Ayodhya* comes from Aroon Purie, editor of the New Delhi magazine India Today. "The tragic event has revealed the shocking state of Indian society . . . a society so hollow that a mockery is made of the highest court of the land, a government so weak that it cannot enforce the rule of law, and a social fabric so tenuous that it soaks itself in blood at the slightest provocation." He also observed that India "has always prided itself, quite justifiably, as the world's largest democracy and a secular one at that. Today that has been put in doubt."

The *Ayodhya* tragedy raises the whole problem of organised religion in a pluralistic state. This is not confined to India but also includes - among others - the U.S.A. The working of the secular state of India have over more than four decades, shown to have been flawed. Questions have long been raised about the "separation of church and state" solution to pluralist, multireligious society in the U.S.A. New approaches merit examination, such as a pluralism along the lines of a "smorgasbord" or "fruit Salad" of separate world faiths instead of the non-spiritual, lowest common denominator of the non-sectarian "religious melting pot." In the U.S.A. both black/white relations and ethnic relations - for example, the role once of Polish/Americans and now of Asian/Americans - are being reexamined. This is not only because of attacks from the "religious right", but because limitations demand being "appreciated", not merely "tolerated".

It is too early to posit any pluralistic polity, but the old relationships merit study and examination as new relationships between and among religious groups in pluralistic societies are proposed.

Today in India, but elsewhere including Bosnia and Herzegovina, a majority people act as if they were a persecuted minority and violate - often violently - the human rights of true minorities. Aryeh Neier, writing in The Nation magazine, attributed this phenomena, not entirely new, partly to a lack of real understanding of democracy.

He insists that democracy must be understood as involving much more than self-determination and includes protecting the rights of minorities. However, today, some majorities, such as some *Hindus* in India, recall that they once were conquered people. They have century-long memories and attribute collective guilt to their erstwhile oppressors.

*Dr. Homer Jack was a U.S. clergyman, writer, and peace and human rights activist. He was a founder and first Secretary-General (1969-84) of WCRP. He published the book **WCRP : A History of the World Conference on Religion and Peace**. A Gandhi scholar **Dr. Jack** died in August 1993, soon after writing **Ayodhya : Indias Greatest Tragedy Since Gandhi's Assassination***.

Science Without Humanity

— Alan Lightman

When I was a young man, and a budding physicist, I grew indignant at people who held Oppenheimer and Fermi and Bethe responsible for the atomic bomb. Theoretical physics is a pure intellectual activity, I said; it is the politicians who decide how to use the inventions of science. As if scientists were ethically neutral, or perhaps lived apart.

But scientists do not live apart. Scientists live in a community, in a culture. Indeed, they are deeply affected by that culture. The humanities provide the store of ideas and images that scientists draw from. Einstein, in his autobiographical notes, credits the Scottish philosopher David Hume with certain critical ways of thinking that helped lead him to the theory of relativity. As another example, the exploding star of 1954 A.D., the Crab Nebula, was sighted and documented by the Chinese, but nowhere mentioned in the West, where the Aristotelian notion of the immortality of stars still held sway. We often do not see what we do not expect to see. Science, in turn, deeply affects the surrounding culture, not just by bombs and by bridges, but by ideas. The great discoveries in science are not just about nature. They are about people as well. After Copernicus, we have taken a more humble view of our place in the cosmos. After Darwin, we have recognized new relatives clinging to the family tree. The great ideas of science have changed our view of the world and ourselves.

Scientists are people, and they cannot be ethically neutral. They must be concerned with the impact of science. Since the Industrial Revolution, we have followed the unquestioned assumption that increasing science and technology automatically improve the quality of life. The more science and technology the better. This assumption ought to be questioned. In less than ten years, we may have hand-held devices that put us within reach of our offices 24 hours a day, 7 days a week. In fifty years, we may be able to design human beings in a test tube. Will these developments improve the quality of life?

Science and technology have a certain feeling of inevitability; they seem to roar ahead like a train careening downhill, with no engineer on board. We must look where we are going. How this will happen, I don't know. Science is a creative activity, and it is difficult to curb the creative imagination. It goes where it wants to go. As for technology it is often driven by economic considerations. If something has a market, it will be built. But unexpected things can happen. Some countries have at last realized that atomic weapons can never be used and are now embarked on dismantling their warheads. Some governments have established guidelines for genetic research.

No human endeavor has more power for good, or for bad, than does science. We must not have science without humanity.

Alan Lightman is professor of science and writing and senior lecturer in physics at the Massachusetts Institute of Technology. He is the author of many books and articles on the human side of science. His most recent book Einstein's Dreams, a work of fiction, has been internationally acclaimed and translated into 20 languages.

When God Takes Care Of You

— Andrew Young

When Martin Luther King, Jr.'s home was bombed in Montgomery back in 1956, the men of the neighborhood came to the scene of the bombing carrying weapons. This was a natural response. Every one in the nation had been conditioned by the violence of that war and beneficiaries of extensive military training.

But Martin, even as a young man of twenty-six, had a vision of another possible approach to the problems and conflicts we faced as human beings. He urged the men to go home and take their guns back to the safety of their closets. If we follow the Old Testament law of 'An eye for an eye and a tooth for a tooth,' we will just end up with a nation that is blind and toothless. "No", he said, "we must discover 'a more excellent way.'"

Martin was using the terminology of the apostle Paul in his letter to the Corinthians as he introduced the beautiful psalm of love in 1 Corinthians 13. Martin was also strongly influenced by the nonviolent ideas of Mahatma Gandhi in his successful drive for India's independence.

Gandhi challenged India to resist evil without resorting to evil. He accepted the spiritual potential of India as worthy of cultivation. "Love of the hater is the most difficult of all. But by the grace of God, even this most difficult thing becomes easy to accomplish if we want to do it."

In our struggles against southern racism, we too chose to accept this moral and pragmatic challenge. We understood that it would not help us to get jobs if we destroyed the factories. Our intent was to be included in the life of America, and this required a moral struggle. We were trying to create brothers, not enemies, so like Gandhi we began to engage in experiments with the truth and power of nonviolence.

When Martin went to jail in Albany, Georgia in 1962, I was a new arrival in the movement. I was given the task of visiting him in jail twice daily to keep him informed of the movement's progress and problems. On my first visit, I entered the jail and said politely, "Excuse me, I'd like to see Dr.King, please." Without even looking up, the desk sergeant shouted to the jailer, "There's a little nigger out here to see those big niggers back there."

I was so taken aback that I didn't know what to do. To express my indignation would only get me thrown in jail or barred from visiting, and someone had to be able to move in and out of jail to keep information flowing if it were at all possible. Violence was no answer. The sergeant was six-foot five-inch, 250-pound, former football player with a stick and gun. I did, however, make a note of his name on his uniform. When I came back the next day, I addressed him by name. "Good morning, Sergeant Hamilton, how are you doing today?"

Now, he seemed shocked, and grunted, "Okay".

From that time on, I never went to jail without addressing Sergeant Hamilton by name and engaging him in some brief small talk before asking to see Dr. King. He never again spoke disrespectfully to me, and we actually became familiar with each other's families and sports interests. Of course, as every one in the southern farm belt does, we talked about the weather. I not only survived, I accomplished my mission and visited the jail daily until Martin was released.

Constant confrontation with people with whom you differ requires some solution. Most of the time, black people just avoided the confrontation and accepted the mutual animosity. That was pattern of behavior before the movement. But for black Americans it was impossible to completely avoid confrontation and humiliation. These problems almost always occurred when we were least prepared and least expected it.

Through the civil rights movement we attempted to change the pattern of avoidance and accidental confrontation which left so many black people intimidated, demeaned, and insecure. Our movement was to change the relationship from one of fear and distrust to a relationship of respect and understanding. That meant we had to aggressively challenge the system and its violence, but with aggressive, organized, disciplined goodwill.

For years we had read the Sermon on the Mount in the Gospel of Matthew :

> *Love your enemies, bless those who curse you,*
> *do good to those who hate you,*
> *and pray for those who spitefully use you and persecute you,*
> *That you may be sons of your Father in heaven;*
> *for He makes His sun rise on the evil and on the good,*
> *and sends rain on the just and on the unjust.*

(Matt. 5:44-45)

Now with nonviolent direct action, we had a method with which to bring alive that radical notion that all men, women, and children belonged to the same heavenly Father. We pursued this method as the means by which we could make Christ's call at least a partial reality and not just a utopian ideal.

Nonviolent direct action seeks to change an unjust situation by addressing it openly and publicly in an attempt to raise it "before the court of world opinion" in the confidence that it can be changed without violence. There is no guarantee, of course, and no method is foolproof. However, with nonviolence or, Gandhi called it "truth force", neither person nor property is destroyed. At times you will be called on to suffer, but never will you inflict suffering.

There is a strange power in innocent suffering. We see it in the Book of Acts with the conversion of the Apostle Paul as he moved to reorient his life after viewing the martyrdom of Stephen. I have never been one to seek suffering, and I believe that God must lead one into the path of suffering. A person's ambition or need for attention will not suffice in the face of suffering. However, one day my number came up in St. Augustine, Florida in the summer of 1964.

St. Augustine was a tough place. Hosea Williams, a chemist with the U.S. Department of Agriculture, had recently joined the SCLC staff, and he had gone to St. Augustine to work with the movement.

Hosea was a disabled veteran of World War II who had been in a foxhole in Germany and suffered a direct hit by a Nazi bomb. Everyone in the foxhole was killed except Hosea. He survived and, after a year in Veteran's hospitals, returned to Georgia where he was roughed up by local police in a Greyhound Bus station for drinking water from the only working water fountain on a hot summer day. Of course, in 1945 even a disabled veteran of the war was still a second-class citizen. Hosea's passion for justice was fired by this incident, and he became convinced that God had saved him in Germany so that he could fight for justice in the United States. This made him an extremely valuable member of Dr. King's team, but one who was always too ready to demonstrate.

In the summer of 1964, the Civil Rights Act was being debated in the Congress, and further demonstrations seemed unnecessary. The SCLC strategy called for a careful marshaling of our limited resources and a deliberate selection of our points of confrontation. The National situation was moving along fairly well in the Congress. The Interreligious Council on Religion and Race had mobilized national religious bodies to support the Civil Rights Bill, and it seemed just a matter of time until the bills passed. How long could the traditional filibuster last? St. Augustine didn't seem to be necessary to our plan of action, so Martin sent me down there to "wind the movement down gracefully" and bring Hosea home.

I arrived in St. Augustine in the late evening. There was a white mob gathered around the town square. I went directly to the church to join the mass meeting in progress. About one hundred people, mostly older women and young teenagers, were gathered in a small church. As Hosea saw me enter the back of the church, he announced, "Reverend Andy Young is here to lead the demonstration", and he called for volunteers to march with me down to the Old Slave Market near the town square.

At that point, I had no intention of leading anyone into that mob. They were shouting and drinking and generally trying to intimidate anyone who might want to challenge the traditions represented by the Old Slave Market. But I didn't want anyone else to lead people down there either. When I discovered that this march had already been announced, and any cancellation would appear to be cowardice, I decided that I would lead the march in order to keep things under control. There had been little or no training in St.Augustine, and that mob was as mean a crowd as I had ever seen.

We marched from the church with just about thirty demonstrators. It was not a very impressive group after the thousands who had marched in Birmingham. But then movements always seemed to start with only the chosen, courageous few. I was trying to decide just how far we could go and yet avoid a confrontation. But what I didn't consider was that these people were standing up against segregation for the first time in their lives. It was not just another march for them. It was their first march towards freedom and they could not turn back. They had been singing, "Oh freedom, Oh freedom over me, And before I'll be a slave, I'd be buried in my grave, and go home to my Lord and be free".

As we approached the street leading to the town square, we were stopped by Sheriff L.O.Davis. He told us to turn around and go back. There was a mob of four or five hundred people in the square, and he only had twenty-seven men on his force, so they could not possibly assure us of safety or offer any protection against the mob. He had already convinced me, but I asked the group to form a circle so that we could pray for guidance.

My prayer was an honest, simple appeal for guidance. I didn't ask God to protect us because I was ready to go back to the church. As far as I was concerned, the risks were too great for a handful of women and children. A march of thirty men would have been much less risky. These mobs seldom, if ever, attacked a group of men, but black men rarely had the courage to lead demonstrations. They had much more to lose.

Typically, individual black men were the primary victims of intimidation, job loss, violence, or even loss of their lives. So, many black men hid behind the macho pose that they couldn't be nonviolent. Occasionally I would shame them by marching. " You and your family are oppressed every day, and you've never been violent to anybody white!" The men were nonviolent daily when confronted by white people. I would go on, "We don't count stabbing your buddies in a crap game or beating your wife and children. That's not being violent, that's being sick. You take your frustration out on the people who love you rather than confront the people who are daily denying you your freedom, your education, your job security, and your advancement just because of the color of your skin".

It was always frustrating that we couldn't get more men, especially young men, to participate. Usually young male SCLC staff members who had been brought in as part of the training team marched with the local people, and they were often the only men in the march.

And tonight was no different; we still lacked men. But much to my surprise, we had a cadre of determined, nonviolent warriors, even though they were mostly women and teenagers.

After I prayed, one of the "good ol' sisters" sang out in a loud, clear voice: "Be not dismayed, whate'er be tide, God will take care of you. Beneath his wings of love abide, God will take care of you".

Then everyone joined in on the chorus: "God will take care of you, Through every day . . . all the way; He will take care of you, God will take care of you".

We sang out an affirmation of faith that was about to be tested. I finally realized that there was no turning back for any logical or pragmatic reason. So I was trapped, but I was still determined that we could finish this march without any one being hurt.

We marched, still singing softly, "God will take care of you". And I thought to myself, It is one thing to sing this in church where it's easy to believe, but the song says through every day, and this is night time in St. Augustine. The mob was still a block away, but they, too, became strangely quite when they realized that we were marching towards them. The silence was broken by the rattle of chains and the shattering of a bottle. It was easy to anticipate what the shattering of a bottle meant. It was easy to anticipate what they had in mind. Mobs could do almost anything under the cover of night, especially when they really had the support of the local law enforcement.

I began to understand what it meant to "walk through the valley of the shadow of death . . . (and) fear no evil" (Ps. 23:4 kjv). I was not afraid for some reason, perhaps because I was determined that none of those good people get hurt.

I remember being very disturbed when one of the ministers walking with me heard the shattering of glass and murmured an expletive. I simply said, "Don't cuss — pray".

Soon we approached a road blocked by a group of burly white men. I stopped the march and decided that I must try to talk with them. There was no turning back, so I walked over to the gang. I later learned the gang was led by "Hoss" Manucy, an underprivileged white man who really thought that his security and survival depended on keeping blacks down. Hoss was seen on national television bragging, "I'm a good Christian. I don't smoke; don't drink; I just beat niggers".

The sheriff was nowhere to be found. I don't think I even got a word out. I was standing there face-to-face with the one man who seemed like the leader, and then someone blindsided me. I didn't feel a thing, but I remember being hit in the jaw with someone's best punch and almost simultaneously being clubbed with what must have been a blackjack. From then on it was lights out. Only several years later did I see a film clip of the beating I took. I was stomped and kicked and probably only spared serious injury because I instinctively rolled into a ball and protected my head and stomach from direct blows.

When I came to my senses, I was being helped to my feet by Willie Bolden of the SCLC staff, who had come to my rescue. I didn't feel any physical pain or fear. I was only determined that we keep on marching. All of our thinking and training had taught us that if you let violence deter you, you're only empowering and encouraging violence. At this point, even though I was probably not aware of what I was doing or what had happened to me, I knew that we could not let this violence stop our march. If it did, it would soon crush our movement.

Martin was fond of preaching, "We will match your ability to inflict suffering with our ability to endure suffering in the confidence that unearned suffering is redemptive".

The mob had left me on the ground and moved back into the park, certain that I had learned my lesson. As I came back to the front of the line I said, "We can't stop now, let's go". And slowly but surely the straggling band of nonviolent marchers continued. I then remember someone in the mob cussing and saying, "Them niggers got some nerve".

I don't know what motivated us to march on, but it certainly wasn't cheekiness. It was closer to faith and determined belief that "the Lord will make a way out of no way". But the way was not to open yet. The same gang moved and once again blocked our way. Again I kept marching slowly and surely until they stood a few feet in front of us.

This time, I did get to utter a sentence. "We are not here to do any harm," I said simply. "We merely want to have a word of prayer at this place where our ancestors were brought and sold as slaves, to ask God to help us end slavery in all its forms".

Just as I finished my sentence, a young boy burst through the crowd and attempted to kick me in my testicle. Fortunately this time I saw him coming and shifted just a bit to the side. As I bent over to avoid the kick, the blackjack again came across my head. This time it merely hurt and left a knot. I did not go down and, thank God, I did not go out, (For months later, I kept wishing I could meet one of these guys alone and away from St. Augustine and the discipline of the movement. I was still struggling with a total commitment to nonviolence, but I had no questions that it was the only tactic that had a chance for success in the South.)

Then, as if by magic, Sheriff Davis appeared and waved the crowd away with one sweep of his hand and said, : "Let 'em through". And we walked on to the Old Slave Market, knelt in prayer, and then returned to the church without incident.

After it was over, I felt a real sense of triumph. No one was seriously hurt. My bruises lasted for months but a new sense of personal confidence also became a part of my life. This had been a real test, and I hadn't faltered.

We demonstrated at the beaches and swimming pools during the day. The marches continued at night. The federal court, under Judge Brian Simpson, ordered the sheriff to protect us. Judge Simpson also exposed the connection between the Klan, the mob, the Ancient City Gun Club and the office of Sheriff's deputies. They were one and the same.

As the movement progressed, St. Augustine may have become our bloodiest struggle. In subsequent demonstrations, we were not able to limit the attacks to a single person; almost everyone suffered in St. Augustine. But I had never seen a more determined people. They went to jail or to hospitals, and when they were released, they were back in the demonstration.

In St. Augustine my wife joined in a march for the first time where I was working, Jean often demonstrated in Atlanta, and I tried my best to convince her that her movement was teaching children — our own three daughters and those with whom she worked in the Atlanta public school system. I argued her task was helping the young to be ready to contribute in an integrated society. She insisted on joining me in St. Augustine. In did not march in the same demonstration with Jean. It was our policy that loved ones not be allowed to take part in the same demonstrations. It put too much strain on one's commitment to nonviolence. It is much easier to suffer yourself than it is to stand by and watch your wife or children attacked.

The experience of marching through the hate-filled mob was frightening. with faces contorted and venomous language flowing from their mouths, the people in the mob waved iron pipes and clenched fists.

But Jean says she will always remember the words of the elderly black women with whom she marched : "Ain't they sad".

On July 2, 1964, President Lyndon Johnson signed the historic Civil Rights Package. Martin went to join Roy Wilkins of the NAACP, Whitney Young of the Urban League, and others for the signing of this bill into law, which committed the United States of America to the enforcement of protection for the rights of all citizens. This legislation also included protection for the rights of women and Hispanic citizens who, though they did not share the legacy of slavery, still experienced wide discrimination.

Hosea Williams and I remained around St. Augustine. We decided to celebrate July Fourth with friends and family and give people a chance to discuss the Civil Rights Bill and its meaning in St. Augustine. Our plan was to test the enforcement and implementation of desegregated public accommodations after the holiday.

After several weeks of having walked "through the valley of the shadow of death", we were pleasantly surprised by the friendly but nervous reception we received as we went to the very places where we previously had been brutalized and arrested and quietly ordered coffee. When the nervous waitress poured coffee to overflowing and offered apologetically to get a new cup, I was filled with joy as I thought: *Thou preparest a table before me in the presence of mine enemies; thou annointest my head with oil; my (coffee) cup runneth over* (Ps. 23:5 kjv).

The refusal to hate, the willingness to forgive and begin a new pattern of relationships under federally enforced law marked a new era for the South and the nation. Southern white churches had not been in the forefront of the struggle for racial justice, but once the law changed, they encouraged and supported compliance. The resistance melted surprisingly fast. We experienced one of the most radical shifts in law and tradition in human history. It was accompanied with very little violence and suffering, when compared with the armed conflict and terrorism which characterized most movements for social change.

The American South almost immediately began to heal its wounds and begin an era in which it would inspire and provide leadership for the nation and the world. The emergence of men and women of talent and vision from the South led to the election of several of the nation's most progressive and innovative governors. One of them, Jimmy Carter, became president in 1976 and made the American Ideal — "that all men (and women and children) are created equal, and endowed with certain inalienable rights" — an important element of America's foreign policy. Over time I moved from a battered form lying in the streets of St. Augustine to the halls of the United Nations as ambassador and spoke for our nation's human rights policy.

This degree of rapid progress and prosperity was possible only because in our struggle we destroyed no resources. We overcame evil with love and discovered that there is a power of the spirit that can change people and nations more effectively than bombs and bullets.

I will always cherish two memories of St. Augustine that symbolize nonviolence at its best. First, that a small group of women and young people had the faith that "God will take care of you". This unwavering belief led them out into the night of hatred and violence with a quiet courage and determination. And second, the beautiful sound of the black community singing as the Ku Klux Klan marched through St. Augustine on a Saturday evening, after having inflicted their hatred and violence on us for weeks.

As the Klan passed by, black people greeted them singing, "I love everybody in my heart".

Ambassador Andrew Young, was the Ambassador of U.S.A. at the U.N., he participated in the Civil Rights Movement along with Dr. Martin Luther King, Jr.,

The Power Of Greed

— Harry Schwarz

The value of peace is not appreciated until it is absent. Many in this world know nothing of conflict and many others live in such violent societies that they have almost come to accept it as part of their existence.

In some societies there is much injury and loss of life through such incidents as motor vehicle accidents and these are accepted as routine because people have become conditioned to them, they make no headlines in the news. Only when a person is affected through a family member or friend is it a cause of concern or grief.

So too people have become conditioned to the environment of violence in which they live. In some cases violence flourishes in deprived communities, in others it is racial, religious and language conflict and again in other instances it is the imposition of power or totalitarianism which results in a striving for freedom.

An examination of most conflict situations however demonstrates they revolve around struggles for limited resources. Often when an economy thrives, people who may be divided on ethnic or other grounds, live in peace together but when conditions of hunger, unemployment or massive wealth gaps exist between groups, these appear to be recipes for conflict.

The attainment of peaceful solutions to conflict must therefore have as an essential ingredient an increase in resources and an ability by all to obtain legitimately, a proper share.

The people of this world claim great progress in many fields. Humans walk on the moon, pictures of the planets are relayed to earth, computers find instant solutions to problems humans would take months to solve but in the field of conflict resolution there is abject failure.

In respect of the distribution of resources, the world has been unable to reconcile incentive and need, reward and greed. While in some regions there are surpluses, they fail to fill the deficits in others.

However, conflict is not restricted in its causes to these matters. There appears to be an inherent desire of some to exercise power over others. The power which some people seek is seen in politics, in business, even in minor organizations where people struggle for position sometimes for status mostly for power.

Businessmen seek to establish vast corporations and amass wealth. Politicians seek power and by simple words and phrases given as orders or by persuasive tongues, change the lives of many people. Leaders of nations seek to expand their authority and sometimes plunge countries into war. The search for power over others whether as an individual or as a group is certainly a major cause of conflict.

Another cause is ignorance. A failure to know what a fellow human's characteristics are, can result in hatred or fear. Much of the world's racism results from lack of knowledge or misinformation. Because there is no knowledge of what a religion which is different to one's own preaches or practices, there is an almost automatic fear, dislike or even hatred. Tolerance appears to be the exception not the rule. It applies to many other characteristics of humans, including colour, race, nationality or language. Instead of seeking to know the persons and ascertain their beliefs and intentions, there is an "anti" syndrome created.

My own country is presently the scene of much violence. There has been oppression and discrimination. It has affected all aspects of peoples lives, not merely their right to vote, but their schooling, their right to occupation and ownership of land, their jobs and much more. There was a struggle for freedom which was carried out in different ways. Some took the route of the armed struggle, others chose non-violent means. Tragically some of those who decided to change the system peacefully are now described by those who chose violence as not real participants in the striving for justice.

Even sadder is the fact that now when there are negotiations to change the system to remove the injustices and considerable progress has been made, There is an escalation of violence. More of our people are dying just when the door to the new South Africa is to be fully opened.

How do we achieve a world without violence? Perhaps we should start with basics, in our own homes, in our communities and in our countries.

In South Africa we need to know each other better. We need to recognise the rights of all people and remember our own obligations, and to know that each human being is entitled to respect.

The resources of our country are great and all who are there should not only contribute their expertise and labour but participate in the fruits. Reward does not come without effort and effort needs reward.

We are a country of many ethnic groups, languages and religions and we need to learn to live in harmony if we are to survive. We can do it if we have the will and the moral values to sustain us. If we do succeed, we may serve as an example to others, if we do not — that scenario is one about which I prefer not to write.

The Hon. Mr. H. H. Schwarz was the Ambassador for South Africa in the United States of America in 1994 while major changes were taking place in that country.

Islam And Nonviolence

— Asghar Ali Engineer

Violence in the name of religion was something. Mohandas K. Gandhi found difficult to accept. No God, he said, would command anyone to kill for any reason whatsoever.

Islam, contrary to general belief, is not a religion of violence. In fact, the word *Islam* means surrender to the will of God and work for peace.

The Arabic word for peace is *"Salam"*. When Muslims greet each other they invoke peace — *"Salam alaykum"*, meaning peace be on you. It is a greeting that Non-Muslims should also use to create an atmosphere of peace. A true Muslim is, therefore, one who surrenders to the will of God and works for peace through his/her action or conduct.

The Muslim God *Allah* is merciful and compassionate — *al-Rehman, al-Rahim*. One who is merciful and compassionate cannot be violent nor would such a one issue commandments for senseless violence. The only violence that a Compassionate One could permit is the violence to remove suffering and injustice. This is what *Allah* means by *Jihad*. More about this later.

Allah is just - *Adil* - and commands his followers to be just also. The holy *Quran* says : "Be just, that is nearer to observance of duty" *(5:8)*. The *Quran* also enjoins upon Muslims not to hate. In the same verse the *Quran* says : "O you who believe, be upright for *Allah*, bearers of witness with justice; and let not hatred of a people incite you to act inequitably."

A Muslim is not permitted to use coercion, let alone violence, in preaching *Islam*. "There is no compulsion in religion," declares the *Quran*. "The right way is clear and distinct. So whoever disbelieves in the devil and believes *Allah*, he indeed has a hold on the firmest handle which shall never break." *(2:256)*.

Clearly, therefore, one can get a firm grip on the "handle" only if *"Din"* is accepted through inner conviction and not through coercion. If compulsion or coercion in any form is used the handle will break.

Maulana Muhammed Ali, a well-known translator of the *Quran*, says : "All the nonsense being said about the Prophet offering the sword as an alternative to pagan Arabs is rejected by this verse. Muslims are told repeatedly that there should be no compulsion or coercion in the matter of religion." *(Holy Quran, Lahore 1973 pp 111, f.n.342)*. The *Maulana* also tells us : "The presumption that this passage was directed to the early converts and that it was abrogated later is utterly baseless"*(ibid)*.

The *Quran* clearly defines the methodology of preaching when it declares : *"Call to the way of the Lord* **with wisdom and goodly exhortation and argue with them in the best manner."** *(Quran 16:125)(emphasis added)*.

The *Quran* also prohibits Muslims from abusing those who believe in Gods other than *Allah*. It says : "And abuse not those whom they (i.e. non-believers) call upon besides *Allah* lest, exceeding the limits, they abuse *Allah* through ignorance." *(6:109)*. The Quran teaches tolerance of others and respect for their beliefs when it tells Muslims : "If *Allah* has desired He could have made you a single community. Instead He chose to create diversity so that we can vie with one another for virtuous deeds."*(5:48)*.

If the *Quran* advocates a philosophy of tolerance and respect how can it also advocate the use of violence to compel non-believers to embrace *Islam*? *Allah* has set down a law for the Muslim community to co-exist in harmony with others and pursue good deeds.

The myth that the *Quran* advocates violence came much later. The reason for this myth can be found in books of history, not in the *Quran*. The *Quran* makes a distinction between faith, which includes ways of worshipping and associated rituals, and the socio-political milieu in which one lives. Violence used for socio-political reasons cannot, in fact, should not, be blamed on faith.

Islam recognizes that those who believe in God, the Day of Judgement and perform good deeds during one's lifetime, will be equally rewarded, irrespective of which religion one follows. No religion can be more tolerant than this. It is, therefore, wrong to say that Islam condemns all other religions. The *Quran* repeatedly says the Prophet came to confirm the Truth that already exists *(mus. . .addigan li ma bayna yadayn)*. He is no bringer of new truth , hence there is no question of his condemning the same truth revealed to other Prophets.

Is *Islam*, therefore, a nonviolent religion? The answer, to be honest, is both yes and no. *Islam* does not advocate violence but does not shun it either. Life is full of contradictions and these contradictions are reflected in what can be called contextual theology. To be true to life the *Quranic* theology recognizes the socio-political pressures of life. Normatively, therefore, the *Quran* opposes violence but contextually it permits violence.

To understand this dilemma one has to study the socio-economic and socio-political conditions of a particular religious group. *Hinduism*, for instance, is a non-violent religion in the ideal sense. Yet, in the context of the circumstances then prevalent *Lord Krishna* had to urge *Arjuna* to fight a war even if it meant killing his relatives and friends.

War, therefore, can be justified in certain socio-political-economic circumstances but definitely not for the propagation of a religion. The concept of *Jihad* in *Islam* must be seen in this light. *Jihad* is a war against oppression and exploitation but there can be no *Jihad* to spread the word of *Islam*.

Explaining what the *Quran* means by the verse calling upon Muslims to "fight in the name of *Allah*" *Maulana Muhammed Ali* says : "while most of the believers who had the means fled from *Makkah* (the city where Muslims were oppressed) leaving behind those who were weak and unable to undertake the journey. These men, women and children still persecuted and oppressed by the *Makkans* had to be rescued. The ensuing war of deliverance can be termed as fighting in the name of *Allah*." *(Holy Quran)*.

One cannot help but emphasize that the concept of *Jihad* in *Islam* is misunderstood largely because Muslims have helped create the misunderstanding. Many power-seeking Muslim rulers fought wars of aggression in the name of *Jihad* and were supported by ignorant and misinformed Muslims. Nothing could be farther from the teachings of *Islam*.

It must also be remembered that *Islam* began as a revolutionary movement to rescue the oppressed and the exploited to give them something to believe in and create a just society. *Islam* is based on four pillars — *'adl, ih.. an, rah..mah* and *h..ikmah* — of justice, benevolence, compassion and wisdom. None of these concepts could lead to violence.

Dr. Asghar Ali Engineer is trained in Islamic theology, tafsir (commentary on the holy Quran), Islamic jurisprudence and Hadith. He has published 35 books on Islam, problems of Muslims, Muslim women's right, communal and ethnic problems in India and South Asia. Has also published numerous research articles in these subjects and in academic and popular journals. He writes articles of current interest in leading national dailies in India.

Caught In A Web Of Negativity

— Rabbi Philip S. Berg

In this age of Aquarius we are all on a journey towards expanded awareness. We are all on this path whether our conscious mind agrees or not. Slowly, but surely the clouds of illusion become thinner and less imposing. For at the end of our journey, at least there is only the true basic reality : Light.

Human beings respond to the magnetism of our environment and of other human beings. For all its action and glamour, today's business world and modern lifestyles generate conditions which wear down the body and spirit. Pressures are taking their toll by taxing body's essential resources and draining its energy. Repeated exposure to the strains of stress bring on a process of heightened deterioration which saps our very foundation.

Most people are falling prey to problems of anxiety, mental illness, drug and alcohol abuse in turbulent search for stimulation. Despite the material comfort achieved through technological advances, technology has thus far failed to enabled man to achieve the personal satisfaction that he craves.

Among the general public today there is widespread dissatisfaction with government in general. Most people are not aware that one of the main reasons for their current state of affairs is the narrow base from which solutions spring forth. The main error, from a kabbalistic perspective, is the approach our leaders take to these problems. Instead of asking the most important and singularly significant question, namely "Why" the problems occur in the first place and then making an attempt to remove these conditions, their thrust is directed toward the manifestated mechanisms through which the problem operates, in order to alter or interfere with them. Directing our efforts towards the symptom rather than the cause is at the very center of all universal problems.

To go beyond them and achieve the *Kabbalistic* model for problem solving will require nothing less than a profound educational revolution. However, most people are afraid of change because this means a re-examination of their lifestyle. Very few people are prepared to change their ways despite the inevitable track record that history furnishes.

What the *Kabbalist* strives for is a change in human behavior. There are but two alternatives - to continue with the same universal model that has always brought chaos, disorder and disease into our lives, or accept the cosmic parallel universe where order, certainty, peace and tranquility reign supreme. *Kabbalah*, a universal teaching, appearing in written form some 4,000 years ago, has over the millenniums made its way into the mainstream of civilization.

Transcending the universal model of chaos wiil be possible only if we learn and practice a method by which we again gain control of our lives and destiny. This, claims the *Kabbalah*, is possible only if the parallel univers is incorporated within our existing system. This system must address itself to the individual in order that he or she can achieve a purer state of awareness and an altered state of conciousness, including as well, control over the environment.

Western thought has programmed the individual to believe that the extrapolition of the laws and principles of our universe is the function of science and government, and that this is not a projec for the individual. However, it is the individual who delivers the mail, not the post office. It is the individual who carries on the act that are environmentally beneficial or destructive, not the government agency.

The misunderstanding of the role of the individual in public affairs is demonstrated by the story recently told by a news commentator. When it was reported to a group of U.S. residents that the cost of guaranteeing the deposits of failed deregulated Savings and Loan banks would be about $1,000?- for each taxpayer, they commented : "Why should we pay for it, why doesn't the government pay the cost ?"

If our attitude toward the condition of the environment and the socio-economic structure is one of helplessness and hopelessness, it is because during the past 300 years the individual has been excluded from the growing knowledge that is needed and has surrendered responsibility for his or her actions. Life experiences are hard proof evidence of the failure to provide a society free of violence, chaos and disorder.

Primal cultures have always practiced methods of transcendence, songs, dances and ceremonies by which they achieved a stress-free society. They were capable of creating security shields that would protect them. What was once a rich social, cultural, and spiritual fabric has been eaten away by empty material concepts, false technological promises, and finally digested by the great, blind myth called "progress". Today, that once intimate relationship we had with nature has been replaced by crass illusions provided by a cornucopia of so-called recreational drugs.

Even the tenacity to achieve so-called freedom from totalitarianism has resulted in chaos and incredible brutality under the guise of "ethnic cleansing". Every action of man is carried by the channels of the cosmos whether man knows it or not. Every earthquake, every supernova, every war is the direct result of violence and hatred in the hearts of men.

Two nations at war with each other spit out their vengeance at one another until they both become exhausted. The cloud of hatred may have vanished but the chaos and the suffering of individual families remains. Mankind should have learned of the futility of war and hatred, but envy and evil still remain a part of our human landscape.

Consequently, pollution, war, hatred and contamination, produced by the activities of mankind themselves, can only be removed by man's ability to change his ways towards a more positive rather than negative approach.

Mankind's polluted, sinful behavior and activity is behind the crises we face today. The preponderance of negativity over the whole of the cosmos. The situation is apparently hopeless without any relief in sight. The future ecology of our civilization might well remain in jeopardy and the end of the earth might be a foreseeable reality.

Were it not for the Kabbalistic knowledge and other metaphysical, spiritual teachings, the future would indeed appear as bleak as one might imagine. The oft quoted *Zohar*, "Woe unto those who will live at that time (The Age of Aquarius), yet happy will be those who will live at that time," attests to the fact of a dual cosmic reality. Thus there appears to exist a cosmos within a cosmos.

Spiritual teachings provide us with the opportunity to segregate ourselves from the polluted physical cosmic reality and connect with the essential unified all-embracing universe of order and harmony. The familiar world around us has and will only afford us the chaos, suffering and pain that is part of the human landscape. There is no way that even kind and positive individuals can look forward to a life of happiness and fulfillment free of chaos unless we all become aware of the fact that there is another reality out there, we shall then experience a change in human behavior.

Unfortunately, due to the overwhelming negative atmosphere and environment, positive people find themselves caught up in the web of this negativity. When human behavior becomes predominantly positive, when the individual begins to understand that his negative activity also affects his own family and environment, we can then look forward to a change in the environment.

One day we will open a door no wider than the eye of a needle, and unto us shall open the supernatural gates exposing the glittering interrelatedness of the universe with all its beauty and simplicity.

Rabbi Philip S. Berg is an ordained Orthodox Rabbi who studied at Torah Va Da' at Yeshiva in the United States and holds a doctorate in comparative religion. He assumed the role of director of The Kabbalah Learning Center in 1969. He is author of over 15 books on the subject of Kabbalah.

Rabbi Berg continues to give lectures around the world on the universal laws of Kabbalah. Privately, many world leaders have met with *Rabbi Berg* to help facilitate the process of peace and positive change in many volatile regions around the globe.

Gandhi The Tactician

— John Kenneth Galbraith

In 1956 I spent some months in India as an adviser in a general way to the Indian Government. I returned in 1959 and then again in 1961 as American Ambassador. I've been back many times since, and India has been a substantial part of my life. So, accordingly, has Mohandas, in a favored reference Mahatma Gandhi. Gandhi and India are inseparable; one lives in India with both.

There were many Gandhis. Perhaps a little exceptionally, I've always been attracted by his sense of humor. In one of his more rewarding moments, there came one day to his ashram a defender of Lord Irwin, Later Lord Halifax, then the Viceroy. The defense was not comprehensive: "Do know, Mahatma, that Lord Irwin never makes a decision without praying over it first". Gandhi, it is said, reflected deeply for several minutes and then replied, "And why do you suppose that the Lord so consistently gives him wrong advice?" One would have enjoyed being there.

But mostly, as have others, I've been impressed by Gandhi as a tactician. Over this talent history has spread a thick sheet of morality; beneath, I belive, is the compelling reality. It is that nonviolence, to gain needed ends, is not only a powerful moral instrument; it is also a weapon of choice.

When some abused, trodden and desperate community resorts to violence, in all ordinary cases it invites its own defeat. For the resort to force is precisely what legitimizes its use by the other side. Men and Women have taken to the streets; there is obvious and justified need for action that restores order. And normally the forces of law and order, as they are called, are better armed, more disciplined and otherwise more effective than those being suppressed. As an expression of discontent violence can be, perhaps usually is, the instrument of its own defeat. It justifies the use of the greater strength that defeats it.

Not nonviolence. With this the repressive and countering force cannot contend. Not only is there no easy course of action against peaceful dissent, but if violent steps are initiated, they bring widespread public rebuke. Peaceful protest, in contrast, is greatly praised. There is a presumption that the cause so defended must be just. Because nonviolence, peaceful protest, has public support and approval, it is assumed to be superior on moral grounds. That is justification. Not seen, or less seen, is the tactical advantage — that this is the most effective design for achieving a purpose, perhaps the only one. The British could put down the Mutiny, as then it was called; they could not contend with the superior Gandhi tactics. Similarly in the American South in yet more recent times. Young black rioters could and would have been surpassed. They would have invited and made legitimate the forceful reaction that would have destroyed them. Marching peacefully in segregated Southern cities, sitting quietly at lunch counters, they were invulnerable.

So I am back to Gandhi. He was of many qualities and dimensions; of that let there be no doubt; but one of these, perhaps the greatest, was in finding and using the only tactic with which superior force could not contend. Perhaps it was part of his genius to give nonviolence a quasi-religious overtone, something good in itself. But there is more than a suggestion in his memoirs that this was a deliberate tactical choice. In England during World War I he did not oppose violence. He urged young Indians to join up and fight for England, and this he later defended. No one, however, should doubt the controlling genius that selected and made nonviolence one and the most powerful political and social instrument of our time.

Dr. John Kenneth Galbraith is Paul M. Warburg Professor of Economics Emeritus at Harvard University. Author of **The Affluent Society**, **The New Industrial State**, *two novels,* **The Triumph** *and* **A Tenure Professor**, *the recently published* **The Culture of Contentment** *and numerous other books. Former Ambassador to India; the organizer of wartime price control in World War II; adviser to Roosevelt, Stevenson, Kennedy, and Johnson in their presidential campaigns.*

Gandhi In South Africa

— Nadine Gordimer

I remark with a sense of wonder on the extraordinary and beautiful circumstance of an occasion when the great man of peace of contemporary South Africa, Nelson Mandela, is here to honour the great man of peace in South Africa and the world in the past, Mohandas Karamchand Gandhi. We are here tonight in the equilibrium of history. It is quite awesome. While celebrating in homage what Gandhi meant to South Africa, in his spiritual philosophy and political wisdom, his immense influence on the development of the liberation struggle that was to come after his time, particularly the long phase followed by the African National Congress according to his teachings, we are in the presence of Nelson Mandela, who in his non-racial philosophy and political wisdom, his leadership at home and international status, means to us the culmination of the liberation struggle.

I once wrote in one of my books that, despite the horrors of apartheid, there was still something remarkable, in modern times, about living in a country where there were still heroes. We have had that privilege. We have had, and still have, the inspiration supremely of the years Gandhi spent in our country, a hero of peace, not war. In our present situation of violence as a tragic accompaniment to vital change, while some resist peaceful negotiation with the gun and the grenade, we realise more than ever that the vision of society that Gandhi formulated first in our country, before he pursued it in his own, is only worth having. Strands of his thinking are there in what is positive in our political thought and attitudes; if we could bind them together in the vocabulary of our actions, between individuals as well as at the negotiating tables, we would be on the way as articulating peace.

*Nadine Gordimer received the Nobel Prize for Literature in 1991. **Ms. Gordimer**, from South Africa is well known as both a novelist and short story writer. Her work centers on life in her native South Africa and is particularly notable for its sensitive probing of apartheid and its effect on the people of that politically troubled country. She has a fine grasp of the language of the black farm workers speak-both among themselves and their masters. She knows their customs, habits, superstitions, holiday ceremonials, and tribal rituals. And she sees right through the deceptive masks they wear for their dealings with the whites and even with the Indian settlers in South Africa. **Nadine Gordimer** is one of the very few links between white and black in South Africa.*

The Nine Sutras Of Peace

— Raimon Panikkar

I would like to introduce the Nine *Sutras* by a general remark. The *Sutras* are threads of a single necklace. The one leads into the other and they depend upon each other. Only together they constitute this jewel which we call peace.

1. Peace is participation in the harmony of the Rhythm of being.

Peace does not mean absence of force or of polarities. Peace does not do violence to the Rhythm of Realities. But nonviolence is not merely a passive attitude of permissiveness. Nonviolence means the non-violation of personhood, the reverence for the inner dignity of everything. It means the participation in and the contribution to the constitutive Rhythm of Reality. We are also responsible for the harmony of the universe. We enhance and transform it by cooperating with it. This cooperation, this synergy is active and passive all in one.

Participation entails an active and a passive taking part in the adventure of being. This adventure is neither a linear progress towards an omega point nor a regression to an original and indiscriminate alpha point. Peace is neither eschatalogical, nor a state of mind which has 'dis-covered' the vanity of all 'transient' things. The meaning of our life is neither to be found only at the end, and the justification of our actions in our final success, nor can we be satisfied with momentary satisfactions. The adventure of being is neither such an evolution towards future, nor a pure involution towards the past. Peace like being is neither static nor dynamic. Being is not even dialectically moving between those two states in more or less disguised schizophrenic fits. Being is rhythmical, it is Rhythm. And Rhythm is the non-dualistic integration of movement and quiet, of striving towards the goal and enjoying it already while pilgrims on the way. Rhythm is the deepest nature of reality, the very becoming of being, which is being precisely because it comes to be.

From such a *Philosophia Pacis* stems, I submit, a deep and constructive critique to our modern predicament visible now in ecological, economic, psychological and political systems.

My conviction is that our technocratic culture, which through the cultivation of acceleration has transgressed the natural rhythms of matter and the mind, is a peaceful society which makes it both urgent and difficult the realization of Peace in our times. Peace does not mean maintaining the *status quo* when this latter has proved to be emancipation from it by several means, and transformation of it into a *fluxus quo* towards an ever new cosmic harmony. All too often discourses about peace tend to become idyllic dreams of an ideal paradise forgetting that the essence of Eden consists in having been lost, and the destiny of man lies in overcoming - not denying - the temporal strictures into which we have the danger to be drowned.

2. It is difficult to live without external peace; it is impossible to live without internal peace. The relationship is non-dualistic.

It is excruciating and dangerous to live in situations of conflict, or warfare of all types. The world is full of institutionalized and non-institutionalized injustices which destroy peace. Over 1000 victims of war fall mortally every day since the last World War - this very year in over twenty major armed conflicts. The refugees in the world are by the millions, so are the street children, and the starving people. And we should not minimize this human degradation of our race. But if there is internal peace there are still chances of survival. Not so if there is no internal peace. Without the latter the person disintegrates. Crime, drugs and many other individual and social plagues come from the lack of internal peace.

But the relationship is non-dualistic. Peace is more than just absence of an armed conflict. If there is no internal peace there cannot be external peace. Lack of internal peace breeds cold wars of all types. Lack of internal peace originates competitions ending in defeats which trigger declared or undeclared revenges of all sorts. On the other hand, it is not possible to enjoy truly internal peace of our human and ecological environment suffers violence and injustice. Without external peace a mere inner peace is a make-believe or an exclusively psychological state of artificial isolation from the rest of reality. The *Bodhisatva* renounces *Nirvana* in order to liberate all sentient beings, the Christ suffers *Gethsemani* for the sake of the world, the saint is not insensitive to the suffering of the universe. No authentic spirituality defends escapism from the real world and no true sage encapsulates itself in its own selfishness or self-sufficiency.

This non-dualistic relationship (there is not the one without the other, we should distinguish, but not separate them) exerts, at the same time, a reciprocal and *Sui Generis* causality. Inner peace produces outer peace, outer peace fosters inner peace. And similarly, internal disorder breeds external strife, and external strife engenders internal degradation. And yet the relationship is *Sue Generis*. Have we not sometimes seen a mysterious and intriguing serenity in catastrophic and unjust situations ? Have we not also witnessed inexplicable depressions in the midst of externally optimal conditions ? The entire universe is embarked in the same venture. The philosophy of life understood as the 'Wisdom of Love' proper to Life helps us to overcome the dichotomy between the inner and the outer, and allows us to enjoy inner peace in the middle of external sufferings and to consecrate ourselves to alleviate unjust situations without losing our internal joy. This was the message of the *Buddha*, the example of Christ, the torment of Luther *"simul justus and peccator"*, the connundrum of *Vedanta* (The *Pratishtha* of *Maya* is *Brahman*), ... revelation of the irreducibility of Reality to an intellectual principle.

3. Peace is neither conquered for oneself nor imposed on others. It is both received, discovered and credited. It is a gift (of the Spirit).

Neither masochistic spirituality nor sadistic pedagogies, on whatever level, bring true peace. You do not fight for peace. You fight for your rights or eventually for justice - not for peace. It is a contradiction. The regimes we impose are not peace for the receiver, be it a child, a pagan, a poor, a family or a nation. We lack a more feminine attitude of receiving, and, by receiving, of transforming what we accept. Christ wanted us to receive his peace, not to impose it on others, or even to force it upon us. The nature of peace is grace. It is a gift.

We discover peace, we unveil it. Peace is a discovery, not a conquest. It is the fruit of revelation : we may experience it as the revelation of love, God, the beauty of reality, the existance of providence, a hidden meaning, the harmony of being or the goodness of creation, hope justice. When in this context I said feminity I mean neither sex nor women. I mean the complementary attitude to what a certain exclusive male mentality has associated with positive values. We accept a gift. But we do something with it. The gift of peace is not a toy. It is an urge, *nixus*, *spanda*, *elan*, an aspiration. Peace is not a ready-made situation, a merely objective dictum. Peace needs to be constantly nurtured, and even created. There is no blue-print of peace, no full-fledged programme is possible. When we say gift we mean also grace. This is why peace is also a creation. Peace is not reached by going back to a primitive state, once the innocence is broken. Peace is recreated each time anew. It is *Gabe* and *Aufgabe*, gift and responsibility.

4. Victory Never Leads to Peace.

This is a theoretical affirmation as well as an empirical statement. Witness thereof are the same eight thousand peace treatises we know of and possess along the millennia of human history. None of those victories has ever brought true peace. It cannot be retorted that this is so, for such is human nature, because most of the wars have started, and found their 'justification', as counter measures against the previous peace treaties. The archetypes of the defeated, when not their immediate children, will sooner or later emerge and demand what was denied to them. Not even the repression of evil will bring lasting results. One is tempted to recall that apparently so simplistic and empirically so unbeatable statement of a young Rabbi of Nazreth about letting grow together the wheat and the tears . . .

Peace is fugitive from the field of the victors, I would say paraphrasing Simon Weil. We know that justice is not 'just us'. But peace is more than mere justice. And peace is richer than *pax*, a mere pact, a sort of balance, often of terror. Peace is not the reestablishment of a broken order. It is a new order. Victory leads to victory, not to peace. And we also know of the deleterious side effects of prolonged 'victories".

But there is also a more theoretical foundation for this *Sutra*. In spite of all our distinctions, victory is always over people, and people are never absolutely evil. So we cannot say that victory is only over the forces of evil or the errors or aberrations on a theoretical level. We may like to kill only evil but we eliminate also the evildoer, we may want to punish the crime, but we imprison the criminal. "Do not resist evil" (or the evil-one) says also challenging and irritatingly that selfsame Son of Mary !

But besides the same caution of not absolutizing anything, because, to begin with, we ourselves are not absolute, there is still another underlying assumption for this *Sutra* : the nature of reality is not dialectical : neither reducible to logistical dynamism nor proceeding by synthesis or opposites. Peace is not the opposite of war, to begin with. Elimination of war does not bring peace automatically. This is why the way to true peace is not the victory on anything real. The defeated do not enjoy the peace of the victors. Peace is not the result of a dialectical process.

5. Military Disarmament requires cultural disarmament.

We have to disarm our own respective cultures alongside with and sometimes previously to a mere elimination of arms. Our cultures are oftentimes belligerent. Treat the others as an enemy, as a *barbar*, *gio*, *maleccha*, *khafir*, unbeliever, and the like. Furthermore, in many a culture reason itself is used as a weapon : in order to win and convince.

Cultural disarmament is not a mere catchy phrase. It is a requisite for peace and certainly for any lasting disarmament in our present state of affairs. First of all it is not by sheer chance that western civilization has developed such an arsenal of weapons both in quality and quantity. There is something inherent in this culture which has led to such a situation : competitiveness, setting our minds for 'better' solutions without considering the possibility of challenging the causes and disolving the problem, sensitivity for the quantitative and the mechanical, creativity in the field of objectifiable entities over against arts, crafts, subjectivity, neglect of the world feelings, sense of superiority, universality, etc. An example' of this spirit is the very fact of political and even intellectual talks concentrating exclusively on reduction of armaments without considering those more basic questions.

Perhaps what has become manifest in the modern technocratic culture was already potentially present in the cultural project of historical Man. We should learn the lessons of History and having come to the 'End of History' begin to contemplete the plausibility of transhistorical Man - as I have tried to explain elsewhere. Our time is ripe for such an anthropological mutation. It is after all a question of survival.

But cultural disarmament is as risky and difficult as military disarmament. We become vulnerable. It is a matter of common knowledge that reduction of armaments is an economic as well as political problem. But economics is a fundamentally cultural problem. The passage from agriculture, as a way of living to agribusiness as means of financial gains could serve as an epitome of what we want to say.

Cultural disarmament does not mean to revert into primitivism. It entails a critique of culture not only in the light of what might have gone wrong in western culture, but also under the perspective of a genuine crosscultural approach.

6. No culture, religion or tradition in isolation can solve the problems of the world.

No religion today is self-sufficient, nor can it provide universal answers (let alone because the questions are not the same). Crosscultural approaches to the problems of the world are imperative. We suffer still from the remnants of colonialism. The essence of the latter is the belief in the monophormism of culture. We need each other and are interdependent on all levels.

Significantly enough when most traditional religions today are prone to lay down the mantle of imperialism, colonialism and universalism, the so-called 'scientific' vision of the world seems to be the cultural heir of such attitudes. Modern astronomy, physics, mathematics, etc., seem, often implicitly, to assume that they are supra-cultural, universal and definite achievements of the human spirit : "Finally we know that Andromeda lies at such a distance, the atoms are no longer *atomoi*, gravitation works in such a way, that the quarks, biomolecules, chromosomes, and what not up to a big bang, represent the real thing, open, of course, to refinements and corrections with possible new parameters". I have criticized enough the technocratic attitude to linger now any longer on the subject. Let me only say Peace on Earth and in the Heavens - and not whether under a very limited context a certain 'Physical Law' is valid or not.

The word to be mentioned here concerning cultures, religions, and traditions is pluralism, about which I have also said enough elsewhere.

7. Peace belongs mainly to the order of the mythos, not of the logos.

There is not a single concept of peace. Suffice to know the resonance and connotations of the different words (*pax, eirene, salam, Friede, santi, ...*). Peace is polysemic, it has many meanings. It is also pluralistic, it has many and doctrinally incompatible interpretations. My notion of peace may not be peaceful to somebody else. Peace is not the ideology. Peace is not synonymous with pacifism. A myth is something we believe in because we take it for granted. A myth is not understandable, the reason reasonable. It is what grants intelligibility in any given situation. Peace is not a mere concept. It is the emerging myth of our times.

'God' was once upon a time a fairly universal myth. Wars were fought in his name and each contender wanted the God at its own side : *"Gott mit uns"*. Peace was also signed in God's name. Peace now seems to be the emerging unifying myth of our times; and wars are also being fought in its name!

But a myth defies a further foundation. It is beyond any possible definition, because the myth is the horizon which makes the definition possible. The *Mythos* cannot be separated from the *Logos* but they should not be identified. This is the explanation why to impose our concept of peace does not bring Peace and this is again a topic so near to me that I may be allowed to cut it short here.

8. *Religion is a way to peace.*

A more traditional notion was that of considering it as a way to salvation. It is a fact that most wars in the world have been religious wars. We are witnessing today a transformation of the very notion of religion and it may be expressed saying that religions are the different ways of approaching and acquiring that peace which is today probably one of the few most universal symbols. *Summa nostrae religionis pax est et unanimitas* (the acme of our religion is peace and concord) wrote Erasmus in a letter of 1522.

Connecting this *Sutras* with the previous one there is no danger of falling into a superficial eclecticism which could chop off all religious denominators. All religions are not the same, first of all, because they do not say it. They say and affirm different things, and speak diverse languages. Secondly, because the same (thing, meaning, . . .) for most of the traditions does not exist disconnected from their saying (it). The word is paramount in most religions.

Yet most religions would agree that their concern is to bring Peace to Man and eventually to the entire cosmos. Each religion understands Peace as a symbol polysemic and pluralistic enough so as to allow the use of it.

But this is no minor step forward because it shifts the emphasis of the religious encounters (in all senses of the word) from the doctrinal issues to a more existential attitude, and thus makes possible a fruitful cooperation of religions in our present human situation. In the past religions have often been factors of inner peace for their followers and external wars for the others. The incongruency is today so manifest that the very self-understanding of religion begins to change in the sense we are indicating.

A difficult word should be mentioned here in this connection between peace and religion. The word is revolution. The way to Peace is not an easy way; it is revolutionary, selfishness, greed. History proves that once religions cease to be revolutionary, first they degenerate and do not fulfil their role; second, the revolution is also degraded to a mere change of the guard. The problems today are formidable.

9. Only forgiveness, reconciliation, ongoing dialogue, leads to Peace, breaks the law of karma.

This is a historical as well as an anthropological and theologico-philosophical truth. Punishment, repayment, restitution, reparation and the like do not lead to peace. To believe that a mere reestablishment of a broken order will put things straight is a crude mechanistic and immature way of thinking. The lost innocence demands redemption, and not the dream of a recovered paradise. No amount of compensation will undo what has been done. Peace is not restoration. Human history is dynamic, The very cosmos moves rhythmically, but does not repeat itself. The status ante is an impossibility.

The only way to Peace is first of all a way 'forward' and not 'backward'. Now, forgiveness is something which transcends the main dogma of modernity : the will. To have the will to forgive is not the same as to forgive. In order to forgive one needs a strength beyond the mechanical order of action and reaction, one needs the Holy Spirit. *Karuna Charis*, love are not just good sentiments of some individuals. They are the pillars of the universe.

It is instructive to remark that each time the Risen Christ appears to his disciples he bestows peace on them and that each occasion when he confers on them the power of forgiveness he gives them the power of the Holy Spirit. Sometimes the law of karma is broken just by putting to shame the holders of justice : "Women, where are (gone) those who accused you?...

The consequences are so far-reaching that it may be improper for me now to spell them out.

The Challenge of The Book

I know how relatively easy it is to quote *Ashoka's* edict on Peace (the victory of *dhamma*, he calls it), or to condemn Flavius Vegetius Renatus dictum, *qui desiderat pacem praeparet bellum* (if you want peace prepare for war), or to cite *Pindar's* famous aphorism *dulce bellum inexpertise* (war is sweet only to those who have not tasted it); or to copy Erasmus' beginning of his *Querela pacis* (peace is the "source of all happiness"), and to recall the many noble souls who have discovered the centrality of peace in all times and latitudes. The real challenge comes when we have to act accordingly without any other support than our conscience.

Dr. Raimon Panikkar himself partakes of pluralistic traditions : Indian and European, Hindu and Christian, Sciences and Humanities. He has lived and studied in Spain, Germany, Italy, India and the United States. His academic achievements include : Ph.D. (Philosophy), D. Sc. (Chemistry), Th. D. (Theology). He is a visiting professor at many universities throughout the world. Member of the International Institute of Philosophy, he has taken an active part in the cultural and philosophical life of Europe, USA and India. He has published over 30 books and several hundred major articles from Philosophy of Science to Metaphysics, Comparative Religion and Indology.

(Excerpted from "Philosophia Pacis", permission to reprint granted by Dr. Raimon Panikkar.)

Give Nonviolence A Chance

— Bishop James K. Mathews

Before daylight on a chilly December morning in 1940 I walked with
two friends from the railway station in *Wardha* (Central India). It was about five
miles to *Sevagram*, Gandhi's "Village of Service". The sun was just rising when
we came to the gate of the *ashram*. Just then there emerged a little man with a
bamboo stick. He was accompanied by some fifteen companions. I remember only
Sushila Nayyar, his physician, and a wonderful woman with whom I was to become
well-acquainted later on.

For about an hour we walked by Gandhi's side. He conversed freely. The
"Quit India" movement was just beginning. Vinoba Bhave, a close associate —
later to become famous for the land gift movement — had just been arrested, the
very first of thousands who were to follow. We talked of that and of the prospects
of the effort. When I inquired whether or not Bhave's arrest saddened him, he
replied in the negative. This was to be expected. He never hesitated to accept the
consequences of his deeds or programs.

When we returned to the *Ashram*, he invited us to make ourselves at home
for the rest of the day, and he turned to his many other duties. During our stay
we glimpsed Mrs. Gandhi, Kasturbai; Mirabahen - Madeline Slade; and his secretary,
Mahadeo Desai. It was indeed a memorable experience.

Since that time I have been privileged to have met two of Gandhi's sons:
the second son, Manilal, Arun's father, and Devadas, his fourth son. Then of course,
I know the grandson Arun and his wife Sunanda; Rajmohan Gandhi, son of Devadas,
and his wife, Usha; and their children — Gandhi's fourth generation. And, finally,
I met little Vivan, Arun's grandson, the fifth generation of Gandhis. It is hard to
keep up with the Gandhis!

In 1952 Manilal Gandhi came to New York to testify before the United Nations
on apartheid. During that time I met him. He invited me to visit the Phoenix settlement
if I ever should come to South Africa. This I did not expect ever to do but the
fact of the matter is that two years later I was in Africa and flew into the city
of Durban. A young man met my plane. I recall that he said that he had received

his driver's license only that day! His name was Arun Gandhi. He showed me around the city and I am glad that I was able to observe the indignities of apartheid for the first time under his guidance.

He took me to the Phoenix settlement where I had a wonderful day with his family and was privileged to meet his mother who spoke my Indian language, namely Marathi. It transpired that I did not see Arun again for thirty years.

I have not forgotten that my topic is ""The Relevance of Gandhi's Nonviolence Today". Arun Gandhi himself has shared with me a statement by his grandfather which shows his broad point of view. It is entitled "Seven Sins":

> *Wealth without work.*
> *Pleasure without conscience.*
> *Knowledge without character.*
> *Commerce without morality.*
> *Science without humanity.*
> *Worship without sacrifice.*
> *Politics without principles.*

The relevance of such a view upon our contemporary situation in this country and in other parts of the world is obvious.

Let me turn now more specifically to Gandhi's method, called *Satyagraha* or truth-force. In Gandhi's view there were only two ways of changing human social ills — by violence or by nonviolence. he chose the latter for his essential remedy for India's ills — internal as well as external. This came as no surprise to those who were familiar with his South African career. Around the concept of *Satyagraha* (truth-force, or derivatively, soul-force) there grew up a complex structure of ideas and activities. Like so many leaders in the field of the spirit he did not himself formulate ideas in any systematic philosophical manner, though he did expound *Satyagraha* almost incessantly.

Gandhi did not claim any originality for the concept of *Satyagraha*. He felt that soul-force was natural; therefore it was taken for granted and not often noted in history. He regarded the *Rishis* (ascetics) who discovered the law of suffering as "greater geniuses than Newton".

Gandhi did not like to define *Satyagraha*, partly because he felt that his knowledge of it was ever growing. He once said, "I have no text-book to consult in time of need, not even the *Gita* which I have called my dictionary. *Satyagraha* as conceived by me is a science in the making". Again, "*Satyagraha* in its essence is nothing but the introduction of truth and gentleness in the political, that is, the national life".

Gandhi always insisted that *Satyagraha* was not a passive force. "It is essentially an active movement, much more active than the one involving the use of sanguinary weapons. Truth and nonviolence are perhaps the activist weapons you have in the world". He goes on to say that while soldiers rest, and fight very little of the time, this internal weapon acts when asleep or awake. By the same token, he regarded that *Satyagraha* was not a negative but a positive force.

Furthermore, Gandhi was constantly at pains to make clear that it was not a weak and cowardly weapon. *Satyagraha* takes more courage and a superior type of courage than that of the soldier, for it involves the possibility of the *Satyagrahi* being killed without inflicting physical harm or death on his opponent. He even said, surprisingly enough, that he preferred violence to cowardice. He also frequently expressed his preference for violence to the "emasculation" of the Indian people.

For *Satyagraha*, Truth is the end and Nonviolence is the means. More attention must now be given to *Ahimsa*. It is undoubtedly one of the most important concepts in *Hinduism* and its related religions. Gandhi regarded it as the "core of Hinduism". Professor Edward Thompson calls it also "core of Gandhi's teaching". The *Mahabharata* terms *Ahimsa* as the supreme duty or religion.

It should be clear what, in Gandhi's thinking, *Satyagraha* is not. It is not Non-Resistance, for they differ as the north Pole from the South Pole. Again, *Satyagraha* and Pacifism are not the same, although the *Satyagrahi* stands opposed to armed conflict. Gandhi regarded pacifism as passive.

We turn now to describe more fully what *Satyagraha* is and to observe the terms commonly used in its exposition, as well as the relationship of these terms to each other. The principal words are : *Satyagraha*, Civil Disobedience, Non-cooperation, Civil Resistance, Nonviolent Resistance, or Nonviolent Non-Cooperation, Constructive Program, besides, of course, Truth and *Ahimsa* or Nonviolence.

In a fairly useful way these terms may be described as a tree. The whole tree is *Satyagraha*. Gandhi himself compares *Satyagraha* to a banyan tree with multiple trunk and many branches.

One "branch" of *Satyagraha* is non-cooperation, a form of civil resistance. The second "branch" for direct action against an oppressive government or for the eradication of injustice or social evil is civil disobedience. All civil disobedience, in Gandhi's sense, is *Satyagraha* but not all *Satyagraha* is civil disobedience. The third main "branch" of *Satyagraha* is the Constructive Program.

Brief consideration must now be given to *Satyagraha* in operation. In the internal sense, it is directed toward realization of Truth through the cultivation of *Ahimsa* in both its negative and positive phases. It has a purifying effect, strengthening moral and spiritual fiber for external manifestation of *Satyagraha*.

Gandhi felt that *Satyagraha* was not a force to be used carelessly or too frequently. It was not to be employed until other and milder methods had been tried, though at other times he speaks of *Satyagraha* as embracing also these "milder methods". In general, however, it was to be the only remedy, for *Satyagraha* is the substitute for violence.

Gandhi liked to stress the simplicity of *Satyagraha* — that even a child can practise it. He thought of it as the extension of a domestic law into politics. It is never to be used for personal gain. It is a deliberate restraint of the desire for vengeance against one's opponent.

Satyagraha used in direct action does not aim at appealing to reason. Rather, it attempts to reach the opponent's reason through the heart. How is this supposed to occur? By self-suffering on the part of the *Satyagrahi*. Self-suffering is represented as a powerful law of life, more potent than physical force. It has an educative effect on the opponent; at the same time it calls attention to injustice and arouses public sentiment — perhaps even world opinion. Gandhi took great and repeated pains to declare that this is not coercion, but that the conversion of the adversary is intended.

Gandhi then reduced this program to an elaborate series of teachings — Preparation, Purification, Promotion, Negotiation, Direct Action, and Constructive Activity.

He regarded *Satyagraha* as "infallible". He made clear that he himself was not infallible. Rather, he grounded this "infallibility" on three factors, all deeply rooted in Hinduism :

1) Because it is based on truth *Satya*. In his view when truth is confronted by untruth, truth must necessarily prevail.

2) Because it is based on sacrifice *Yajna*. According to *Hinduism*, a sacrifice carefully rendered must inevitably obtain its intended purpose.

3) Because it is based on austerity *Tapas*. Here again, according to *Hinduism*, the thorough practice of austerity must command the gods.

These three terms *Satya*, *Yajna* and *Tapas* are constantly used by Gandhi. To him they would finally overcome all barriers.

It goes without saying that for him this viewpoint was very sustaining and comforting. It gave him great confidence as to the outcome of his campaign. Likewise, it inspired confidence in his followers.

For Gandhi, his political methods had a religious base. He wrote: "My politics and all other activities of mine are derived from my religion. I go further and say that every activity of a man of religion must be derived from his religion, because religion means being bound to God, that is to say, God rules your every breath. If you recognize that truth, naturally God regulates every activity of yours".

Moreover, he regarded *Satyagraha* as universal in its application. Therefore, there would have been no doubt in Gandhi's mind about nonviolence being relevant today. Yet this notion seemed to have collapsed when independence came to India.

Hardly had the goal been realized before violence broke out between the religious communities of the two new countries of India and Pakistan. No one knows how many were slaughtered as *Hindus* and *Sikhs* attacked *Muslims* and as the latter attacked *Hindus* and *Sikhs*. Nor is it possible to say who initiated the disturbances. Millions of *Muslims* fled India for Pakistan; other millions of *Sikhs* and *Hindus* sought refuge in India. After months of confusion, the principal author of freedom and the leader of efforts to restore harmony himself succumbed to violence.

A small flat stone in the garden of *Birla* House in New Delhi marks the spot where Gandhi fell at the hand of an assassin on January 30, 1948. Inscribed on the stone are two words in *Hindi* : **He Rama**, "O God", the phrase on his lips as he died on his way to his regular evening prayer meeting. These same words appeared as a wall-motto in his hut in *Sevagram*.

Still, his contributions were many:

1) He brought freedom to his country.

2) He prepared Indians for freedom to a very considerable degree by awakening them; by restoring their self-respect and self-confidence; by giving them a renewed sense of nationhood.

3) He focused attention in a new degree upon the poor and oppressed of India and took steps in the direction of their relief.

4) He developed into a practical, nonviolent mass method, ideas of resistance. Whether or not his techniques are universal, they will continue to serve as a model and inspiration to those who would secure rightful ends but are either denied use of force of arms or do not desire to employ it.

Nonviolent non-cooperation campaigns are not restricted to Gandhi alone. This method was used by Vinoba Bhave — *Bhoodan Yajna* — in 1951 and thereafter.

Is *Satyagraha* universal in its application? The question is by its very nature unanswerable, for it must be attempted in specific instances. The indication is that it would be and is effective widely, given a strong cause, and adversary to whom moral appeal can be made, a case in which violence is impossible or imprudent, and by nonviolent resisters who are disciplined and patient. This would more likely be true of a clear, specific and local issue. It is less likely to be true in a complicated, ambiguous and general issue such as has commonly resulted in war.

Nevertheless, when one considers violence in our homes, widespread murder on the streets of our cities, instances of terrorism, oppression of the poor, repeated outbreaks of warfare and fighting (Israel, Iraq, Bosnia, Cyprus, Lebanon, Iran, Afghanistan, Northern Ireland — the list is long), and an annual world-wide expenditure on armaments exceeding one trillion dollars, should not nonviolence be tried?

James K. Mathews is an American but also a life-long friend and admirer of India and of the Indian people. He first came to India in 1938 and lived there for more than eight years.

Dr. Mathews is now retired bishop of The United Methodist Church. His travels and work have carried him to six continents. He is the author of seven books and many articles on a wide variety of subjects.

Violation Of Gender Rights

— Ellen Goodman

The floor in front of the podium was covered by stacks of petitions bearing half a million names from 124 countries. In 21 different languages, people of the world had joined together to make a single plea to the UN Conference on Human Rights : "We demand gender violence to be recognized as a violation of human rights".

This bank of petitions may have served as a psychic shield for the women who came to that podium all day long to tell their stories. While bureaucrats and dignitaries debated words and compromises upstairs in the cavernous Austria Center, women in this room took part in a powerful and emotionally exhausting tribunal on women's human rights. They shared just a token number of the abuses against the world's women that have gone unnoticed, unnamed and unpunished.

Perveen Martha, a poor Pakistani woman, came to tell how she had survived her husband's attempt to kill her by burning and then lost her children to him when he won a divorce. *Bok Dong Kim*, a dignified elderly Korean, "comfort woman", told a hushed audience how she had been taken as a sexual slave for Japanese soldiers when she was 14 years old. Gabrielle Wilders, a young American, told how her stepfather, a former priest, served only 18 months in jail for years of sadistic sexual abuse that began when she was 12.

Witnesses as well as survivors came to testify. A Russian photographer who covered the unheralded conflict in Ossetia, once a part of the Soviet Union, told of tanks decorated with severed women's heads and breasts. An activist from Zagreb talked of the women refugees from Bosnia, including a woman who was compelled to make a Sophie's Choice and leave one of her twin babies behind with just a pacifier and a note. Above all else, there were witnesses to rape in every imaginable circumstance — in war, at home, in police custody.

But this tribunal was not just a chronicle of horrors, a parade of the world's failures. It was, in its own way, a tribute to the "success" women have had in breaking the silence that has surrounded this violence.

In Vienna, the sophisticated city of Mozart and Freud, Women's rights groups from every culture and country have come with a unifying theme — stop, the violence. Unlike many diplomats divided along economic and cultural lines, they have formed the most organized and cohesive force at this conference. For the first time, they have succeeded in getting their message onto the UN's agenda — and perhaps the world's.

The deceptively simple idea that women's rights are human rights has been a long time in coming. After all, human rights philosophy was originally written by men seeking protection against the state. They created a list of the things they feared the most: repression by the state, violence by the state.

When women were included, they won the same protections as men. But over the years it has become clear that women's fears of human rights abuses are not always the same as men's.

In the months when she was helping to organize this tribunal, Charlotte Bunch of the Center for Women's Global Leadership at Rutgers discovered that when "you ask women what is the form of inhuman and degrading treatment they are most afraid will happen to them.. it's that they will be raped or battered".

If men fear the state, women also fear their husbands. They fear the male traditions in which, as Stella Mukasa of Uganda told the tribunal, "domestic violence is viewed as the normal wear and tear of marriage".

If men need protection from torture for their political beliefs, women need protection from torture for their gender: from rape or genital mutilation, beatings or bride-burning.

The women's agenda brought to this conference is not, then, just a matter of equality. The UN's Universal Declaration of Human Rights gives the world the moral authority to look inside borders at the way countries treat their citizens. But women are demanding that the world look across another threshold at crimes that were once as private as family and as personal as sex.

This view is not pretty or easy. But as Judge Elizabeth Odio of Costa Rica put it during this searing tribunal, "We must make sure the absurd division between the public and private sphere disappears."

Here, at last, survivors baring their scars and women activists sharing broad moral vision are taking off the world's blinders.

*Internationally known Washington Post columnist, **Ellen Goodman**, submitted the preceding piece as a tribute to Mohandas K. Gandhi's concept of a World Without Violence especially since Gandhi believed so long as 50 per cent of humanity suffered gender discrimination and violence freedom and peace will be meaningless.*

*This article was initially written for Boston Globe, dated Sunday, June 20, 1993 in the OP-ED section. **Ellen Goodman** is also a columnist for Boston Globe.*

A World Without Violence?

— Richard Ernst

I am convinced that the eternal words of Mahatma Gandhi could pave a path towards a world without violence, if only they would be followed. I recognize, sadly, that I am not more advanced than others, and that I will hardly ever be able to follow this path without compromise.

I have myself acquired in the past wealth without work.

I have enjoyed pleasures without much conscience.

I possess, although in a very narrow field, more knowledge than character.

I have been involved in commerce without morality.

I am often persueing science without taking into consideration humanity.

I was involved in politics without deeply rooted principles.

Thus I have no right nor intent to preach or to influence by words my surroundings. All I can hope for is to serve with my past as a deterrent example for the future conduct of myself and, perhaps, also others.

To be honest, even the writing of these emphatic words is not without self-seeking intent. The egoistic desire to stand out is shining though disdainfully.

Indeed, the ultimate destiny of all our superfluous, eloquent rhetoric should be silence in modesty and compassion.

Prof. Dr. Richard R. Ernst *from Switzerland, received the Nobel Prize for Chemistry in 1991, for his contribution to the development of the methodology of high resolution Nuclear Magnetic Resonance (NMR) Spectroscopy.*

The Kingdom Of God

— Richard Deats

Muriel Lester was born into a wealthy British family near London. Growing up she led a life of privilege, with piano and tennis lessons and extended travel abroad. She loved the military exploits of the British Empire and kept a scrapbook of wars and battles. But when she was 18, she read Tolstoy's The Kingdom of God Is Within You. "It changed the very quality of life for me," she later wrote. "Once your eyes have opened to pacifism, you can't shut them again."

This religious conversion led Muriel and her sister, Doris, to found Kingsley Hall for the impoverished residents of London's East End. Despite its remarkable ministry to the area, World War I brought great criticism against Muriel's outspoken pacifism. She said, "We, at Kingsley Hall, refused to pronounce a moratorium on the Sermon on the Mount for the duration of the war. We could not conceive of God as a nationalist. We could not suddenly look upon our brother man as an enemy just because he chanced to have been born on the other side of a river or a strip of sea."

Hit by a German bomb, Kingsley Hall was rebuilt and it flourished, bringing poor Cockney children music, art, poetry, drama, camps and outdoor life. In time Muriel Lester became an nondenominational minister to the area and also served as socialist alderman in the London borough of Poplar where she worked with her colleague George Lansbury.

In 1926, Lester made the first of many trips to India and became a close friend of Gandhi, working for the independence of India from the British. When Gandhi came to England for official talks with the government, he chose Kingsley Hall as his residence for three months.

Lester often preached at Hyde Park and spoke for the fellowship of Reconciliation and the way of nonviolence and service. In 1934, she was named ambassador–at–large by the International FOR; for the next 30 years she travelled all over the world on its behalf.

She was in the United States when World War II broke out but she remained steadfast in her opposition to the slaughter of modern warfare. She went from the U.S. to Latin America where she received word that Kingsley Hall had been bombed in the London blitz. She cabled home : "From Kingsley Hall's broken body, the bread of life can be better and more widely distributed. Christ is in the midst of her. God has all in his hands."

Lester's pamphlet, "Speed the Food Ships" and her speeches came to the attention of the British government. Winston Churchill, zealously carrying out the food blockade, ordered her arrested. In Trinidad, she was removed from the ship in which she was travelling and interned there for ten weeks. She wrote in her diary, "Excess in drink, vice or gambling won't draw attention to you, but thinking independently will. If it leads you to act generously, to identify yourself with the poor or the prisoner or the foreigner or the Negro, the vested interests will be displeased."

Finally she was transferred to London's Holloway jail : she had been there before, but as a lecturer. After she was released, she continued her work at Kingsley Hall. With the war's end, she resumed her world pilgrimages for the International Fellowship of Reconciliation, witnessing to the way of life that removes the occasion for wars.

Muriel Lester went around the world nine times in the work of peacemaking. She travelled extensively on the continents. In 1950 she visited South Africa to establish the FOR there and to visit *Manilal* and *Sushila Gandhi* (second son of Gandhi and his wife) at the Phoenix Settlement. The Japanese called her "Mother of World Peace" and in America she was called "the Jane Adams of London." A practical mystic who combined the life of prayer with the life of service, she wrote, "The job of the peacemaker is to stop war to purify the world to get it saved from poverty and riches to heal the sick to comfort the sad to wake up those who have not yet found God to create joy and beauty wherever you go to find God in everything and in everyone."

She died in 1968 at the age of 84.

Richard Deats is editor of Fellowship magazine and has worked for the Fellowship of Reconciliation since 1972. He is the editor of Ambassodar of Reconciliation: A Muriel Lester Reader, and member of the Advisory Board of The M.K. Gandhi Institute for Nonviolence.

The Pilgrims Of Peace

Ann & John Rush

We have loved Gandhi for many years. My earliest memory of him is sixty years ago when I heard a great pacifist Methodist minister, Dr. Henry Hitt Crane, extol the virtues of this saintly man and yet tell us that Gandhi would not call himself a Christian because he believed that unless all Christians live according to the teachings of Jesus Christ, (The Sermon on the Mount) he does not see any reason to call himself anything but a Hindu.

John and I have spent 45 years working in one way or another in the peace movement for a nonviolent world. In the 1950s we lived in a small Quaker community in California. We had been deeply inspired by reading Gandhi's autobiography and his experiments with truth. Three couples of us studied Wilford Wellcock's booklet, *Gandhi As A Revolutionary*. This was an important factor inspiring us to move to Argenta, in the backwoods of British Columbia, to raise our children away from our materialistic, militaristic society. Always Gandhi was the shinning light in our lives.

We met another shinning light, Peace Pilgrim, on her one trek across Canada. She came to our Argenta Quaker community to speak to our Friends Meeting on the shores of Kootenay Lake. We were delighted with her dedication and identified with her desire to save our world from a nuclear holocaust.

She said, ". . . I didn't know exactly what I was here for. It was out of a very deep seeking for a meaningful way of life, and after having walked all one night through the woods, that I came to what I now know to be very important psychological hump. I felt a complete willingness, without any reservations, to give my life, to dedicate my life to service. I tell you, it's a point of no return. After that, you can never go back to completely self-centered living."

We kept in touch for her remaining 24 years. While on her pilgrimage she would stay with us in different parts of the United States where we happened to live.

We tried to get her to write a book but she would never take the time. Finally John wrote to her, "You better write that book, you won't live forever." Two months later she was killed in a car accident while being driven to a speaking engagement. Before she died she had written back to John, "Well, I've really written enough for a book, its just not in book form." It was not easy to be joyful about her "glorious transition" as she repeatedly called death. But it was very easy to bury ourselves in the joyful task of compiling the book of her life and work in her own words, with three of her other friends.

We are spending the rest of our lives filling requests for Peace Pilgrim books and tapes. It has been such an incredible experience to have 258 people in India ask for Peace Pilgrim books, many write glowingly of her message and repeatedly request more books and tapes. At first I could hardly believe it - people from the land of Gandhi actually loving a book we helped compile about an American woman who walked this country like their *Sanyasins*. The simplicity and devotion of Peace Pilgrim inspires Indians much as their Gandhi inspires people world wide. Many have written their astonishment that a woman would (could) go on such a devoted pilgrimage in this materialist, militaristic country.

Once she was asked by a friend, "Why do you carry a tooth brush and comb? Gandhi didn't." She replied, "Gandhi didn't have any teeth and he didn't have any hair."

Peace Pilgrim loved Gandhi as all of us do.

Here in Hemet during our Quaker Meeting, a quotation from Gandhi comes to mind about once a year, and I repeat it during the silence :

"When that fineness and rarity of spirit which I had longed for has become perfect natural to me, when nothing harsh nor haughty occupies, be it momentarily my thought world, when I have become incapable of evil, then and only then will my nonviolence, my *Satyagraha* move the hearts of the world."

Gandhi and Peace Pilgrim were deeply moved by the poor of the world. Gandhi said, "Whatever you do, ask yourself if this will help the poor." Peace Pilgrim said, "I do not want more than I need while others have less than they need."

Dr. Arunachalam of Gandhigram University, after visiting us, established an Indian Friends of Peace Pilgrim. They translated into *Tamil* the little Steps Toward Inner Peace booklet by Peace Pilgrim and printed 10,000 booklet. Steps has been translated into *Hindi, Malyalam, Kannada* by other Indian friends of Peace Pilgrim.

Dr. Arunachalam has said many wonderful things about Peace Pilgrim - that her message is so similar to Gandhi's. We feel deeply moved that one who has lived and worked in the Indian Gandhian movement most of his life and lived with Gandhi in his Ashram for a year, thinks so highly of Peace Pilgrim.

"I travel a lot and carry Peace Pilgrim books and Steps to be distributed to friends with whom I stay. This time I had a bunch of Tamil Steps for emigres from Sri Lanka, Fiji, Malaysia and I have to mail additional copies to these countries. Recently we have printed 5000 more Tamil Steps to meet the increasing demand. India also needs the message of Peace Pilgrim. The youth of India will be inspired to hear from the vibrant voice of the Pilgrim the words "non-violence and Gandhiji".

Following are a few excerpts from letters from the many hundreds we received from India :

Shambhu Dass writes from Pilani, India : "Peace Pilgrim has been a saint par excellence of this century, and all souls across the globe ready for an awakening are deeply touched and moved and guided by her message, of which she was a living demonstration for well over four decades".

Navin Kumar from Pune wrote : "Thank you so much for the two copies of Peace Pilgrim. They are being circulated among friends. Yesterday we took up this book for study in the meeting of the Theosophical Society. The book is most inspiring and I have read it many times. I am deeply impressed by the Friends of Peace Pilgrim in spreading the message of Peace".

From a student of *Gandhian* thought at Gandhiji's *Sabarmati Ashram* : "You can't imagine how I felt when I went through the Peace Pilgrim book. I've been much impressed by her life and I've kept her book as a treasure. It is so interesting and inspiring! Though small, the book has tremendous educative value. This is not merely a travel account or autobiography, but also a scripture that contains the concerns of all religions and preaches universal brotherhood.

"I was glad to know that you've read Mahatma Gandhi, one of the greatest souls of this century. In fact there is not much difference between the thought and ideas of Gandhi and Peace Pilgrim. Both were the messengers of Peace and love who come to the earth for the salvation of humankind. Gandhi preached and practiced truth and nonviolence throughout his life, and so also Peace Pilgrim. For both Truth is God, and God realization of the ultimate truth is the primal goal of life. The path they laid down for getting inner peace and outer peace is essentially the same. If we want to make this world a better place we're to tread the paths of people like Gandhi and Peace Pilgrim.

"After reading the book it seemed that though Peace Pilgrim was a Christian [she never belonged to a religious group] by birth she was a Hindu by practice. She had absorbed all the philosophy of the Hindu religion. Her ideas about birth, rebirth, Karma, God, etc., are the same as described in the Hindu scriptures".

He offers to translate Steps into his native tongue, *Oriya* and continues : "I would consider myself fortunate to preach the message of love and peace of that good woman of the west".

A Tibetan Buddhist nun wrote from India that she found the Peace Pilgrim book in their retreat library. She writes that though Peace Pilgrim did not study their texts, she found the same principle from within. She asked us to send a book to the Dalai Lama.

Ann & John Rush *are recipients of the Courage of Conscience Award of 1992 given by the Peace Abbey, Sherborn, Massachusetts; for their dedicated work for peace for more than four decades.* *Ann & John* *are completely immersed in Peace Pilgrim work.*

The Eighth Blunder

— Sir Ranulph Fiennes

Gandhi stands for love and for peace as did Jesus Christ. Christ used a whip to clear the Temple and I do not know what Gandhi would have done in that position.

When evil can only be prevented by violence, and we can all think of examples of such situations, what is the answer?

Let us all be pupils, Gandhi said. Did he ever learn and pass on the least answer to this conundrum?

When I next come upon a man beating or killing or raping, do I stop him by rendering him unconscious in as gentle a way as possible once I have ascertained that no other less physical alternative will save his victim? I believe Gandhi would say "Yes" for he was not narrow-minded, and he knew that the exception proves the rule.

Nonviolence, I think he would agree, encompasses minimal violence when applied expressly to quell violence.

Gandhi's Eighth Blunder might have been "Doctrine Without Realism", and had this been so, nonviolence *per se* would, I believe, have fallen foul of it.

Sir Ranulph Fiennes has thrilled audiences of all ages all over the world for many years, with superbly illustrated lectures and presentations. In the 1980s he was chosen as Chief Motivational Speaker in the USA. Sir Fiennes trekked to the North Pole unsupported and on foot. His greatest expedition took ten years from conception to completion, during which he and Charles Burton became the first men in history to reach both the Poles.

A Vision Quest

— *Rev. Lila C. Forest (Rabiya Majid)*

Gandhi named "religion without sacrifice" as one of the seven blunders of humanity. What might the *Mahatma* have meant by this? The word "sacrifice", when looked at through its Latin roots, means "to make sacred or holy". Taking this meaning, religion without sacrifice can mean observing the outer forms and rituals of religion without inner meaning. When persons go through the motions of religious observance without engaging the inner being, the central purpose of religion is lost. But when one uses the precepts and the inspiration of one's religion to seek the sacred in each person, each aspect of reality, one enters into a different life, one which offers to the whole of humanity and the earth community the possibility of a universal peace, respect, and harmony. For when one sees all and everything is sacred, one must necessarily treat all as worthy of respect and consideration. And this is the foundation of *Ahimsa* (nonviolence) and of a world at peace with itself.

The word religion itself means "to bind again", or "to reconnect". So if religion is performing its function in human life, it reconnects us to each other and to the world in which we live, as well as to the Divine, (or whatever it is that we hold as central meaning). When we can see how we are all interconnected - I like the word "interbeing" used by the *Buddhist Thich Nhat Hanh* - or, even further, to see that we are all aspects of One Being, then how can we intentionally cause harm to others, without serious consideration and reflection?

But sacrifice also has the meaning of relinquishing something we value for the sake of someone or something greater or more valuable. What is it that we sacrifice when we are living our religion most fully and deeply? I would answer, such things as ego gratification, personal comfort or convenience, the satisfaction of wholly selfish desires and aims. It can mean the surrender of all one is and has to the Divine, or Truth, or Love, or Peace or one's fellow human beings. This kind of surrender is seen by most religious and spiritual traditions as the Royal Road to happiness and bliss. If this is true at the individual level, it is even more true at the level of society and the whole human family. As more and more individuals dedicate their lives to the service of the One, the Whole, the quality of human interaction at all levels transforms, replacing strife, war, cruelty, and selfishness, with conflict resolution that benefits all concerned, peace, respect, love and harmony.

In many traditional tribal societies, such as those of the American Indians, youths at the brink of adulthood undergo a vision quest in order to discover who they are and what their place is in their society and in the cosmos. The adult members of their community prepare for them a rite of passage into full participation in the life of the people, some kind of experience that demands from them the full extent of their courage and strength. When these rites are performed successfully with full power and intention, the young emerge as fully commited members of their community, worthy of inclusion and respect, and ready and willing to give their energies, their talents, and their lives for the good of the whole group to which they belong.

Without some kind of experience such as this, societal or religious, which helps each of us to know who we are and to feel completely a part of our community, be it the family, the tribe, or the whole human family, each one wanders without a sense of purpose and meaning. Often, by sheer grace, we stumble onto our own unique spiritual path at some point in our lives and begin our journeys, but all too often the sense of connection to the rest of humanity never really develops, and thus are possible all the destructive behaviors that arise from a basic sense of alienation.

There is, of course, another element that is crucial to the development of a person who is willing and able to sacrifice for the greater good, and that is being loved in early life. Generally, loving persons have been well-loved as children. So we have the tremendous task in our present world to break the cycles of family violence, physical and emotional, that are the root cause of violence perpetuated.

I believe that a world without violence will be a world in which each individual is guided, by family, by society, by religious forces, to develop a positive sense of self and his/her place in the entirety, and thereby to be capable of gladly sacrificing, making holy, transforming hatred, the use of power over others for personal gain, self-indulgence, the superfluous and the nonessential, in order to serve the well-being of all. I believe that, sooner or later, such a world will come to be, because it is essential to the fulfillment of our reason for being. And, with the committed action, to the fullest extent of our capacity, of all who so believe, it will come sooner.

The Rev. Lila C. Forest (Sheikha Rabiya Majid Chishti) is a Unitarian Universalist minister and a teacher in the western Sufi tradition. Her work is focused on social, economic, and spiritual evolution, as well as the restoration of the Earth.

From Lenin To Gandhi

— Robert L. Holmes

A_S the final pieces of the 20th century fall into place, we can begin to ask what the century has meant for human history. Historians, theologians, and political scientists will differ as to what that is. But no account can be complete which fails to recognize that this century has posed definitively the basic choice in the approaches to change in the social, economic, and political realm.

That choice was given intellectual-expression near mid-century by Arthur Koestler, who wrote of the *Yogi* and the Commissar : the two representing idealized conceptions, respectively, of change from within and change from without. The Commissar sees humankind's salvation coming through revolution and social, political, and economic engineering - a restructuring of the social order so as to make it answer better to essentially material human needs. The end, here is all important. And the commissar is prepared to use all necessary means to its attainment, including violence. The *Yogi*, on the other hand, believes that change must come from within, and that only by transforming individuals will social structures begin to reflect the deeper spiritual realities with which we are all connected. And he believes with equal conviction that means rather than ends are all important; and that to be truly effective, means must be nonviolent.

But more important than Koestler's definition of this issue is the fact that the 20th century witnessed the embodiment of these outlooks in two of history's most important figures : Lenin and Gandhi. They both launched great experiments.

Lenin and his followers, in their renovation of Marxism, sought to transform the newly formed Soviet Union (and eventually the world) by manipulation of social and economic structures. Central control, social reorganization, and enforced economic equality were the prescriptions. The scheme was a grand one. And the end - a progressive, economically prosperous world free of exploitation - a splendid vision. But with the collapse of the Soviet Union in the century's closing decade the experiment proved to be a failure - as complete a failure, perhaps, as any massive social enterprise ever undertaken.

Gandhi launched a very different experiment. It was an experiment in truth

- truth in word, thought, and deed. It did not by any means forego efforts at social change; indeed, one of its most notable dimensions was the struggle to liberate India from British rule. But its ultimate message was that change must come from within and involve a commitment to nonviolence. "As human beings," Gandhi said, "our greatness lies not so much in being able to remake the world as in being able to remake ourselves". And, like Thoreau, an optimism about the value of even one person's efforts at effecting social change. As he said, "even a tiny grain of true non-violence acts in a silent, subtle, unseen way and leavens the whole society".

Gandhi was not, therefore, a pure *Yogi* in Koestler's sense - certainly not to the extent that Lenin and his followers were very nearly pure Commissars. His was a principled nonviolence to transform not only the individual, but also society — and ultimately, the world as well. But it was the need to begin with ourselves, through discipline and purification, that he stressed. And he regarded the enterprise he was engaged in as truly an experiment, one whose outcome was far from certain.

It is this which presents humankind with its greatest challenge as we approach the beginning of a new millennium : to continue Gandhi's experiment with non-violence. For what sets this experiment apart from others is that it will work if we make it work. And it is in our power - that is, in the power of humankind collectively - to make it work. What it requires is moral and spiritual effort on the part of each of us, in our own way, according to our circumstances, and according to our capacities. There is no other way. If we learn this from the 20th century, we may yet find our way to redemption and renewal from its unprecedented destruction, cruelty, and violence.

Dr. Robert Holmes is the author of War and Morality, (1989), and Basic Moral Philosophy, (1993), as well as the editor of Nonviolence Theory and Practice. After receiving his under-graduate degree from Harvard, Dr. Holmes obtained his Ph.D. at the University of Michigan. He is both a member of the Advisory Board of the M.K. Gandhi Institute for Nonviolence and on the National Council of the Fellowship of Reconciliation.

The Power of Love

— *Rev. Jose "Chencho" Alas*

There are two ways to resolve a conflict among people; one is through the power of the mind and the heart, the other one is through the power of the canons. The first one has to do with conviction, the second is the fruit of imposition. The first one has a instrument the power of the words, the second the power of the bullets.

These two ways of resolving conflicts can not avoid violence, that is part of our spirit. But there are two kinds of violence, one that is irrational, based in greed, and the other one that is rational, based in love. Jesus said: " Do not think that I have come to bring peace to the world. No. I did not come to bring peace, but a sword." (Mt. 10, 34) what kind of sword is Jesus speaking about? Certainly, not the one that serves to kill people. He prevented Peter, his disciple, from using the sword, when he was arrested " All who take the sword will die by the sword ". (Mt. 26, 52).

The violence of the spirit means that we denied ourselves. That we are " the change which we wish to see". " As human beings, our greatness lies not so much in being able to remake the world as in being able to remake ourselves." M. K. Gandhi

The prophets have the power of the worlds. They denounce the structures of sin, what is wrong in society, in ourselves; and announce the kingdom of love, understanding, reconciliation, solidarity. They proclaim a world without violence against others. It doesn't matter where they come from, what their origin, religion or faith, they have in common the only "salvific" word for human beings: Understanding and love. Jesus, Mohandas Gandhi, Martin Luther King, Archbishop Oscar Romero affirmed their faith in mankind, that is what they shared and for that they gave their lives.

They do not silence the others with guns, they open their ears and hearts to hear the others and walk together in this life, on this planet. That is the difference between a general and a prophet.

My dream is that there will be a day when in our schools, we will teach the history of the prophet and less the history of the generals and their instruments of war.

Rev. Jose "Chencho" Alas is a former advisor to Archbishop Romero. He is international representative for the Institute of Technology, Environment, and Self-sufficiency in Round Rock, Texas. He periodically visits his native country, El Salvador.

When, When, O God, Shall Men be Brother to Man?

— *Swami Nirmalananda*

I often feel like crying when I hear of the tragic happenings in this country (India). All religions, started with the best of good intentions, have outlived their purpose. Religion which should have been a blessing has become a curse. Each religion by erecting its separate enclosures has built barriers between man and man. Sitting in these little narrow cages, the adherents of different religions are calling others to their cages which they consider to be a better cage than all cages instead of asking people to break down these man-made barriers and to come out of these cages that keep them bound so that all may live as free men and women. This is the need of the hour. So long as these cages and enclosures exist, the followers of one religion will continue to live as the sworn enemies of another faith. This is what we have been observing in human society. We may stretch our hands across the separate walls of different religions and shake hands with others saying piously that we are all brothers. Yet as long as this wall of separateness exists, man will not be able to realise his true relationship and unity with all. As long as blind belief is actively promoted from pulpits and platforms, we are thereby sowing the seeds of religious fanaticism in the minds of the masses. Although we may be extolling the virtues of brotherhood of all men, in actual life we are inwardly at each other's throat and often behave as unbalanced insane individuals. It is far better to be sincere and honest non-believers than to be blind and fanatical believers in God.

We are blindly clinging to the shadows of religion rather than to the substance, more concerned with the shell of religion than the kernel and more interested in chasing cheap pleasures of life than discovering the truth of God and we are waging war in the name of religion combined with politics. Our clear stream of reason is getting lost on 'the dreary desert sand of dead habits'. When, when, O God, shall man be brother to man?

Mixing religion with politics is like playing with fire. But, by doing so, it is easy to become great and famous by cleverly exploiting the weakness of the masses and by scratching on their religious sentiments. But at what cost? The result is here for all of us to see. Frankly speaking, it was Ram-Nam and Allah that divided India and made India and Pakistan as two hostile nations. Jehovah and Allah, even when they both stress on the oneness of God, will always fight, as we have been seeing with our own eyes.

It is time to realise that violence with violence, hatred with hatred, will not foster amity and understanding. According to Buddha, the cream of religion is Compassion. It is this healing balm of Divine Compassion in man, but not of a particular faith, that is sorely needed in India and elsewhere in the world, for applying on the wounds which are being blindly inflicted on others. It is vitally important to know the Truth that makes man free and happy. Then each religion will have to bow to the Truth of all religions.

Swami Nirmalananda, the none-too-noticed Sage of India, after quite some restlessness in his worldly life when young, sought and achieved eternal blessedness, wisdom and peace in the teachings of the most spiritual personalities of many different cultures around the world, his spiritual quest taking him all around the globe.

*Following an inner call, **Swamiji**, at the impressionable age of fourteen, made a deep study of the world's major religions. He was greatly influenced by the lives and teachings of Ramakrishna Paramhansa, Vivekananda, Mahatma Gandhi, Thoreau, Tolstoy, Schweitzer and many others. Like Sankaracharya, Jesus and Buddha, he became a wandering monk. On his way to Europe, he visited all of West Asia, particularly Israel. In Jerusalem he met and discoursed with the Existentialist, Martin Buber who reminded him of Jesus, both in looks and charisma.*

The Degradation Of The Master

— David Dellinger

My friend the American poet Kenneth Patchen once made the following criticism of the U.S. Pacifist Movement: "They want to get rid of war without getting rid of the causes of war." It was his way of saying that there can be no peace without justice and the pacifist movement should devote as much effort to eliminating injustice as to eliminating the latest weapons of military warfare.

The truth is that the two primary reasons for war are greed and need. The greed of those whose aim in life is to appropriate for themselves (or their country) a disproportionate (unjust) amount of money, power, privilege etc. And the need for the losers in that unworthy competition to get back some of the things that have been stolen from them, things that they would have access to in a more loving (and, therefore, more egalitarian) society. One has only to think of the basic necessities of life — food, decent housing, health care, useful work, respect and participation in the decisions that affect one's daily life.

And there was another point to Patchen's critique. The injustices and oppressions that cause wars are in themselves acts of violence, even apart from the patriotic wars that create or defend them. A recent estimate is that in the United States the total deaths every month from causes related to poverty are greater than the total number of deaths of U.S. soldiers during the entire Vietnam War. Of course the deaths of Vietnamese from the U.S.'s chemical warfare, massive bombing and My Lai type massacres was greater than either of these figures. But so are the numbers of deaths from poverty (and U.S. - trained death squads and U.S. - supported dictators) in countries that are dominated by the U.S. military-corporate empire.

To understand why this is true, consider a top secret document (PPS23) of the U.S. State Department in 1948. It laid down the policy that the United States military-corporate empire has followed ever since: "We have about 50 percent of the world's wealth but only 6.3 percent of its population. In this situation we cannot fail to be the object of envy and resentment. Our real task in the coming period is to devise a pattern of relationships which will permit us to maintain this position of disparity." By now, the United States's proportion of the World's population is only 4.5 percent but it still controls about 50 percent of the world's wealth.

Meanwhile, in 1965 President Lyndon Johnson, in a rare moment of candor, told the U.S. troops at *Cam Ranh Bay* (Vietnam) that "The trouble is that there are only 200 million of us and nearly three billion of them and they want what we've got and we're not going to give it to them."

Speaking pragmatically, my own studies and experience have convinced me that major advances in nonviolent force have come not from people who have approached nonviolence as an end in itself but from people who were passionately striving to free themselves and their fellows from social injustice. Gandhi himself originally discovered the method not through someone who preached or wrote about it but when he went to South Africa as a young, British-trained lawyer in search of a career and was "sidetracked" by the shock of experiencing the galling injustice imposed on all Indians, as "coolies." This does not mean that one should not use every possible method of deepening one's understanding of the method and its spiritual undergirding, including study, acts of communal solidarity, opening oneself to the Natural Universe, meditation, prayer and creative experimentation in the midst of concrete struggles. Gandhi certainly followed this course. But I shall never forget the words I heard from a Black man in Birmingham, when that city erupted in major nonviolent struggle in 1963. He said: "You might as well say that we never heard of Gandhi or nonviolence, but we were determined to get our freedom and in the course of struggling for it we came upon nonviolence like gold in the ground." He also said, as the mass meeting at which he spoke was ending: "We're going out to face the police dogs and the water canon so that we can win our freedom, and in course of winning it we are going to free our white sisters and brothers too."

That last statement reminds me of something the novelist Virginia Woolf once said: "The only degradation that equals that of the slave is the degradation of the master." Real nonviolence understands that none of us is free until everyone is free. It is not enough for us to refrain from acts of direct physical violence if we do not simultaneously work to get rid of the injustices that deny any of our fellows any human right that is available to anyone else. Or, as an Aboriginal African woman is reputed to have said: "If you have come to help me, you are wasting your time, but if you have come because your liberation is bound up with mine, then let us work together."

Nonviolence is not significantly advanced if our devotion to nonviolence is limited to our refusing to commit overt acts of violence in our own lives and relationships. In the end Gandhi dedicated his life to proving that loving nonviolent resistance is the best way to work for justice. But he also said that it is better to resist injustice violently than not to resist it at all. And an American judge, David Bazelon, after 35 years of hearing criminal cases, concluded that "Society should be as alarmed by the silent misery of those who accept their plight as it is by the violence of those who do not."

Nonviolent force comes alive only when we live and act in ways that express a positive, overpowering love for all of our fellows, even those whom the society considers to be "the least" of our sisters and brothers. After all, as Gandhi said, "I know that God is neither in heaven nor down below, but in everyone."

*Now in his 79th year, **Dave Dellinger** is a long-time nonviolent activist for justice and peace. An author and editor, he has written six books, including **Revolutionary Nonviolence** and his memoirs, **From Yale to Jail** : Pantheon 1993. He has taught part time in a number of universities in their Adult Degree Independent Studies programs. In 1940 he refused to register for the draft even though as a seminary student he was exempt from military service. He served a year and a day before the U.S. - provoked Japanese attack on Pearl Harbor led to U.S. entry into World War II. Later he served another two years. From these and other prison experiences, he says that he learned more things of value in prisons than he did at Yale or in seminary. But he is actively working to replace punishment and prisons with centers of loving rehabilitation. In 1992 and 1993 he participated in lengthy fasts that called for Columbus Day to be re-named Indigenous Peoples Day and demanded full human rights for Native Americans, the descendants of the kidnapped African slaves — and all other oppressed people.*

Experiment With Truth
in The Nuclear Age

— *Pamela S. Meidell*

A world without violence would be a world without nuclear weapons. When *Gandhiji* was asked what he thought about the bombing of Hiroshima, he reportedly said, "We have yet to see what it will do to the soul of the destroying nation". As we approach the 50th anniversary of the beginning of the nuclear age, we have a clearer vision of the damage we have wrought to our souls by unleashing the power of the atom.

Fortunately, the *Mahatma* gave us a clear view of what we can do to unleash and harness the power of the human spirit. One of Gandhi's great gifts to the world is his habit of conducting experiments with truth in his own life. *Satyagraha*, which is often translated as nonviolence, more accurately means soul-force or truth-force. In a world without violence, we would all be experimenting with this force. Gandhi showed us that anyone can do what he did if that person has but the will. In the introduction to his autobiography, ***The Story of My Experiments with Truth***, he says :

"I simply want to tell the story of my numerous experiments with truth . . . my life consists of nothing but those experiments . . . My experiments in the political field are now known. For me, they have not much value . . . But I should certainly like to narrate my experiments in the spiritual field which are known only to myself, and from which I have derived such power as I possess for working in the political field.

". . . Whatever is possible for me is possible even for a child, and I have sound reasons for saying so. The instruments for the quest appear quite impossible to an arrogant person, and quite possible to an innocent child. The seeker after truth should be humbler than the dust. The world crushes the dust under its feet, but the seeker after truth should be so humble himself that even the dust could not crush him. Only then, and not till then, will he have a glimpse of truth . . ."

In the arrogance of abrogating to ourselves the power unleashed in the atom, we have nearly destroyed ourselves. If we in the nuclear age are to restore our souls, we need to become "humbler than the dust", activating the force of soul and truth in our lives and experimenting with it creatively and playfully. We need to become *Satyagrahis*, using the resources of prayer, meditation, fasting, reflection, liturgy, ritual, drama, music, dance song, standing vigil, and the practice of witness and pilgrimage.

To begin this process of experimentation, the Nevada Desert Experience has proposed an International Year of Reflection on *Satyagraha* (Soul-Force) in the Nuclear Age. We offer the idea as an experiment and as a gift in the 125th anniversary of Mohandas Gandhi's birth, with the fervent hope that the end result will be the creation of what Martin Luther King, Jr. called "the beloved community".

When the former archbishop of Brazil, Dom Helder Camara, visited the Nevada (Nuclear) Test Site in 1986, he said, "This is the site of the greatest violence on earth,* therefore, it should be the site of the greatest nonviolence on earth". Again at the gates of the Test Site in 1991, he called on people everywhere to work toward a new millennium with no weapons of mass destruction, and enough food, clothing, shelter and education for everyone on the planet.

In 1995, the people of the earth will remember the 50th anniversary of the beginning of the Nuclear Age on July 16, 1945.

We will remember each child born since the dawn of the Nuclear Age, the miracle and sacredness of each living being.

We will remember the images of the first mushroom cloud of the Trinity atomic test rising above the earth in Almogodo, New Mexico.

We will remember the words of Robert Oppenheimer, director of the Manhattan Project, "I am become Death, the Destroyer of Worlds."

We will remember "Little Boy" and "Fat Man", the bombs that destroyed the Japanese cities of Hiroshima and Nagasaki on August 6 and 9, 1945.

Fifty years later, the people of the earth will remember the terrible destructive power and violence latent within us and made manifest in the bomb. We will meet this power of destruction by drawing on the rich sources of our human spiritual tradition and the deep wells of faith, beauty, humor, and creativity of the human spirit to nurture the growth of a culture of nonviolence, health and peace.

We will remember the visionaries who have come before us, calling us to our deepest and highest selves, and we give thanks for their witness and their commitment to life.

We will remember the cost to all life of our commitment to death.

We will remember the Indigenous peoples, on whose lands we mined for uranium, tested our nuclear weapons, and filled with nuclear waste.

We will remember the Downwinders, the Atomic Veterans and all radiation victims, knowing that in the global community, we are all downwinders.

We will remember the desert of New Mexico, Nevada, Lop Nor, Maralinga, Algeria, Rajasthan, and Kazakhastan where atomic violence creates deserts in our hearts and souls; we will remember the island of Bikini, Christmas, Eniwetok, Fangatauta, Johnston, Monte Bello, Moruroa and Novaya Zemlya where atomic destruction makes us islands of ourselves.

We will remember the plants and animals of the earth, whose waters, soil and air we contaminate in the "name of security".

We will remember our children and grand children and all beings of the future whose toxic radioactive inheritance we cannot keep from them.

We will remember our nuclear history so that we will not repeat it.

Therefore, we call on the people of the earth to ponder in our hearts where we have been and what we can do.

We call on our religious leaders and spiritual teachers to think and reflect on this matter and to lead us by drawing on humanity's deepest teachings to set the context of our thinking and acting.

We call on our cultural leaders - artists, writers and musicians - to help us to face our agony and pain and to tap the wellsprings of joy and creativity by moulding new forms that will allow us to mourn and celebrate together.

We call on our scientists to remain true to their quest for the truth and knowledge, to forgo research for death, and to find productive and life-enhancing uses for their discoveries.

We call on our political leaders to remember the people of the earth when they make their decisions, and to act courageously to chart new and just ways where we can work and live together in peace.

Therefore, we call on the people of the earth to ponder in our hearts what we can do, and then do it.

* Nearly 1000 nuclear weapons have been exploded at the Nevada Test Site since 1952, making it the most heavily bombed nuclear battlefield on earth. The Nevada Test Site, equal in size to Rhode Island, lies within the boundaries of the tribal lands of the Western Shoshone Nation.

Pamela S. Miedell is the Director of the Nevada Desert Experience (NDE), an interfaith organization with Franciscan origin that has been working since 1982 to end nuclear weapons testing through a campaign of prayer, dialogue and nonviolent direct action. NDE is a violence in the desert calling people to nonviolence in the face of violence, truth in face of illusion, hope in the face of despair, love in the face of fear. NDE works with groups around the world calling for a Comprehensive Test Ban Treaty.

Gandhi : The Political Moralist

— *Dr. Raghavan Iyer*

"I have not conceived my mission to be that of a knight-errant wandering everywhere to deliver people from difficult situations. My humble occupation has been to show people how to solve their own difficulties.... My work will be finished if I succeed in carrying conviction to the human family, that every man or woman, however weak in body is the guardian of his or her self-respect and liberty."

— *Mahatma Gandhi.*

In assessing the thoughts of Gandhi, it is essential to see that he was mainly a political moralist who wrote from the standpoint of a rebel, who did not concern himself with the ethical and practical problems facing men in authority. The significance of his conceptual formulations is necessarily limited by this fact. He was a man of action rather than an abstract theorist, and he had far more to say about the moral problems facing the citizen than about the tasks and purposes of government. It would be wrong, however, to assert that he was mainly concerned with resistance to authority or with problems at the fringe of political life. He tried to apply his basic concept of *satya* and *ahimsa* to a variety of practical matters - the relation between capital and labor, the decentralisation of political and economic power, social inequalities and different types of exploitation, the connection between individual liberty and national independence, the promotion of collective welfare and village self-government, attitudes towards work and the problem of full employment, the alienation of intelligentsia and the universal obligation of manual labour, the problem of educational and social reconstruction.

If we take into account the entire body of Gandhi's writings, it would be impossible to conclude that he was an essentially negative thinker. No assessment of Gandhi as a thinker would be complete or just without adequate consideration of his practical recommendations concerning the many problems facing Indian society. His ideas have considerable relevance to the societies of the future, even if his measures cannot be regarded as valid or feasible in differing conditions. Behind Gandhi's practical proposals there lay a vision, roughly sketched rather than worked out in detail, of a reconstructed polity and a regenerated society in which the pursuit of *satya* and the development of *ahimsa* are carried to their fullest fruition. His political vision was ultimately based upon the classical Indian myth of *Rama Rajya*, the ideal polity, ascribed to *satya yuga* or *krita yuga*, the Golden age lost in the mist of antiquity and prehistory. Gandhi's active political imagination took him some times entirely out of the region of existing realities into the realm of utopian fantasy, the anarchist's paradise and the city of God.

Gandhi's practical proposals cannot be examined without full consideration of the Indian context in which they were formulated. Such a study would affect our view of the range of his moral and political thought. It would not, however, modify our assessment of the most significant element in his thought - his concern with a universal political ethic founded upon his concept of *satya* and *ahimsa*. He was led to this concern with political ethics by the problems he faced as a man seeking to become a saint while never ceasing to be a politician. Although his thinking as a political moralist was not dictated by mere expediency, his formulation of his views was at times coloured by his missionary fervor and his role as political propagandist. He did not, however, function in the level of practical exhortation. He was also deeply concerned to transcend the limitations of time and space and to view political society *sub specie aeternitatis* in the classical tradition of political thought. He was much more *engage*, far more committed and active than most political thinkers, but he was no less inspired than the greatest thinkers by a coherent and exalted conception of the ends of human activity, man's place in the cosmos and the moral responsibilities of the citizen. A careful study of Gandhi's writings shows that he cannot simply be regarded as a politician and saint. He was certainly given greater thought and written more concerning "metapolitics" or "pre-political" matters than any other politician or saint, or any other political thinker in the twentieth century.

Gandhi's standpoint as a political moralist may be summed up as follows. Early in life, reacted strongly against modern civilisation and saw a contradiction between our deepest moral values as individuals and the moralistic criteria by which we tend to judge our institutions and our collective progress. He thought that the "sickness" of modern civilisation is reflected in our "soulless" politics, owing to a segregation between religion and politics and the prevalent doctrine of double standards. He redefined both "religion" and "politics" so as to emphasize the distinction between sectarian beliefs and religious commitment, between power politics and *sattvic* or "pure" politics. Politics is corrupted by power-seeking and it could be purified by introducing the monastic ideal into the sphere of political activity and social service. All men must come to accept certain values as absolute, especially truth and nonviolence. At least, some men must pledge themselves by vows to upholding these absolute values in public life. The reason for such drastic remedies is that human nature is so constituted that it must either soar or sink, and it will increasingly connive at untruth and violence if the quest for self-perfection is abandoned. Individuals should not abdicate from social responsibilities in their quest for personal salvation.

It is possible to combine an appeal to conscience with heroic action I the midst of society, to yoke freedom with commitment.

Gandhi proclaimed *Satya* as the supreme moral value and the common end of human endeavor. He stressed action as the means to *satya* and distinguished between absolute and relative truth. He also declared *ahimsa* to be the only valid basis of all political and social conduct. He distinguished between the acceptance of *ahimsa* as a creed and a policy, regarded some violence as unavoidable, and held that it is possible and necessary for the state and all social institutions to reduce progressively their reliance upon coercion. He further regarded *ahimsa* as the necessary means to the pursuit of *satya* in personal and social life. He also pointed out that we cannot make a hard and fast distinction between the means and the end, and we must not merely reject the doctrine that the end justifies the means, but also come to regard the purity of the means we employ as all-important. The individual always retains his moral authority in relation to the state , and while he must actively support the laws of the State and serve the needs of the society, he must be ready to offer nonviolent resistance to injustice and untruth. The doctrine of *satyagraha* lays down the qualifications required by a *satyagrahi*, the criteria needed to distinguish between *satyagraha* and its abuse *duragraha*, and the prerequisite for the legitimate application of appropriate modes of *satyagraha*, especially of civil disobedience and non-cooperation.

In the last analysis, Gandhi's political ethic rests upon his metaphysical presuppositions, which introduce a strong subjectivist element into his basic concepts, as well as a sustaining conviction that the morally right must necessarily be the most effective of conduct in the long run. Those who reject Gandhi's presuppositions may come to regard all his views as questionable and unrealistic. Even those who share his presuppositions and overlook his ambiguities in his formulation of basic concepts, could point to the practical difficulties and dangers implicit in their unqualified application by the great majority of men. It is, further, possible to hold that the consequence of an uncritical adoption of Gandhi's attitudes to politics and society could be very different from what he intended.

It is not surprising that a saint or a moralist should react as Gandhi did to the social institutions and the political methods of modern civilisation. It would be tempting but unworthy to respond to his moral indictment by dismissing him as a "reactionary" or a latter day Puritan or a moral fanatic. Even if we think that his attack was intemperate and exaggerated, we could safely concede its value as corrective to complacency. The difficulty with such indictments lies deeper. As a passionate moral reformer, Gandhi intended his attack to arouse people, especially in India, from their uncritical acceptance of all that goes by the name of "modernisation" and "progress". Is there not, however, a danger that such attacks on modern civilisation could and do produce two undesirable consequences? Given Gandhi's own moral diagnosis of modern man, only a few are likely to respond to his indictment with moral earnestness and reformist zeal. Such people may come to enjoy the luxury of moral indignation over contemporary institutions without even trying to set the moral example that Gandhi gave to his fellow men. This could lead to much frustration on their part, as well as considerable annoyance among those who do not share their views and resent the plane of false moral superiority from which they are delivered. Secondly, and even more important, a moral indictment such as Gandhi's could undermine the prevailing loyalty to imperfect institutions among people who are not morally prepared to follow Gandhi's positive injunctions or the example he set. This difficulty is particularly important at a time when defeatism is more common than complacency. It is easier to encourage the defeatism of the weak than to disturb the complacency of the strong, especially when the social structure is relatively stable.

The same point holds, but even more sharply, in regard to Gandhi's stress on "pure" politics. In appealing to greater involvement in the political activity which is untainted by power-seeking, Gandhi may unintentionally be responsible for "apolitical" attitudes, for political disengagement by morally worthy people. Furthermore, the attempt to introduce religion (in its finer forms) into politics may merely result in exploitation of religious emotions of baser variety) by unscrupulous politicians. One of the consequences of Gandhi's importation of religious spirit, which he exemplified in its exalted sense, into Indian politics was the increased stimulation of religious fanaticism by petty politicians among *Hindus* as well as *Muslims*. On the whole, those in the West who have emphasized religion in politics - thinkers like de Maistre or Murras - have been identified with authoritarian attitudes. Tolerance and civility came to be generally stressed in Europe at the very time when politics became secular in tone and vocabulary.

Similarly, the taking of vows, despite all the precaution which Gandhi stressed, by people who are not ready to carry them out, would merely result in greater cynicism than existed before. In India today, wearing of a "Gandhi cap" evokes suspicion, rather than respect. This may well reflect the instinctive suspicion of idealism in a corrupt and cynical age. In our century we can see all too clearly how easily and often the best becomes the enemy of the good. Similarly, the appeal to conscience commands respect in the case of rare individuals, but the very word loses its significance when it is over employed. Galdstone may have been a man of conscience but his opponents could not help their amusement or annoyance at what they termed "salamander conscience."

We can see this difficulty even more strikingly in regard to the heroic ideal. At its best, it is indeed admirable, and even today there is spontaneous appreciation everywhere for genuine instances of individual heroism in personal life or in arduous public sports. In politics, however, appeals to heroism often sound too fantastic, at the worst, or too smug, at the least, for our comfort. They serve their purpose in wartime or in period of national crisis, but in more normal times they sound either hollow or dangerous. Repeated references to heroism even in support of deserving causes are self-defeating.

The distinction between absolute and relative truth is important and useful, but in practice people may come to hold to what they call relative truths with considerable dogmatism and inflexibility. If no man can ever possess absolute truth, by its very definition, the views regarding the relative truth by all men may be marked by conflicting views regarding the relative respect that must be shown to various relative truths. it is very difficult for most human beings to adhere firmly to their relative truths without bringing their feelings into it. The ideal of detachment, much stressed in India, is admirable in itself, but if most men could come to show it there would be no reason to respect it as we now do.

The difficulty in regard to the concept of *ahimsa* is that it appears too all-embracing and too demanding in its reference to thought, word and deed for it to be meaningfully employed. Further, the creed of *ahimsa* requires so exacting a discipline that it might seem safer to avoid the term altogether in politics than to encourage people to set themselves so high a standard that they are unable to take difficult decisions involving a choice of relative evils. The same objection could be raised, but even more strongly, in regard to *satyagraha*. Only a very few people seem to be capable of taking upon themselves considerable suffering in support of a worthy cause without becoming embittered in the process. The doctrine of *satyagraha* demands such a high standard of compliance with the laws of the community — compliance out of the highest motives, without a trace of fear or self-interest — that very few · people would really qualify for its exercise.

Altogether, all these objections to the practical adoption of the Gandhian standpoint in politics turn upon assumptions about human nature. Even if we do not presuppose the unverifiable notion of the constancy of human nature, why should we expect that human being would change more readily in response to the doctrines of Gandhi than they have been able to do in the past as a result of the exhortation of the religious prophets? Gandhian concepts have nothing in common with the Buchmanite or Evangelical notion of a sudden transformation of human nature, but is there not a danger in practice that the doctrines of Gandhi could degenerate into some form of Buchmanism? Gandhi himself told Dr. Buchman once that his experience in his Ashrams showed him that changes in human nature are harder to come by than Buchman thought. In any case, does Gandhi's political ethic merely amount to a renewed attempt at moral exhortation? Was Gandhi ignoring the weakness of the flesh, which are important factors in politics, in stressing the willingness of the spirit, which may be very necessary in mysticism? Did the saint in Gandhi prevent him from becoming a sage, in the Indian tradition? Was he too good a man to be politically or spiritually wise?

All these questions may be raised even by those who sympathise with Gandhi's standpoint. In the eyes of those who are positively unsympathetic to his views, such objections could be made the basis of the claim that Gandhi was a failure as a thinker and perhaps even as a saint. On the other hand, several Indian mystics, like Ramana Maharshi, thought that Gandhi was a good man who sacrificed his spiritual development by taking on too great, too Atlas-like, a burden upon himself. Such a line of reasoning could be reinforced by using Max Weber's distinction between the mystic and the ascetic. The ascetic, in the view, makes what the mystic would regard as mistake of recognising the corruption of the world but continuing to dabble in worldliness. The mystic may have chosen what seems to be the easier way, but the ascetic may actually come to harm others by his self-righteousness and obstinacy.

Gandhi's standpoint could also be criticised by employing a totally different line of attack. It is possible to rid his concepts of their religious overtones and to dilute them so as to make them correspond to the essentials of good liberal doctrine. One could then argue that what is valuable in the Gandhian standpoint amounts to no more than liberal truisms in an inflated religious language. The jargon may serve its purpose among illiterate, devout peasants, but we should not let it conceal the commonsensical and unoriginal nature of the Gandhian attitudes.

All the above criticism - from pragmatic, mystical or liberal viewpoints - contain an element of truth but they ignore a vital concideration. While the best may often be the enemy of the good, an appeal to the best may be the only way, in certain circumstances, of arresting a rapid moral decline or even of securing some good. The distinction between guilt and shame is relevant in this connection. In societies which give importance to the notion of sin and guilt, a general awareness of human weakness could result in the common attempt to establish minimum standards below which people usually do not fall. The reasons for such compliance may be frankly mixed - based in part upon the presumed or actual self-interest, in part upon the competitive spirit and in part upon pleasure in self-approbation which Hume stressed. These minimum standards could be justified both by the argument from survival and collective or long-term self-interest (notions that are not free from difficulties) and by the appeal to supernatural sanctions or some transcendental concept. It is then possible to argue as Hume did that the latter argument is based on a convenient fiction and that the effective factor is self-interest. Men may come to believe this and distrust every form of high-mindedness, while zealous in the performance of the duties of their station.

In such societies there is no need to set extremely high standards, while it is possible for minimum standards to be maintained. The appeal to higher than normal standards may be made only at times of exceptional crisis. Even this may be no more than rising temporarily the minimum standards that men feel entitled to expect of each other. Normally, there would be reliable convention that would prevent politics from becoming too impure or corrupt, while no one would be particularly bothered about raising it to an impossibly high level of purity. It is enough if people in public life silently cherish religious values, and it would be improper for them to bandy about religious terms in every day politics. Politicians must be seen to be people who will not obviously misuse their position for personal advantage or to crudely seek power. They must be relied upon to keep their word in the normal way, and to respect their legal or ceremonial oaths. There is no need for them to take vows of publicly abjure all private property. They may be expected to refrain from conduct which offends their conscience but they may not talk much about "conscience". They may do heroic deeds while seeming to take them in their stride as though they were part of their essential obligations. They will avoid untruths though they might be rather hypocritical. They will regret the use of force, though they have no qualms about it in instances that are generally regarded as requiring such use. In such societies some men may be willing to suffer for their beliefs and even go to prison, while hating the thought of being regarded as rare martyrs. The authorities will put them in jail as a matter of course but avoid exulting in their action or appearing insensitive to the resister's appeal to their conscience. Altogether, in such societies men may seek to improve themselves morally without any wish to become more perfect.

On the other hand, there may be societies in which notions of shame and perfectibility, rather than guilt and sin, may be deeply rooted. The heroic ideal may be kept alive by national folklore. Men may respect goodness more than anything else and may respond to it even if they feel no compunction about falling below minimum standards. They may expect so much morally from their leaders that those who are found wanting by these very high standards may deeply disturbed and may become responsible for the rapid spread of cynicism and demoralisation. There is no need to elaborate on this model; the details can be filled in. In such societies the Gandhian standpoint may produce more results than mere appeals to commonsense and duty.

It is not suggested that India necessarily corresponds to the later model. In a sense, the country had become so demoralised when Gandhi entered the political scene that the traditional notion of "shame" as well as the Western notion of "guilt" were inoperative. His heroic appeal to the forgotten language of tradition produced results - but not for long, as he discovered to his cost. Also, Gandhi had become imbued with Christian notions of sin and guilt while he was also filled with traditional Indian notion of shame and perfectibility. By the end of his life, his faith in the readiness of the Indian people in regard to *ahimsa* was profoundly shattered and he began to feel that his ideas might have a better chance in other parts of the world.

It would in fact be wrong to suggest that the Gandhian standpoint was culture bound and applicable only in India. Several elements in his doctrine are already precious in the West - the reduction of *Himsa* in particular spheres (capital punishment, cruelty to animals, nationalist support of violence used against a hostile power in peace time) as well as the use of certain techniques of mild *satyagraha* - and they are more respected today than in his lifetime. This is not to say that these are signs of the spread of Gandhian ideas, but rather that in some ways the soil has already been more prepared for their absorption by the West than in the new climate of opinion in the post - Gandhian India. Appeals to a mere sense of duty are losing their former force with the decline of conventional religions, and even the notions of sin and guilt are weaker than before. On the other hand, the ideal of heroic action and self-denial is coming to have a new significance in countries which have to find new forms of expression for the missionary zeal fostered by messianic religions and spent in empire-building.

Gandhi's fascination as a thinker lies in his inward battle between two opposing attitudes - the Tolstoyan socialist belief that the Kingdom of Heaven is attainable on earth and Dostovskian mystical conviction that it can never be materialised. The normal *Hindu* stand point has generally been anti-utopian : *Rama-Rajya* lies in the bygone *satya yuga*, and *kali yuga* is the age of unavoidable coercion. Gandhi began by challenging this view under the influence of Tolstoy, but he ended his life with more of a Dostovskian pessimism. This does not mean that he abandoned either his imaginative, Utopian, political vision or what he called his practical idealism embodied in concrete programs of immediate action. He did not feel that he was wrong to urge men to set themselves, as he did in his own life, seemingly impossible standards, but he came closer to seeing that it was wrong to expect them to do so. In July 1947, six months before his assassination, he felt that he had been betrayed by the Congress leaders and let down by his countrymen. But he did not blame them for not living up to standards that he had set them but which they never chose or really accepted for themselves.

Dr. Raghavan Iyer *was professor of Political Science at the University of California, Santa Barbara. Educated in Bombay, India and at Oxford, England, he was Rhodes Scholar and President of the Oxford Union. He taught Political Philosophy at Oxford for eight years and was visiting Professor at the University of Oslo, Ghana and Chicago. He was a Consultant to the Fund for the Republic and a member of the Club of Rome and Reform Club. He is President of World Culture and Pythagorean Academy. He has written several books.*

(Excerpted from " The Moral & Political Thought of Mahatma Gandhi", Permission to repirnt granted by Dr Raghavan Iyer.)

Would You Ever Kill?

— Bruce Kent

Perhaps I am a bit of a heretic in circles devoted to non violence. The other day at a conference for teachers on peace education I was asked if I was an absolute pacifist. I always find that a difficult question. My response was that I believed in the nonviolent settlement of conflict. That answer did not satisfy my questioner. Would I, or would I not, ever kill anyone, he wanted to know.

Proving the shallowness of my nonviolence I began to get a little cross. How can anyone truthfully answer that question? If in some very unlikely situation the only way I could save my wife from being murdered by some maniac was to get hold of a gun and shoot to kill then I think it highly likely that that is exactly what I would do. It seems to me that I would be choosing for the lesser of the two evils, which is often the only choice we get in many situations.

There were a number of reasons for my rising indignation. By pushing people to give absolute answers to hypothetical questions we can often make nonviolence look like an impossible option. Morever, it is illogical to suggest that nation states are no more than individuals writ large. They are not. Sovereign nations are simply units of people in a particular form of political organisation which happens to have been generally acceptable for a couple of centuries.

Nonviolence applied to problems between nations is a different and a more complex matter than nonviolence between individuals. Who in a nation represents it anyway? Who is supplying weapons? How much is conflict due to economic injustice? Have attempts been made to dialogue with those opposed to government policy? Has the media created enemies? What international solutions have been sought?

In my time in the British Army I spent some months in Northern Ireland. It was at the time a very peaceful place - or so it looked, since we were not even armed when on sentry duty. Only long years afterwards did I learn about the structural violence of the discrimination which was setting one community against another. Nonviolence within that area meant much more than the 'would you ever kill?' question. It should mean working for justice and reconciliation long before anyone took to bomb or gun.

Furthermore I realise that I was getting a little irritable because my questioner was putting nonviolence on a level of spiritual renunciation which most people just think impossible. We ought to start from the other end and help people understand how normal nonviolence is. Most people most of the time do live their lives in nonviolent ways. Even in America where a gun seems to be an object of domestic veneration, killing people to settle arguments is still unusual.

Because we believe in nonviolent settlement we have courts, lawyers, mediation, counselling, and arbitration. The areas of the globe within which nonviolence is the norm is expanding all the time as more and more people realise how interdependent in the fragile world we all are. Even at levels above the nation state wars are the exception, not the rule.

The task of those who believe in nonviolence is, of course, to declare their own spiritual values and not to be afraid to talk about love and forgiveness. But it is also to help to build the structures between human beings which make nonviolence more and more normal and possible.

I remain therefore a rather pragmatic pacifist. It took me forty years to get to my present position from the days when as a young lance corporal, I would have obeyed any military order I was given. Since my progress has been slow I want others to have their space in which to move forward in their own way. One step forward usually leads to two more in the same direction. I am, therefore, more interested in the beginning of a journey rather than in arguing the details of the end.

Bruce Kent is a member of the Advisory Board of the M.K. Gandhi Institute for Nonviolence, past President International Peace Bureau, Vice President Pax Christi and the British Campaign for Nuclear Disarmament.

Human Rights In China

— *Fang Li-Zhi*

As a veteran Chinese activist, who has long been involved in the democratic movement, I feel that today's world needs to evaluate what Mohandas K. Gandhi called the Seven Blunders, especially "Politics without Principles". This is because one of the principles of human rights is sometimes being distorted.

I would like to address one of such distortions, because it is circulating among some foreign policy makers. It says that economic development will automatically lead to a democratic society. In China, the release of market forces has indeed led to economic growth. We should, of course, welcome this growth. But some people have gone further and said that China now needs only economic development, because more economic growth will lead inevitably to democracy. The Chinese communist authorities clearly like this theory, because they can use it to cover up their record of violation of human rights. It would be wonderful if democracy did indeed grow automatically out of economic development, but history gives us, un-fortunately, no such guarantees. In the history of both China and the rest of the world, it is easy to find counter examples to the theory of the automatic generation of democracy.

When China's 1989 pro-democracy movement was crushed by the Chinese government, some China policy makers argued, and many people also hoped, that continued investment would lead to both economic reform and gradual improvement in the human rights situation. However, after four years of business as usual the Chinese Communist government continues to imprison citizens for their political and religious beliefs. And in the actuality of China today, the economic growth that we see has not in the slightest moved Deng Xiaoping and his associates to alter their autocratic rule. There have been on substantive changes in Chinese political life since the protest in 1989. It is naive to expect that the dictators will control their own behavior in the area of human rights abuse as a repayment for business as usual. 'Keep the human rights principles on' is the only way to save the victims of human rights violations. We have no reason to conclude that economic development can substitute for progress toward democracy.

I feel the need to stress this point because this "theory" about the primacy of economy pops up from time to time in world diplomacy. In times like ours, when the world economy is sluggish, the place of human rights as a basic principle in international affairs is frequently down-played, whether intentionally or not. Any foreign policy that intentionally or unintentionally down-plays principles of freedom and human rights will increase the factor of violation in our world. Therefore, it is time we send a strong message to all governments in the world that we do not support a policy which overlooks the principle of human rights. For this reason we need to provide politicians with a live reading of Gandhi's conviction that our world will be violated if we continue to practice "politics without principles."

Fang Li-Zhi, *was born on February 12, 1936. During the cultural revolution (1966-1976), he was sent to the labor camp. With the rise of student unrest in 1987, the government accused* **Fang** *of promoting "bourgeois liberalization" and discharged him from the University of Peking. Subsequently he was transferred to the Bejing Astronomical Observatory to work as a research fellow. In June 1989* **Fang** *felt compelled to seek sanctuary in the U.S. Embassy in Bejing, where he remained for 13 months.*

Fang *is Guest Research Professor of the Royal Society at London, senior visiting fellow of the Institute of Astronomy of Cambridge University, and research fellow at the Institute for Advanced Study at Princeton. Since 1992* **Fang** *is professor of Physics and Astronomy at the University of Arizona.* **Fang** *has published more than 190 scientific articles and is the author, co-author and editor of 23 books.* **Fang** *has received 27 awards and honors.*

Violent Means = Violent Ends

— *Alvin F. Poussaint*

If we want to create a world without violence, we must begin at home. Government decrees or compassionate legislation are meaningless unless the values they espouse are practiced in the family.

With what is known about child development, and the publicity of child abuse, we continue to condone, and use, physical punishment for our children. A recent survey indicates that approximately fifty percent of American parents admit to spanking their children. Parents who advocate the use of physical punishment often quote the proverb : "spare the rod and spoil the child." A quote from Gandhi more appropriately reflects the damage done to a physically abused child:

"I object to violence because when it appears to do good, the good it does is temporary, the evil it does is permanent".

When parents argue that they hit their children to "teach them", what do they teach them? They may teach them to stop the behavior, at least when they are around. They also teach them that violence is acceptable, in certain situations. By their action, they teach that "might makes right". Yet, there is abundant evidence that children who are treated violently become fearful and anxious; in several cases, developing post-traumatic stress disorder. Those who are abused may develop behavior and conduct disorders that damage their ability to learn. Consequently, such youngsters are at a high risk to become school dropouts and, thereby, short-circuit their life opportunities.

To prevent the development of violence related neuroses we need to begin by practicing nonviolent parenting. Adults do not know how to be good parents instinctively; they learn by the example of their own parents, and by acquiring knowledge as they develop their relationship with their children. There are many effective methods of discipline which teach self- control and self discipline without having to strike a child. Smacking a child because she hits her brother does not really teach her not to hit, it teaches instead that violence is an acceptable way to resolve conflict.

When we discipline our children using nonviolent means, such as taking away privileges, or sending the child to his room, we teach self-control. When we punish our children physically, we simply invite their resentment - they may have been punished for a behavior, but they really haven't learned how to control themselves. Far from developing a nonviolent child, such abuse leads to a child filled with rage and anger.

Children cannot learn to control their own violence and aggression when they do not see their parents control theirs. Through imitation and identification, children adopt their parents' model as their own. This internalized message can lead a child to become a bully or an abuser of others. If our homes are places where no one can physically harm another under any circumstances, then we will be a long way towards a world without violence.

Often when children are physically punished by parents, it leads to violent emotions on he part of the child toward them. It is not uncommon for severely abused children to murder their own parents. Such hostile feelings are easily displaced onto broader community, leading to high rates of physical assault and homicide. When displaced onto other nations, this rage can lead to war and genocide that is fueled by interpersonal conflicts and pathological needs. Many individuals, unfortunately, actually believe they are using violence for righteous and good causes. They are mistaken. Gandhi's objection to violence was based on the understanding that violent means always lead to violent ends.

Dr. Alvin F. Poussaint, *MD is a clinical Professor of Psychiatry and Faculty Associate Dean for Student Affairs at Harvard Medical School. He is also a Senior Associate in Psychiatry at the Judge Baker Children's Center in Boston. He is author of* **Why Blacks Kill Blacks**, *1972, co-author of* **Black Child Care**, *1975, and co-author of the revised edition of* **Black Child Care**, *entitled* **Raising Black Children**, *published in November, 1992. He has written dozens of articles for lay and professional publications.*

Guns are as American as Applepie

— William Lucy

In the half-century since the end of World War II violence has continued to be one of humankind's most common denominators. There are so many conflicts at any given time — bloodlettings rising out of tribe, clan, nation, culture, or religion — that most American news media don't bother to report on anything more than the most monstrous atrocities. Distance lends disinterest.

But if Americans are mentally able to tune out savageries in Belfast, or a Bosnian village it is almost impossible to ignore the blood that washes through the streets of our own neighborhoods. The cruel fact is that on the brink of the 21st Century, America is drenched with violence, and a typical school kid these days is as familiar with its vocabulary — of AK-47s, drive-bys, crack, skyjackings, Saturday Night Specials, knee-capping — as any Libyan terrorist.

By the end of 1993 homicide had become the leading cause of death on the job in six of the 50 states and in Washington, D.C., the nation's capital. Within our borders some 20,000 men, women, and children are slain each year. All too often, adolescents are the perpetrators and the victims; in 1991 teen-agers were being murdered at the rate of 15 a day. What is most troubling is that much of the violence is random, with no purpose other than a momentary thrill or of acquiring status in a street gang.

It is currently popular to assign part of the blame for this malign epidemic to the mass media, and particularly to television; critics say that vivid and unending portrayals of mayhem encourage violence, and that may be so. But I'm struck by a possibility that is infinitely more depressing — that television's gore-soaked "entertainments" only mirror an American society that has lost its way.

President Clinton has already proposed such counter-measures as more police and harsher penalties, and we shall probably spend more billions of dollars trying them again although neither approach has worked in the past.

Those who ask why there is so much violence in America or anywhere else immediately arm an endless debate over nurture vs. nature. The nurturists hold that violence is rooted in poor education, or unemployment, or the loss of family values. The naturists argue that violence has genetic roots and may be a testosterone flavor.

Whatever the cause, we have to find a cure, and soon.

There is another way, I've seen it work. In 1968, as a young staffer for my union, I was assigned to Memphis, Tennessee, where sanitation workers were on strike for union recognition. The strikers were, for the most part, middle-aged black men with sore feet and aching backs, and each day they marched peaceably through downtown Memphis to air their grievances. Before long they became the targets of official violence. Police clubs, tear gas, and dogs quickly transformed an obscure local labor dispute into a gripping national story — a major chapter in Black America's struggle to win the civil rights guaranteed them by the Constitution of the United States.

It was a show down that inevitably drew into it the leading figure at that time on the moral dimensions of discrimination, the Rev. Martin Luther King, Jr. Dr. King was an apostle of *Gandhian* nonviolence, having applied it in Montgomery, Alabama, and elsewhere. He called nonviolence "an experiment in love" and "a creative force". I am convinced, he wrote, that for practical as well as moral reasons nonviolence offers the only road to freedom for African Americans. He brought his strategy of nonviolence with him to Memphis.

Dr. King went to Memphis despite indications that he knew it would be his golgotha. His speech to us on the eve of his assassination — a message of strength and faith — was, in retrospect, both a farewell and an exhortation for us to continue the struggle in Memphis and anywhere else that injustice rules.

Since that day in 1968 the nature of the struggle in America has changed. The focus has shifted from civil rights to epidemic violence: to a wave of mayhem that makes our inner-cities living hells and that is tearing the nation apart.

Late last year [November 13, 1993] President Bill Clinton went to Memphis, Tennessee, to address a convocation of Black ministers. Referring to street violence, Clinton tried to imagine what Dr. King would say:

"I did not live and die to see the American Family destroyed. I did not live and die to see 13-year-old boys get automatic weapons and gun down 9-year-olds just for the kick of it. I did not live and die to see young people destroy their own lives with drugs and then build fortunes destroying the lives of others. That is not what I came here to do."

There are today signs of a resurgence of nonviolence. Leaders as disparate as Lewis Farrakhan, Jesse Jackson, and Benjamin Chavis are urging the revival of activism in the nation's African American families and communities. Similar stirrings are evident in Latino and Asian-American communities. In Congress our lawmakers are debating measures that would better prepare young people for a life of work and create job opportunities for them.

It is unlikely that I will live to see the day when we have a world without violence, but I hope that in my time I will see an America in which violence is no longer the driving force behind our political, religious, and social debates.

William Lucy is International Secretary-Treasurer of American Federation of State, County and Municipal Employees, AFL-CIO based in Washington, D.C. since 1972. He is executive member of several organizations connected with Employees Unions. Mr. Lucy worked with Dr. Martin Luther King, Jr. in the struggle for Civil Rights and is member of the National Leadership Conference on Civil Rights. He is actively connected with the needs of African-Americans and minority workers.

What Did Gandhi Mean By Satyagraha?

— Sissela Bok

"I have nothing new to teach the world.
Truth and nonviolence are as old as the hills."

— Mahatma Gandhi.

Gandhi's words, carved on a wall at the *Satyagraha Ashram* that he founded in Ahmedabad, are at once accurate and far too modest. To be sure, there is nothing new about the ideals of truth and nonviolence to which he dedicated his life. They have long been stressed in every major moral and religious tradition. Nevertheless, he did have something utterly new to teach the world about them : how to implement them on a large scale in the practices of nonviolent but forceful resistance for which he coined the word *Satyagraha*.

What exactly did Gandhi mean by *Satyagraha*? He continued to develop its methods and to comment on them and explain their purpose and potential to the end of his life. In 1920, a British commission of inquiry asked him whether he was the author of the *Satyagraha* movement — a movement which had already become known the world over for carrying out the first nationwide campaign of civil disobedience in history and under that banner — and how he might explain it. Yes, he answered, he was indeed its author. And as for an explaination, it lay in what the movement intended to accomplish: "to replace methods of violence and (to be) a movement based entirely upon truth."

The word "replace" is crucial in this context. After first trying out a Tolstoyan approach of passive resistance in his South African campaigns, Gandhi concluded that it would not suffice. Instead, nonviolent resistance should reject not only all recourse to violence but also mere passivity so as to play an active, forceful, even militant role. By means of *satyagraha* thus interpreted, Gandhi sought to bring about profound social and individual change without the fanaticism, the hatred, and the slaughter that attends so many violent struggles. As Jawaharlal Nehru pointed out, Gandhi thereby brought an entirely new dynamic into the political and social field, which in the end transformed not only the history of India but also the lives of all who took part in his campaign.

Since Gandhi's death in 1948, his example, his writings, and the militant nonviolence he advocated have continued to "teach the world." They have influenced liberation movements as diverse as the American civil rights struggle, the Polish Solidarity movement, and the Philippine "people power" that overthrew the Marcos regime.

In 1925, when Gandhi undertook to write his autobiography, he had no way of anticipating such developments. Fifty-six years old, he felt uncertain and at times despondent about his own future as well as about the prospects for Indian independence. Three years before, he had been sentenced to jail for six years by the British, only to be released early following an attack of acute appendicitis that required hospitalization. Now he wanted to take stock of his life and consider directions for the future. In this way, he hoped to achieve greater self-knowledge and come closer to the goal of self-realization that he equated with truth, with moral and religious insight, and with seeing "God face to face." This effort would require him to describe his experiences in detail and with ruthless honesty, omitting no ugly truths "that must be told".

The result is an extraordinary account of a lifelong moral and spiritual quest. Every incident, every educational and working experience, every human encounter is examined from the point of view of how it affects that quest. In this sense at least, Gandhi's book has more in common with such works as the confessions of St. Augustine and the Vita of St. Teresa of Avila than with most contemporary autobiographies. It especially resembles the former as it combines expressions of deepest humility with a full awareness of the importance to readers of personal revelations it contains. Gandhi could have echoed St. Augustine's words.

"Many people who know me, and others who do not know me but who have heard of me or read my books, wish to hear what I am now, at this moment, as I set down my confessions. They cannot lay their ears to my heart, and yet it is in my heart that I am what I am. So they wish to listen as I confess what I am in my heart, into which they cannot pry by eye or ear or mind."

Gandhi subtitled his account "The Story of My Experiments with Truth." Since his life, he said, consisted of nothing but such experiments, recounting them would amount to writing his autobiography. He experimented, as a scientist might, by purposely introducing into his life or that of others new ideas, ways of living, challenges, and constraints, and then examining the consequences and considering their significance for further exploration. Gandhi refers to such experiments-with diets, for example, ways of coping with disease, spiritual exercises, forms of communal living, and political advocacy. Some were soon discarded, others modified, still others adopted for the long term.

Gandhi's experiments also served the purpose of testing his own character and moulding it in directions he saw as desirable. The words "trial" and "test" often enter into his characterization of these experiments. He shows how the most minute, most ordinary, and sometimes most intimate aspects of his own life offer opportunities for testing himself. Nothing, he implies, prevents readers from viewing their own lives as likewise open to choice and experimentation, making them able to participate in equally astounding personal and social transformation.

Some of Gandhi's early experiments involved purely personal change, as in his trying a diet including meat only to reject it or in seeking, as an adolescent, practical ways to return good for evil. Other endeavors involved his wife Kasturbai, whom he had married at thirteen. In his autobiography, Gandhi looks back with pain at having been thrust so prematurely into the married state and at the passion, the possessive jealousy, and the desire to dominate her in their early years together. He details his struggles to achieve celibacy and the evolution of their relationship to one greater mutuality and comradeship.

Gandhi's well-known experiments in the communal, educational, and political realms are closely linked to his efforts at personal change. However different, his experiments in several realms cannot be pried apart, he claims, since at bottom they are all moral experiments. They are all, moreover, embedded in a still more general form of experimentation and search: the continuous inquiry into what, in his own background, he could cherish and what he must reject on moral grounds-the unjust treatment of India's untouchables, for instance. At the same time, he always weighed what he could agree with in other traditions, such as Christianity and Islam, and what he must, on the contrary, leave aside. The writing of the Autobiography, finally, was itself an experiment that encompassed and re-examined all the others in memory.

As we look back at Gandhi's life and consider its importance for us, close to the end of the twentieth century and nearly fifty years after his death, it is well worth adopting that same attitude of experimenting, of testing what will and will not bear close scrutiny, what can and cannot be adapted to new circumstances. We can pick and choose from among his views just as he did from those of others. If we take seriously his approach to conflict resolution and social change, for example, we must surely stress, as he did, the twin principles of truth and nonviolence. But we do not therefore have to go along unquestioningly with his idiosyncratic, sometimes obsessive, views on diet, sexuality, or bodily hygiene. Nor need we cling to his economic certainties, a number of which were oversimplified and poorly informed even in his own day. And we have every reason to challenge-as he might well have done himself, had he lived to see India's and the world's unprecedented population growth-his opposition to all family planning methods save celibacy.

Even as we might wish to reject or modify particular aspects of Gandhi's thinking, his Autobiography remains invaluable for its account of the shaping of a new path to collective resistance to injustice. We can draw on it as well, for three more general legacies that will matter as greatly in the decades to come as they did in his own time. Gandhi would say that these legacies, too, are as "old as the hills," just as much as the principles of truth and violence that he sought to further. But his Autobiography exemplifies them in a strikingly vivid manner.

The first of these legacies is simply his strong belief that all people can shape and guide their lives according to the highest ideals, no matter how insignificant and powerless they might feel themselves to be. Gandhi lived his life, from childhood on, as someone convinced that his decisions about how to live mattered and that he had the power to make those decisions conform to what he believed right.

The second legacy matters to us more than ever as we witness mass atrocities against civilian populations purportedly carried out in the name of ethnicity and religion-as in the former Yugoslavia and so many parts of the world including Gandhi's own India. It is the example Gandhi set of someone deeply rooted in his own culture and religious heritage who still remains utterly opposed to all forms of social, ethnic, or religious intolerance. Evil means, he insisted, corrupt and degrade not only the purposes for which they are undertaken but also the persons who stoop to such means. Overcoming the urge to resort to such means is hardest when one aims to rectify past injustices. It is because "hate the sin and not the sinner" is a precept so rarely practiced that "the poison of hatred spreads in the world"

The third legacy is Gandhi's insistence that personal change and the ability to bring about social change are linked. He warns that it is no use striving to implement principles such as nonviolence or injustice in public affairs so long as one neglects them in one's personal life. And it is wise to begin in small and piecemeal ways. Everyone can carve out, should they so wish, "zones of peace" in their own lives-territories where every effort will be made to banish violence and untruth. By so doing, one will be preparing the ground for "the world of tomorrow" which will be, must be, society based on non-violence. It may seem distant goal, an unpractical utopia. But it is not in the least unobtainable, since it can be worked from here and now. An individual can adopt the way of life of the future- the non-violent way-without having to wait for others to do so. And if an individual can do it, cannot whole groups of individuals? Whole nations?"

Sissela Bok, *a writer and philosopher, was born in Sweden and educated in Switzerland and France, before coming to the United States. She received her Ph. D. at Harvard University in 1970. Formerly a Professor of Philosophy at Brandeis University, she is currently a Distinguished Fellow at the Harvard Center for Population and Development Studies. She is the author of the Foreword to the 1993 Beacon Press reissue of Gandhi's Autobiography:* **The Story of My Experiments with Truth**.

(Excerpted from "Gandhi : An Autobiography,
Permission to reprint granted by Sissela Bok.)

Transforming Relationships In The Balkans

— Margareta Inglestam

Centre for Peace, Nonviolence and Human Rights is the name of a small centre in Osijek Kroatien very close to the Serbian border. In July, 1993, the Centre organised a peace week, Days of Peace Culture.

A sign of hope in the middle of war zone.

I must admit that it was not without some anxiety and fear that I decided to accept an invitation to participate in the peace week. But from the first minute when I got off the train in Osijek and was met by a small group from the Peace Centre — with openness and affection and warmth — from that first minute I felt safe and secure.

Many times afterwards I have wondered: How is it possible that this little group at the Centre can do what they do and be what they are?

The Peace Week was a week full of serious discussions on a high academic level as well as games on an equally high but children's level, exhibits with children's drawings, songs, music, dance and play, a week of compassion and passion. One evening, during a public meeting on the Possibilities of Nonviolence, we heard distant firing from the other side of the border.

Half of the house where I lived had been bombed when Osijek was besieged in November, 1990. The husband of the family had been wounded, the husband of his niece, who also lived in the house, had been killed.

Osijek is a city of conflicts. Between majorities and minorities. Between Croats and Serbs. Between Catholics, Orthodox and Moslems. Between those who left the city during the war and the very few who stayed. Between employed and unemployed.

The Centre was founded by a small group in May, 1991. There is still a core group of five people and altogether they are 20, including Croats, Serbs and Moslems.

This little group is involved in quite a few activities. They work with women in one of the nearby refugee camps, they have tailor's and machine knitting courses integrated with social rehabilitation work. Together with the people in the same refugee camp they are building green houses for vegetables and they will organise courses in agriculture.

One of the projects of the center is called the Laslovo Multicultural Restoration Project. The aim is to prepare the refugees from the village of Laslovo – a Hungarian minority, Croatians and Serbs – to return and to live peacefully together.

A group of teachers from the Peace Centre, together with unemployed refugees are active in a very ambitious programme in peace education. After quite a lot of negotiations with authorities they work now with both teachers and children in eight elementary schools. On the agenda is play therapy reconciliation and creative conflict resolution.

One of the main activities is the Human Rights work, which mainly concerns the small Serbian minority who has dared to stay in Osijek. People have appealed to the Centre for help and protection — When they have lost their jobs, when their requests for citizenship have not been acted upon, when their social benefits have not been paid and when they have been evicted from their apartments. The Human Rights group of the Centre has responded to these requests by initiating legal procedures and protests. The members of the Centre have also practised sitting in apartments with Serbs so that they could confront soldiers who came with orders to evict them.

Consequently, they themselves have been threatened. They have been accused by the authorities of being unpatriotic traitors, taking sides with sworn enemies. One of the heads of the local government has said he had been restraining soldiers from shooting them, but would stop doing so if they continued doing their work. He could also encourage angered widows to lynch them and he would destroy the Centre and ensure that its members lost their jobs. Also in the media there have been insults and accusations.

But the members of the group all agreed on continuing the work and step by step they are reaching out to others in the community, and people are coming from other parts of Balkan, from Krajina, from Split, from Bosnia and Slovania, even from Serbia, learning how to resist oppression and violence.

Why have I told this story about this little group in Osijek? Because I think that this group so very well illustrates the ideas of Mohandas K. Gandhi. A true Peace Service in the midst of war.

But how is this possible?

I asked the question to Katarina Kruhonja, the chairwoman, a physician, and to other members of the Centre. And all of them gave the same two answers.

The first answer was : education, training, preparation.

In only one year, starting 1992, the group has participated in approximately twenty workshops. Educators, trainers, facilitators come from different parts of Europe and the United States sharing knowledge and skills. The agenda has included Human Rights education, negotiation, decision making, conflict handling, healing the traumas of victims of violence, group dynamics, communication skills, computer use and electronic communication, etc.

The second answer from the members of the Peace Centre was that the support, the advice and the inspiration from Adam Curie has been crucial for the growth of the group and for the individual members.

Adam Curie is a Professor Emeritus of Peace Studies at Bradford University - he built up that department after his time as a Director of Harvard's Center for Studies in Education and Development at Harvard. He is also a Fellow of the American Academy of Arts and Sciences. During more than thirty years he as been called upon as a mediator in conflicts in Asia, Africa and Europe, between governments and governments, between governments and guerilla groups and between people on the local level.

Exploring the situation during his first visit to Osijek in May, 1992, he saw less scope for mediation or working himself as an intermediary. On the other hand, he thought, if the few people he met were to become a group , it would have quite a few problems to deal with: e.g., technical – devising the right provisions for refugees; social - the prevailing militaristic atmosphere; psychological – the anxiety and uncertainty of working against the stream of popular opinion. For this reason he hoped that it would be possible to devise a form of training which would provide a firm foundation upon which could be built up conflict resolution abilities and other appropriate skills.

Adam Curie has written reports from his continuous visits and workshops during 1992 and 1993.

The word "empowerment" has been important in this process. To be empowered according to Professor Curie, means to recognise confidently that we can take charge of our own lives. For that we need knowledge of the facts of our situation and we need skills enabling us to increase different capacities. We need the self-confidence that comes from the use of these skills. And above all we need the self-awareness to understand what has been done to us and what we must do – and be to escape the poverty-oppression trap and so to exercise some influence in our community.

But can empowerment be educative?

Let me quote from the report of Adam Curie, from his second visit, which included a five—day workshop :

"We examined the conditions I refer to as the fist around the heart – the worries, fears, prejudices, egotism, vanity, guilt, irritability, etc, that reduces our awareness and our sensitivity to others. We worked with various mediation and awareness exercises.

In the same way we tried to become aware of some of our blind spots, irritating reactions, especially anxieties and dislikes; things that could impair both our judgment and our relations with those we were working with.

We considered our connections with all human beings, with all life, with the planet. In so doing we tried to rid ourselves of the conventional concepts of self, other and enemy.

We related what we had been considering to the human, social and economic problems associated with violent situations – refugees, homelessness, psychological and physical traumas of war, separation of families, social dislocation, deprivation and poverty. We examined these particularly in relation to Osijek. We studied the basic principles of nonviolent protest, conflict resolution and mediation. We considered how these might be applied in our specific situation. Throughout we devised appropriate listening exercises and roleplays."

In spite of being one of the most experienced people in mediation and conflict resolution Adam Curie never assumed the role as a "foreign expert" initiating ideas or projects or trying to give his solutions to people's problems. Together they were making "experiments with truth".

Together they discovered that it was possible to move from insecurity to self-confidence, from feelings of worthlessness to dignity, from mistrust to trust, from guilt to forgiveness, from independence to interdependence, from fear to love. They moved from powerlessness to the power of reconstructing themselves and their communities.

These are experiments and insights inspired and shared by Mohandas K. Gandhi, who claimed that every experiment had deepened his faith in nonviolence as the greatest force at the disposal of mankind and challenges everyone of us saying : "I have not a shadow of a doubt that any man or woman can achieve what I have."

For many years and to many people the expressions of nonviolence which have attracted most attention have been big marches, meetings and demonstrations, creative protests, civil disobedience and heroic actions against oppressors. And then, because the changes were achieved through nonviolent means this might have led people to expect that just, free, peaceful and democratic society would hold up nearly by itself.

History has taught us that true democracy asks much more from people. Future peace history may show the significance of what is taking place in Balkan today. The continuous training and preparation, the mobilizing of people's inner resources, the continuous strategic analysis and planning, the step by step and bottom-up approach, the "collective effort of the people", all this work of active nonviolence will be counted as important contributions to a just, peaceful and democratic Balkan and as important contributions to a new culture of peace.

The contributions come from the group in Osijek and other courageous groups working in similar fashion, groups in Zagreb, Belgrad, Pancevo, Sombor, Maribor, Ljubljana, Split, Pacrec and many other places. Members from these groups have started to meet together. They share experiences and plan for the future.

Already in 1922 Mahatma Gandhi founded the *Shanti Sena*, the Peace Army, in India. A few decades later, in the 1960's Martin Luther King Jr. and James M. Lawson Jr. drew up plans for a "ten thousand person nonviolent army" for service in struggle for civil rights in the United States. Since then similar ideas have been presented by individuals and organisations from all over the world.

The contributions to the Global *Shanti Sena* at work in Croatia come from Adam Curie, and 30-35 skilled, courageous and compassionate women and men with various skills and capacities, from different churches, religious organisations and other non-governmental organisations.

The contributions come from people in peace services in conflict areas in different parts of the world, Peacemaking Teams, Peace Brigades International, Witness for Peace, Peace Monitors, Listening Teams, International Nonviolent Peaceforces, International Fellowship of Reconciliation, etc – they all have different shapes and include various activities. They are building more than a network, a community, across all borders.

We live in a transforming age which needs transforming people.

Now is the time for people to understand and believe in the true meaning of the words of Gandhi: "A nonviolent resolution is not a program of seizure of power. It is a program of transformation of relationships, ending in a peaceful transfer of power."

Now is the time for ordinary people to discover and use the extraordinary power of nonviolence in all its dimensions. The key to a World Without Violence for our children and future generations.

A Follower In Osijek

The apartment where he lives has been bombed twice. His grandmother's house was nearly totally destroyed. His uncle has been seriously hurt. Relatives and friends have been killed.

He lives in Osijek in Kroatia, in a war zone – listening to the sounds of fighting from "the other side". He is nine years old. His name is Hrvoje.

"Do you know who is my best friend" he asked his mother one day.

"Jesus is my best friend. Then comes you. Then father. Then grandmother. And then my friends."

"Do you know why Jesus is my best friend", he asked, thinking that his mother might be jealous.

"When I am afraid I pray that Jesus shall take away my fear."

But if the fear is good for something – if the fear is there to make me aware of something - then I tell Jesus that it is OK, I tell him that the fear can stay.

But every time the fear goes away.

"The prayer has saved my life", Mohandas K. Gandhi said. "The prayer has saved my life. Without it, I should have been a lunatic long ago."

Margereta Ingelstam, is Secretary of a Swedish ecumenical working group for Global Peace Services, exploring the content of different curricula for Peace Services. She is member of the Swedish Fellowship of Reconciliation and a former member of the Steering Committee of the International Fellowship of Reconciliation. She has written several books on media and media policy and is also a member of the international committee of Churches Human Rights Program.

A Call For A Resistance Church

— Frank Cordaro

Despite our nation's Judeo-Christian roots, and although a majority of our citizens claim a Christian background, we live in an increasingly faithless society. If there is a dominant faith experience, it's wrapped up in our individualistic addictive First World consumer lifestyles and expressed through our imperial national myths. Sadly, there is little difference between the lifestyle and ethics of those who claim a faith in Jesus and those who do not.

Within our mainline Christian churches we have allowed the powerful Good News of Jesus to fizzle. The salt of our Christian message has lost its counter cultural flavor. What is needed is a renewed commitment to the radical, counter cultural message of the Gospel. This renewed commitment will come about when more and more people begin to reclaim the spirit of the nonviolent activism of Jesus.

The quickest and surest way to rediscovering the nonviolent activism is by asking : What did Jesus do in his lifetime? How did he act? Who did he hang around with? Who were his friends? Who were his enemies? What were the conflicts in his life? And how did they get resolved?

The lone source available to answer these questions is the biographical sketches of Jesus' life found in the Gospels of Mathew, Mark, Luke and John.

The four Gospels give us a picture of a Jesus who works and lives among the common people. He is a lay person with no credentials or formal education. Yet he has unsurpassed knowledge of the scriptures and his Jewish faith. He teaches and acts on his own authority, preaching a radical interpretation of the scriptures.

We also find that Jesus clearly sees himself as a nonviolent social reformer with a social program of his own. The Sermon on the Mount, justice for the poor, unconditional love and unlimited mercy were his social tenets.

Throughout his public ministry, he identifies with the under-dogs, the poor, the down and out and the marginal people in his society. He challenges many of the laws and the prevailing social norms of his day. No friend of the rich and powerful, he was a thorn in the side of the status quo throughout his public life.

When the time was right, he took his radical message to Jerusalem, leading a major street demonstration in his capital city. Later, he carried out a dramatic assault on the Temple. Later still, he was arrested, jailed, put on trial, found guilty, and sentenced to death for being subversive. These actions taken against Jesus were all carried out legally by legitimate authorities. Crucified, Jesus dies between two thieves, abandoned by all, except for a few good women and one male disciple.

For sure, our Christian faith is based on a belief that Jesus is the Christ, son of God, second person in the Blessed Trinity and resurrected Savior and Reconciler of the World. We believe in the miracles and signs Jesus performed in his lifetime.

Without diminishing those more cosmic and spiritual aspects of our faith, it is of equal importance that we believe and follow a Jesus who was an active nonviolent resister to social injustice. The four Gospels paint a picture of a Jesus who was an advocate for the poor, a social activist who confronted the "powers that be". His tactics included ecclessiastical/civil disobedience.

It is clear Jesus expected his disciples to do the same. Any fair reading of the Book of Acts, the sequel of the Gospel of Luke, will show his disciples picking up where Jesus left off. According to the Book of Acts, the first followers of Jesus often found themselves in jails and prisons, dragged before the judges and governors of their time. Like their master, they are branded "outlaws" and "subversives", and put to death for their faithful witness.

Adapting this unique spirit of Christ for our own time and situation is crucial to reclaiming a needed faith integrity that is woefully lacking in U.S. Christian Churches today.

What is needed is living example of people, set apart from the dominant culture, yet in the midst of that culture, living lives of faithful nonviolent resistance. What is needed is what I have come to call a Resistance Church. This Resistance Church, a church within the larger church, has four distinctive marks: 1) downward mobility, 2) direct identification with the poor and the oppressed, 3) direct nonviolent resistance to existing unjust social, economic and political structures, and 4) small, faith-based, intentional communities, committed to a radical biblical social justice agenda.

Downward Mobility : On a basic level, the unjust distribution of the world's wealth is at the center of our human family's suffering. We in the U.S. live in a country with 6% of the world's population. Yet, we consume 30-40% of the world's developed resources. Within our borders there is a great disparity between the rich and the poor. Quite literally, our consumer habits fuel a national addictive spirit. This spirit holds our First World souls captive. When much of the world is starving to death, we are consuming ourselves to death.

While the majority of people in the dominant culture strive for more and more things to consume, people in the Resistance Church will learn to live on less and less. There is enough thrown away in our society to easily provide for the physical needs of a Resistance Church. Members of this Resistance Church will serve as counterpoints to the larger society's piggish First World consumer habits. In doing so, the Resistance Church will provide for the larger Church an example of how people can live below the poverty line and live well.

Identification With The Poor And The Oppressed : Direct identification with the poor and the oppressed means making the lives and the struggles of the poor and the oppressed part of our everyday lives. It means taking on the same risks and uncertainties that the poor and the oppressed live with every day.

We know that Jesus had direct contact with the poorest and the most oppressed of his day. He often performed miracles and signs benefiting them. In their defense, he took on the rich and powerful. He virtually became one of the poor. In addition, the early church was made up mostly of the under-class and the persecuted of the Roman Empire. It was from and for these "outlawed" early Christian communities that the New Testament was primarily written.

If we hope to get in touch with the radical nonviolent activist spirit of Jesus, we need to be reading the New Testament in its original context — through the eyes of the poor. Standing in solidarity with the marginal, poor, outlawed, outcast and underground people of the world is the surest way to find the person of Jesus today.

Direct Nonviolent Resistance To Unjust Social, Economical and Political Structures : This is the most noticeable, flashy mark of the Resistance Church. It is also the one that can land you in jail. Is the public violation of civil and ecclisiastical laws necessary? Yes, if we are going to stay true to the example Jesus set for us in the Gospel.

During his ministry, Jesus broke a number of social mores and religious laws when he associated with known sinners and social outcast. He had unacceptable and familiar relationship with women. Throughout his ministry he broke many a Jewish purification and Sabbath Law.

According to the three synoptic Gospels, in the last week of his life, Jesus took on the civil and religious authorities directly. His Palm Sunday street demonstration and his follow up Temple Cleansing witness were acts of direct nonviolent resistance.

In John's Gospel, the Temple Cleansing takes place in the second chapter, at the very beginning of Jesus' public ministry. In John's Gospel, Jesus is in open rebellion against the Church and State officials of his day from the very beginning of his ministry.

Indeed the prime act of salvation, the ultimate statement of our faith, the resurrection itself was an act of civil disobedience. For when the Roman Empire executed Jesus, he was supposed to remain dead. Rising from the dead put Jesus outside the law. I'd insist that the Resurrect Spirit of Jesus has been outlawed ever since.

In any society dominated by unjust structures and systems, the legitimate legal system is used to protect the unjust structures and systems. Jesus understood this. That is why he took on the institutions and structures of the rich and the powerful through direct and public acts of nonviolent resistance. If we are to follow in his footsteps, are we not called to do the same?

To this I would add that nonviolent resistance is one of the most patriotic actions a citizen of the U.S. can perform. I'm often asked, "Father, do you have to do civil disobedience?" I say in response, "No, one doesn't have to do civil disobedience, but it's the American way."

If we take a look at our nation's 200 plus year history, we find almost every social or political advancement was initiated and sustained by campaigns of protest and dissent that included civil disobedience. It is how we "do social change" in the U.S.

Small, Faith–based, Intentional Communities, Committed To A Radical Biblical Social Justice Agenda : This is the most difficult aspect of the Resistance Church. Why is this fourth mark the most difficult? After all, downward mobility, direct identification with the poor, and prophetic nonviolent civil disobedience appear to demand much more than living in a supportive, like–minded community.

Unfortunately, we live in a very sick society. A "rugged individualistic" spirit dominates our communal life. We no longer know how to live in community with each other. We constantly live our lives alienated from each other. This is most apparent in our families. The rate of divorce, broken families and family abuse in the U.S. is epidemic.

The Murderer Nation of the world, we are admittedly the most personally violent people on the earth. In the U.S. you are more apt to be killed by someone you love than by a stranger.

For certain, our selfish consumer habits and addictive behaviors foster this violent communal environment. Addiction and violence are different sides of the same problem.

If community is so hard to pull off, why insist on intentional communities? Simply because it is the way Jesus expects us to live our lives. Community is essential. It is, if you will, in the script. The New Testament was written by and for people in the faith communities. To truly understand and live the way of Jesus, we need to do it in community. Despite our failed attempts, we must live in community to be in community with Christ.

Will It Work? The Church's history is replete with examples of how Holy Spirit has renewed the Church in troubled times. Through Church history special people, filled with the Holy Spirit, came forth to revive a radical Apostolic way of life. We need only look to the long list of saints, movements and religious orders in Church history to see this dynamic in action.

St. Benedict and St. Francis are two good examples. Both were charismatic leaders. Both started major renewal movements that later became religious orders. And both had a major influence in renewing and recreating the Church of their day. Today, most religious orders in the U.S. are dying out. Their numbers are shrinking and their membership is aging. I believe the Holy Spirit is clearing the table for a whole new spiritual direction and renewal in the U.S. Church. I believe the Resistance Church I am writing about is the part of the new direction and renewal.

In truth, it's already happening. There are many people living out one or more of the four marks of the Resistance Church in grass root's peace and justice communities throughout the country.

This Resistance Church I'm promoting is connected to a much larger movement of the Holy Spirit that has its modern roots in the experience of Third World poverty and the work of Liberation Theology. Born in the midst of dire poverty and under the yoke of brutal political repression, Third World Liberation Theology has set a standard by which all other authentic theologies are measured today.

Still, we can't just mimic the Christian liberation movements in the Third World. We must develop our own First World models of liberation communities based on our own stories, histories and unique settings. The Resistance Church I advocate is just such an effort.

How many people will it take to join the Resistance Church before it can make a difference? We know that one person, whose faith is strong can move mountains. And we know the world could use few good mountain movers right now. But how many?

It's always dangerous to pick up exact numbers needed to effect social change. But as an exercise in what is possible, I tell my Catholic brothers and sisters that all Resistance Church really needs is one percent of the Roman Catholics in this country. One percent would be just over 500,000 folks ! Could you imagine that many "Catholic Worker types" in the cities and villages scattered across the country? What could half a million nonviolent activist Christians living below the poverty line, identifying with the poor, living in intentional communities, and 'in and out' of jails and prisons, do for our churches and nation? I am certain that if this were to happen, we could help change the spirit and heart of the Christian churches in this nation, if not the course of history.

Father Frank Cordaro dropped out of the seminary track in the Summer of 1976 and helped co-found the Des Moines Catholic Worker Community. He spent seven years with the D.M.CW'er. While at the D.M.CW'er, he participated in many public protests and acts of nonviolent civil disobedience. He was arrested numerous times and spent a total of ten months in jails and prisons for his protest. His protest covered a wide range of issues including nuclear weapons and the arms race, US foreign policies, nuclear power and issues surrounding poverty in the U.S. **Fr. Frank** *has been associate pastor at St. Patricks parish in Council Bluffs Iowa. since his release from Yankton Fed. Prison Camp in South Dakota in November of 1992.*

The Things That Make For Peace

— Michael Boover

There are things that make for peace, just as there ARE conditions that make for war. The *Mahatma* knew these things, promoted the former and discouraged the latter. And we do too.

A very dramatic rendering of the distinctions to be made between the works of mercy and the works of war are provided us by Catholic worker artist, Rita Corbin. The juxtaposition of the works of mercy and war make many complicated lessons very simple. Essentially, the diametrical opposition of the works makes us more aware of the better path we may choose.

The *Mahatma's* "Seven Blunders" likewise point out directions which make for peace. In each case, the exercise of the missing virtue makes a vast difference in the kind of prospects for peace the human family might enjoy.

In the west, people of faith in the Jewish and Christian communities have the invitations found in Denteronomy XXX, 19 and Matthew 25:31 - 46 to choose life-giving rather than death-dealing paths. These are paths I have increasingly come to appreciate as grace or gift, not only the fruit of great discipline which also is required. The *Mahatma* recognized this when, despite his failings and subsequent weeping, his taking of refuge in God gave him heart that ultimately the good would prevail, a belief akin to the Hebrew understanding of Divine Justice and the christian sense of the vindication of nonviolent love found in the resurrection of Jesus.

The practices of *"tzedakah"* and Christian charity constitute good (and effective in a mysterious way) remedies for what ails us in the West, particularly with regard to our economic lives. Because life in the United States is so closely enmeshed with, epitomizes and promotes a consumer culture, a vast market, often with little or no regard for ethical checks, we are particularly threatened by and threatening because of our "COMMERCE WITHOUT MORALITY." This condition has led some Americans to envision and seek out morally sound economic alternatives. In my boyhood, as a young Roman Catholic seminarian living at a former Shaker settlement in New Hampshire, a sense of being part of an American alternative began early. This sense has served as a pole-star in my life, directing me to and along paths of simplicity and service, loving attitudes to an increasingly fragmented, "buy and sell" culture.

As a Catholic Christian, I have given some voice to these concerns in several poems, two of which I share with you as modest summons to the path trod by the prophets, Jesus, Tolstoy and Gandhi and celebrations of the great spiritual wealth we found in voluntary poverty. The first was inspired by a trip to Leo Tolstoy's country home, "Clear Glade"; the second by reflecting on the meaning of Jesus' disruption of the money-changing in the Temple.

Having spent my earliest years in the small township of Linwood in Central Massachusetts, not far from Hopedale, that mid-19th century community founded by Adin Ballou whose Christian pacifist convictions had an enormous influence upon Tolstoy, who in turn so influenced the Mahatma, who in turn so influenced Martin Luther King, Jr., who in turn influenced so many, I am amazed at how grand these seeds of good do grow, at how wide they scatter o'er the earth and of how much hope they yet contain for the most blessed of harvests.

The Kingdom Of God Is Within Us

Michael Boover

At Tolstoy's country home, in a birch wood forest...
It was the summer of '80. It was western Russia.
It was a pilgrim with a good monk's question...
And it was here that I asked it.

"What do I need to know?"

Immediately my eyes were led to a pillow
resting on the couch where all the Tolstoy children were born.
There embroidered upon the pillow —
the Lamb of God, standing, holding the banner of victory.

So tired this American pilgrim that inner lights burned dimly
and matched that primitive lightbulb that was the gift of Edison.
Our sorrows met there. Lev Tolstoy's last family meal is
preserved under glass and tells the story.

He set out on foot, making it only to the train station.

Throughout a lifetime of taking account,
this Count had lost his appetite for counting.
And so he donned peasant robes and began his sad journey of the soul.

Repentance. Repentance. A new accounting —
the accounting of the reigns, his own and that of the lamb.

I confess, my soul-mate, that I too have an empire in me...
and veer so sadly and awkwardly toward the death of self,
all our deaths.
Yet you would have it told-
Every cross is worth its weight in gold!

You can weep if you want. But take good heart.
The worst is done. The Lamb has won.
To share his sorrow, our remorse, is blessing.
Though a strange way to joy, here it is.

Song For The Cleansing
The Cleanser And The Cleansed

Michael Boover

The people for years came up
over and over, longer than memory.
The years passed, each Passover to Passover.

*Then **he** came, descended full of fire and light to the people.*
*He, himself, was the gift — the sacrifice of sacrifices laid at **our** feet.*

We did not know how to handle him then or handle him now.
We turned and turn his kindly whip back — back upon his back.

But, as Merton wrote, and Christmas cards quote:
"Into this world, into this demented inn, He has come, uninvited."

And that, that coming continues to this day-
means the tables get tipped and so the children play :
"Hosanna to the Son of David",
an uneasy song, even for the poet in tatters.

There always seems to be treasures to keep us run round,
keep the noonday dim. And so his judgments we fear.

But, somewhere, even in this mad race-
We hear along the rim: "This light shines on. This Light will win."

You are the lonely, lowly sanctuary-pursuing inhabitants.
How different from all we know of building, for
we remain blind to nearly all but our own blocks shouldered
high, side by side.

And so carry within us all the greediness and pride.
Forgive us our closedness, our commerce, our sin.
You are our Justice. You are our Mercy.
We learn so slowly. Still, you beckon us in.

Indeed, Lord, You Yourself are our Inheritance.
All else is parcels not the field, pearls not the Pearl,
Words not the Word.
You would have this blindness brushed aside-
animals and doves scattered around, coins on the ground...
and our hearts beating with Yours. Amen.

Michael Boover is an extended family member of the Mustard Seed Catholic Worker in Worcester, Massachusetts. He lives with his wife Diane and their children Atta, Ben, Joey and Greg at the edge of the city on what might be described an "urban farm." Michael has worked in and for the Catholic Church in various capacities, from gardening and teaching to working with and beside the hungry, sick and homeless of Worcester County. He lived for a time on a Catholic Worker Farm in the Sierra Nevada foothills. His spirituality has been nourished by Trappist monks, the ecumenical movement and especially Catholic Worker priest, Reverend Bernard E. Gilgun. His politics, inspired by the youth movements of the sixties and seventies, owe a great deal to Worcester's own radical son, Abbie Hoffman.

Permission granted by **Rita Corbin** to utilise the print of **The Works of Mercy.**

Light Of Love

— Edward M. Eissey

The quest for a society free of violence is a quest for truth, justice and the acceptance that we are all joined, by a divine plan, into the brotherhood of man. To exist in peaceful harmony, man must accept the premise that we are dependent on one another, that, as the poet John Donne once said, "No man is an island, entire of himself; every man is a piece of the Continent, a part of the main."

Truly, for every action by man there is a reaction. Decisions made by one group or country are oftentimes felt by another, either across geographic boundaries or around the globe.

As men and women, we must all learn to work together, pool our God-given resources and strive to promote the common good. Indeed, it is only through love, mutual respect and construction, and not destruction, that we can enhance the quality of life for others.

The eradication of disease, famine and poverty are paramount in the quest for a society based on peace and nonviolence. The lessons of history show us that, too often, society elects to take up the sword rather than arbitrate differences in a peaceful manner. As long as one drop of blood is shed in conflict — whether in military, police or private confrontation — society must accept the terrifying consequences that are wrought when violence is considered the norm, and the only means by which results can be achieved.

Without question, violence begets violence. It is an age-old story, and one that involves a dream for peace in a promised land. Whether we are living in that promised land is highly debatable, but in any event, it is time to plant the seed of love that will one day yield a harvest of compassion, understanding and acceptance.

To accept others, we must first accept ourselves, acknowledging our own human frailties and weaknesses. By continuing to polarise communities, we build boundaries and walls — walls which ultimately rise so high that the light of compassion is forgotten — and the sense of justice is replaced by one of injustice.

Again, it is important to remember that we are living in a global community

. . . a global society. Each man and woman is different, yet very much the same, for each is created in the divine image. Hopefully, through the attainment of mutual understanding and spiritual introspection, we can learn to appreciate and respect these unique differences, choosing the role of peacemaker rather than warmonger.

United together, we can work peacefully in the world to form a more perfect union, to lead us all from the darkness of despair, towards the light of love. It is only when humanbeings learn to replace violence with nonviolence, to seek justice rather than injustice, that they become totally free.

Dr. Edward Eissey, *President of the Palm Beach Community College, North Campus, West Palm Beach, Florida, is also on the Advisory Board of the M.K. Gandhi Institute of Nonviolence.*

Peace Starts With Me

— Jean Bethke Elshtain

When I was a student of Political Science, I was told that the whole point of the "scientific study of politics" was to clear away the cobwebs of foggy thinking, the sort of thinking induced by those who persist in finding politics with principles an impossible proposition. Not so, said many fine men with their self-certain arguments and elaborate mathematical models for what politics is all about. They refused the earlier warning of the Western political philosopher, Jean-Jacques Rousseau, that he who would separate politics from morals must fail to understand both.

Fortunately, I had come from a solid background that included Christianity and my own wide-reading, including the autobiography of Mohandas K. Gandhi. I often thought of what my parents taught me and what I had learned from reading Gandhi, and other wise men and women when during my college years, I was told, in effect, to give up this unscientific or even childish way of thinking and come to my senses about what politics is "really about." What it is really about, the argument went, is power — who gets what, when, where and how. Ethics does not really figure into this equation. Some political scientists went even further and claimed that the expert could "predict" what human beings would do politically by calculating their unfailing determination to "maximize their utilities," which means, roughly, gaining some marginal advantage over their fellow human beings in pretty much each and every situation.

This is a very impoverished view of politics, clearly. Small wonder Gandhi called it one of the Seven Blunders of the World. But I think we should be forewarned as well that if we formulate our principles too narrowly or too rigidly we might be unable to respond creatively, compassionately, and moderately to new situations. Part of Gandhi's genius as a leader was his rock-solid commitment to unchanging verities, on the one hand, and his canny openness to rapidly transforming situations and realities, on the other. Politics with principles does not mean becoming moralistic and judgmental of others. It means accepting the inviolability and dignity of each and every human being. It means building politics on that simple but profound recognition. It means being open to how one might implement that recognition in a bewildering number of very different circumstances. We cannot be universal except in our own backyards. Gandhi was not what is sometimes derisively called a

Luftmensch, someone with his head in the clouds, someone disconnected from the concrete realities of a time and a place. That is not what Politics with Principles means. It means taking responsibility for the here and now, for the very real place in which one finds oneself and for human beings that inhabit it.

My Father, who was a very gracious and kind man, died recently. I recall his words, written for a book his grand daughter, my daughter, put together for a family book on "What the Heart Means to Me." My father said: "I am reminded of a bumper sticker I once saw, 'Peace Starts with Me.' I think that says it all Wouldn't it be nice if we really behaved and lived by that motto? If you really think about it you come to the realization that love and respect (having a heart) are the bases of peace in our personal relationships with other human beings and in our political activities on the local, state, and national level. Differences can be solved peacefully, without hatred." These are idealistic words, no doubt, but in a cynical and violent world they are words we very much need.

*Jean Bethke Elshtain is the Centennial Professor of Political Philosophy at Vanderbilt University. She is the author of many books, including **Women And War** (Basic Books, 1987), **Power Trips and Other Journeys** (Wisconsin, 1991) and co-author of **But was It Just? Reflections On The Morality of The Persian Gulf War** (Doubleday, 1992). **Professor Elshtain** first read the work of Mohandas Gandhi when she was twelve years old and discovered his autobiography in the "bookmobile" that visited her small town in Colorado.*

Great Contemporary Tragedy

— Dr. Eknath Easwaran

During my days as a professor of English literature, one writer with whom I felt a special kinship was Gilbert Keith Chesterton. Not only did he do keen studies of favorites of mine such as Robert Browning and Charles Dickens, but he wrote a fascinating portrait of Saint Francis of Assisi which shows that Chesterton had some personal grounding in matters of the spirit.

On one occasion, it seems, friends of Chesterton's were complaining that people today have nothing to believe in. "The real problem," Chesterton replied, "is that when you don't have something to believe in, you will believe in anything at all."

This is our great contemporary tragedy. If something is presented seductively, if it appeals to our society's carefully cultivated taste for profit or pleasure, most of us will believe in anything that comes along. Millions of people of all ages and occupations, out of intentions which for the most part could not be called wrong, are entangled in activities that in the long run will injure their health, impair their peace of mind, inflict suffering on their families, and eventually threaten the very life of our society - all because, in the depths of their hearts, they lack something to believe in that is loftier and more meaningful than personal pleasure and profit.

Contrast this picture with the scene five thousand years ago on the banks of the Ganges. The sages of ancient India used to pray every morning as the tropical sun rose in glory:

> *Ya atmada balada yasya vishva*
> *Upasate prashisham yasya devath*
> *"To that radiant Being, who gives life and strength,*
> *I offer all my desires, all that I am."*

This shining being within is what gives meaning to life. Nothing in the world of change outside us can provide the abiding purpose that we seek. "He is the source of my strength, my very self," this prayer implies; "so I owe my life to him. Everything I do, everything I desire, everything I am, should go to serve him in the rest of his creation. Understanding this gives purpose to life; practicing this brings fulfillment."

Sanskrit describes this core of divinity as *Satyam, Shivam, Sunderam* : the source of truth, of goodness, and of beauty. The seas surge with the flow of his love; the mountains reflect his glory. All the loveliness we see in nature is his. Yet although we may admire the beauties of his garden, the mystics say, very, very few of us actually seek to discover the Gardener, who dwells in the heart of every creature.

Different religions use different names for this aspect of divinity which is the very core of our being: *Krishna*, Christ, the *Buddha*, *Allah*, the Divine Mother. But the reality referred to is one and the same. In *Sanskrit* the term is simple and universal: *Atma*, the self, radiant, loving, immortal, infinite, who is the same in all beings, in all creatures, in all of life.

"The soul has two eyes," says Meister Eckhart: "one looking inwards and the other looking outwards. It is the inner eye of the soul that looks into essence and takes being directly from God." It is because we do not know how to look to the Shining Being inside us that we try to light up our dim lives from outside in any way we can. Not knowing how to turn inward, we look for meaning and fulfillment in the fickle realm of sensory experience.

Those who are sensitive to what goes on inside them know how much of this effort is generated by a nagging sense of desperation, of emptiness within. Such is the nature of the human being, such is our very constitution, that we have to have a purpose greater than the endless struggle to satisfy personal desires. We have to believe in something more lasting than creature comforts. Otherwise we will eventually feel driven to do anything, try anything, to find fulfillment - as Chesterton implies, to do anything at all.

We need, in short, a central force to hold us together; otherwise we fly apart, pursuing our separate goals. The *Sanskrit* word for this force is one of the oldest the most meaningful in the *Upanishads* : *Dharma*, "law" - the law of unity, that life is one indivisible whole. The *Buddha* did not talk about God; he said simply, "*Esa dhammo sanatano* : the fact that all of us are one and indivisible is an eternal law." Unity is the very law of life. In that law lies our growth; in it lies our future; in it lies our fulfillment. And today, in the world of medicine, we are discovering that in unity also lies our health, our longevity, our vitality. When we live just for ourselves, we are stunting our own growth and courting illness. It is in living for all that we rise to our full potential of vibrant, vital, creative action.

Much of the art of living, rests on the rare ability to discriminate between what is in harmony with this central law of life and what violates it. To act wisely we must see clearly. "Does this particular choice bring me closer to my partner or my family? Does it resolve a conflict, foster clean air, bring peace to my mind or to people around me?" If the answer to such questions is yes, that course of action is in harmony with the unity of life. If the answer is no, it is not - however pleasant it may be.

To grow spiritually, we need both the detachment to see clearly and the discrimination to know what is of lasting value - and of course, the willpower - determination. Discrimination is the third of my three Ds, and it flows directly from the second, detachment. Discrimination is pure, detached love in action.

Without discrimination, by contrast, "anything goes." The only basis for choice is personal conditioning - likes and dislikes. One of the grimmest warnings in the Sanskrit scriptures states, "Lack of discrimination is the source of greatest danger" - to health, to security, to personal relations, to life itself.

Despite the tremendous achievements, one of my lover's quarrels with modern industrial civilization is that it is so lacking in discrimination, that it cannot see how its choices and values are violating the unity of life. In focusing on manipulating the world outside us, it has lost sight of the world within; yet only there can we find meaning, purpose, and value. More than any other quality of modern life, it is essentially this lack of discrimination that is sending our world on a collision course with disaster.

In daily living, discrimination means making wise choices — knowing what to do and what not to do, not so much in moral terms as in the terms of where our choices lead.

One of the most stirring of the *Sanskrit* scriptures, the *Katha Upanishad*, uses two marvelous words to help us see which course of action will lead to trouble in the long run and which will lead to detached, loving living. I say "marvelous" because these words apply to every choice, in every circumstance, so they dispel the haze that often surrounds a difficult situation. Wherever you have a choice, ask yourself this question: "Which is *Preya*, that which pleases, and which is *Shreya*, the long-term good?"

Preya is what we like, what pleases us, what offers immediate gratification to senses, feelings, or self-will. *Shreya* is simply what works out in the end. *Preya* is the "pleasure principle" : doing what feels good, whatever the consequences. *Shreya* means choosing the best consequences, whether it feels good or not – often forgoing a temporary pleasure for the sake of a lasting benefit.

When we learn how to look for it, we see that choice between *Preya* and *Shreya* comes up every moment, in virtually everything we do. There is no escaping it. The moment dawn breaks the choices begin : "Shall I get up for my meditation, or shall I pull the blanket over my head and stay in bed a little longer?" It starts there, and it goes on until you fall asleep at night.

Early morning, therefore, have your meditation right on time. It sets the tone for the rest of the day. The *Bhagavad Gita*, in a verse that is etched on my heart, assures us that regular meditation will protect us from life's gravest dangers. "*Svalpamapasya dharmasya trayate mahato bhayat* : Even a little meditation will guard you against the greatest fears" : against physical ailments, emotional problems, disrupted relationships, spiritual alienation. Most critical, perhaps, meditation slowly opens our eyes and hearts to the needs of those around us. That is discrimination, and I know of no better protection against the mistaken choices that can so burden life with guilt and regret.

After meditation, of course, more choices come in a flurry, generally at the breakfast table. With all the conditioning of the media, where eating is concerned, right choices are not easy. Food has become a kind of religion, and business is quick to cash in on it. To choose wisely, your senses must listen to you. That is essential pre-requisite. And for your senses to listen to you, your mind must listen to you. That is why, as you train your mind in meditation, your eating habits come under your control. Likes and dislikes begin to change, the choices open up everywhere.

Yet determination, of course, extends not only to eating but to everything. In the *Sanskrit* scriptures, we are said to eat through all the senses. Just as we learn to be discriminating about what we put into our mouths, we learn to be vigilant about the books and magazines we read, the movies and televisions we absorb, the conversations we indulge in, the company we keep: in short, everything we do and say. Ultimately this extends even to what we think. We have a choice in all these things; that is what is meant by intentional living.

We have to be exceedingly judicious about what we put into our minds. The fact that a book has become a best-seller is no guarantee at all of quality. I am not talking about morality now but simply about the effect on the mind. When you are training a puppy, you don't try to teach its limits for an hour and then say, "All right you are off duty now. Go do whatever you like for the rest of the day." It is the same with training the mind. Why spend half an hour every morning in meditation, going through the agony of teaching an unruly mind to be calm and clear, and then go out and stir all its appetites again in the name of relaxation?

Some years ago, a man who honestly thought he was doing people a service wrote a best-selling book on sex. The subtitle might well have been "A Guide to Disputed Relationships and a Bloated Ego." His theme was simple: "Your need comes first. Don't hesitate to impose them on others; everybody will be happier for it." When has this ever worked?

Anybody who takes this kind of advice seriously is going to become more lonely, more frustrated, and more estranged. Physical appetites can never be satisfied for long; the more we want, the less they can be fulfilled. Gradually the mind becomes unruly in everything, and other people become things that either please or hinder us. Then, where two people sincerely sought love, they find only anger, bitterness, and regret. Yet the books and magazines and movies go on promising; satisfaction lies in sex, and it's just around the corner; just try again. Many years ago, for the Fulbright orientation program, I spent a beautiful summer month at the University of Kansas, where I visited the home of a colleague who had a twelve - or thirteen-year-old daughter. In the course of the evening I got acquainted with the girl and said, "Let's see what you are reading." After looking over the row of books piled up on her desk for the summer vacation, I went privately to her father, just as I would have done in India. "Do you know what kind of books your daughter is reading?"

"Oh, sure," he said casually, as if amused by my provincial Indian attitude. "This is a free country, you know."

I had already heard this a few times before. "By the way," I said, "I notice you lock the bathroom cabinet. Is that an American custom?"

"No," he laughed. "That's where we keep dangerous drugs, so the kids don't get into them."

"There are drugs that injure the body," I said, "and there are books that injure the mind."

Today, of course, my young friend's summer reading would look tame compared with what is available to teenagers now. Books and magazines and much more explicit and potent mind-drugs are available at the touch of a button and acted out for us on the screen so that everything is reduced to its lowest level. The real problem raised by this kind of mass distribution of mind-drugs is spelled out in two verses in the Gita:

> *When you keep thinking about sense objects,*
> *Attachment comes. Attachment breeds desire,*
> *The lust of possession which, when thwarted,*
> *Burns to anger. Anger clouds the judgment,*
> *And robs you of the power to learn from past mistakes,*
> *Lost is the discriminative faculty,*
> *and your life, is utter waste.*

X-rated material aside, consider ordinary TV fare. If a child spends an hour a day with a parent and five or six hours watching the fantasies of MTV and the so-called realism of soap operas, what images of people and of personal relationships are going to fill that child's mind? What makes up the bulk of his or her experience? Whether we like it or not, this is the world that child will live in; those experiences are teaching that child how to act.

There was a time when, saying these things, I felt my voice was crying in the wilderness. Today I am very glad to say that I am not alone. Excellent books like Marie Wynn's *Unplugging the Plug-in Drug* relate the experience of many, many families who have "gone straight" : either locked the television in the basement or thrown it out altogether. After a short period of deprivation, people discover suddenly that they have time again - time for being together.

One gentle, effective way children can be weaned from the set is for their father or mother to take a good book and read to them. If that sounds old-fashioned, try it. Many families of TV addicts will tell you that it works. Younger children love to have a story read or told to them, and if older children want to read to themselves, encourage them and set an example.

Every day, in everything, we have a choice. Nobody can say, "I am not free to choose." Those two words from *Upanishads* can always help us see our choices clearly : *Preya*, that which is pleasant but which probably benefits nobody, even ourselves; and *Shreya*, that which is of lasting benefit to all. Shall I reply curtly to her remark, or shall I speak kindly? Shall I spend the afternoon doing something I like, or shall I work at something that helps a few others?

Everywhere we have choices like these, and discrimination comes when we start choosing what brings lasting benefit even at the cost of a few private, personal satisfactions.

As you start doing this, you will feel the chains of conditioning on your wrists and ankles slowly falling away. Do you remember Charles Dickens's *Christmas Carol* ? In an eerie scene, which I still recall vividly from the movie, the ghost of Scrooge's old partner Marley comes into Scrooge's bedroom rattling his chains. Scrooge looks up and exclaims in fright, ""Marley ! What happened to you? How did you come by all those chains?" And Alec Guiness, with that sardonic grin of his, replies grimly, "I made them all myself. Link by link. Every one of them."

That is what selfish pursuits become in the long run: chains. Though we never intended it, though we may have taken it up only as recreation, every selfish activity becomes a chain. At the outset we have no intention of disliking and avoiding and deprecating and manipulating. But in the end we find ourselves with very little choice. In matters of this magnitude, an ounce of discrimination is worth pounds and pounds of effort it takes to cut off chains with the dainty jeweler's file, which is the kind of work that is required when selfish habits are allowed to grow rigid and strong.

"I found thee not, O Lord, without, because I erred in seeking thee without that wert within." Augustine speaks for us all. When we do not know that life's fulfillment lies within us, we cannot help reaching for what is outside. And the more these attempts fail to satisfy, the more insecure we become. That is why so many spend their lives in some kind of hoarding: money, possessions, pleasures, memories, always trying to reassure themselves with something more.

Do you remember *Fiddler on the Roof*, when Tevye exclaims, "Lord, if money is a curse, strike me so hard that I may never recover from it !" This is probably a universal sentiment. It is the basis of the confusion in which civilization so often functions: make as much money as you can; it will make you happy, secure, loved and respected.

Of course, money has a place in life, even in the spiritual life. But to ascribe to money these impossible magic qualities, to make it the measure of things or the very goal of life, is to disinherit ourselves from the divine trust fund we all have stored up inside. Our real wealth is our inner resources, which are infinite because the core of our personality is divine. And the purpose of life is not to accumulate physical tokens of wealth but to mine these deeper resources for the good of all. That is the supreme goal of our existence and the only source of lasting value.

This is not simply a matter of economics. It is a clear sign we need to look for a wiser religion than materialism. The idea of growth for growth's sake, which has been the driving motive behind civilization for hundreds of years, can now be likened to what one writer calls a "creed of cancer."

The vast majority of us, of course, are not so greedy that we would choose to let others suffer to get what we desire. But when a person gets wrapped up in personal interests, other people become shadows. And as far as most of us are concerned, our love is constrained to what we can see. If we are not aware of anybody suffering on our block, or on our own side of the town, we feel content not to think about it further; our thoughts are already full. The plight of those living in desperate conditions in the inner city districts of our own home town does not touch us appreciably. Nor does the sight of so many of our young people, our hope for the future, feeling they have nothing to pour their energy into except the search for chemical thrills and aimless acts of violence.

Thousands of good people today, I am told, live in boredom and loneliness, looking for some kind of meaning in their lives. Why not pour at least a little of that time and energy into making life better for the homeless street-dwellers in the cities near them, for the runaway young, for the abandoned elderly who literally have to choose each month between food and heating? For many, the answer is pitiful: This religion of grabbing, of "looking out for number one," does not allow for fellow-feeling. It only deadens our sensitivity, building the walls of loneliness and alienation higher and higher.

To fail to live up to this great challenge, my spiritual teacher used to say, is simply being irresponsible. This is not asking for perfection but merely expecting us to do our best to grow. If we do not do this much, we are depriving life of a contribution that only we can make. Spiritual living is responsible living. I am responsible not only for myself but for all of you, just as all of you are responsible for me.

The ideal of discriminating action flows spontaneously in those who know the spiritual basis of life. It comes when we live in the highest state of awareness, when our lives become a benediction to every person and creature around us. We live then a truly selfless life, one in which we think never in terms of personal profit or pleasure but always in terms of global prosperity and world peace. For even these grand goals ultimately depend not on governments but on the selfless efforts of little people like you and me. In the long run, friendly persuasion is the only effective teacher. Human being are educable; human beings can always grow. "If one man gains spiritually," Gandhi said, "the whole world gains with him."

A beautiful prayer from the ancient *Hindu* scriptures echoes in my heart always: "May all creatures be happy. May people everywhere live in abiding peace and love." For all of us are one, and joy can be found only in the joy of all.

*Dr. Eknath Easwaran was a successful writer, lecturers, and professor of English literature when he came to U.S. on a Fullbright exchange in 1959. In 1961 he founded the Blue Mountain Center of Meditation in Berkeley. At the University of California, he taught the first credit course on the theory and practice of meditation. He is the author of over a dozen books, including **Meditations, Gandhi the Man, Dialogue with Death**, and **The Bhagavad Gita** for **Daily Living**, a practical commentary on India's best-known scripture.*

The Dove Of Peace

— Fredrick Franck

I feel it to be more than just an honor; rather an opportunity to pay a debt of gratitude, to join the contributors to this book in homage to a man whose life was devoted to peace and even beyond that, a life that appealed to what is most human to human beings. Mahatma Gandhi was one of that handful of truly human spirits who have lightened the opaque darkness of this appalling century, the twentieth after Christ.

What comes to mind in this context is a quotation of Gandhi's reply to the question of what he thought of Christianity : . ."that it was an admirable idea, well worth being tried in practice."

Of the handful of true humans I had the privilege to meet on my way, and whom I regard as my spiritual mentors, *Mohandas Gandhi* was the precursor. Two of these were Christians : the Protestant doctor who lived his principle of "Reverence for life" for almost a century, Albert Schweitzer, on whose medical staff I served in Africa, and the Catholic Pope John XXIII, whose love of life and of humanity knew no bounds, so that thirty years after his death he is still a living force for freedom, tolerance and sanity. Last but not least I must mention *Daisetz Teitaro Suzuki*, the *Buddhist* sage who almost singlehandedly initiated the West in Wisdom/Compassion, the *Prajna/Karuna* of *Mahayana Buddhism.*

Instead of adding more words to this miniscule tribute I venture to enclose this Dove of Peace and of Spirit, which symbolizes the modest trans-religious sanctuary *Pacem in Terris* — Peace on Earth — which I built in Warwick, New York, and of which, I feel confident, *Mahatma Gandhi* would not disapprove.

Dr. Fredrick Franck lives with his wife, Claske, in Warwick, New York, where they have created an oasis of peace and spirituality called Pacem in Terris (Peace of Earth).

(The Dove Of Peace Is Reproduced with the dedication at the beginning of the book)

Dilemma Of A Politician

— Ien van den Heuvel

During the years I spent in politics I never met anyone who told me that she or he was in favour of a world with violence. Though people often react sceptically to my plea for a pacifist attitude, they always assert they too favor non-violence. It is just that they also believe that peace can only come through the strength of weapons.

I take this seriously. In my opinion people like myself, who call themselves pacifists, don't have the right to under-estimate the earnestness of those who take a different position. Many of my (political) friends really hold the view point that sometimes only violence can put an end to oppression and dictatorship.

Against my arguments that history shows that through violence you never can really solve problems and that violence always creates more violence, they refer to the experience of World War II, and how we, as western Europeans would have suffered under the Nazi regime, if the allied forces had not been there to achieve peace.

I must admit that this is a difficult point for me to refute. I personally have struggled (and still am struggling) with a lot of questions concerning this argument. Growing up in the years after the war, I tried to find an answer to the question how to combine my desire to follow Jesus Christ and to reject use of violence, with the needs of the Jews in the concentration camps.

At such times, I resolved one could not avoid the use of violence. I am deeply convinced that we have to avoid situations giving rise to Nazism at any price. I saw how the threats of the communist world increased and, being a member of the Netherlands Social Democratic party, I accepted the policy of mobilising effective military counter forces.

I was young and really believed for a while that in accepting this political policy, my questions were answered. Now, after almost a life-time experience in politics, I am very grateful that people like Mohandas Gandhi demonstrated that there are nonviolent possibilities. I look upon people like Gandhi with great admiration.

He helped me understand my own doubts. I realise the possibilities of a nonviolent attitude depend upon one's conviction and that my choice of democratic socialism is the best contribution to fight the seven blunders mentioned by the *Mahatma*.

I lived through the experience of the cold war and saw how populations were turned to hate and enmity. People in power on both sides created stereotype images to ensure their constituents supported the high cost of arms build-up. The armaments became increasingly deadly and sophisticated. At this point it became clear to me that this was a diabolical game and responsible for much of the hunger and poverty in the world. I came to a new position : the Devil's circle had to be broken. We had to say "NO" to further armament.

It was not easy to live with that attitude in my political life. I became president of my party, member of the Senate and later on member of the European Parliament. I had to deal with a party policy that was not completely in line with mine and, therefore, I had to make a compromise, between my choice for nonviolence and the party policy which favored a decrease in armaments. However, I did not reject it entirely.

Many of my friends did not understand that, in spite of my personal feelings, I was prepared to defend the party policy. I think this is the only way pacifists can put into practice what they believe in. Of course, it is easier to declare categorically that you are against use of violence. The question is by taking such a hard stand can we help people and governments around the world understand and appreciate the philosophy of nonviolence?

I know that I dirtied my hands in politics. Also that I had, together with others, some influence on party policy. I was proud that in the 80's my party supported the campaign of the peace movement against deployment of cruise missiles in Europe. (I was no longer the party president at the time).

The peace movement of the Dutch churches (of which I was also the president for some years) was also not on an absolute nonviolent line, but I am convinced that all together we made a contribution to what was called the "Dutch disease" in those years.

On the other hand I am aware that history is replete with cases of many compromises of principles. Especially in politics one deviates too much from one's principles. Perhaps I have done that sometimes in my life. The alternative, however, is to stand aside with clean, but empty hands.

Are my problems solved, now that I am no longer in a political position? Far from it ! What should I say, for instance, to my friends from the former Yugoslavia, to the women who are humiliated and violated when they plead for military intervention to stop the war?

There I am again. It is the same dilemma as I had to cope with in my youth. And, like then, I do not know the absolute answer.

How happy I would be to be able to speak about these questions with the great Mohandas Gandhi . . . .

*Ien van den Heuvel of Tiel, The Netherlands, was President of "Rooie Vrouwen in de PvdA" (women's organisation of socialist party) from 1968 to 1974. She was President PvdA (socialist party) member Earnest Kamer (senate Dutch Parliament) from 1974 to 1979. During the years 1979-1989 she was member of European Parliament, Vice President Socialist Group, a.o. President of Committee on Human Rights. In 1992 Ien van den Heuvel left as President of Inter-church Peace Council IKV) where she worked from 1986. **Ien van den Heuvel** is a member of the Advisory Board of the M. K. Gandhi Institute of Nonviolence, Memphis, Tennessee.*

Reflections On Gandhi And Democracy

— Benjamin R. Barber

Nonviolent resistance bears a paradoxical relationship to democracy; for on the one hand, democracy is that form of government that relies on deliberation, participatory politics and peaceful conflict resolution to create the conditions for common life; a way to resolve differences by talk and reason rather than brute force or coercive authority. That is to say, democracy is precisely the politics of nonviolence — a politics with principles that avoids what Gandhi understands as the most egregious political "blunder" of politics without principles.

Yet on the other hand, democracy is a form of popular sovereignty which, like all forms of sovereignty, legitimizes coercion by giving the democratic state a monopoly on all uses of force. Without the right and power to enforce, a democratic state lacks the essential attribute of sovereignty and is presumably without the capacity to maintain law and order (its first and primary responsibility) either from within or without.

So democracy both eludes coercion by its defining reliance on a participatory politics of rational deliberation, and legitimizes and amplifies it by giving sovereign forces the added legitimacy of popular sanction. The democratic state not only has the right to kill (to put to death external enemies as well as internal outlaws) which is the right of every sovereign, but it may tend to do so with great impunity because of its democratic legitimacy (this is the essence of the classic liberal critique of majoritarian tyranny from Tocqueville and J. S. Mill to modern America advocates of "limited government").

The cherished strategy of nonviolent resistance pioneered by Gandhi in South Africa and India, and pursued by Martin Luther King, Jr. and others in the American civil rights movement, is obviously in the first instance an antipolitics intended for use by individuals and groups rather than states. It is a way to resist legitimate state authority, whether exercised by an internal government (say the State of Alabama enforcing "legal" but immoral Jim Crow laws in the 1950's) or by an external colonial conqueror (say the British exercising "lawful" but oppressive dominion over India). Is there or can there also be not just an anti-politics but a politics of nonviolence? Can a democratic state eschew violence, or is nonviolence always an anti-politics aimed at the abuse of political authority? If we define politics by sovereignty and sovereignty by the legitimate use of force, then nonviolence would seem to have little relevance to state politics. Switzerland maintained "neutrality" for several centuries, but it was an armed neutrality prepared to resist aggression with every available instrument of war. Costa Rica is perhaps one of the few nations that has resorted to a remarkable and unprecedented act of collective national nonviolence.

After World War II, it ratified a constitution that abjured violence: quite literally, it refused to constitutionally authorize an army. A pacific policy was also foisted on the losers of World War II, Germany and Japan, by the winners although it would be hard to argue that either of those countries has developed an ethics of nonviolent resistance as a consequence. Indeed, both countries have hurried to reacquire the full credentials of their sovereignty, which for both has meant rearmament. In general, nations — especially democratic nations — do not and cannot eschew violence. The best they can do in honoring Gandhi's principles is to insist on principled politics.

They do not prohibit war but they do insist that war requires special justification and that traditional national interest arguments are insufficient. Democratic nations (as well as other states with moral basis — Christian or Muslim, for example) that seek to keep their international politics "principled" have thus sought "just war" rationales when they have felt forced to pursue coercive strategies. If violence cannot be prohibited to states whose sovereignty is defined by the legitimate use of violence, it must nonetheless be legitimized in special ways. One might say that the discourse of just war does honor to principles of nonviolent resistance without adhering to nonviolent behavior. Nonviolence is the default mode of democratic politics — the norm unless pressing and principled moral arguments justify a temporary departure from the norm.

Traditionally the United States had an unusual affinity for nonviolence in its international relations in its first one hundred and fifty years, perhaps in the main because of its natural isolationism (although the Civil War was bloodier and costlier than all of America's foreign wars put together!) When the country has gone to war, it has always required special justifications that have deployed the language of democracy and morals. "We went down to Mexico to save democracy" said Woodrow Wilson. In the eyes of America's cold warriors, enmity with the Soviet Union rested on opposition to what Reagan called "an evil empire." Intervention in Somalia is justified by a war on hunger, in Haiti by the struggle to establish a democratic order.

Cynics will argue that such moralism merely rationalizes and conceals national interests, and makes international relations more problematic and renders war more vicious. War fought for simple purposes of national interest can be adjudicated and terminated when the purposes are served. Wars animated by moral fervor and principled righteousness may become holy wars, a *Jihad* that brooks no compromises and can end only in total victory (or defeat). True pacifists may be led by this to argue that nonviolence allows no compromise, that its power lies in its absolutism. To think that nonviolence can be served by calibrating violence as a means to securing just ends is worse than simple coercion used without rationalization.

Yet democrats will insist that if we are to avoid the blunder of politics without principles and commerce without morality, we will have to find ways to make the use of force principled; to make the application of sovereign coercion, even though intrinsically legitimate, subject to further moral and political (i.e., democratic) debate and justification. Nonviolence works for individuals but not for states, but states must nonetheless seek principles surrogates for nonviolence which guarantee that the use of violence will be minimized and political coercion will be principled rather than merely self-interested.

Indeed, for individuals and nations alike, Gandhi's principles stand as aspirations and normative parameters rather then codes for practical behavior. Like Lincoln, Gandhi spoke to the "better angels" of our nature not because he thought all men could become angels but because he knew that without the insistent voice of better angels, we would succumb all too easily to the siren song of demons for whom war, slaughter and death are not tragic compromises with reality but felicitous ends in themselves.

There is one other argument against trying to introduce nonviolence into the politics of nations that is more difficult to answer. From Machiavelli to George Kennan, political realists have insisted not just that the principled morals of nonviolence are irrelevant to politics, but that they can be perilous as well. This "consequentialists" perspective, which looks at the outcomes of political decisions rather than the good will of those who make them, is hostile to nonviolence as political strategy because however admired it may be as a moral posture, it often has political consequences that seem to contradict its own objectives. That is to say, nonviolent resistance may actually contribute to overall suffering when the aggressor being resisted is an absolute tyrant or a civil terrorist beyond the pale of the kinds of moral persuasion that Gandhi or Martin Luther King thought nonviolent resistance could endanger. The ultimate faith of nonviolent resistance is that it will transform not just the resister but the oppressor. When it fails to do that, it loses much of its political virtue (though it may retain a powerful personal and moral virtue).

Consequentialism raises tough questions : how does Sophie (in Sophie's choice) resist the choice forced on her by the Nazi to select which of her children will live and which will die, since to refuse the choice is to condemn both children to death? How, asks Machiavelli, does the prudent Prince justify "mercy" towards a rebel condemned to death when mercy will spare the rebel and leave him free to spark another civil war in which thousands of innocent citizens will die? When non-action turns out to be a kind of action with moral consequences, goes the argument, nonviolence becomes a species of irresponsibility: I will not hurt anyone even though my action may lead to suffering and hurt for others. Isn't this kind of behavior a sort of moral narcissism in which, as long as my hands are clean, I am indifferent to real suffering in the world? And are not political rulers subject to different standards than individuals since they are by definition officially responsible for all of the consequences of their acts and non-acts? The individual may say "yes, people may suffer and even die because I refuse to do violence to an evil oppressor, but people die and suffer anyway, and my doing wrong, even in the name of right, cannot finally make it a better world." But the sovereign, whether a benevolent Prince or a sovereign people, must say, "my responsibility is precisely to the people, and if I must dirty my soul and violate my personal moral principles in order to save my people from suffering and death, that is my duty. I cannot afford to save my soul if it costs me the safety and security of my people."

Thus, President Harry Truman might have argued that in dropping the atomic bomb on Hiroshima he committed a horrendous act of violence and mass murder (he did), and yet suggest that not to have used the new weapon to end the war would have meant a prolongation of war and an invasion of the Japanese islands that would have cost far more lives — both American and Japanese. One might even hazard the guess, from a long-term consequentialist perspective, that the one awful use of the bomb in World War II offered an example to the world of such hellish devastation that it rendered all subsequent uses of the bomb unthinkable. In this logic, the people of Hiroshima and Nagasaki died as part of a lesson to humankind that spared the race any further use of nuclear weapons.

Nonviolence is a powerful moral posture for individuals resisting states but once again seems of limited use by states whose ends are necessarily calculated in con-sequentialist terms. This may be particularly true for states committed to democratic principles and the preservation of common good. At the same time, nonviolence remains a potent ideal, a constant warning against the easy rationalizations of power and violence by those in power, a token of the regret democrats must feel when employing coercion, however justifiably. It would be too much to expect mere mortals and the democratic governors who have taken on responsibility not just for their own souls but for the welfare of whole peoples, to act in perfect accord with the principles of nonviolence. But it is a blessing that those principles are there not just as a theoretical warning to the abuses of power, but as an expression of the careers of men like Gandhi and King who dedicated and ultimately sacrificed their lives to nonviolence. The rest of us may never fully live up to such principles, but we are inevitably improved by our efforts to do so. We cannot live as our better angels counsel us to, but we still listen to them and so keep human hope alive.

Dr. Benjamin R. Barber is Walt Whitman Professor of political science at Rutgers University, and the Director of the Whitman Center for the Culture and Politics of Democracy. Recent books include Strong Democracy (1984), An Aristocracy of Everyone (1992) and the forthcoming Jihad Versus McWorld.

Reflections On Violence In Northern Ireland

—Richard R. Fleck

A number of years ago I spent a half year in Ireland assessing the influence of Henry David Thoreau, Mohandas K. Gandhi and Martin Luther King Jr. on the Northern Ireland Civil Disobedience Movement which sponsored a nonviolent tax revolt of some twenty thousand persons refusing to support what was perceived to be an unjust government. My contact person across the border in Belfast was Frank Gogarty, one of the leaders of the movement. What I discovered was that every attempt was made early on to conduct a nonviolent peace march a la Dr. King (inspired by Thoreau and Gandhi) with hopes that the discriminatory policies in the work-place against Irish Catholics by Irish Protestants in the North would be reduced over the months and years.

The day after I spoke with Mr. Gogarty, his luckily empty house was blown up by the underground Protestant army called the UVF (Ulster Voluntary Force). Such an action followed suit with the years of turmoil since 1969, the year the peace march failed. The marchers, who attempted to walk in peace from Londonderry to Newry, were intercepted and brutally beaten with boards and nails. Tragically, Gandhi's dream expressed in the words "In the midst of darkness, light persists; in the midst of despair, hope persists; in the midst of death, life persists" suffered a setback. The temperament of these beaten people reversed from meekness and acceptance to horror and anger. It has been that way ever since.

Now, twenty years after my visit, it seems that the way people can refuse to be angered and frightened by terrorists' bullets from the IRA and UVF is for there to be a transformation of spirit from hatred to love and acceptance even if it means risking the death of many more people as during India's struggle for independence. Love must overcome hatred. I will never forget the hatred in the eyes of a Catholic woman coming out of church in Northern Ireland and seeing a British soldier on patrol. She spat in his face saying he was no good dirt. And I remember well talking with a Protestant gentleman in a pub up in Crossmaglen. He expressed the notion that Catholics might be alright if they weren't so dirty and lazy and such a lot of rabbit-like breeders. Love must overcome hatred and it must come from within that society. We people from far across the sea should heed and pray for Mohandas Gandhi's words to filter into the hearts of those treading the rainy streets of Belfast or, for that matter, the sunny streets of Los Angeles or Denver :"When your opponent is in the wrong you can afford to keep your temper. When your opponent is in the right you cannot afford to lose it."

*Richard F. Fleck is currently Dean of Arts and Humanities at the Community College of Denver. His writings include **Critical Perspectives on Native American Fiction, Henry Thoreau and John Muir Among the Indians**, a novel **Clearing of the Mist** (set in Ireland), **Bamboo in the Sun** (poems of Japan), and numerous essays. He spends his time off climbing the 14,000 peaks of Colorado.*

The Power of Personal Example in Overcoming Racism

— Holly E. Hanson

"*We must be the change which we wish to see.*"

— Mahatma Gandhi

"*It is through your deeds that ye can distinguish yourselves from others.
Through them the brightness of your light
can be shed upon the whole earth.*"

— Baha'u'llah

Social movements seeking the redress of racial injustice have been among the most visible applications of *Mahatma Gandhi's* belief that people have the capacity to create a world without violence. As thousands of Indians, Africans, and Americans took actions that asserted the dignity of all human beings and met hatred with love in very visible ways, they have released a moral power that led to significant changes in the legal and economic structures of ethnic and racial oppression in some nations. It is appropriate to remember these achievements in commemorating the 125th anniversary of *Mahatma Gandhi's* birth.

Thirty years after culmination of the Civil Rights movement in the United States, however, it is apparent that its victories were only partial. Barriers of racial animosity and habits of racial segregation seem unchanged, despite the evident progress in creating structures for affirmative action and undoing Jim Crow laws. This essay proposes a further path of loving action through which groups of people can overcome racism. It suggests that in order to create a world without racial violence, we have to take the battle within ourselves. Institutional changes are not enough; we must also eliminate the patterns of racial segregation that characterise people's thoughts and actions. Commitment and conviction give vitality to a legal framework of desegregation and affirmative action. As Gandhi wrote, "we must be the change which we wish to see".

A path of social action which emphasizes the role of self examination and personal transformation in overcoming racism begins with the somewhat contradictory perception that racism is a powerful force that is based on illusion. Humanity is one family — we are all the children of God; prejudices are fictions which have their origin in human self-interest. This assertion does not deny the harmful consequences of people choosing to believe in imaginary racial or ethnic differences. Racism is a corrosive, deadening force that deprives victims of their dignity, diminishes the perspective capacity of perpetrators, and undermines the economic and social health of whole societies. It is important to acknowledge that this palpably destructive force does not come out of nowhere, it comes out from us.

Racism is an assertion of self-interest that infects people's patterns of thinking and action. It is a negative impulse of human nature which, over generations, permeates the cultural, political, and economic structures of a society. It exists because human beings have the capacity to be selfish, but it is not inevitable because human beings also have the capacity to rise above their selfish inclinations.

The conviction that racism is not inevitable rests on an appreciation of the transcendent qualities of human nature and the power of those qualities in the world. Spiritually focussed human beings do not have to be limited by the tendencies to injustice and prejudice which they inherit from the past. They can choose to think and act differently. There is no limit to the progress people can make when they choose to confront racism in their own lives, because nothing can impede the determination of people to change themselves.

The action that people take to eliminate racist thoughts and actions in their own lives can have broad social consequences. People who are consciously trying to do something about racism on a personal level make social programs more effective; they can act to prevent the subtle sabotage of affirmative action or anti-segregation laws. People who locate the problem of racism within themselves can recognise the way their actions perpetuate patterns of racial separation, and actively seek to change the way they participate in racist social structures. The new ways of interacting that they develop can provide a model that challenges assumptions that racism is ubiquitous and insuperable. When people take responsibility for racism instead of blaming it on forces that are beyond them or outside of them, they assert the power of people to create and transform social institutions. Instead of protesting the existence of social institutions that express and perpetuate racism, they choose to act purposefully to create economic, educational, social and political structures that affirm the oneness of the human family.

The potential of social change inherrant in this perception of how to overcome racism demonstrates Gandhi's admonition that people must integrate sacrifice into worship. The power of divine assistance is essential. An attempt to eliminate racism, to create new patterns of thought and action which are based on love of others instead of selfishness, must begin with a higher source, a power that transcends human understanding and motivates human beings to overcome their innate selfishness. "For self-love is kneeded into the very clay of man", "it is impossible for a human being to turn aside from his own selfish advantages and sacrifice his own good for the good of the community except through true religious faith". People can turn to the many lights of faith that God has provided in order to find the tools that are needed to unite the human family.

The strength and self-assurance that comes from faith enables people to look honestly at their own lives and see their own prejudices. A desire to manifest the transcendent qualities of humankind motivates people to make the sacrifice and take the risk that are necessary to change racist patterns of behavior. Devotion to God enables people who have been oppressed to give up their fear, bitterness, and habits of self-protection; the same spiritual commitment enables people who have been dominant to sacrifice their privileges and their complacent sense of superiority. Love of God is the fire that burns away the barriers of racism and ethnic hatred.

A clearly articulated expression of the steps in a spiritual path to overcome racism can be found in the focussed efforts of the followers of *Baha'u'llah* in North America to heal the profound wounds of American racism and to create a united spiritual community. *Baha'u'llah*, a nineteenth century Persian nobleman who claimed the station of a Messenger of God, thought that humanity will attain the capacity to create a peaceful, just and dynamic world civilization through infusion of spiritual power and insight that accompanies a fresh revelation of divine wisdom in human affairs. His followers, the members of the *Baha'i* Faith, are diverse, broadly-based grass root network of spiritual communities, engaged in action at many levels. As the oneness of humankind is the central teaching of *Baha'u'llah*, *Baha'is* have been working to eliminate racism in their midst since the religion was established in the United States at the turn of the century. In 1993, most of the outreach activities of *Baha'i* communities centered on the goal of creating racial unity.

Baha'i scriptures and the instructions addressed to believers in North America by the leaders of the Faith assert that making efforts to eliminate racial distinctions is among the most significant expressions of obedience to God. Writing to insist that the *Baha'is* integrate all their activities, despite the tension and social disapproval this provoked in the early twentieth century, *Abdu'l Baha* (the son of *Baha'u'llah*) stated it is God's purpose that in the West union and harmony may day by day increase among the friends of God and the handmaids of the Merciful. "Strive earnestly and put forth your greatest endeavor towards the accomplishment of this fellowship and the cementing of this bond of brotherhood between you. Such an attainment is not possible without will and effort on the part of each . . . .". The conviction that creating a racially united community was the intention of God which gave *Baha'is* the vision and courage to act in ways that transcended their own habits and conceptions.

Another aspect of the *Baha'is* approach to dealing with American racism has been the sense that different kinds of personal change are required by those who have been the perpetrators and the victims of racism. *Shoghi Effendi* (the great grandson of *Baha'u'llah* and the leader of the *Baha'i* community after the death of *Abdu'l Baha*) delineated these tasks for members of the dominant group :

"Let the Whites make a supreme effort in their resolve to contribute their share to the solution of this problem, to abandon once for all their usually inherent and at times subconscious sense of superiority, to correct their tendency towards revealing a patronising attitude towards the members of the other race, to persuade them through their intimate, spontaneous and informal association with them of the genuinness of their friendship and the sincerity of their intentions, and to master their impatience of any lack of responsiveness on the part of a people who have received, for so long a period, such grievous and slow-healing wounds".

A distinct but complementary set of challenges face African American believers :

"Let the Negroes, through a corresponding effort on their part, show by every means in their power the warmth of their response, their readiness to forget the past, and their ability to wipe out every trace of suspicion that may still linger in their hearts and minds".

Every one together is charged to recognise the difficulty and complexity of the challenge of overcoming racism, and the maturity it requires.

"Let neither think that the solution of so vast a problem is a matter that exclusively concerns the other. Let neither think that such a problem can either easily or immediately be resolved . . . Let neither think that anything short of genuine love, extreme patience, true humility, consummate tact, sound initiative, mature wisdom, and deliberate, persistent and prayerful effort, can succeed in bolting out the stain which this potent evil has left on the fair name of their common country".

These guidelines have proved to be tremendously useful in circumventing many of the stumbling blocks that can impede efforts to overcome racism.

There is a momentum for change inherent in the statement that white people must confront their inherent sense of superiority and African-Americans must confront their sense of suspicion and mistrust; progress is impossible when people deny these negative emotions. The alienation that often arises when well-intentioned white people do not recognise the patronising quality of their actions can be reduced when white people accept that they will have a tendency to act this way and must make efforts to correct it. The statement that everyone's participation is necessary prevents the stagnation which results when people see racism as some other group's fault and responsibility.

The assertion that creating racial unity is an extremely difficult challenge which can only happen through drawing on sources of spiritual strength gives people courage and helps people to alleviate the frustration they feel when their efforts are not immediately successful. It is not easy for white people to be diligent in recognising and rooting out their negative attitudes; it is not easy for people of colour to be willing to extend themselves in the way that may cause disappointment and hurt. An atmosphere of love and acceptance of each other, and acceptance of each one's own self and own limitations, has to be cultivated; without the affirmation of the powerful, positive, capacities human beings inherently possess, this process would be impossible.

In the authoritative *Baha'i* texts regarding American racism, people are to complement their efforts to change their own attitudes with efforts to transform the patterns of their lives that uphold subtle and pervasive racial separation. Calling for "a close and intimate social intercourse" *Shoghi Effendi* told the American *Baha'is* in 1926 that fidelity to the principles of their faith required them to ensure the unity of blacks and whites *"in their homes, in their hours of relaxation and leisure, in the daily contact of business transactions, in the association of their children, whether in their study-classes, their playgrounds and club rooms, in short under all possible circumstances, however insignificant they appear . . . . "*

Holly Hanson is currently working on a book on the actions and attitudes of North Americans working to overcome racism. A Ph.D. candidate in American History at the University of Florida, her research is on the social and moral dimensions of land tenure in Uganda. Ms. Hanson spent almost a decade facilitating social and economic development activities of Baha'i communities around the world and has published a book and numerous articles on Baha'i religious teachings and rural development.

Lessons From Sri Lanka :
Politics Without Principles

— *John M. Richardson, Jr.*

The world began to experience a wave of political change in 1989. Entrenched authoritarian regimes in many nations have crumbled in the face of popular dissatisfaction with repressive policies that failed to deliver on promises of economic opportunity. Many nations are now experimenting with the forms of democracy; popular elections to choose leaders, accountability of leaders to elected parliaments, freedom of expression and freedom to compete for power within organized political parties.

Democratic experiments have begun with high expectations and aspirations. Czech dissident, Vaclav Havel, in his memorable New Year's address of 1990 spoke of democracy as "innate within human beings" and "reflecting a capability always to be striving for something higher". Burmese leader Aung San Suu Kyi, writing from confinement in 1991, spoke of democracy as expressing the highest aspirations of the human spirit. "It is," Aung said, "man's vision of a world fit for rational, civilized humanity which leads him to dare and to suffer to build societies free from want and fear". Others have expressed the view that democratization would usher in a "new world order" in which human society would move toward Mahatma Gandhi's vision of a world without violence.

Tragically, the fall of authoritarian regimes has often been accompanied by an intensification of violence rather than giving birth to societies "fit for rational civilized humanity." the names Angola, Armenia, Benin, Bosnia- Herzegovina, Georgia, Romania and Somalia must now be added to an already long list of nations where democratic regimes have succumbed to violence or where high levels of violence and some forms of democracy coexist. These include Guatemala, India, Lebanon, Haiti, Philippines, and Sri Lanka. Even Western nations with long democratic traditions fall short of Gandhi's ideal. Northern Ireland's decades long ethnic conflict shares many characteristics with those in India and Sri Lanka. In the United States, a rising tide of violence has not been political, but has been intense.

Why do democracies fall short of *Ahimsa* (nonviolence)? Why does democratization sometimes intensify violent political conflict? How can democratization and sustainable development be achieved nonviolently? For more than five years, I have been trying to find answers to these and other questions about violent political conflict through an in-depth study of India's neighbor, Sri Lanka. This beautiful island nation has suffered two civil wars, one ongoing, that have consumed vast resources, killed thousands and impoverished hundreds of thousands.

At the time of independence, achieved peacefully in 1948, Sri Lanka's people viewed the future optimistically. All Citizens (including women) were given the right to vote in 1935 and exercised their franchise vigorously. Sri Lanka's four major ethnic communities — *Burgher, Muslim, Sinhalese* and *Tamil* — had mostly lived at peace with one another. Nonviolence was a major tenet of both dominant religions, *Theravada Buddhism* (practiced by most Sinhalese) and Hinduism (practiced by most Tamils).

Optimism seemed justified in Sri. Lanka during the first decades of independence. Enlightened social policies demonstrated that a developing nation could, with modest economic resources, become a world leader in meeting the basic needs of its people. Sri Lanka's democratic institutions coped successfully with economic problems, two military coup attempts, the assassination of a Prime Minister and a violent insurrection by youthful revolutionaries. Political power was transferred peacefully following regularly scheduled free elections, with wide popular participation and with major offices contested by strong, well organized political parties.

By 1988, however, Sri Lanka had come to exemplify violent communal conflict in the eyes of the world rather than democracy or development. The northern part of the island was occupied by Indian "peace keeping" forces engaged in a bitter struggle with Tamil secessionist guerrillas. In the south, Sinhalese Marxist revolutionaries controlled many rural areas, assassinated political leaders almost at will and challenged government authority in the capital city, Colombo. Five years later, Sri Lanka still has a viable democratic government and the Indian peacekeepers are gone, but there is no peace. Secessionist guerilla warfare and political assassinations continue. Military spending, rather than meeting basic human needs, now received top priority in the national budget.

What explains Sri Lanka's transformation from a nation epitomizing peaceful development and democracy to one epitomizing violent communal conflict? What can be learned from Sri Lanka's experience that might help to build nonviolent societies? No short paper could answer these questions fully. However decisions by influential political leaders that rejected two interrelated principles central to Gandhi's political philosophy, provide part of the answer. The principles are *Ahimsa* defined as nonviolence, or the avoidance of hurt by lying or evil thoughts, and

Satya defined as truthful or moral conduct. Like politicians in many nations, top Sri Lankan leaders who were personally decent, principled and intelligent, chose imperfect means to pursue worthy goals that seemed to require political power as a prerequisite. They fell prey to the seventh of Mahatma Gandhi's seven blunders of the world: politics without principles, and contributed to consequences that all of Sri Lanka's people have endured.

The practice of politics without principles is not unique to Sri Lanka, it is pervasive in all nations. Those who engage in this practice often do so with the best of intentions — Sri Lanka's post independence leaders were genuinely concerned with the well being of their people and pursued that goal energetically, even courageously. That a pursuit of worthy goals by principled leaders contributed to the island nation's slide into violent communal conflict makes the outcome all the more tragic and all the more deserving of careful study.

The Sri Lankan case points toward two generalizations that are both informed by Mahatma Gandhi's philosophy and, I believe, widely applicable. First is that practicing politics without principles, even in pursuit of principled goals, is likely to push a society toward violent conflict. Ethnically diverse societies are particularly susceptible to this pathology. A second generalization is that processes of democratic political campaigning and elections pose nearly irresistible temptations to practice politics without principles. The more worthy the aspirant, the stronger the belief that his or her leadership is needed to deal with crises or achieve worthy goals, the more irresistible will be the temptation to compromise the principle of Satya and commit the seventh blunder. Decisions of three respected Sri Lankan leaders - S.W.R.D. Bandaranaike, Dudley Senanayake and J.R. Jayewardene — during a pivotal juncture in their nation's history illustrate these generalizations.

Our story began in 1955. General elections to choose a new Parliament and Prime Minister were scheduled for the following year. Since before independence, Sri Lanka had been governed by the conservative United National Party and guided by the Party's vision of a secular, multi-ethnic society. Members of the majority Sinhalese community dominated the government, but the rights of the minority Tamils to use their language, practice their Hindu religion and hold coveted positions in the government civil service were protected.

Although their nation had been independent for more than seven years, poor members of the Sinhalese majority community had experienced little change in their daily lives. For many, the post independence years had been embittering and dis-illusioning. Most galling, was the fact that English remained not only the nation's official language but the gateway to economic opportunity. A Sinhala speaker could not seek higher level employment in government or business, plead a case in court, understand Parliamentary debates or even use a telephone directory in his nation's capital. The elite schools that provided instruction in English rarely enrolled rural Sinhalese and were often controlled by Roman Catholics who combined education with religious instruction that was offensive to Buddhist beliefs. Only in Tamil areas was English language instruction, provided by Roman Catholic missionary schools, widespread. This was seen to give the Tamil minority, who had also been favored by the British colonial rulers advantages over the Sinhalese. By 1955, many Sinhalese saw the need for greater political power to achieve the interrelated goals of economic opportunity, cultural revival and a special place for their Buddhist religion in Sri Lanka. However they lacked strong leadership and were not effectively mobilized.

Among Sri Lanka's political leaders, the charismatic S.W.R.D. Bandaranaike had greatest empathy for the Sinhalese rural poor. In 1936, he founded the Great Sinhalese League (*Sinhala Maha Sabha*) to promote a Sinhalese political agenda. Although Oxford educated, he wore Sri Lankan "national dress", gave speeches in Sinhala, practiced Buddhism and publicly opposed British customs. As Local Government Minister and then Health Minister, he had travelled extensively in rural areas and managed a successful malaria eradication campaign. In 1951, he resigned from the government, founded a new opposition political party and began an aggressive campaign to become Prime Minister. The party grew in strength, but did not gain the public support necessary for victory until Bandaranaike chose himself, in 1955, with strong advocates of Sinhalese-Buddhist cultural revival.

In this new alliance, Bandaranaike discovered an issue that could be extraordinarily effective in arousing hitherto politically apathetic rural Sinhalese, the issue of language. "I am amazed at how this language issue gets people worked up," he is reported to have said. In spellbinding speeches, Bandaranaike promised followers that he would make Sinhalese the official language throughout Sri Lanka "within twenty four hours" following his elevation to the office of Prime Minister. However as a former government minister with years of experience, he knew that keeping his promise would be impossible. Bandaranaike soon discovered that using the minority Tamils as a scapegoat for the failure of Sinhalese to achieve a better life was also effective in arousing his followers. Personally, Bandaranaike respected the Tamils and he knew that many of his charges were exaggerated or false, but this did not deter him. As election day approached, Bandaranaike's speeches became increasingly strident and more focused on Sinhalese resentments and fears, which were directed against the Tamils. Bandaranaike's campaign succeeded. The election results gave him a Parliamentary majority and the Prime Minister's office, but his campaign tactics had violated the principles of Satya and Ahimsa. To gain power he had practiced politics without principles.

Once elected, Bandaranaike, as he had always intended, attempted to deal sensitively with the anxieties among Tamils that his campaign rhetoric and proposed language policies had aroused. His true vision was of a more responsive and egalitarian government for Sri Lanka, within the context of British liberal traditions and including protection for minority rights. Once elected to office, he saw himself as leader of all the nation's citizens. His goal was to respond to Sinhalese aspirations, but arbitrate contentious issues according to principles of "fair play" that would benefit everyone. In keeping with this philosophy, government initiated legislation to establish Sinhala as the official language proposed an implementation process of several years, rather than twenty four hours, along with an end result that included "reasonable use of Tamil". Bandaranaike also sought common ground with Tamil political leaders on other issues and successfully negotiated a "pact" for limited regional autonomy and power sharing that would provide some protection for minority rights.

Tragically, Bandaranaike could not, despite good intentions, free himself from the tactics that had brought him to power. In the face of threats and demonstrations from his radical followers, the Prime Minister was forced to back down on both his more moderate language policy and proposals for limited power sharing. In response, the disillusioned Tamils began a civil disobedience campaign that would, much later, escalate into a full scale armed guerilla movement advocating secession.

Like Mahatma Gandhi, Bandaranaike died at the hands of extremist supporters of his own religion. In contrast to Gandhi he was the victim of forces that he had played a pivotal role in unleashing. On September 29, 1959, the Prime Minister walked out of his house to greet a group of well wishers. A Buddhist Priest stepped forward and as Bandaranaike bowed in the traditional gesture of greeting and respect, drew a pistol from beneath his saffron robes and fired. "The people's Prime Minister" died twenty four hours later after appealing to Sri Lankans to treat his murderer with compassion.

Bandaranaike's task of following a moderate path would have been easier were it not for the decision of the principal United National Party leaders, now in opposition, to oppose his proposals in the hope of weakening the Prime Minister. Both Dudley Senanayake and his principal deputy, J.R. Jayewardene, were sympathetic to Sinhalese aspirations but had favored moderate language policies and protection of minority rights. When Bandaranaike proposed moderate language policies and power sharing to protect minority rights, however, Senanayake and Jayewardene formed an improbable alliance with Sinhalese nationalists, political Buddhist priests and other radical groups that had played key roles in the United National Party's 1956 election defeat. Opposition focused on the beleaguered Prime Minister's power sharing pact with the Tamils leadership. The normally sensitive, temperate Senanayake denounced the pact as "act of treachery" that would mean the partition of Ceylon and avowed that he was willing to "sacrifice his life : to stop it" . The sophisticated, politically astute Jayewardene labeled the pact a "betrayal of the Sinhalese" and organized an abortive protest march, billed as a religious pilgrimage, to stop it. At a critical juncture, both men had chosen politics without principle in the hope of regaining political power.

The UNP leaders' decisions, which contributed to the failure of the pact, marked the beginning of what Bandaranaike biographer James Manor has called a "poisonous" cycle of Sri Lankan politics that has polarized the society along communal lines. When in power, leaders of both parties have advocated reasonable concessions to the Tamils minority in order to maintain national unity. But when in opposition, these same leaders have used uncompromising advocacy of Sinhalese Buddhist nationalism as a tactic to gain political support. Opposition to proposed concessions, often taking the form of disruptive, violent demonstrations, has pushed successive Sri Lankan governments toward more extreme positions on communal issues, with tragic consequences. Moderate Tamil leaders have felt betrayed and either radicalized their own positions or been supplanted by proponents of more aggressive, violent responses. Today, Tamil majority areas are controlled by the most radical, aggressive and violent faction, the "Tamil Tigers".

One of the three has personally experienced the long-term consequences of policies that, after 1956, began dividing the Sinhalese and Tamils. Twenty years after the power sharing pact failed, J.R. Jayewardene, then Sri Lanka's President, reluctantly invited Indian forces to take control of Sri Lanka's Northern and Eastern Provinces in the hope that the world's fourth largest army could pacify the Tamil Tiger guerrillas. To gain India's support, he was forced to concede to the Tamils much more than Bandaranaike had proposed in 1957, but Jayewardene's concessions failed to end the conflict. Simultaneously attacks of the radical Sinhalese People's Liberation Front in the South made even the Colombo suburbs unsafe.

Jayewardene's retirement from public office in 1988 did not bring violent conflict to an end in Sri Lanka. He was succeeded by Ranasinghe Premadasa, a man of humble origins who, like Bandaranaike, characterized himself as the "people's Prime Minister". Premadasa made further concessions to the Tamils and successfully negotiated the Indian Peace Keeping Force's withdrawal. Then, Tamil Tiger leaders betrayed the agreement they had made with the new President and fighting began a new. In the South, Premadasa's Defense Minister, Ranjan Wijeratne was given the task of restoring order. His successful strategy was to create government sanctioned death squads. With considerable public support, the death squads were given a free hand to crush the People's Liberation Front and their supporters. For several months Sri Lankans found bodies or only the severed heads of death squad victims alongside public roadways, where they had been placed as a warning. Wijeratne argued that it was impossible to fully protect innocent people and realize the greater good of destroying a threat that had totally disrupted the Sri Lankan society and economy. Eventually, the top People's Liberation Front leaders were betrayed, arrested and killed.

In August, 1990, President Ranasinghe Premadasa, reflecting on conditions in his troubled nation, shared the following fable with a group of supporters:

A lion and a tiger lived in a certain forest. One day, both those animals got together and hunted another animal for their food. Unable to have the prey divided among themselves in a fair manner, they fought with each other. They fought so hard that they ultimately injured each other and lay beside their prey helplessly. A fox who had been observing this fight came out and took away the animal hunted by the lion and the tiger. Thus both lion and the tiger lost the animal they had killed.

"It is because I have learned the moral of this story," the President concluded, "that I have always been sounding a warning about this sort of fighting".

In the Spring of 1992, Defense Minister Ranjan Wijeratne was killed by a car bomb. Tamil Tiger guerrillas were implicated in the killing.

On May Day, 1993, Ranasinghe Premadasa was leading a parade of his followers through the streets of Colombo when he was assassinated by a Tamil Tiger suicide bomber who had evaded the President's security guards on a bicycle.

A chain of events that began with the practice of politics without principles had claimed two more victims.

The guerrilla war in Sri Lanka's Northern and Eastern Provinces continues.

Dr. John Richardson writes, lectures and consults in the field of applied analysis, international development and Third World political conflict. He is presently Professor of International Affairs and Applied Systems Analysis and Director of Doctoral Studies in the School of International Service at The American University, Washington, DC. He has written numerous books including **Ending Hunger : An Idea Whose Time Has Come**.

Anger, Retribution and Violence

— *Raymond M. Smullyan*

The role of anger and hatred in violence does not appear to be adequately recognized. Violence is more usually associated with desire for material gain, and although this is certainly a factor, the importance of the other two should not be underestimated. I once asked a professional psychiatrist whether it is not possible to live without anger. To my amazement, he replied : "I wouldn't want to." When asked why, he replied : "Because I enjoy expressing my anger ! Life without anger would be too bland." The last sentence struck me as particularly astonishing! Aren't there an enormous number of exhilarating things in life that don't require anger? Does one need anger to enjoy good food, good music, good literature, good love-making? Another friend of mine once said : "I want the privilege of expressing my anger!" I can understand his wanting that privilege, but wouldn't it be more of a privilege not to be angry in the first place? If I have a pain, I certainly want the privilege of doing something to alleviate it, but it is obviously better not to have the pain to begin with. And I think that this is really analogous, since anger is definitely painful, (often causing headaches) and its expression is certainly a relief. And so, I am not advocating repression or suppression of one's anger so much as analyzing its cause, which would tend to dissipate it without harming others (unlike the direct expression of it). Anger is really a weakness. As one psychiatrist once wisely said : "Anger is really an evasion".

Anger and violence surely constitute two of the world's major problems. Furthermore — and I cannot stress this too strongly — all this is closely tied up with retributive ethics! One of the wisest insights of Mahatma Gandhi was that retribution only brings more retribution in return. By retributive ethics I mean the doctrine that evil doers deserve to suffer for their evil deeds. This is not to be confused with the Eastern notion of Karma, which is that evil deeds do indeed bring inevitable suffering to the doer, not because he or she deserves it, but that is simply a law of nature. In other words, there is no agent who punishes one for his evil deeds; it is the evil deeds themselves that bring suffering to the doer. The psychology behind this is profoundly different from that behind the idea of retribution. The phrase : "Vengeance is mine, saith the Lord" strikes me as unfortunate. I believe that when the religions of the world become more mature, the phrase will be replaced by : " 'Vengeance is nobody's, not even mine,' saith the Lord".

I wish to go on record as predicting that the decline in retributive ethics, the decline in war, and the decline in crime will all come hand in hand. Most everyone hates war and crime, but few realize the evils of retributive ethics and its tie–up with the other two ! It is amazing how many people who claim to be pacifists are nevertheless in favour of capital punishment : "The murderer deserves to die for what he has done !" As to the tie-up with war, can you honestly imagine any normal person going to war trying to kill the enemy without believing this enemy is somehow evil and deserves to be killed? Without the belief, wouldn't one's conscience make fighting unbearable?

What I have said so far is comprehensible in purely secular terms, though I don't believe that religious consciousness is completely irrelevant. Some orthodox religionists claim that the evils of the world will never cease until we abandon a purely secular approach to life. I think this is putting the cart before the horse! I would rather say that the decline in violence and retributive ethics (which I insist are closely tied together) will come hand in hand, not only with each other, but also with something somewhat like religious consciousness — not in the sense of any organized authoritarian religion, but rather more like *Cosmic Consciousness*, in the sense of Richard Bucke's excellent book of the title. This book, published in 1901, deserves to be far better known today than it appears to be. Bucke's thesis is that a more advanced type of consciousness — called 'Cosmic Consciousness' — is slowly coming to the human race through the process of evolution and that the mystics and spiritual leaders of the past were evolutionary sports. He believed that one day we will all be in direct sight of that which we formerly believed only on the basis of authority or faith. (This idea, incidentally, comes much closer to Eastern religious thought than Western). He also believed that Cosmic Consciousness will come hand in hand with the decline of what he calls two of the world's greatest evils : riches and poverty. To this I would like to add : "and the decline of retributive ethics".

In conclusion, let me emphasize that I am not blaming people for having desires for retribution, which I realize is part of human nature. The unfortunate thing, though, is that so many people approve of these desires, instead of recognizing them for the evil that they are.

Dr. Smullyan is Oscar Ewing Professor Emeritus of Philosophy at Indiana University and author of several books. He writes a bi-monthly column on logic for The Sciences (published by the New York Academy of Sciences). He was appointed a Sigma Xi lecturer for 1984-85.

Religious Intolerance Leads To Violence

— Udo Schafer

Translated from the German by Dr. Geraldine Schuckelt

The world has not become a more peaceful place since Mahatma Gandhi, shot down by an assassin, surrendered his spirit on 30 January, 1948. Violence, as old as mankind itself, has taken on a new dimension in modern industrial societies — it has become an integral part of our lives. Just as fever indicates sickness in the body, the increasing tendency towards violence point to a serious malady in society. It is a society lacking orientation, in which traditional value-systems have lost their authority. It is a world characterised by Nihilism and Hedonism, in which fear and hopelessness are spreading — ideal conditions for the growth of individual and collective violence. In a world so overshadowed by darkness, the figure of Mahatma Gandhi with his message of nonviolence, his unspeakable faith in a future world of justice, peace and harmony, is a ray of light, a sign of hope.

One of the most ancient and apparently ineradicable causes of violence is religious fanaticism. From Cain's murder of his brother right up to the present day one can trace through human history a trail of blood resulting from religious persecution, religious wars, "Holy Wars" and religiously motivated acts of violence. The Enlightenment, it is true brought about the postulation of religious freedom as a universal human right, a right now written into the Constitution of every democratic state, thus removing claims to religious truth from the domain of state power. Yet, at this very time, bloody conflicts are being conducted in the name of religion in Lebanon, Northern Ireland, Bosnia, Sri Lanka and Sudan. Religious fanaticism periodically flares up in riots and massacres, as in India and Egypt, and often atrocities committed under direct invocation of God and in His name. In the name of the "true" religion minorities are subjected to persecution, oppressions and harassment — the violent persecution of the Baha'is in Iran is, even today, a sad example of this phenomenon.

The tragic end of the Mahatma's life demonstrates that fanatics are provoked by the acts of peacemakers. In Gandhi's case his co-religionists could not bear the thought of treating the "Untouchables" equally and that Hindus and Muslims should live in harmony and mutual respect. The fanatics considered Gandhi's murder an act of piety, praying in the Temple prior to the crime. As Pensees Pascal says, hatred is never so profound and irreconcilable as when its motives spring from the deepest levels of consciousness, from religious beliefs *(Jamis on ne fait le mal si pleinement et si gaiement que quand on le fait par conscience).*

There is, however, no basis for committing such deeds : none of the religions legitimises violence against those who think or believe differently. Religious fanaticism, the bitter fruit of narrow-minded dogmatism, is the worst deformation of religion, the perversion of one of the most noble virtues, that of steadfastness in faith. Its psychological roots lie in vices such as arrogance, pride, and tacit envy, attitudes which are condemned in all religions as "sin" or even "mortal sin". Intolerance, fanaticism and religious hatred are "destructive to the foundation of human solidarity" profoundly contrary to the spirit of true religion : Baha'ullah, the Founder of Baha'i Faith, called it "a world-devouring fire", "a desolating affliction", and impressed upon his followers that "The religion of God is for love and unity; make it not a cause of enmity or dissension". Abdu'l Baha even went so far as to state that: "If religion becomes a cause of dislike, hatred and division, it were better to be without it, and to withdraw from such a religion would be a truly religious act. For it is clear that the purpose of a remedy is to cure; but if the remedy should only aggravate the complaint it had better be left alone."

Fanaticism is incompatible with the commandments of justice and love. Love requires tolerance, and this noble virtue means respect for the opinion and beliefs of others, not out of religious or moral indifference, but, irrespective of one's own standpoint, out of respect towards one's neighbour as a free and equal person with the inalienable right to his own convictions.

For numerous centuries the spirit of irreconcilable rejection was reflected in the behaviour of one group of believers towards members of other denominations, or, worse still, of other religions. Yet in all religions, from the Emperor Ashoka to the present,there have been individuals who have defined the dominant *Zeigelist* and stood up for understanding and tolerance towards other faiths. Casanus, a Cardinal of the Catholic Church, who in 1453 coined the sensational phrase *"Una religio in ntuum varietate"*, the Protestant theologians Fredrich Scleiermarcher and Fredrich Heiler, the Lutheran Archbishop Nathan Soderblom, the Indian philosopher, Sarvapalli Radhakrishnan, the Catholic theologians Raymondo Panikkar and Hans Kung, among others, have raised their voices for the overcoming dogmatic claims to exclusivity, for a fraternal relationship between religions, for the spirit of love and tolerance in keeping with the demand in the Qur'an : "Let there be no compulsion in religion!" Among these protagonists of religious tolerance, Mahatma Gandhi was undoubtedly the most significant.

The "Declaration of the Church to non-Christian Religions" of the Second Vatican Council and the "Guidelines on Dialogue with People of Living Faiths and Ideologies" produced by the World Council of Churches in 1979 were both of epochal significance in providing a new orientation based on the spirit of reconciliation. They marked the beginning "of a serious dialogue of the World Religions", "a slow awakening of a global ecumenical consciousness" which, according to Hans Kung, is "one of the most important Phenomena of the twentieth century". This development is a sign of hope that in our world of violence, genocide and religious discrimination, the spirit of tolerance and respect for the inalienability of human dignity and human rights will triumph over the spirit of irreconcilability, prejudice and hatred. World peace depends upon it : "There will be no peace among the peoples of the world without peace among the world religions".

The formulation of sublime principles alone is, however, of little benefit. The significance of Mahatma Gandhi lies above all in the fact that — despite long years of incarceration — he exemplerily lived out his principles of all-embracing love for mankind, religious tolerance and nonviolence, engaging his whole personality fearlessly in corresponding political action : "The world is tired of words; it wants examples".

Dr. Udo Schaefer *received his degrees at the law faculty of Ruperto-Carola University, Heidelburg. He was a chief public prosecutor at the State Court of Heidelburg. His publications on the subjects of religious studies, religious sociology and religious philosophy have been translated into five languages. He is a member of the National Assembly of the Baha'i's in Germany.*

Is Fearlessness Possible?

— Gordon C. Zahn

Civics classes in Milwaukee's public schools in the middle and late 1930s included frequent reports of the doings off Mahatma Gandhi : his fasts, his arrests, his boycotts — in short, his peaceful campaign to achieve independence for India. An already convinced pacifist, I was an admirer from afar but one who shared what Thomas Merton would later describe as the view that "Gandhiji was some kind of eccentric and that his nonviolence was an impractical sensational fad." If this exotic Indian and his movement claimed any direct engagement with my personal political sentiments and convictions, the link lay in the added justification they provided for my generalized suspicions and resentment of what I saw as the British Empire's unrelenting efforts to lure the U.S. into foreign entanglements serving the Empire's own world interests. My "Free India" sympathies, I am ashamed to admit, was based more upon that distinctly anti British taint than upon awareness of, or concern about, imperial injustice.

The subsequent involvement of the United States in World War II seemed to confirm my Anglophobe prejudice, and I accepted assignment to alternative service as a conscientious objector secure in that confirmation. Fortunately, a going away gift from a friend was a copy of *Shridharani's War Without Violence*. It was this book which introduced me to the fuller vision of *Gandhian* nonviolence. At first, of course, to this Roman Catholic (in a Catholic sponsored camp — itself a distinct religious anomaly at the time!) *Satyagraha* remained an exotic unrealistic concept. Nevertheless my pacifist convictions helped me to recognize important parallels between my Christian values and beliefs and those advanced by this strange, but obviously revered, man in his simple loin-cloth with his ever-present spinning wheel. Only later, through the writings of Dom Bede Griffiths, Thomas Merton, and others were those "parallels" elevated into their rightful status as expressions of essential and universal truths of the human spirit.

Even today, I must confess, my personal commitment to nonviolence tends to be more political and sociological than religious in nature. This is not to say, however, that I agree with those who discount or actually deny the valuable contributions and added strength of commitment that can be found in religious beliefs and sources. For me, my Christian teachings and models provide the foundation even though I am not given — as so many of my fellow pacifists are — to scheduled periods of meditation and contemplation or similar devotional practices. I respect, even envy, the strength and fervor they draw from them but, try as I may, my mind wanders too easily and refuses to be chained.

This same secular social science perspective leads me to take issue with Gandhi's insistence upon "unadulterated fearlessness" as an essential and necessary characteristic of nonviolent commitment and practice. If this were true it would have the effect of restricting participation in nonviolent campaigns and movement's activities to saints or innocent simpletons who are unaware of and, it would follow, unprepared for dealing with the risks and consequences nonviolence will involve. Instead I would argue that one must not only experience fear but be able to recognize it and be prepared to handle it.

It is that element of "preparation" which presents today's crucial challenge to all the formative institutions of society and most particularly to the combined agencies of religion and education. In a world increasingly keyed to violence from the most intimate interpersonal level to planet-threatening, international tension and conflict, Gandhi's vision of nonviolent order seems unreasonable and beyond any serious hope of attainment. Even so every possible effort must be made to reach the goal.

What is involved is essentially a philosophical difference that must be resolved, two contrasting views of human nature and capacity and their interpretations of behavioral "breaking points" of individuals under stress. One interpretation holds that effective domination is to be sought and ultimately obtained through threatened denial of physically satisfying needs and desires coupled with threats of (or, if need be, even resort to) violence-induced pain and injury. The other, the nonviolence option, centers upon the recognition of common identity expressed through the power of self-sacrificing love which, however hopeless the situation, cannot be completely or permanently suppressed. In this ineterpretation one finds the very real promise that everyone (even the Roman tyrant, the Buchenwald guard, the brutal thug terrorizing his neighbourhood!) has a "Breaking Point" beyond which participation in parrened inhumanity cannot be forced or endured.

In 1932 as he prepared to start on a "fast unto death" Gandhi described the difference between the two approaches: "Violent pressure is felt on the physical being and it degrades him who uses it as it depresses the victim; but non-violent pressure exerted through self-suffering, as by fasting, works in an entirely different way. It touches not the physical body, but it touches and strengthens the moral fiber of those against whom it is directed". A half century later those words may seem even less reasonable than they did then, but this makes the truth they contain even more compelling. And its acceptance much more necessary. Instead of continuing our present descent to total inhumanity, this world and its inhabitants must somehow be persuaded to make a significant and long overdue turning in the direction of a renewed act of faith in the humanity of every potential enemy — and our selves.

*Dr. Gordon Zahn is a distinguished scholar and educator with several books, **Thomas Merton and Peace** (1971), **German Catholics and Hitler's Wars** (1962), and several awards, "Courage of Conscience", Pax Christi "Ambassador of Peace", to his credit.*

Nonviolence In The Context of Palestinian Independence

— *Mubarak Awad, Laura M. Bain, David T. Ritchie*

Nonviolence is a positive action for social change — a mechanism to move us from empowerment to development, and to look to the future and see the challenge of stopping violence in our homes, streets, and all facets of life; including our political life. Nonviolence is a challenge to build a better society, and also have the energy to spot injustices and find ways to prevent and resolve them before they become a destructive conflict.

Nonviolent action is a process for eliminating violence. Changing social conditions and finding practical ways for people to work on overcoming injustice, and in so doing, empower themselves to do these actions without fear. The power of nonviolence is within every person.

Palestinians have long been disappointed and rejected, and everyone must realize that this can no longer occur. In 1984, a nonviolent strategy for occupied territories was outlined. It was a serious and comprehensive strategy for Palestinians in the West Bank and Gaza to resist the Israeli Occupation. This call also detailed the means and tactical methods of implementing these strategies, as well as the problems and obstacles which would face Palestinians.

The condition in the West Bank and Gaza have changed since 1984. For those who are constantly looking for changes, they are able to see them not only among the Palestinians but also among the Israelis. These changes were prompted, in no small part, by the largely nonviolent actions of thousands of Palestinians which is widely known as the *Intefada*.

The *Intefada* brought a new era from which Palestinians cannot turn back. *Intefada* means "to quake," and expresses an intention to try to shake the shame and fear of a people's occupiers, as well as build self-respect and assertiveness as human beings with dignity to resist occupation. It was resisting occupation that became as much a part of the daily life of Palestinians as possible, and included all segments of Palestinian society. The *Intefada* miraculously achieved this, but

Palestinians still need to go even further, to develop a political purpose. The Palestinian grassroots resistance of occupation challenged Israelis to recognize Palestinians as humans — with dignity and respect.

The *Intefada* has been such a successful experiment in the Palestinian community, that the Israeli government (with all its means) was, and still is, unable to control the uprising, destroy it, or change its own political directions to account for the fact that its responses to the Intefada have been completely unsuccessful. The uprising influenced the political leaders on both sides, and brought the issue of the Palestinians who are under occupation to the conscience of the world. In a very real sense, the actions of the Palestinian people brought on talks which eventually led to the signing of the Declaration of Principles (DOP) in Washington. We would like to express our opinions on precisely what the Intefada did for Palestinians as a people:

1. It forced confrontations — on a daily basis — between members of the Israeli government, the Israeli military, and Israeli society. This significantly strengthened the Palestinians as a people;

2. It illuminated, for the world, the Israeli ideology (as found in the general public) that Palestine is theirs to live in and inhabit freely. Settlers used to think that they could come at anytime to these areas and "picnic" in leisure (with an Israeli Flag) without noticing the Palestinians. This resulted directly in the purposeful devastation of the of the Palestinian nation and culture. Israelis can no longer do this as a result of the *Intefada*;

3. It forced the Israeli government to bring in as many soldiers as possible to control the Palestinian population. In 1978, one military jeep could control twenty villages. With the introduction of *Intefada*, the number of soldiers multiplied substantially. This succeeeded in making the occupation expensive for the Israelis, and they certainly felt the pinch of the increased expenses;

4. It energized the Palestinian people in the Diaspora. They have developed a stronger feeling of kinship between people living inside Palestine, as well as others in the Diaspora.

5. It gave the Arab masses (this does not necessarily include Arab leaders or Governments) evidence that Palestinians could resist Israeli occupation without weapons, in the face of the violent Israeli opposition. This has given hope to Arab peoples that they can resist their own corrupt governments;

6. It gave Palestinian women the ability to raise the consciousness of other women world-wide that women have a full role in a struggle against occupation. Resistance is not only for men and guns;

7. It provided children and youth with the outlet for pride and resistance. Even though the sacrifice has been great (including death, broken bones and jail), their spirit could not be stopped. Children and youth have learned that they can utilize tactics available to them to reject living under occupation;

8. It revealed to the international community that the Israelis have been a barrier to change. The *Intefada* brought the Palestinian cause to the forefront of the international media. It also challenged Western peace groups, who for a long time would not discuss the Palestinian cause because it carried a taboo. But most of all, the *Intefada* challenged the Israeli people. Even though it polarized them, they were forced to make a decision for themselves rather than have the government do so for them; and

9. Finally, the *Intefada* challenged the Palestinian leadership to recognize the need to talk peace, which in turn challenged the international community to recognize the urgency of the peace process and peace talks between the Arabs and the Israelis.

As a result of the *Intefada*, it has become clear that Israel cannot control the West Bank and the Gaza Strip without the cooperation of the Palestinians. The *Intefada* made it hard for the Israelis to have this cooperation. Palestinian non-cooperation was, therefore, the highlight of the *Intefada*.

Throughout its development, the *Intefada* displayed four major characteristics, non-cooperation, obstruction (including harassment and resistance), parallel institutional alternatives, and civil disobedience. It is time for Palestinians to move beyond these tactics, and develop other tools of change.

The signing of the DOP marked a change in the Palestinian resistance to the Israeli occupation and Palestinian efforts for self-determination. Palestinians are now changing their strategies and formulating new goals to reflect the new stage ushered in with the signing of the DOP. In this stage, *"Kaufsa,"* Palestinians are "leaping and moving forward" towards self-determination and independence. It is very important, however, to realize that although the *Intefada* brought on the talks which led to the signing of the declaration of Principles, there is still much to be done in order for the Israeli occupation to cease and for Palestinians to capably organize and administer their society. Nonviolent action of the Palestinians will be crucial during this period to continue to move towards self-determination, to develop a role for the new Palestine in the international nation state arena, and to create a more fundamentally just Palestinian society.

Economic, resource and political development are all nonviolent means with which the Palestinians can continue to fight against the Israeli occupation. Development in these areas will allow Palestinians to build a strong society, empowering themselves and gaining self sufficiency and independence from Israeli occupation·and foreign intervention. Action must be taken, however, in all of these areas, as the circumstances of each one determines the success or failure of the other. Palestinians must undertake efforts to mobilize their institutional, intellectual, professional and grassroots resources in order to address basic economic and resource needs, as well as to create the vital institutional and political structure and stability.

With democratization, Palestinians can achieve a stable and just society and reduce violence — both within the Palestinian state and between the Palestinian and Israeli peoples. By nature of its characteristics of equal participation and representation, the institutional structure that results from democratic participation has legitimacy and stability that it might not otherwise posses.

In addition, the relationship between citizens and their leadership that democracy entails — rule by the people — and the guarantee of personal freedoms including human and civil rights, all reduce the level of frustration and fear that often result in violent action. Democratic and electoral processes would offer Palestinians a nonviolent constructive and creative way with which to bring about social and political change in their leadership as it participates in domestic and international context.

In January 1994, we conducted town meetings in villages, towns and refugee camps in Palestine to raise the issues of democracy and elections among the Palestinian grassroots population and to give them a forum in which to freely express their opinions. We used the town meeting strategy because it is founded in a strong belief in the legitimacy and strength of a Palestinian democracy that begins at grassroots level. Although many people at the meetings verbally criticized democracy and dismissed it as a foreign and/or Western idea, the same people unknowingly participated in and supported the democratic process. They respected majority opinion, contributed their ideas, cooperated with the discussion process, respected others and completed a survey. Both Nationalists and Islamists expressed their interest in election and democracy.

A survey was also conducted in the West Bank and Gaza to assess grassroots opinion regarding democracy and elections. An overwhelming majority supported the development of a democratic process and electoral system. Majority opinions expressed including support for general elections, a democratic republic, political election, direct presidential and mayoral elections, multi-party system, referendum for election law, and the right of women to vote and run for office.

Clearly, Palestinians were interested in proceeding with discussions and preparations for democracy and elections. However, within the time frame of elections for an interim government, Palestinians are not yet sufficiently prepared. There is a strong need for civic education, training, voter registration, commodities procurement and party organization in order to organize elections. Palestinians also need to select and build consensus on electoral formulas (i.e. proportional representation or single member district and ballot structures), constitutional structures, and a commission for elections.

The quest for democratization continues to challenge Palestinians to look to the future and to build a just society free of violence.

As we have said, the power of nonviolence is within every person. When each of us faces the inner reality that brings freedom and liberation through nonviolence, it is a commitment not only a noble thought, that as humans, regarding our past and thousands of years of changes, we are able to live in a nonviolent world starting from our children, our schools, and communities. Nonviolence can advance the dream of a new generation that there will be no soldiers to kill, and that no artificial lines and claims of nationalism will be used to divide the peoples of the world.

*This paper was originally delivered by **Mubarak Awad** at a conference entitled "Possibilities for Nonviolence in the Palestinian-Israeli Conflict," convened by Palestinian and Israelis for Non-Violence on September 7-8, 1993.*

*Permission granted to reprint by **Mubarak Awad**, Executive Director, Nonviolence International.*

***Mubarak Awad** is the Executive Director of Nonviolence International based in Washington, D.C. He was deported from Israel in 1989 for his nonviolent activities in the Occupied Territories.*

***Laura Bains** is NI's Project Coordinator.*

***David Ritchie** is Managing Editor of the "International Journal of Nonviolence".*

In Search Of A Definition

— *Paul Lansu*

Nonviolence is, in fact, very different from what public opinion imagines it to be. To be sure, it makes itself known first in negative guise as the refusal to violence. But this refusal suggests neither weakness nor passivity. Nor should nonviolence be identified with an absolute pacifism or with non-resistance.

Gandhi the apostle of nonviolence, put it this way : "I would prefer to see India defend her honour by armed force than to see her stand like a coward, watching her defeat without an attempt to defend herself. But I still believe just as strongly that nonviolence is infinitely superior to violence." Nonviolence is not cowardice. On the contrary, as Eustave Thibon wrote : "The violent person is simply a coward who pretends to be bold."

Nonviolence is, above all, a critique of violence. It denounces its misdeeds and contradictions. Far from redressing injustice, violence adds further injustice. Even when it does not kill people, it shows scant respect for their integrity or dignity. Violence is a force which escapes the control of reason. Put positively, nonviolence is the affirmation of an alternative view of force. It is a clear-sighted power which uses means proportionate to the goal it sets itself. For, as Gandhi wrote : "The end is in the means as the tree is in the seed." It is the power of reason and truth, the power of morality and the human spirit. It is what in Brazil is called principled firmness and in the Philippines the power of the weak, the power of the soul. And it is in this way that Pope John Paul II defined nonviolence in 1985 in Guatemala: "an active commitment to achieve justice."

Nonviolence is not mere passivity or an internal disposition, but a constant way of acting which names acts of violence for what they are, as Pope John Paul II consistently did before, during and after the Gulf War. Nonviolence refuses to cooperate with evil and injustice. Nonviolent reaction to acts of violence is reaching out in goodwill towards the perpetrators of violence together with a willingness to suffer ourselves rather than make others the victim of violence in retaliation.

Thus, nonviolence is a series of acts of choosing life rather than injury or death - whether physical, psychological, social or cultural. Habitual nonviolence results in a deep peace of heart based upon an integrated love of ourselves, of God's gratuitous nature, of our neighbours in our one world and of God the creator, redeemer and sanctifier.

This definition has been confirmed by subsequent events. In the Third World we saw it in the overthrow of President Marcos in the Philippines in 1986. In 1989, we saw it in Central and Eastern Europe with the "velvet revolution" in Czechoslovakia and the destruction of the Berlin wall. In his *encyclical Solicitudo rei socialis*, John Paul II puts it this way : "The events of 1989 in Eastern and Central Europe give an example of success achieved by the will to negotiate and gospel values in the face of the enemy who has opted to remain unhindered by moral principles. . . Many people learn to strive without violence for justice, having recourse to the class struggle in national conflict and no recourse to war in international conflicts!"

At the end of August 1991, the failure of the coup against President Gorbachev endorsed this analysis. The military coup leaders were divided and finally retreated before the determination of the Moscow crowds, which peacefully deployed their strength in defense of their Parliament and their human rights. The military hesitated to use its full violent might.

It was defeated by people power. It was not western armour which overthrew a communism which the realists called immovable. It was peace power of a newly awakened people, convinced of their intrinsic worth and rights. Principled firmness and people power proved stronger than military might.

Can this nonviolent power experienced in those actions and strategies be used to defend a nation against a foreign aggressor? What is certain is that all the Popes have consistently affirmed that "the theory of the just war as a way of resolving conflicts is now outdated" (24 December 1944). It is even "the most barbaric and least effective means" (1 January 1982). The Gulf War showed the accuracy of these statements. The Lithuanian resistance to the aggressors from the (former) USSR hinted at a new way forward.

However, the problem that the champions of the nonviolent cause have to address is how to find new ways of resolving international conflicts, ways which are in accord with human dignity and more effective than outmoded war. This quest has been initiated by some researchers in France, for instance, Christian Mellon, Jean-Marie Muller and Jacques Senelon in their book on civil defense. They agree that "nonviolent defense alone cannot prevent an enemy from entering a country and occupying it militarily." But they also point out that "the heart of the conflict is in everyday life." The most recent events confirm the wisdom of this fresh approach.

They show too that real possibilities exist for civil defense. The expressed will of the people to resist an armed intervention from outside prevented such an intervention from happening. Starting from examples such as these, it remains for us to analyze the means adopted, in conditions which allowed them to succeed and the possibility of improving them and extending their influence. What happened relatively spontaneously must now become the product of careful preparation. So it is that nonviolent defense will no longer be a dream but a meaningful formation process based on experience and good practice.

Nonviolent action brings the power of love into play in the arena of conflict. Nonviolent action uses only means that promote the well being of all parties to the conflict. Those who act nonviolently seek to overcome enmity rather than to impose their own will on their adversaries. To the extent that nonviolent action succeeds in any given instance, it changes the situation itself from one of dominance and submission to a state of mutual respect for human rights and active concern for the genuine need of all parties to the conflict. As Gandhi pointed out. Nonviolent action seeks to overcome the enemy, and make the enemy a friend.

Paul Lansu *is a political activist connected with Pax Christi International in Brussels, Belgium.*

Reverence For Life

— Bernie S. Siegel

"In the midst of darkness, light persists;
In the midst of despair, hope persists;
In the midst of death, life persists."

— Gandhi

Recently I read an article stating that extra-terrestrials have not contacted earth because they found no signs of intelligent life here. My response was that they were looking in the wrong places and instead of looking at people they needed to look at nature.

As a physician I learned what science without humanity did to people. I saw and heard from my patients their need to learn how to live and it was often their disease, their darkness, that became the gift that led them to find their true path in life and heal their spirit and soul.

I have seen what hope does when dealing with life threatening illness. I know what it does for the human body and spirit and how necessary it is if we are going to survive adverse circumstances.

I also know that accepting death as inevitable frees us to truly live fully in this moment and contribute to life in our unique way. We thus became a beacon and light the way for others.

The Bible tells us that after God created the universe He said, "And it was good." After creating humans no such statement was made. So what can nature teach us.

Communicate with nature and you will learn how to deal with life and all its difficulties. Most people feel life is unfair but I disagree. It is fair. The rules are the same for all of us. However, it is difficult, painful and full of problems. That is life. How does nature survive? Observe it.

I have learned lessons from our two cats, Miracle and Penny. Miracle is an

Orthodox Jew, short-haired, black and white. Penny is Catholic, long-haired, brown and yellow. What have I learned from them? I have learned that despite their differences they can live together, nurture each other and share food, warmth and love. We are all the same color inside.

From nature I have learned a reverence for all life and that our creator loves us. I am in awe as a scientist. I see something as simple as a wound heal. I see the incredible universe and I know the Creator loves me and all of creation. There are no exceptions, to His love and there should be none to ours.

Because humans are imperfect we have been given the opportunity to become God-like. When we love, accept, forgive and realize the earth is our gift to our children we approach a point where God may look and say of us, "and it was good".

Let us understand there are deeds that we will not like but that all people are loveable.

Let us become aware of the child in each of us and love and nurture that child so it grows to be a loving human being.

Let us treat each other and the earth as a loving mother would and let us commit ourselves to love and revere all life without exception.

Let us be there to support, nurture and love one another through our actions so that every living thing will achieve its greatest potential and we will live in harmony and peace.

Darkness, despair and death will still exist but in the presence of love they cannot destroy nor defeat the human spirit.

Dr. Bernard S. Siegel *is a surgeon, an author and God's child.*

Nonviolence - A New Way for Russia

— *Andrey E. Serikov*

Many people in Russia share a stereotype that the quality of their lives totally depends on the political system in the country. For more than seventy years communists were 'building' socialism, and now the new government is 'building' capitalism. People are so used to radical constructions and reconstructions of the political system that many of them cannot think about solving social problems in any other way. They believe that an ideal social structure must exist and as soon as it becomes reality all societal blunders will go away.

This stereotype is very dangerous : if an ideal society exists and promises to everyone, why do people not use the most effective means to get there? Unfortunately, many people think that the most effective means of social change is the use of force, so they are ready to tolerate violence today in the name of a better society of tomorrow. In practice it turns out to be violence forever.

History demonstrates that no political system, nor any social structure, can guarantee that all people will be kind to each other. No law can define all possible human activities as either good or bad. So no law can prevent us from 'commerce without morality', 'politics without principles', or 'science without humanity'. Under any political conditions people need to defend their freedoms, economical independence and health. Only by doing it nonviolently can they escape creating new social problems. There is no pure capitalist or socialist society on the Earth, but there are societies more violent and less violent.

Mohandas K. Gandhi believed that the Seven Blunders of the World he pointed out were the cause of violence. On the other hand, the first Russian apostle of nonviolence, Leo Tolstoy, argued that all social evils were caused by the use of violence. Many other prominent people saw violence as very essential to all societal blunders and thought that only consistent nonviolence can be a real tool for improving society. As Leo Tolstoy put it, 'all attempts to end slavery by violence resemble extinguishing fire with fire.'

As to effectiveness of nonviolence, I do not have to remind you about M.K. Gandhi's, M.L. King's, and other successful nonviolent movements. Maybe a comparison of two recent episodes from Russian political history would be also of interest. During the coup in August 1991, supporters of the Parliament gathered in front of 'the White House' to defend it nonviolently. Their consistent nonviolence became one of the crucial factors that prevented the army from fighting against them, so finally the Parliament won. In September—October 1993, new defenders of the Parliament gathered at the same place for the same reason. However, at that time only some of them intended to be nonviolent and too many were ready to use guns. Were the defenders of 'The White House' consistently nonviolent again, the majority of the public and the army would probably support them sooner or later against those who violated the Constitution. But on October 3, supporters of the parliament were the first who spilled blood, and after that the majority of the Russian population silently watched tanks firing at the Parliament.

The more violence there is in a country's history, the more violently people live in it because they are used to violence. There were too many wars and revolutions, too much blood spilled in Russia during the last century. So the message of nonviolence is of special importance in this country. And since politics here is strongly associated with violence, I think that Russian people can get the best experience of nonviolence by taking part in nonpolitical nonviolent movements directed towards solving some particular problems of their lives.

Probably the most vital need now is that for clean environment. Industrial growth, pursued at reckless speed, without effective measurement of economic or social costs, has put 70 million out of 190 million Soviets living in 103 cities in danger of respiratory and other life-shortening diseases from air that carries five and more times the allowed limit of pollutants. Almost three-fourth of the nation's surface water is polluted; one-fourth is completely untreated. The new 'democratic' government continues to build nuclear power plants, radioactive wastes are still being dumped in Russian seas, and unique forests are being decimated at an even faster pace than before.

Being traditionally nonviolent, the environment movement can become a real 'school' of nonviolence in such situations. Greenpeace, for instance, has since 1971, been using bearing witness, civil disobedience, direct actions, demonstrations and remonstrations, boycotts, drawing public attention, and other nonviolent methods to make governments and corporations stop environmentally dangerous projects and operations and to promote ecologically sound alternatives. The Russian branch of Greenpeace has been working for three years on ocean ecology, forests, toxic trade, disarmament, and nuclear energy issues; there is also a plan to start a Volga River campaign. All these problems are vital for Russians and many of them want to take active part in the Greenpeace movement. Participating in Greenpeace activities they learn how to use nonviolence and how to be nonviolent in different situations.

For thousands of Greenpeace supporters in Russia a new experience was to collect signatures against building nuclear plants. But let me show one more interesting example. In September 1993, Greenpeace together with local green activists blockaded a courier that illegally operated on the territory of the national nature preserve Samarskaya Luka. As a part of preparations to the action, all participants discussed to what extent they must be nonviolent if the courier workers would fight against the blockaders. It turned out that the local greens wanted to fight back, but Greenpeacers insisted on complete nonviolence in any case; and that was the final decision. Fortunately, the workers did not start fighting that time, but it was extremely important that all blockaders were ready to resist only nonviolently.

To conclude, nonviolence is not only a new way of acting for many Russians, it is a new way of thinking. That is why it is so important to show everyone that :

No political system itself can be a paradise;

Nonviolent step-by-step transformation of society is more reliable in the long term than any rapid, but violent change;

Consistent nonviolence is effective.

Andrey E. Serikov was born in 1963 in the Moscow region. Upon graduating in 1982, from a technical school in Odessa, Andrey worked and served in the army. In 1986-1991, he studied at Moscow University, in the Department of Sociology. Then in 1989-1990, he took classes on sociology at Indiana University, in the United States of America. Since 1992, he has been a graduate student of Moscow Institute of Philosophy and takes an active part in Ethics of Nonviolence. He is also an activist in the Russian branch of Greenpeace.

Pursuit Of True Knowledge

— Glen Lockhart

For one to have a wealth of knowledge on which to draw upon is a wonderful thing. Yet, it seems, many who are in this enviable position fail to use this in such a way that it could be even more beneficial potential than they know it to be. They fail to discover or to unlock the full potential of what possessing this knowledge can do, and so, rob it of a large amount of good it could accomplish. Because of this, one would have to question whether that person was aware of what knowledge really is.

Knowledge can be taught, but what one learns is not necessarily knowledge. There is a point, though, where it can become knowledge.

To illustrate this, I offer the following example. Back when I attended school, I had one classmate who was undoubtedly intelligent. He could process and retain information; he could apply it in a logical way to any problem, even those that were, to the rest of us, seemingly impossible to solve. He always received very high marks, and the teachers doted on him, for he was something rare — a star pupil. He graduated from high school at the top of the class and went on to one of the most prestigious universities in Canada, where he continued to excel at his chosen field of study. Here, too, he was gifted. Learning came easily to him and he never had any difficulty in his pursuit of knowledge; he graduated very highly here, also.

Did he truly have knowledge? Some would say yes. I would venture to answer no, that he was merely book-smart. There is a difference.

The tragedy of the situation was that while he was busy enriching his mind, he failed to cultivate a personality. Always busy studying, he never really became "one of the gang" and seemed to give the impression that everything the rest of us did was trivial in comparison to his all-consuming pursuit of knowledge. However, while he realized dividenda from this personally, he paid dearly for it.

It was not debatable that he was very intelligent; in fact he was held in awe by many because of this, but he had missed out on a lot and this became evident whenever anyone asked for either his opinion of something or for his help to explain something not understood. Unfortunately, he did not know how to bring himself down to the level of the person requesting the assistance and speak to them in a way that they could understand. He always talked somewhere above them. This was not done purposely to show off or to irritate people, it was just that he really did not know how to relate to anyone.

In reality, by doing this, he showed a lack of knowledge. Perhaps if he had participated more in those after supper touch football and road hockey games, he would have become more relaxed and at ease with people, and then been able to pass around his knowledge for everyone's benefit.

Knowledge is useless when it resides in only one persons mind, especially when that person is either unable or unwilling to share it. Knowledge should be something open to all, and all should avail themselves of the chance to pursue it and gain it.

Knowledge, though, is not just what one learns from a book. Book learning can supply one with fact, but fact does not equal knowledge. True knowledge is only arrived at when fact from learning is combined with life experience. Only the person who is interested in other people as well as in learning stands the chance to achieve true knowledge. Embracing one without the other is to fall into a trap, for life is not just about pure fact, and human beings are social animals. Failure to recognize this only serves to make one half a person. When one can relate to other people, no matter what their status or circumstances or interest, then one gains true knowledge, for true knowledge also includes wisdom, which is achieved only by recognizing the experience of others.

The *Mahatma* believed that knowledge without character was one of what he referred to as the Seven Blunders of the World, which were (and still are) responsible for contributing to the violence we see around us. I have illustrated what the consequence is of only one person guilty of this blunder, but it is obvious that many in our society are also guilty of doing this. With this magnification of occurrences comes a compounding of the problems to the extent that society as a whole tends to follow the same misguided path.

However, let us not be too harsh regarding this, In many cases, this may not be intentional, it may be human nature. This is something though, that we must all work to eradicate in ourselves. We must become enlightened enough to see this fault, and when we can say that we ourselves no longer harbour it, we must help others to identify and eliminate it in themselves, also. Only in this way will we all become truly knowledgeable, truly wise. When we realize that those things that divide us are ultimately only petty differences, we will be freed to embark upon this task without reservation. Only through understanding, gained from knowledge with character, will we be successful in accomplishing this.

This does not have to be a slow procedure, nor does the task have to be long and arduous. If a large percentage of us are willing, at this moment, to see the fault and folly in ourselves and improve upon this, we can become a truly global people in a relatively short period of time.

Through understanding gained with knowledge, we can change those negative things that we do not like about ourselves and the society we live in. If we could all, as human beings, do this and come to some kind of consensus on the situation, there would be no need for tyranny, no opening in which injustice may flourish. But only when we are able to see and correct our own shortcomings will we be comfortable to see those of others. This is something that can be done simultaneously, in every country of the world. The creation of an internation knowledge with character, containing that of ourselves in combination with that of our neighbors, must be our ultimate goal.

It seems we are already off to a good start in achieving this, As I make these observations in September 1993, the prospect for a world of peace and justice have never looked better. In fact, the events of the last five years have brought us closer to this goal than the events of the five hundred years to this point in time. We are making significant gains, but we can not afford to reduce the pressure even for a moment.

There are still trouble spots in our world that must be cleared up, and we must realize that there will be more in the future unless we channel our energies into avoiding any more of these occurrences. We must not allow ourselves to get frustrated or discouraged in this task, rather we must be relentless in our pursuit. How wonderful it would be if we could achieve this before the year 2,000. Let us all now commit ourselves to this.

Let us not worry about being accused of having too much optimism, for as we all know optimism is something we could use a lot more of in our world. No one ever sets out on a journey full of doubt, for that would be counterproductive to the goal. Any positive accomplishment is better than lack of accomplishment.

Can the *Mahatma's* vision become reality? Yes, we are prepared to make it so, but we must realize that the first step begins with ourselves.

Glenn Lockhart is a North American Aborigine, Ojibwe (Chippewa). He is a Postal Clerk and an active worker in the Canadian Union of Postal Workers. His hobbies include history and political science as well as labour studies. For relaxation he does woodwork.

Ten Fringe Benefits In A world Without Violence

— Steve O'Donnell

1. Retooled electric chair waffle irons.

2. Aircraft carrier Midway now known as The Love Boat

3. Cartoon cats & cartoon mice given separate houses in which they can peacefully pursue their respective hobbies.

4. Kickboxer Jean Claude Van Damme comes to your house to give your malfunctioning TV a good whack.

5. Remodeled "Pentagon Motel" boasts a thousand rooms.

6. Worked-up crowds leave soccer matches and neatly repaint the stadium.

7. Top-quality lawn care by former Green Berets.

8. New Arnold Schawarzennegger hit : The Big Fluffy Teddy Bear Who Came To Life And For Some Reason Spoke With An Austrian Accent.

9. Unexpected Terrorist hugs.

10. Nerf Missiles.

Steve O'Donnel is a humorist who lives in New Work. His work has appeared in The New York Times, The Rolling Stones, and Spy. He is currently a writer for The Late Show with David Letterman on CBS-TV.

Morality And Politics :
The Lessons Of Gandhi

— Grazina Miniotaite

If I can say without arrogance and with due humility, my message and methods are indeed, in their essentials, for the whole world.

— M.K. Gandhi

It is not the bloody revolutions, the devastating wars the advanced industry of destruction of life, but rather nonviolent victories against violence that will be the mark of the 20th century. Recognition and activation of the power inherent in active nonviolence, its purposeful use for the solution of social and political conflicts is indeed a new turn in human history.

It is no accident that the beginning of the turn is associated with the name of M. Gandhi. A. Einstein called him the teacher of mankind. Gandhi was the first to break the paradigm of violence, to lay the intellectual foundations and to practically implement the option of nonviolent social and political change. The subsequent story of the success of nonviolence is alive in every culture, in every human being, that it does not need to be imported (as arms), it only needs to be awakened and then cultivated and prudently used. Nonviolent liberation of Eastern Europe has proved the case of nonviolence once again.

Yet sooner or later nearly every student of the history of the use of nonviolent means in politics finds himself confronted with the baffling question : "Why it so happens that after a goal has been achieved by nonviolent means, there is often a reversal to violent, military solutions of social and political problems?" India, the Philippines, Russia, to take only some recent cases, are the obvious examples. Well, in every particular case one is offered a particular justification for the use of violence. Yet a more penetrating analysis, based on the experience of Gandhi, helps to identify the common cause of the phenomenon, namely, the dominant conception of the relation between morals and politics.

It is usually taken for granted that in politics, concerned as it is with the attainment of immediate goals, the most important thing is the practical efficiency, not the moral purity of methods used. The means are seen as neutral instruments which can be used both for the good and the bad. Gandhi has decisively rejected this kind of attitudes. In 1919 he started a nonviolent campaign for the liberation of India - the so called *satyagraha*. After several years of effort, when the mass campaign was already in full sway, he put on the brakes, despite a strong opposition from his followers. This was because he found it altogether unacceptable, both from the moral and strategic point of view, that the campaign was acquiring violent forms. Having chosen a nontraditional way of achieving political goals, the one based on peoples reason, goodwill and solidarity, Gandhi saw his task as nothing less than a revolution in people's mind. "Nonviolence to be a potent force must begin with the mind", he wrote. And he stressed that real understanding of the essence of active nonviolence leads to an essential change in the relations between people.

The power inherent in nonviolence is the power of truth, of good and of love. Yet since no one is able to comprehend at a glance the whole world and its essence, there can be no absolutely right or absolutely wrong point of view, and it is primarily the means used, the concrete actions, that show the justice or injustice of the ends: "the means is the end in the making". Gandhi saw, as few saw before, and has practically shown the whole world the importance of the means, the role of morals in the art of choosing the means, in politics. He wrote : "As the means so the end ... Our progress towards the goal will be in exact proportion to the purity of our means. This method may appear to be long, perhaps too long, but I am convinced that it is the shortest." The quotation concentrates the main lesson that Gandhi has taught his contemporaries and future generations. One can also discern in it the answer to the question why nonviolent victories have usually been rather short episodes in human history. For once a nonviolent victory is achieved, the arena is occupied by professional politicians whose "great" goals — the supremacy of the nation, of the state, of the empire - can only be achieved by violent means. So long as the moral reason (in the Gandhian, the Kantian sense of respect for persons) does not penetrate the domain of politics, violence remains the dominant means of conflict resolution.

Grazina Miniotaite (b. 1948), Ph.D. in Philosophy from Moscow State University. Senior research fellow at the Institute of Philosophy, Sociology and Law of the Lithuanian Academy of Sciences, President of Lithuanian Centre for Nonviolent Action. Research interests : history of ethics, morals and politics, the theory of nonviolent action. Major publications include : **Kantian Ideas in Recent Moral Philosophy** *(1988);* **Civil Disobedience : Theory and Practice** *(1991);* **Nonviolent Strategy in the Liberation Movements : The Case of Lithuania** *(1993).*

Resist Not Evil

— Martin E. Hellman

The Russian writer, Count Leo Tolstoy, was credited by Gandhi as being one of the key influences in development of nonviolent resistance. Gandhi even named his South African commune, Tolstoy Farm. Tolstoy had wrestled with spirituality, first rejecting religion in favour of modern "scientific" view of creation, then turning back to the Russian Orthodox Church of his youth, and finally rejecting the Church's dogmatism in an essay that led to his excommunication. Tolstoy gives the following account of the moment when the veil was lifted and he first understood true spirituality and the path to nonviolence:

The passage which served me as a key to the whole was Mathew, v.38,39: "Ye have heard that it was said, An eye for an eye and a tooth for a tooth; but I say unto you, Resist not him that is evil.". . . . These words suddenly appeared to me as something quite new, as if I had never heard them before. Previously when reading that passage I had always, by some strange blindness, omitted the words, "But I say unto you, Resist not him that is evil"' just as if those words had not been there, or as if had no definite meaning. Subsequently, in my talks with many Christians familiar with the Gospel, I often had occasion to note the same blindness as to those words. No one remembered them, and often when speaking about the passage Christians referred to the Gospel to verify the fact that the words were really there. (Leo Tolstoy, A Confession, The Gospels in Brief, and What I Believe, translated by Aylmer Maurde, Oxford University Press, 1971, pp 316-317).

What could Tolstoy (and Jesus) possibly have meant? Is it not our duty to resist evil? In his flash of inspiration, Tolstoy saw that, in resisting evil, we usually become the very evil we seek to destroy, perhaps worse. In resisting the evils present in communism, the United States built 30,000 nuclear weapons. These actions created an evil far greater than those it resisted; the real danger that civilisation will be destroyed.

Similarly, in resisting the evil of nuclear weapons, many people made war on President Reagan, the military, or the scientific community - all of whom had some responsibility for the mess in which we found ourselves. But, in resisting the perceived evil, these people often created their own "evil empires" whose destruction would make the world safe - not an effective way to pose the possibility that love of neighbor is the path to salvation.

In learning to "resist not evil", the playing field need not be international politics, with daily interpersonal relations providing perhaps the best workout. It is easier to "resist not" when the perceived evil is distant and abstract, but much harder when it is an angry spouse in the same room !

I will never forget the day my wife, Dorothie, told me that I had to love her even when she was angry. Going further she informed me that at such times I had to love her, not in spite of, but because she was angry. After my initial shock and resistance, I realised that, while it was extremely uncomfortable for me when she was angry, I would not eliminate her angry times even if I could - which of course I could not. Many things that she needed to say, and I needed to hear, only came out when she was angry. I later came to see another benefit of Dorothie's demand; I could ask her for the same consideration, and was thus able to be heard in a way that before had seemed impossible.

As we learned to hear each other better, we came to see that our anger was usually a result of not having been able to say things that needed to be said, or not having been adequately heard. Once we could express ourselves and be heard, the anger had less chance to build.

Learning to "resist not" - or at least to "resist less" - proved extremely valuable when, from 1984-88, I acted as Director of the Beyond War Foundation's "International Scientific Initiative", an attempt to bridge the gap between a book entitled *Breakthrough : Emerging New Thinking*, published simultaneously in Russian and English in late 1987, during a marathon, two week trip to Moscow in June 1987. In the middle of this exhilarating but physically draining experience, a crisis arose. Alexander Nikitin, one of the Soviet participants, requested a seemingly impossible change in the opening lines of Yale Professor Paul Bracken's paper :

No single dictator, no single event pushed Europe into war in 1914. But during the preceding decade, the nations of Europe had institutionalised the potential for catastrophe. They had built interlocking alert and mobilisation plans that, once triggered, swamped and outran the political control process. It was a disaster waiting to happen.

Nikitin objected, "It makes it sound as if war were a big accident, yet we all know that there were strong historical forces at work". I was furious. The requested change seemed to contradict the thesis of Bracken's Paper : even though no one wants a nuclear war, it is an accident waiting to happen. This was a key paper. There wasn't time to get Bracken to rewrite it. And I didn't want it rewritten. Labouring under my massive resistance to Nikitin's request, I also felt that he had violated a key agreement, not to inject either nation's propaganda into the book, since the phrase "strong historical forces" in this context was often a Soviet code word for "Western colonialism and imperialism". I was incensed but, recognising that expressing my fury would do little to bridge the gap between Soviet and American world views, I muttered something like "I'll have to think about it", and went to cool off. Good thing!

As I dropped my resistance to Nikitin's objections and thought about what he had said, I realised that I had read much into his few words and that I needed to check things out. Moving out of resistance, I could become more creative. I called Nikitin and suggested adding a phrase so the second sentence of the paper read : *"But during the preceding decade, motivated by various political and economic self-interests, the nations of Europe had institutionalised the potential for catastrophe"*. Nikitin agreed that this minor change took care of his objection, Bracken approved the change, and the book came out on time.

On many similar occasions, I have found "resist not evil" to magically bring forth a bountiful harvest from seemingly barren soil. In order for you to decide for yourself if there is truth in this adverb, I highly recommend trying "resist not" as an experiment and seeing how it works in your life. On this celebration of the one hundred twenty-fifth anniversary of Gandhi's birth into this world, I will seek trying to read the mind of a departed soul, and say that I believe Gandhi would second the motion.

__Dr. Martin E. Hellman__ is currently Professor of Electrical Engineering at Stanford University, where he has also served as Associate Chair of The EE Department and Associate Dean of Graduate Studies concerned with minority student affairs. __Dr. Hellman__ has authored over 60 technical papers, 5 US and a number of foreign patents and has a strong interest in the intersection of ethics and technological development. In this capacity, he has been a spokesman for ensuring privacy in the rapidly growing telecommunications field, with Prof. Anatoly Gromyko of Moscow, co-edited __Breakthrough: Emerging New Thinking__, a book dealing with issues of war and peace, published simultaneously in Russian and English during the rapid change in Soviet-American relations.

Get Rid Of The Prophets

— Bernt Jonsson

Visionaries and prophets are rare. They are bold enough to challenge the wisdom of the day. They are charismatic enough to get committed followers. They are persistent enough to struggle with deeply rooted resistance.

They are often the result of a simultaneous appearance of societal oppression, political forces, economic exploitation, religious beliefs and personal gifts and dedication. They tend not to appear in true democracies. It seems as if people can only be ennobled in situations of oppression. As a consequence, the price visionaries and prophets pay is often very high, not seldom with their lives.

Conventional wisdom has it that conflicts normally are dealt with in a violent way. Therefore you had better prepare yourself - as an individual, as a group or as a nation. In the best case, you are supposed to be able to deter your adversary. In the worst case, you will have to teach him a lesson. Your right to self defence is a part of the UN Charter.

Thanks to conventional wisdom called "realism" the world experienced an incredible arms race after World War II, wasting not only money but also natural resources and human lives. In the name of security, nuclear arms made the world more insecure than ever before. And thanks to the same conventional wisdom, a number of conflicts have over the years erupted into violence, hatred, human suffering and even massacres.

History has seen quite a few prophets of nonviolence: Jesus, Mohandas K. Gandhi, Martin Luther King - just to mention a few. They and several other anonymous advocates of nonviolence have been killed. Their challenge and provocation has been too difficult to cope with. Therefore, the conclusion among the powers that be: get rid of the prophets, quick fix, and gone with the wind is the concept of nonviolence - that has been the idea, the unrealistic idea.

We may dream of a world without violence, even if the odds are bad, but should we dream of a world without conflicts? Would we like to live in such a world? Would we live in such a world? No! It would be the peace of the grave.

The overwhelming majority of conflicts between individuals, groups and nations, however, are solved in a peaceful, nonviolent manner, that should not be forgotten. Democracy is basically a doctrine about conflict management.

It is often understood as just being majority decision, but an overwhelming majority as such - be it the result of a democratic election process - it not enough in itself to make a decision truly democratic. In order to be a democratic decision it has also to be consistent with democratic values like respect for minority rights and other basic human rights. Democracy is therefore above all a method for solving conflicts with peaceful means.

This fact should not be overlooked by advocates of nonviolence, when they search for a bridge-head for a political strategy. There is another possible bridge-head available too: The doctrine of common security.

It's true that the Palme Commission in their report "Common Security" in 1982 only proposed a number of military measures to de-escalate the then very dangerous nuclear arms race, but the philosophy of common security is much more far-reaching.

The very starting point of this thinking is the shared interest in human survival, which is not only more positive but also more realistic as a frame of reference than the threat of mutually assured destruction - MAD - the basis for the doctrine of nuclear deterrence. In contrast to the old "realism", based on arms (hard ware), the new one could be termed "soft ware realism", i.e. based on mutual interest and relationships.

In the common efforts to build up in stead of threatening to destroy, nonviolent methods have to be used - in the enlightened self-interest. As the use of violence becomes too dangerous and self-destructive as a way of solving conflicts, the Gandhian vision becomes the only realistic one for the future.

Bernt Jonsson *is a mathematician, theologian and social scientist from Sweden. He worked in the Student Chrisstian Movement in the 60s. He is a well known journalist in press, radio and TV and political advisor to the Swedish Government on education, foreign affairs and disarmament issues. Presently he is Director of the Life & Peace Institute, an international ecumenical peace research institute based in Uppsala, Sweden.*

The Causes Of War

— John M. Swomley

The goal of history is a worldwide community of men and women who have been liberated from war, racism, poverty, imperialism and other major structures of violence, including the destruction of non-human life that is a part of our total environment.

The elimination or the conversion of violent individuals does not deal with the war system or other structures of violence, which all of us have inherited. These structures which humans have collectively erected have attained a dynamism and virtual autonomy of their own. Almost 2,000 years ago a Christian writer said, "Our fight is not against any physical enemy; it is against organizations and powers ..." *(Ephesians 6:12, Phillips translation).* Another translation of the same statement says : "For ours is not a conflict with mere flesh and blood but with the despotisms, the empires, the forces that control and govern." (Weymouth translation). A concentration on changing systems does not mean that persons are less important; they are so important that they must not be used as tools of any system. Moreover, it is human who must change systems, and that requires a change of thinking.

The primary form of violence in our world is war. However, there is no cause of war that lies outside the war system. Injustice, oppression, human greed, and other so-called causes of war have existed without causing war, The one indispensable component or ingredient for making war is the institution of war itself, with its armies, navies, air forces, missiles, weapons which destroy towns, cities and human beings; and the military economy and industry that make those weapons. Until that institution or system is dismantled in nation after nation, wars will continue.

A disarmed world is a world without national or regional armed forces. It is not a world without police forces. Most previous disarmament proposals permitted some form of internal national militia for riot control, but without offensive weapons that would be used against other nations. In a disarmed world there would be no justification for a world organization or government to have a world armed force to be used against cities, states and regions. In fact, cities or states without private possession of guns could have unarmed police, along the lines of the traditional London "bobby".

The war system is undergirded by political and economic structures that permit some people to have unusual power and cause others to have little. Government structures put the war-making decision in the hands of a relatively small group of persons whose interest are determined by their positions in the military, financial and political systems. Decentralization of power is essential to ending the war system.

The pacifist analysis of history differs from the Marxist analysis. The Marxist analysis is based on the assumption that wars will end with the abolition of capitalism. In other words, the way to peace is through justice. Pacifism, however holds that justice is a by-product of a disarmed or nonviolent state. As A.J. Muste put it, "There is no way to peace, peace is the way". Injustice is therefore a by-product of structural violence and must be opposed by nonviolent means.

Pacifists advocate nonviolent methods rather than the idea that violence must be met with violence. Nonviolent struggle such as strikes, boycotts and disobedience and sit-ins can be said to be successful if they accomplish a limited purpose and if that achievement results in some transfer of power or in partial demonstration so that new demands can be made from a position of greater strength. The concept of nonviolence requires the paying of the price for liberation rather than exacting the price from others by killing or enslaving or oppressing them.

The term "nonviolence" as used by both Gandhi and Martin Luther King was not the mere absence of violence but shorthand for the social and economic power of non-cooperation plus the moral power of voluntary suffering for others.

History records not only the use of violence in the conquest of other people, but the use of nonviolent methods for liberation. Nonviolent methods not only freed India from British rule but were responsible for the ending of colonial rule in scores of countries around the world. African-Americans in the United States and rights for women were won by nonviolent methods. Nonviolence is not utopian, but the ultimate effective form of power, since imposition of military force is eventually unstable and breeds antagonism and resistance.

*John M. Swomley, author of **Liberation Ethics, The Politics of Liberation**, and other books; National Secretary of the Fellowship of Reconciliation 1953-60; Professor emeritus, Saint Paul School of Theology, Kansas City, Missouri. Ph D in Political Science.*

Commitment To A Culture Of Nonviolence

— Hans Kung

Numberless women and men of all regions and religions strive to lead lives not determined by egoism but by commitment to their fellow humans and to the world around them. Nevertheless, all over the world we find endless hatred, envy, jealousy, and violence, not only between individuals but also between social and ethnic groups, between classes, races, nations, and religions. The use of violence, drug trafficking and organized crime, often equipped with new technical possibilities, has reached new global proportions. Many places still are ruled by terror "from above", dictators oppress their own people, and institutional violence is widespread. Even in some countries where laws exist to protect individual freedoms, prisoners are tortured, men and women are mutilated, hostages are killed.

a) In the great ancient religious and ethical traditions of humankind we find the directive: You shall not kill! Or in positive terms : Have respect for life! Let us reflect anew on the consequences of this ancient directive : All people have a right to life, safety, and the free development of personality insofar as they do not injure the rights of others. No one has the right physically or psychically to torture, injure, much less kill, any other human being. And no people, no state, no race, no religion has the right to hate, to discriminate against, to "cleanse," to exile, much less to liquidate a "foreign" minority which is different in behavior or holds different beliefs.

b) Of course, whenever there are humans there will be conflicts. Such conflicts, however should be resolved without violence within a framework of justice. This is true for states as well as for individuals. Persons who hold political power must work within the framework of a just order and commit themselves to the most nonviolent, peaceful solutions possible. And they work for this within an international order of peace which itself has need of protection and defense against perpetrators of violence. Armament is a mistaken path; disarmament is a commandment of the times. Let no one be deceived : There is no survival for humanity without global peace!

c) Young people must learn at home and in school that violence may not be a means of settling differences with others. Only thus can a culture of nonviolence be created.

d) A human person is infinitely precious and must be unconditionally protected. But likewise the lives of animals and plants which inhabit this planet with us deserve protection, preservation, and care. Limitless exploitation of the natural foundations of life, ruthless destruction of the biosphere, and militarization of the cosmos are all outrages. As human beings we have a special responsibility — especially with a view to future generations — for Earth and the cosmos, for the air, water, and soil. We are all intertwined together in this cosmos and we are all dependent on each other. Each one of us depends on the welfare of all. Therefore the dominance of humanity over nature and the cosmos must not be encouraged. Instead we must cultivate living in harmony with nature and the cosmos.

e) To be authentically human in the spirit of our great religious and ethical traditions means that in public as well as in private life we must be concerned for others and ready to help. We must never be ruthless and brutal. Every people, every race, every religion must show tolerance and respect — indeed high appreciation — for each other. Minorities need protection and support, whether they be racial, ethnic, or religious.

*The Parliament of the World's Religions in Chicago promulgated this text on September 4, 1993. This text is an integral part of **The Declaration Toward A Global Ethic**. **Dr. Hans Kung** is the author of the draft of this declaration. **Dr. Kung** says he can witness to the fact that for this part of the declaration he felt greatly encouraged by the great teaching and life model of Mahatma Gandhi who himself was inspired by the message of nonviolence of Jesus of Nazreth.*

(Permission to reprint granted by Dr Hans Kung.)

The Recipe For Violence

— Anita Roddick

Trading is one of the oldest human activities. It developed to satisfy the mutual needs of the peoples of the ancient world. But once need is supplanted by greed, you have commerce without morality which simply divides the world into camps: exploiters and exploited, with the latter dependent on the former's arbitrary largesse. And, as Gandhi pointed out, that is a recipe for violence.

I'm a great believer in business as a force for social change. Just imagine what could be achieved if the combined wills of multinationals were bent towards leaving the world a better place than they found it. But such change can only be brought about if profits and principles are inextricably interwoven. A company needs core values and the way it does business should express those values.

The most fundamental must surely be a respect for basic human rights, which increasingly encompasses environmental issues as well. This whole area becomes even more topical as the need of big business for resources takes it into undeveloped regions in the majority world, where the precedents — if they exist — for commercial relationships tend to be petarnalistic or, worse, unscrupulous. But if we accept self-determination as a basic human right, then we in the developed world need a whole new approach to our trading relationships with those in the majority world. Rather than simply taking what we need, we have to look at giving something back, such as help for communities to acquire the tools and resources they need to support themselves. When a company as big as The Body Shop trades with a small community somewhere in the majority world, the benefits must flow both ways for the relationship to be useful in the long term.

The benefits are clear for the indigenous community. You can be pragmatic as you like about what constitutes benefits for the trading partner in the developed world. Take The Body Shop as an example : we have tried to educate our customers to know the story behind what they buy, so that they can use their purchasing power to make informed, responsible choices. By endeavoring to establish complete cradle-to-grave product stewardship, we can reassure our customers that our trade supports neither exploitation of an underclass nor environmental degradation.

Awareness of the consequences of one's actions hopefully steers one away from shortsighted or short-term courses of action. That makes excellent sense in a business world which gets more competitive by the minute. So values are not just an antidote to the violence bred by commerce without morality. They are an aid to success.

Anita Roddick has successfully demonstrated that nonviolence and humanistic approach could be practised in commerce through her enterprise. The internationally well-known Body-shops have lived that experience and Anita now speaks on this subject all over Europe and the globe.

Nonviolence Does Work

— Walter Wink

The way of nonviolence and love of enemies has frequently been dismissed as impractical, idealistic, and out of touch with the need of nations and oppressed people to defend themselves. No such irrelevancy is charged against violence, however, despite the fact that it always fails at least half the time. Its exaltation of the salvific powers of killing, and the pledged position it is accorded by intellectuals and politicians alike, to say nothing about theologians, make redemptive violence the preferred myth of Marxist and capitalists, fascists and leftists, atheists and churchgoers alike.

Then came 1989-1990, years of unprecedented political change, years of miracles, surpassing any such concentration of political transformation in human history, even the exodus. In 1989 alone, thirteen nations comprising 1,695,100,000 people, over 32 percent of humanity, experienced nonviolent revolutions that succeeded beyond anyone's wildest expectations in every case but China, and were completely nonviolent (on the part of the participants) in every case but Romania and parts of the U.S.S.R. The nations involved were Poland, East Germany, Hungary, Czechoslovakia, Bulgaria, Romania, Albania, Yugoslavia, Mongolia, the Soviet Union, Brazil, Chile, and China. Since then Nepal, Palau, and Madagascar have undergone nonviolent struggles, Latvia, Lithuania and Estonia have achieved independence nonviolently, the Soviet Union has dissolved into a Commonwealth of Republics, and more than a dozen countries have moved toward multi-party democracy, including Mongolia, Nicaragua, Gabon, Bangaldesh, and Benin. If we add all the countries touched by major nonviolent actions just since 1986 (the Philippines, South Korea, South Africa, Isreal, Burma, New Calcedonia, and New Zealand), and the other nonviolent struggles of our century — the independence movements of India and Ghana, the overthrow of the Shah of Iran, the struggle against authoritarian governments and landowners in Argentina and Mexico, and the civil rights, United Farm Worker, anti-Vietnam and anti-nuclear movements in the U.S. — the figure reaches 3,340,900,000 : a staggering 64 percent of humanity!

All this in the teeth of the assertion, endlessly repeated, that nonviolence does not work in the "real" world.

It appears as if the nonviolent way has finally found a following. The dream of abolishing war, like child sacrifice and exposure, galdiatorial combat, slavery, cannibalism, colonialism and dueling, seems to be finally approaching the first stages of realization.

Dr. Walter Wink is Professor of Biblical Interpretation at Auburn Theological Seminary in New York City. In 1989-1990 he was a Peace Fellow at the United States Institute of Peace.

(Exerpted from "Engaging the Powers" by Dr. Walter Wink, Permission to reprint granted by Fortress Press, Minneapolis.)

"*Whom To Be Blamed*"

— *Kate Lebow*

"*It will not be denied, that a child, before it begins to write its alphabet and to gain knowledge, should know what the soul is, what truth is, what love is, what powers are latent in the soul.*"

"Real education," to Gandhi, was teaching that love is stronger than hate, truth is stronger than violence. Certainly, the school system in South Africa is not designed to teach those things.

"Bantu Education," as it is called, expressly sets out to convince black South African children that they are stupid. It is like a series of hoops they must jump through — but the hoops are crooked shapes and set at uneven heights.

White authorities expect black children to fail; so, too, often, do teachers, parents, and the students themselves. In 1991 (the year I arrived in South Africa), only one in three high school seniors passed the state-set final exams. Few of those who passed received "exemptions", or high marks enabling them to apply to universities; fewer still of those found funding to further their studies.

As an English teacher, my job was to help boost students over the hurdle of the Queen's tongue. Most of my kids were already very expressive — even eloquent — in English. The problem was that they were like Elizabethans : because each one had learned more from radio, TV and each other than from books, school, and elementary-school teachers (who themselves may not have graduated high school), each followed her own unique rules.

I could not keep up with the varied and creative ways my students used prepositions and verb forms. In written work, capitals got sprinkled about with abandon; other punctuation was catch-as catch-can; and as for spelling, "live" and "leave", pronounced the same way in South Africa, "this" and "these", were interchangeable.

"Whom to be blamed?", as one young man wrote; but it was my task to enforce linguistic uniformity, and it was joyless and often less than successful. Students continued to "leave" in Soweto and get "feelings" in their teeth, if they were lucky enough to afford the dentist.

At times it felt viciously absurd to be correcting spelling mistakes, given the violent context of all our lives in South Africa. My red pen held back its blood-like ink on Rudolph's essay about how his best friend had been killed in a tavern shoot-out; on Thulile's, about sexual abuse she had suffered at the hands of her uncle; on Sanny's piece about an armed attack she had witnessed on commuters waiting for the train; and on Grace's mid term exam, in which she wrote about being abducted into an *Inkatha*-supporting men's hostel and being beaten until "the days were over to her".

But the more I read and learned of students' experiences, the more I realized they did not need to come to school to learn "what the soul is, what love is, what truth is, what powers are latent in the soul." That lesson is present everywhere.

For instance :

I spent one night in a tiny village in the foothills of Lesotho. My host lit a small fire in the cornfield behind her house that chased away frosty winter air. All else in the unelectrified village was pitch dark, and we didn't see Mme Mathato and Ntoetsi, a woman and child of the chieftainess's household, until they appeared in the circle of light cast by the fire.

We crouched together in silence, watching the flames leap, feeding them fronds of dry grass when they began to grow dim; and Mme Mathato stood up and stuck her foot in the fire.

After she felt the foot was warm enough, she took it out and put the other in. Then she said goodnight and walked away in bare feet over the stubby field.

Ntoetsi, ten years old, dressed in bright red slacks and sneakers, decided to copy Mme. She let the flames caress her leg and foot, all the while glancing shyly at us. I was terrified that her red pants would burst into flames at any movement. But she just smiled. She was showing us how grown-up she was, and reassuring us, as if to say : Don't worry; I am strong and brave. I will not be hurt.

Kate Lebow is a freelance writer and substitute teacher living in New York City. She taught at the educational Programmes Center, a private high school for township youth in Johannesburg, from 1992.

In 1992, students and teachers at the Educational Programmes Centre in Johannesburg, South Africa, formed a creative writing magazine, called "Eye".

The magazine got its name, according to Thulile Ngidi (then in tenth grade), because it should see all, and also because through it students could express their individual "I's".

Much of the writing in "EYE" concerns the violence that is a part of daily life in the townships. The following three poems contemplate, with remarkable insight and compassion, imaginary perpetrators of such violence. (They are unedited and unexpurgated.)

Magic Man of Soweto

Tebogo Mekgwe

He is the magic man.
He lived in Soweto location in Orlando.
He was unknown man.
He used to walk in the night.
The people called him night man.
He is a dangerous man in Soweto.
The people hate him.

He lived alone in the house.
The neighbours were afraid of him.
The people say he is a killer.
He killed several people of Orlando East.
He is not walking in the
street day light.

Most people say he
is changing in the night.
In the night he looks like woman
That's why people called
him magic man some
times he looks like hose

The police are afraid of him.

He is not the friendly man
His parents were killed by K.B.S.
He doesn't have any member of his
family in Soweto and his name
is Makwero.

The Killer During the Darkness

Lusanda Ntsele

It was dark the night
was human and the
wind was blowing very
strongly in our village
called Sodoma. You
could not see the
palm print of your hand.

The people always stay
Scared. No one knew
the time or the place
he could get in.

He was beaten by the world
so he wanted to take
his anger to the people
of our village. No one
had seen him or his face.

He came during the night
and was scary. No help
was given and everyone
was waiting for his death.

The Death of Makhanda

Tom Buthelezi

He comes from Soweto
A rich place full of happiness
Where people rejoice.

But police are after him.
He is charged with murder and rape.
They are after him as he sleeps in
a cold place.
He is getting diseases,
Dangerous diseases, he is suffering.

His mother cried as she saw him
lying dead in the cold ground.
Freezed as a frozen chicken.

❖ ❖ ❖

The following poems were written as part of an assignment on "color". The last one, "House with beautiful colours", reminds Kate Lebow of the explanation for a better and more peaceful future.

❖ ❖ ❖

Red

Dorah Ramela

Red rose in the garden,
Red blood,
It's beautiful,
It's the brightest of them all,
It's for danger
Dark in the night
It's that red heart
Red for red hot!

Black Colour Poem

Junior Maseko

*the black colour is the colour
that the people show how it
is strong and someone
said i'm going to find
you at night because no
one should see me when
i want to kill you.*

House with Beautiful Colours

Portia Sinhala

*I would like to paint
my home. With red panes
and red burglarproof.
Brown door and black
gates. The beige colour
for the house,*

*Red colour for the
roofing and white walls
Black number for my
house. My house
with beautiful colours.*

World Without Violence

— Terry Michael Tracy

I belive on planet Earth everyone steps to a different drummer. The beat I hear is one of non-violence, but that is what I want. In my world the oceans are blue, the water clear. The rivers run deep, the fish plentiful. Mountains are a majestic purple in the afternoon sun, their peaks mantled with glacier white snow caps. Green meadows, grass blades vibrating in the summer breeze, spread as far as the eye can see. I live with peace and tranquility in a snug harbor of wind chimes and fluffy clouds. We neither watch television nor read newspapers. There is no violence to be seen or felt here. That is how we want it.

On the other hand some people hear a different drummer. They live in a world of violence, guns, bombs and Molotov cocktails. Their streets are littered with trash and the homeless souls are everywhere. They riot and loot and murder. Their avenues are chocked with smoke and haze. Buses and garbage trucks belch fumes. They are bodies in bedlam — but that is how they want it.

For a world without violence they must have that burning desire to cross over the line. I know the world without violence, but do the violent ones dare embrace serenity and non suffering?

*Terry Michael Tracy spends most of his time writing short stories and weighing the outcome of the human race. He is a true champion of nonviolence. He has appeared in American motion pictures as well as in TV commercials. He has contributed to Time Life Books, **The Meaning of Life**; and writes for Surfer Magazine; "Baja Times" Newspaper and several other publications.*

Peace Through Religion

— Zena Sorabjee

As we look at the world scenario today, there is a near anarchical condition where violence has become a way of life. Law and order appear to have collapsed and often the very upholders and custodians of the law themselves, perpetrate crimes of violence. Sociologists tell us that the major contributors to the development of aggression and violence are factors such as injustice, fear, anxiety, anger, prejudice, frustration and discouragement in individuals. It is also obvious that the human character has become debased and the number of God-fearing people is on a sharp decline.

How can we reverse the trend, is the question on every one's mind. Leaders of thought and leaders of nations bemoan the crises of character in human beings and nations, but are bankrupt of ideas and impotent to offer solutions.

The Founder-Prophet of the Baha'i Faith, *Baha'u'llah* said over a hundred years ago :

"We can well perceive how the whole human race is encompassed with great, with incalculable afflictions. We see it languishing on its bed of sickness, sore-tired and disillusioned. They that are intoxicated by self-conceit have interposed themselves between it and the Divine and Infallible Physician . . . . They can neither discover the cause of the disease, nor have they any knowledge of the remedy . . . . The all-knowing Physician hath His finger on the pulse of mankind. He perceiveth the disease, and prescribeth, in His unerring wisdom, the remedy."

Is there a remedy which can eliminate the above-mentioned factors which contribute to a violence-filled society? For the Baha'is, residing in over 210 countries, islands and dependencies of the world, there is a God-given solution.

"Religion is the greatest instrument for the order of the world and the tranquillity of all existent beings . . . . whatever lowers the lofty station of religion will increase heedlessness in the wicked, and finally result in anarchy."

A vitally religious society vigorously enforces moral sanctions, whereas in an irreligious one the question of right and wrong become intermingled with self-interest and passion and moral confusion and chaos ensue. Religion also develops in man a firm conviction of future existence which is the greatest motivation that a person can have for right conduct. An acceptance that there is accountability after death strongly restrains a person from wrongful acts. Religious laws of conduct help in the emergence of spiritual man.

Unfortunately the word religion in today's context has become distasteful. Crimes of violence against individuals and groups, in the name of religion, have made people shy away from religious beliefs, believing rites, rituals and dogmas to be religion. These outward trappings have hidden the fundamental truths which have been enshrined in the teachings of the founders of religions.

Gandhiji said, one of the blunders of the world today is the practice of "worship without sacrifice". Worship has taken the form of going to temples, mosques, churches where God is given a few minutes to propitiate Him for wrongs done, or to selfishly ask for something for oneself. There is no element of sacrifice at all. One is not willing to forgive or forget or give up one's anger, prejudice or hatred which is driving us to all forms of violence. There is no atonement. We repeat the same crimes then return to the place of worship believing these visits wipe the slate clean!

Religion as the Baha'is see it, is worship of God not only in payer, but mainly in the form of service to humanity. Religion is a mighty bulwark. There are two safeguards which prevent man from wrongdoing.

"One is the law which punishes the criminal; but the law prevents only the manifest crime and not the concealed sin, whereas the ideal safeguard, namely the religion of God, prevents both the manifest and the concealed crime, trains man, educates morals, compels the adoption of virtues and is the all-inclusive power which guarantees the felicity of the world of mankind".

All the major religions existing today appear to have lost their vitality because of the irreconcilable schisms that have developed amongst them, and the moral sanctions of religion are rapidly disappearing. The founders of these religions foreseeing such conditions, assured their followers in their holy scriptures that there will be another Divine Teacher to guide mankind again. There appears to be a dire need at this time for another Prophet who will teach human beings to turn to the Creator with a commitment to the belief that a crime against man is a crime against God. Baha'is believe that this assurance to mankind has been fulfilled by the coming of Baha'u'llah in the last century, who has once again renewed religious truths and emphasized the need for deeds not words.

Gandhiji wrote, *"We must be the change we wish to see"*. This change is what the world wide Baha'i community, several million strong, representing most of the nations, races, religions and languages of the world is successfully undertaking. An example of such a change would not be out of place here. The Daga people of Papua New Guinea have a reputation for tribal infighting and sorcery. By tradition, any kind of transgression would invite an immediate and often lethal vengeance. However, reports of dramatic changes have begun to emerge. One Mr. Levi George, a retired official of Papua New Guinea lived in fear of death for himself and his family, as his son had accidentally killed a member of the Daga people in an automobile accident. According to custom, there would be a "payback killing". After hiding for some time he was forced to return to work and found a group of Daga people waiting for him. These people who Mr. George regarded as the worst known killers of the area, to his great surprise, smiled and walked towards him, extended their arms and shook hands with him. They said "Brother, we are from the area of the dead boy. We came to tell you that you and your family must not be worried. We are brothers and sisters. We are from the Baha'i Faith and we want to assure you and your children that there will be no payback killing".

According to regional government officials in the Daga area, several of the tribes are acquiring a reputation for peace-making and inter-tribal harmony. At a Baha'i conference for these people where a thousand representatives of some 60 villages had gathered, the local officials were surprised at the lack of even nominal security since, in the past, it would have been impossible for such a gathering to have not been violent. Mr. Thomas Ilaisa, an attorney said, "It is indeed a historic moment for the Daga people to come together in such large numbers, as has never happened before, in a genuine spirit of love and friendship. This type of large public gathering with a common unifying zeal is something which some could call a miracle".

The Baha'i community provides the milieu where to think of a violent act against another would be considered an act against God and functions on the principle "the earth is but one country and mankind its citizens".

Gandhiji's mentor. Count Leo Tolstoy. on reading about Baha'u'llah and his teachings wrote, *"We spend our lives trying to unlock the mystery of the universe. But there was a prisoner (Baha'u'llah) in Akka, Palestine, who had the key".*

*Ms. **Zena Sorabjee** is Chair of the Baha'i House of Worship Management Committee in Delhi, a member of the Continental Board of Counselors of the Baha'i of India, and a trustee for the Lotus Charitable Trust in Bombay. She authored Nabil's Narrative Abridged on the early history of the Baha'i as well as contributes to newspapers and journals. **Ms. Sorabjee** has travelled to over sixty countries and she has been involved in numerous rural development programmes in India.*

The Face Of Greed

— *Barry Sanders*

I live in Pasadena, in the northwest quadrant, within the city's black and Chicano ghetto. At eight or eight-thirty in the morning, as I head for the freeways — like most cities, the freeway here deliberately skirts the slums, unrolling like a red carpet through the heart of the city — black or white, old vets or young ones, lots of them holding, in a styrofoam cup, what is most likely hot coffee. Winchell's lets you sit for only short time, two doughnuts' worth at most; Denny's enforces a minimum. Styrofoam, lethal for the environment and not too healthy for humans, has become the nomad's best friend.

These are the modern-day, urban poor. In the very neighborhoods where most people can barely afford a cup of coffee, others score grams of crack-cocaine. Young men and women who have been closed out of jobs and professions drive brand-new BMWs. They can make out better by saying screw the system. In the sixties, many of those young people directed their anger at the system. Lots of them plugged away week after week in demonstrations, and hour upon endless hour in political meetings. Scores of young men and women truly "served time". Today, a teenager can make hundreds, even thousands of dollars, in a single drug deal that takes no longer to transact than a TV commercial. No wonder young people are only about half as likely to vote in national elections as their elders.

We have to ask : What could alter a human life so radically; what could work with such intensity to erase hope and ambition and love? Who knows such powerful violence? The culprit has remained hidden from view for a very long time. More and more these days, though, one can hear it talked about, not by scientists in labs or by experts in universities, but by plain folks out on the streets. What has taken control of the body politic, sapping its strength and vigor, is nothing less than greed. And it kills more efficiently and effectively than any weapon. The casualties are easy to spot — young folks falling before their time, adolescent refusing to bloom, mature men toppling over — but the victims never get counted in the homicide rate. Some people, however, have read the symptoms correctly : In late October 1990, two hundred demonstrators took to the streets of San Francisco, carrying placards denouncing corporate greed; the police arrested sixty-eight of them. A few people have made the symptoms easier to notice : On November 19, 1990, a Federal Court

Judge sentenced Michael Milken to ten years in prison for what was surely the boldest act of greed in this century — perhaps all time — by an individual. So fantastic was his junk-bond swindle that it landed him a place in the Guinness Book of World Records for the most money amassed by an individual in a single year — 550 million dollars. In one way or another, Milken affected the financial history of virtually every person in this country, That's the terrible monster, greed.

Greed has wormed its way through history with astonishing speed. The word doesn't even make its first appearance in writing until the seventeenth century. It comes into the language through a rare linguistic process called back-formation in which an existing word is mistakenly analyzed, and its supposed base pressed into service as a new, back-formed word. The seventeenth-century coined the word greed by analogy with an adjective that had been in circulation since the tenth century, greedy, "a ravenously voracious appetite". That is the word initially referred to eating, to ingestion and consumption. A greedy gut can never be satisfied, its hunger never slaked. It churns with such ferocity, in fact, that it devours everything in sight. How could such a consuming frenzy ever be stilled and quieted., contained in something so intent as a common noun? The idea sounds impossible. Yet, that's exactly the paradoxical history that greed describes — a process that quietly turns invisible, all the while wreaking more and more havoc.

By the seventeenth century, the apparatus of capitalism — banks, capital, interest -- had settled firmly into place. As if it were the most natural thing in the world, usury became much more universalized at roughly this same time. Even churchmen like Luther and Calvin begin to openly justify its existence. A tremendous social change had been taking place, which manifests itself linguistically. The word beggar undergoes its back-formation into beg — shifting attention from people on the street to the intrusive activity of beggars working those streets. At the other extreme, wealth shifts its meaning from describing a person's spiritual state, or the health of a country, to an abundance of material possessions. Immediately, a word was needed to describe "an inordinate or insatiate longing for wealth." In one decisive moment, like the climactic scene out of a mediaeval morality play, "Monstrous Appetite." meets "Worldly Goods" to create a new gruesome noun: Greed.

While economics gave the world of finance a theoretical framework, early seventeenth-century science-mathematics, chemistry, and especially astronomy — began uncovering a whole new world, and its images, tantalizingly surreal, piqued the popular imagination. The church foundered against such a formidable enemy, leaving the poets once again to sound the alarm. "The New Science," John Donne warned, threatened to "call all in doubt". Science promoted free experimentation with the aim of controlling and dominating nature. It went after its goal with a vengeance. While Gallileo brought the planets down to earth, Copernicus predicted their movements through the heavens. Speed and acceleration could now be found everywhere — in the cosmos and in commerce. Dramatists like Christopher Marlowe smelled trouble : In a God-less world, a greedy-minded scientist could play havoc. Worse yet, he might play God. Doctor Faustus, the hero of Marlowe's Tragical History of Doctor Faustus, cares only for what he calls the new "manly fortitude". He wants total domination over his nakedly secular world so desperately that he commits the ultimate, detestable sin — sells his soul to Mephistopheles, the devil's representative, for the promise of instantaneous and infinite power.

The supreme salesman of mumbo-jumbo, Mephistopheles convinces Faustus that he can turn his every dream into a shining reality, and so guarantee him heaven's own happiness. And he promises to do it fast — indeed, immediately. To tantalize him, Mephistopheles produces pictures — of Faustus's own fantasies — placing on display everything he has ever imagined, but never thought possible. Then Mephistopheles pulls out all the stops by offering Faustus both the crown jewels and the crown itself — the entire world. He moves beyond human imagination by dangling God's own power in front of Faustus. And Faustus salivates at the very idea. like a Hebrew prophet, Marlowe sees into the present. Everyone gets hungry that's obvious. Some people act like gluttons and gorge themselves — that's obvious, too. But Marlowe sees people restless with that new hunger, greed and he knows it must be stirred up by skillful pitch man; that it must be attractively packaged; and that it must be sold. People need to see wealth — bright, shiny pictures win them over. Without those visual aids, greed remains abstract and dead.

So Marlowe never mentions money. In Faustus's hallucinatory world, money encumbers; it smacks of the mundane world of avarice. Outside the confines of the theater, of cource, it takes money to set greed into motion. Once it circulates, money not only talks, it works miracles. Breathing fiery new life into the archaic, tenth-century appetite, money reduces gluttony to fool's game. For gluttony must actually obey fairly narrow restrictions. Only a limited amount of food can be safely hoarded before it soon rots and begins to stink — before the earth reclaims it as compost. Money lifts all restrictions on hoarding. With money, a greedy gut can indulge to its heart's content, not by continually devouring like a field rat or even hoarding like a pack rat, but by stockpiling an infinite amount of buying power — in the form of cash — like a fat cat. Cash never molders or rots. Quite the opposite : It grows bigger by gathering interest — the more cash the better.

A fat man eats, but a big man consumes. The former fills up, but the latter fills out — sprawls across the land on huge estates and in stately, expensive manor houses. No one in the Renaissance thought of measuring this new brand of consumption by what they saw digested, but rather in what they saw accumulated. The signs of material consumption excited them : They spill over in grand displays of objects

— in fancy new things, in more things even than God dreamed of creating. In the game of power, money carries more weight than food, for it not only buys food, but holds the key to a rich, aristocratic life.

Marlowe dramatizes the danger of such greedy thinking; indeed, he shows how such an appetite can overwhelm a person's good sense, sending him directly to the devil. But Marlowe never once uses the word greed : in 1604, when he published *Doctor Faustus*, the word did not yet exist. Just five short years later, however, greed found its way into print, in an anatomy of the bodily humors, an archaic version of physiological psychology : "...whose avarice and greed of geare (goods) is such that they care not whom they joyne, so being they ritch." Notice that even in this early seventeenth century line, avarice and greed live a strangely amoral life of their own, refusing to socialize with anyone but the most wealthy.

First mentioned in print in 1609, greed immediately exerts such a disfiguring influence that everyone it touches takes on a monstrous look. Marlowe, the earliest historian of greed, also gets credit in a 1598 citation in the Oxfords English Dictionary for the first calling human behavior "monstrous". Describing Tamberlaine, a king of unbounded ambition, Marlowe refers to him as a creature "monstrous as Gorgon, Prince of Hell". In the next century, Alexander Pope warns of the social fiends he fears will soon emerge : "Vice is a monster of so frightful a mien as, to be hated, needs but to be seen". Without naming the vice, he adds to the picture a more frightening, modern prospect of inevitability — that we will all become monsters ourselves — and not necessarily against our wills : "Yet seen so oft, familiar with her face, We first endure, then pity, then embrace."

By the begining of the ninteenth century, Pope's warning comes true : Men have transformed themselves into monsters. A new disease enters the medical lexicon, Pleonexia, a pernicious greed that threatens to redefine the boundaries of human behavior. Like ghosts of the medieval usurer, ghoulish, greedy pawnbrokers haunt the pages of ninteenth-century fiction. Jacques Le Goff, in describing the medieval usurer, saw him as a "pre-capitalistic Dracula . . . a doubly frightening vampire for Christian society." On close examination, Le Goff's comparison does not seem far-fetched or sensational. Count Dracula, the Golem, and the Wolf-man — similar in appearance to men — all evolve directly out of the earliest monsters of greed. Like Grendel, their forebear, they stalk the pages of popular literature, determined to satisfy an awesome appetite — "the universal wolf", as Shakespeare calls it — unconcerned that they will surely waste the world in the process. A de Maupassant character in "The Flayed Hand" even sounds shockingly like the first violent monster in English literature, Grendel : "All men are my enemies. I will rob, burn, murder until the world is destroyed." All these fiends are driven by a greedy lust for one thing — power. None of them, however, can match the terror of Mary Shelley's

Frankenstein, or the Modern Prometheus. Perhaps only someone so far removed from the competitive, commercial world — a young woman of twenty-one — could gain enough distance to understand contemporary events at such a fundamental level. For Shelly describes, in minute detail, how Doctor Victor Frankenstein, through his macabre scientific and technological manipulations, takes great delight in playing God by creating life from a cast-off cadaver. But Frankenstein can imbue the corpse with only the darkest side of his own personality; his creation turns out to be a greedy monster. He reproduces his own lustful nature.

Doctor Faustus encourages Mephistopheles to work his guile on him. He slides easily into greed — miring himself more and more deeply in it — because he yearns so desperately for power. He quickly takes Mephistopheles lesson to heart; and then he chomps at the bit to work his own magic. Victor Frankenstein knows he can rival God in only one way — by creating life. But he creates nothing more than his splintered self, deformed by greed beyond all recognition, set into perpetual motion to destroy everything and everyone in its way: A hideous automation, incapable of feeling, willing, and even acting, except in the most limited, one-track way — an amalgam of man and machine. In modern terms, he has been programmed. The back-formation from greedy to greed — perhaps more accurately the "throwback-formation" — completes its devolution with Mary Shelly's modern hero, that frustrated "Victor", Doctor Frankenstein.

But to describe humans with animal metaphors, or to represent them as master implies that abhorrent behavior remains alien to them — not innate but unnatural. Human beings have to learn to act in a debased, depraved way. Indeed, nineteenth century monster-men all depend for their transformation on some outside power. The Wolf-Man cannot shape-shift without the influence of the full moon; Count Dracula cannot drain a single drop of his victim's blood without first lying the night in a wooden casket; the Golem remains a lifeless goon until four Hebrew characters, a Kabbalistic tetragram, have been inserted in his forehead. Monstrousness always requires some outside agent to set it into motion. Even Frankenstein's monster must be shocked into life, in his case with the miracle of that age — electrical currency. Only Robert Louis Stevenson's character, Doctor Jekyll, seems to present something new : Not only does he want to bring his evil, dark side to life, he figures out a way to make it happen. But even he must ingest something, a concoction or rare salts, before he can stalk the night as his alter-monster, the evil Mister Hyde.

Jekyll has a mentor in Victor Frankenstein, the scientist turned technological wizard who dares eat from the new "Tree of Information". He lusts after God's ultimate power — the power of creation. Doctor Frankenstein takes the first tentative step into the new, complicated, modern world, a world in which greed is incipient, ready to be jolted into life — in the form of Frankenstein's monster. Victor Frankenstein acts monstrously, for he has long since undergone transformation. He merely clones himself into this literary fragment, the monster. So Doctor and creature merge — so closely that most people mistakenly call the creature by the name of its creator, Frankenstein. Robert Louis Stevenson's innovation is to introduce a modern, psychological reality into the monster business : Jekyll and Hyde are really one person, a suggestion that each one of us is capable, under the right circumstances, of splintering into polar opposites.

These ninteenth-century monsters represent the new, modern individual, who, having succumbed to greed, develop enormous appetites for consumption. Transformed, they feel alive and powerful only when the flames of desire are continually banked. But how to keep such an engine fed? In the mid- twentieth century, scientists rallied to the cause with a technological solution. Without intending to, perhaps, they went Shelly one better and put Doctor Faustus in every home. Using a stronger bolt of electrical power, they quickly transformed every person into an all-consuming monster and installed greed as the capital sin of the modern world.

At the close of World War II, scientists completed a project they had been working on since the thirties, but had shelved because of the war — a new-fangled contraption that could broadcast not only sound but pictures as well. They created television, and it scored an immediate hit, TV provided the way for America's economy to move at an accelerated rate, forestalling any possibility of a post-war depression. But TV out-performed everyone's wildest expectations. It promised satisfaction and a more complete and easier way of life, by showing tantalizingly real pictures -- just as Mephistopheles had done — of "The Good Life". Moreover, to the delight of corporations, it accelerated consumer demand for goods and services at an ever-increasing rate.

While physicists were busily experimenting with nuclear accelerators, TV emerged as the fastest, most effective, and most efficient accelerator of consumption. Today, 99.7 percent of American homes are wired for television — the ultimate greed meter. Some homes, of course, have more than one, more than two sets. Which means that, in practical terms, we have all plugged ourselves into race. The moment we acquire the latest gadget, another time-saving, beautifying work : In 1989 alone, Americans purchased $1.4 billion worth of goods through the TV shopping channels. They also bought TV's straightforward, no-nonsense lesson : If you want to keep ahead of the pack, then pay close attention — especially to its power — has technology been employed to impress images into the minds of so many people, particularly with such astonishing speed.

Just as a farmer broadcasts seeds, TV broadcasts greed. Poor people do not get poor reception; they see the same images, at the same instant, as people in Beverly Hills, and Westchester County, and West Palm Beach. They just can't afford all those neat, new things. And so greed victimizes them. One can see the fallout from greed in the streets, and one can breath it in the air. Marlowe had the luxury of pursuing greed as the stuff of literature; for him, it made interesting reading. But only recently has the hellish transformation of the planet smacked us so forcefully in the face. Only recently has greed moved from an interest of literature and the cinema — recall D.W. Griffith's nine-hour extravaganza, *"Greed"*, at the opening of this century — to real-life crisis at the close of the century. The "Bomb", the "Red Menace", the "Yellow Peril", the "Cold War", even the "Mid-East Crisis" — all these pale against ozone holes the size of Alaska, stretching over the continent of Australia. It has taken a long time — several hundred years — to feel the full effects of greed, to finally realize that we may be running out — of animals, of trees, of air, of time. We have let it happen, unfortunately, by running out on the planet.

No one needs to be told how ravenously we have been devouring the planet. But we need to be told to stop. And we need to know the enemy : Greed. Sure, life feels a bit more secure with miniaturized computers built into everything, from cars to towing machines; and sure it feels a bit more comfortable to call on a myriad of electronic gadgets; but it should also feel a bit more lonely with fewer species of animals, and less fish, and only two-thirds of the Rain Forest. Greed breeds violence — of the most insidious, pernicious kind. The alarm has gone off : We are running out of time. It's time to wake up and bring our great gobbling life to a halt. Salvation will clearly not arrive with another politician's promises, or with nuclear or solar energy, or through space technology, or with the peace dividend, or with cars that get slightly better gas mileage. Any plan to effect change — to live in a world, that is, freed from violence — must go directly for the heart : It must aim at digging up the roots of greed. Radical change can occur. Greed itself tells us that. Its own history points out that greedy, monstrous behavior is unnatural; and that means we can shed it, moult our lives like snakes.

If we don't stop the spread of greed, we will continue destroying lives and running the environment, like runway Frankenstein monsters, we can cripple our creator, in one simple and deft stroke — by simply pushing the button. We can turn off television — even if it's just for one week, both day and night. No TV. Imagine the set turned off : Families, friends, neighbors, lovers, even total strangers, literally taking the time to talk, sing, or tell jokes, instead of watching all those programmed programs, all those glitzy commercials. How refreshing to imagine groups of folks sitting around telling stories to each other — hopefully, made-up ones, but even a short story read aloud would be preferable to a sit-com. The phrase "entertaining an idea" reverberates with hope; it suggests that the mind is warm and friendly : not a bad place to spend some time. Warm and friendly do not admit of violence. Noisy, boisterous sessions, punctuated by finger-pointing and sudden interruptions — I envision all the confusion and exhilaration of old-fashioned social intercourse.

Turning off the television could have wonderful economic benefits : families might suddenly find themselves getting by on less, consuming fewer gadgets and goodies and appliances. As consumers, we have something called "buying power". We forget, however, that power is sometimes best expressed in its potentiality, greatest when we withhold it. Resisting temptation and authority both exert their own special kinds of violence. Even if only one percent of TV viewers played possum for seven full days, they would be handling a frighteningly powerful message to corporate America. If that one percent increased, corporations just might take notice. They have the government's ear; let them lobby for affordable housing and decent jobs; let them worry about drinkable water and breathable air; let them take charge for a change.

I am suggesting something akin to Gandhi's stance of passive resistance that he adopted for his work in the forties. Passive resistance does not really assume any enemy; rather, it focuses on the power and dignity of the individual. Don't think of TV as the enemy, except in so far as it colonizes viewers, undermining their dignity and power. TV breeds a most insidious form of electronic violence, a form that creates an ethos of "everyone for himself", a form that can eventuate in one thing only — in greed. In this country, at this time, turning off the TV represents the most dramatic, the most singular brand of passive resistance. The surest way of not falling under the spell of TV is to avoid watching it — all of it. Any of it.

Every evening Americans have their perceptions shaped — scripted and programmed — by TV broadcasts. I call this an act of violence of the most punishing, most invisible sort. No one clubs the viewer on the head, no one holds a gun to the viewer's temple; but the effect is nonetheless brutal. The most effective, dramatic and efficient way of regaining independence may lie in turning off the TV. Only in that way, I think, can we begin to turn back greed.

Barry Sanders lives in the black ghettos of California to experience the pain and sufferings of the economically deprived people and understand their anger. He tries to resolve their conflicts with human goodness and nonviolence.

Where Happiness Hangs Like A Fog

— *Bill McKibben*

Among the more revealing statistics I have come across recently is this : in the mid 1980s, when the Soviet Union's economic paralysis was at its height and every necessity meant a wait in line, the average American was spending more time shopping then the average Russian. The average American was visiting the mall more often than the church, which raises the question of which is the church. For teenagers, home and school occupied more hours than the mall. The YMCA in suburban Washington last year began running their summer day camps inside shopping malls, because they were convenient for parents.

For me the great power of Gandhi's example has always rested in pleasure he seemed to take, the satisfaction he seemed to gain, from the everyday mundane, The chuckle not far below the surface. Told by thousand advertisements a day where to find this joy, we in the overdeveloped West prospect for it endless with our wallets full of credit cards, doing along the way great inadvertent violence to the earth and each other.

The enormous unspoken truth of the consumer age, though, is that while our acquisition binge has made us more comfortable, it has not made us particularly happy — the vague sense that there must be something more to life than this hangs like a fog over our societies. And of course there is more to life. One need only look at our biology — clearly we did not evolve this outstanding collection of muscles and bones, this stunning coordination between hand and eye, this collection of emotions and insights, merely to recline in front of the television searching for distraction. We did not evolve as the gregarious species as we are in order to shut ourselves off in the miniature castles of suburbia. We are built for things quite different, and we cannot be fulfilled until we find them.

It is insufficient to say : our consumer lifestyle is destroying the earth. We have shown ourselves unable to think far enough into the future for that truth to be very powerful. It is insufficient to say : How can you be out buying a large screen TV when there are people starving in Somalia? We, quite clearly, can bring home the large screen TV from the mall, watch people starve in Somalia, and not lose much sleep over it. Moralism is not subversive any more — we are trained by television to defend ourselves against it, to think of the world as too large to effect, to think of the forces around us as inevitable. Irony and cynicism are our armor, as impregnable as ignorance in an earlier day.

But is it deeply subversive to say : I am having more fun than you are. You could have more fun — more joy, more satisfaction — living in the state of sufficiency. A state where you needed to do some work with your hands (for why else do we have them?). A state where you did some for others (for there is deeper pleasure in changing the sheets at a homeless shelter than people who have never done it would guess). A state where you took your pleasure cheaply — from the woods and waves around you, from talking with friends, from a musical instrument you have learned to play.

The great and enduring oddballs — Jesus, the saints, Gandhi, Buddha, the mystics, and so on — owe their powers less, I think, to the specifics of their programs than to the joy those specifics produced in them. We live at the interesting age — the recommendation towards simplicity from eons of such *gurus* meshes neatly with the emerging advice of our atmospheric chemists and physicists, the chroniclers of our violent assault on the planet. But it is not just the advice we need, it is the example. The joy that does not fade.

*Bill McKibben is the author of **The End of Nature**, **The Age of Missing Information**, and a forthcoming book on environmental hope. A former staff writer of the New Yorker, he lives in the Adirondack Mountains of upstate New York.*

Christian Perspective Of Nonviolence

— *Milan Opocensky*

In commemorating and honoring the legacy of Mohandas K. Gandhi we remember those who throughout history have defended non-violence as an effective and genuine approach to solving conflicts in the human community. For example, in the earlier Christian period there was a man called Maximillanus who declared : *"Non possum militare, Christian sum"* (I cannot be a soldier, I am a Christian). There were many who suffered and were marginalized because they did not comply with the prevailing ethics of their society.

In this commemorative volume I would like to introduce Petr Chelcicky of Bohemia who was a prophet of this time and defended non-violence on the basis of Christian faith. He lived roughly during the period between 1380-1450. He experienced the beginnings of the Hussite movement. First he lived in Prague and witnessed the rise and peak of the influence of Jan Hus. After the death of Hus at the stake in Constance the Hussite parties gradually evolved and Revolutionary mood swept the country. Although highly educated and versed in contemporary polemics, Chelcicky was a free farmer and withdrew to his property in South Bohemia, from where he exercised the role of emphatic critic of the turbulent events of his time. He was close to the Taborite movement in the Hussite spectrum. At the outset the Hussites rejected war, but later, war was imposed on them in spite of that. When the crusaders invaded the country they saw no other solution but to take up arms and to defend their Reformation and their revolutionary stance by force. Chelcicky never endorsed this decision and developed a courageous critique of the concept of Christian society.

In the Middle Ages it was generally accepted that secular power is one of the functions of the Church and therefore God's law can and should be defended by the sword. However, the question was repeatedly raised whether a Christian war can be justified. In this respect, Chelcicky was unique. He saw a basic difference between the Old and the New Testament. The Old Testament admits violence but the New Testament forbids it. Chelcicky realistically counts on a secular power. It has the function of being a "strong fence" without which the world could not exist. However, Christ's church cannot use violence. The highest law of Christians is the commandment of love. A Christian should love his/her enemies and pray for them. Christians do not take vengeance but leave that to God. The most radical form of violence is war, and according to Chelcicky the most godless form of war is the war which is waged in defense of faith.

This specific question of war led to the broader problem of whether or not the idea of a Christian society can be justified. The New Testament presupposed that Christians live in a non-Christian milieu. Viclef, who was in many ways highly influential in the Hussite movement, accepted the mediaeval decision of society in three parts : lords who should defend and fight; priests who were supposed to pray; farmers who should labor and feed "these two fat Baals".

Chelcicky rejected the generally accepted division. According to him the Christian Church is a Spiritual community which cannot be identified with any social grouping. No social phenomena should be concidered Christian way. A secular order which uses violence is incompatible with the Christian commandment of love. Christian who should love each other. This is the ultimate reason why Chelcicky rejected the division of the three parts ("three-fold people"). The exploitation and oppression of simple people committed by priests and secular rulers is in sharp contradiction to the law of love. In this way Chelcicky very effectively attacked the medieval myth of Christian society based on two pillars : Pope and Emperor. Chelcicky revolted against the compromise between the secular order including war and force and the syncretism which had far-reaching consequences. The spirit of war and violence prevailed in the world. There was no place for the order of love and forgiveness.

It is to the greater merit of Chelcicky that he applied biblical thinking to the social structure of his society. He drew attention to some questions which are still vital in the ecumenical discussion. He protested against the attempts of the Constantine epoch to chain the power of the Gospel through medieval, social and culture forms. According to him the biblical message itself revolts against such tendencies. The idea of Corpus Christianum was a grandiose attempt to establish a synthesis between the church and the world, between Christ and Culture. Chelcicky was not able to express the relationship of the Gospel and the world in a positive way. In spite of this fact his approach was purifying, inventive and revolutionary because he radically rejected such a simple synthesis and drew a line clearly dividing the two levels. He understood that biblical witnesses struggle constantly with the temptation to integrate God in various human models and plans despite their religious features.

Sometimes Chelcicky is concidered as being antirevolutionary, if not reactionary. However, it is necessary to see his contribution in a historical context. It was primarily his input that Hussitism represented not only a shock to medieval thinking but the entire social order was under unprecedented critique. The Church was responsible for the creation of a sacred social formation which in fact did not reflect much from the liberating dynamic of the gospel. Chelcicky was delineated anew the boundaries between the rule of Christ and the corrupted human world, between sovereign rule and the power of this world which, according to him, were mixed and intertwined in an impermissible way. He stripped society of its religious and Christian haze. War and violence were accompanying factors of the muddled situation. Whoever did not want to be governed by the "city law" has to leave the world behind. It is not possible to follow Christ and at the same time be obedient to the secular laws which include war, violence, oppression and exploitation.

When the followers of Chelcicky organized themselves in the Unity of Brethren (from 1457 onwards), they withdrew from the world and for several decades they lived in secluded places where they tried to fulfill Christ's commandments of love and forgiveness. In the beginning of the sixteenth century they returned to the world and actively participated in shaping the cultural, educational and social life of Czech society. However, by their example they influenced many other communities which have trodden the same path. Quakers, Mennonites, Hutterites and other communities witness to the fact that there exists an alternative to the world of war and violence. Other Christians should learn to value the contribution of the peace churches. The legacy of Chelcicky is still very timely and it is not incidental that some great thinkers (e.g. L.N. Tolstoy) highly praised his contribution. In times of continuing war and civil strife in many parts of the world the question is justified whether in the era of nuclear arms and ever more sophisticated weapons Christians and religious people in general should not embrace the idea of Chelcicky, and later of M.K.Gandhi, that war should be excluded from the moral code of humanity. Only then can we hope one day we ill live in a world without violence.

Let me finish with a story which is proof that people long for non-violence and that even major change can be achieved in a peaceful way. During the eventful November 1989 in Prague graffiti appeared on the walls remembering Jesus, Masaryk (the founder of modern Chekoslovakia) and Gandhi. T. G. Masaryk used to say: Jesus, not Caeser. But also Gandhi and the famous film about him certainly had a great impact. The example of three men from different times has probably contributed to the velvet character of the revolution which marks a new beginning in the history of two nations in Central Europe.

Milan Opocensky is Professor of Christian Social Ethics at the Protestant Theological Faculty of Charles University in Prague and currently serves as General Secretary of the World Alliance of Reformed Churches in Geneva.

The Oneness Of Humankind

— Nathan Rutstein

In pondering what I should write in commemoration of Mohandas Gandhi's 125th birthday, the thought that he gave so much to others, including his life, crossed my mind; it was time the world gave something to Mr. Gandhi.

What would he want, I wondered. Certainly, nothing material like a statue or museum. It had to be something that would help fulfill a personal hope that never materialized during his lifetime.

Since he was an avid seeker of truth, a universalist who yearned for the day when all peoples would live peacefully and in harmony, the appropriate gift would be the creation of a way to unite the human family. After all, science has discovered what God has always known, that earthlings, regardless of skin colour, texture of hair or geographic location are related to one another. Everyone, all five and half billion human beings, are at least 50th cousins, according to world renowned geneticists. But you don't have to be a genius to figure that out. All it takes is simple arithmetic; double your ancestors with each generation and you'll discover that all of the people on earth living in 700 A.D. were our ancestors.

Yes, the Inuit of Alaska, the Hasedic Jew of Jeruslam, the Watusi of East Africa, the Lakota Indian of South Dakota, the Chinese, the Japanese, the Pacific Islanders, the Mexican, the Arab and the white Anglo-Saxon Protestant industrialist of Greenwich, Connecticut, are our cousins.

While Mohandas Gandhi had internalized the principle of the oneness of humankind, most people hadn't, Why? Mainly, because of prejudice — which I believe is an emotional commitment to ignorance, a condition that generates in the human mind a distorted view of reality. In essence, those prejudices have embraced falsehood as the truth. Mr. Gandhi knew this, and dedicated his life to a rigorous pursuit of truth, sharing openly with others what he discovered, and that included the reality of the oneness of humankind.

In doing so, some men and women overcome their race and religious prejudices. But the great majority of people never met him or internalized his teachings and remain prisoners of beliefs that foster intolerance and bigotry.

Since a way of overcoming race and religious prejudice is by internalizing and practicing the principle of the oneness of humankind and unity and diversity, I propose a world-wide educational campaign, promoting the reality of the oneness of the human family as a gift to Mohandas Gandhi on his 125th birthday.

What better place to teach this reality than in schools, which are charged with the responsibility of exposing students to the truth. As the Universal House of Justice, the world governing body of the Baha'i Faith, stated in its 1985 message to the peoples of the world, entitled The Promise of World Peace, oneness should therefore be universally acclaimed, taught in schools, and constantly asserted in every nation as preparation for the organic change in the structure of society which it implies.

Because of the magnitude of racism, the principle of the oneness of humankind should be woven into the school's curriculum from kindergarten through the 12th grade, and reflected in every course a child takes for the next 12 years, even electives such as art, music, home economics, physical education. Why the saturation approach? Because for hundreds of years people have been led to belive that Caucasians are inherently superior to everyone else. Imagine — kindergarteners, Africans, Asians, Europeans, North and South Americans, Pacific Islanders, Hindus and Moslems learning about the oneness of the human family, discovering that their classmates are actually relatives. The seed of truth will have been planted in five year old minds and nourished for the next 12 years. The children will be fortified to repulse the assault of the prejudice that they encounter in their homes and in the streets; in fact, they could become catalysts in overcoming the prejudices of the elders they are so close to, like their parents, relatives and neighbors. A new generation of adults will emerge, whose hearts are free of race and religious prejudice, and who have internalized the principle of the oneness of humankind. Only then will the race unity dream of Dr. Martin Luther King Jr. a follower of Mohandas Gandhi, be realized. In the end, all of us will be the beneficiaries of the gift we give to Mohandas K. Gandhi on his 125th birthday.

Nathan Rutstein *is a well-known author involved in all branches of the media - newspapers, radio, television, films and video — and has particular interest in their uses in education. He had been Director of the Communication Media Center at the University of Massachusetts School of Education and has written two books on the effects of television on children.*

Tolstoy, Nonviolence And Russia

— *T.A. Pavlova*
Translated by R.M. Iluchina

It would be good to start with one paradox in the social life of modern Russia. Our society tries now to recomprehend in different forms the moral problem of violence and nonviolence and the value of historical progress in the past, in the present and in the future. Whatever questions could be raised : either of the history of Russian Tzars, or of Communist dictators, or of modern leaders, the problem of violence is inevitably touched upon. Although all political parties and their leaders proclaim their desire to act in a nonviolent way, they do resort to violence as the first alternative. Re-establishing priority to nonviolence in a country where the word "nonviolence" was thrown out of the Russian vocabulary 70 years ago will be a significant achievement in itself.

This makes it all the more imperative for the Russian people to discard the stereotype that the history of Russia represents a long train of permanent wars, riots and irreconcilable class struggles. Marxist ideology of violence was based mainly on punitive motives — rebellions and revolutions — taken out of historical context and idolized as true national features which influenced the movement. All the other traditions were rejected and proclaimed as unacceptable. Moreover, creative work of our thinkers, writers and artists, who represented nonviolent tradition, were cruelly persecuted.

The 20th century which is coming to an end was one of the most bloody in Russian history. Totalitarian dictatorship was established in 1917 and millions were murdered. Revolutionary violence, like a red wheel, ran through Russia bringing up generations of Russians in spirit of hatred and aggression.

The fundamental moral law — evil never destroys evil only good can destroy evil — which Leo Tolstoy formulated in the beginning of the century, was ignored.

In reality there are only two methods of conflict resolution : to resist violence by violence or, according to Christian teachings, resist violence by nonviolence. Tolstoy believed that true nonviolence means not to be passive, not to reject active resistance and not to ignore reality.

"Not to resist evil by violence," he wrote, "does not mean not to resist evil at all ... We cannot put out fire with fire nor can we resist evil with evil although people have been trying to do so since time immemorial and have led us to the present unhappy circumstances."

We assume that the moral credo of Leo Tolstoy may be the base for the understanding of the Russian psyche. Early in this century Leo Tolstoy expounded the belief that Russia could give the world a nonviolent alternative. However, this belief remains dormant.

What did Tolstoy expect from the State and from the government? The main purpose for any power, he believed, is "service to the common will of those people over whom it has authority." Tolstoy believed that a government can stay in power not by cunning, cruelty, executions and guns.

"Offer ideals of justice, honesty and integrity better than anyone else," Leo Tolstoy wrote in 1906. "What is more, don't make this offer to save your skin but make it seriously and sincerely and you will save not only yourself but Russia also".

Leo Tolstoy believed that the main element of nonviolent development of Russia could be the giving back to the people their natural and legitimate right to own land, a right which was enjoyed for centuries by the people of Russia.

The Russian Empire, Tolstoy felt, with its conglomeration of different ethnic people could exist only through oppression of the people. "To hold on to Russia as it is now it is necessary to keep the obedience of the Polish, Finnish, Latvians, Georgians, Tartars, Armenians etc... it is necessary to forbid them to live as they like to ... But, you working people don't need that. You need only to own enough land, you need the assurance that nobody could take your property violently or take your sons to military service and, most of all, you need the assurance that nobody can force you to make other things".

The thesis of social and political non-cooperation with injustice was an important element of Tolstoy's doctrine of nonviolence. "..... there is only one alternative for Russian working people : refuse to submit serenely and humbly to any violence."

The basis of social non-cooperation rests on separating different political ideologies. People who stop at nothing — murder, mayhem, wars and torture — to maintain their hold on power are few but in powerful places.

"Some people think," Tolstoy wrote, "in the best interest of the Russian state the '*Duma*' should go on undisturbed with its activity, others think there is need for another '*Duma*', the third group think that we need a republic, the fourth group believes it should not be just a republic but a socialist republic. Because of these conflicting messages we encourage civil war."

In general Tolstoy believed that political strife takes a human being away from his or her inner spiritual life, reducing the "level of social morality." This makes it possible for "the most immoral people like Danton, Marat, Napoleon, Taleyran, Bismark" and others become heros of their time. True morality is possible only outside the State and political parties, in the invisible heart of heart of individual human beings.

Leo Tolstoy equated abolishing of violence in the human mind with religious revolution, with the creation of a new Christian self-conciousness based on the concept of renunciation. Tolstoy's philosophy of nonviolence is based on radical antimilitarism. The great thinker believed universal peace could only be established with the destruction of the State "which demands taxes and military services for organized violence and murder."

Leo Tolstoy believed compulsory military service was extreme violence used to support state power. "This is the foundation-stone that supports the walls, remove it and the whole edifice would crumble," he wrote. His struggle against compulsory military service, his angry speeches against military budgets and growth of armaments started the tradition of radical antimilitarism in Russia.

Even this very superficial and brief exposition of Tolstoy's social ethics shows what a profound vision Tolstoy had of 20th Century Russia. He accurately gauged the sore points in Russian life.

Why did Russia reject its own eminent philosopher and his wisdom? For the answer to this question we need to go back again to the beginning of the 20th century, to the tragic changes which took place in 1917 and which were close to the theme expounded by Leo Tolstoy.

One of Tolstoy's many paradoxes was that he, considered a prophet by some an initiator by N. Berdysev and a mirror of the Russian Revolution by Lenin, was a much maligned and misunderstood philosopher. Tolstoy described the dilemma best of all when he wrote : "The conservatives oppose nonviolence because it hinders the energetic suppression of a revolution; revolutionaries oppose it because it hampers the overthrow of conservatives."

The philosophy of nonviolent change in Russia was utterly defeated by the violent revolutions of the 19th and early 20th Centuries. The violence of the October, 1917, coup was the ultimate in the ideological delusion. Socialism assumed various different forms and identities and political scientists tried to justify the violence of the Socialist revolution by reverting to the myth of the Russian revolt, the Russian spirit and the "primordial values" of the Russian way of life.

Tolstoy, like others of his genre, was not understood by his own people. Followers who attended Tolstoy's funeral carried placards proclaiming their allegiance to their master and his philosophy of nonviolence. And, even before his body was interred they began to express their doubts at the efficacy of nonviolence and soon indulged in looting, burning and destroying homes of landlords, in the violence that preceded the 1917 revolution.

Many peasants rejected the faith of their forefathers and joined the Bolsheviks who promised them land, bread and peace if they first helped the revolution. Others who remained devoted to the Christian faith and became martyrs did not accept the dry rationalism of Tolstoy who denounced the mystical essence of Christianity, rejected miracles and the very idea of Resurrection.

Consequently, Tolstoy, a nonviolent rationalist, was not accepted by the Bolsheviks nor by the religious people. During the Soviet regime Tolstoy was only accepted as a great writer but not as a great thinker. His religious writings were not published and his philosophy was suppressed. Students studied Tolstoy and his philosophy through the abusive article by Lenin entitled "Leo Tolstoy as a mirror of Russian Revolution."

However, Tolstoy did have a small but faithful following who kept his memory, and his message, alive in spite of the pressures exerted on them. According to W. Edgerton the most amazing aspect of Tolstoy's followers was that they never reacted with anger, hatred or even mockery towards those who persecuted them, falsely accused them, unjustly arrested them and inhumanly killed them. This did not save the Tolstoyans. By the end of the 30's they were either dispersed or were decimated.

Against this background to what extent will post-Communist Russia accept Tolstoy's nonviolence, especially the moral aspect, remains debatable. Significantly, the changes instituted since 1985, ignore the very important component of spiritual and moral integrity. The change to democracy comes without repentance. It means that the Russians still subscribe to violent means of achieving violent ends.

The turmoil caused by the change to democracy spawned a new and terrifying power — Russian fascist troupes — who demand "Russian National Unity" and "Russia for Russians". Theses are hardened troops who participated in the military conflicts in Riga, Vilnius, Tiblisi, Pridnestrovie and Abschasia and have tasted blood. The future of democracy in Russia is in the balance. Will the Army be able to protect democracy violently or will the angry and hungry people, caught in the wild and ambitious market system, destroy it violently.

The poor and hungry, according to latest statistics, make up one-fifth of the Russian population. The number may not be large enough to win elections, but it is large enough to spark a national tragedy. Russia also cannot ignore the segment of the population who grew up in the communist ideology and are unwilling to accept democracy. This is another potential source of violence.

Eighty years ago Tolstoy wrote : "The conditions in Russia are terrible not because of its economic situation, nor decay of its industries, nor the disorder in its land distribution, nor the proletariat, nor the financial disorder, nor the violence. It is terrible because the people live without any moral or religious law." If this was true eighty years ago it is even more true today.

As in any other country there are numerous small groups working for nonviolent change in Russia. They are small and face many difficulties but they are persistent. The Tolstoyan pacifists have a new vision of Great Russia. The true grandeur of the state, according to them, is not its military power, not the size of its territory but the spiritual well-being of its citizens, personal freedom and value of human life. To achieve this objective the Tolstoyan pacifists are working for a "Russia Without Nuclear Weapons".

If Tolstoy's philosophy of nonviolence evoked a small response at the beginning of this century it evokes no more at the end of the century. The philosophy still remains unacceptable to both the elite and the masses. The Tolstoyan pacifists remain a small group, splintered, have no material base and are subjected to inordinate pressures from the power structure. Just as during Tolstoy's life-time people still continue to speak about nonviolence in the privacy of their apartments. Consequently, its propagation is limited and its influence on the State negligible. However, these are the first steps towards moral ascendancy and, perhaps, the realization of Tolstoy's dream of a moral, ethical and peaceful Russian society.

T.A. Pavlova is a member of The Centre for the Ethics of Nonviolence Institute of Philosophy in Russia. She is also on the Advisory Board of the M.K. Gandhi Institute.

The Imperative Of Revolutionary Nonviolence

— *S. Brian Willson*

Nonviolence is a way of life, an external manifestation of an internal peace. Nonviolence is mindfulness and consciousness of the sacred, of the inter-connectedness of ourselves with everything and every being. It is an attitude, an awareness, an understanding, a manner of expression and interaction operating from a deep internal integration that honors this sacred interconnectedness. It motivates intervention in our confrontation of forces destroying or harming sacredness of life, utilizing consciousness of the sacred in the means of intervention. When we embrace nonviolence we willingly take great risks with courage, enabling a freedom to love unconditionally, even if unsentimentally. The nonviolent practitioner is prepared to endure suffering and hardship as an alternative to inflicting harm or violence upon others.

This sounds, I am sure, wonderful. Is it realistic ? Having been born and raised a white Euro-American male in the United States of America means that I have been Intensively conditioned by nation, sex, race, and class with deeply rooted sense of superiority over the remainder of the world. Values and practices of comfort, privilege, domination, patriarchy, chauvinism, and separateness die hard. Even when I intellectually and logically know how destructive the layers of conditioning are, the emotional and psychological patterns and addictions don't automatically vanish. they are deeply inprinted.

Our civilization, the United States of America, as with other empires, was founded on an original "sin" of racism. It has been built through many successive "sins" of racism, sexism, classism, and worldwide imperialism. Millions of people in many ancient indigenous cultures inhabited their lands in the "New" world for 40 millenniums before the first invasion by the Europeans. The acquisition of the territories that now comprise the United States, as with all other countries in the Americas, occurred through violent theft of all the lands by use of deceit, force, and genocide of millions of the native aboriginal people. Perhaps the most agregious genocide in human history, the native population in what is now North America were reduced in numbers by at least 97% by 1900, while the European-American population had zoomed to over 80 million from zero in 1492. Similar tragedies occurred in Central and South America.

Subsequently, the brutal kidnapping and transporting of millions of indigenous African people from their ancient cultures provided chattel slavery for the economic "development" of the "new" world. Half the African native population is believed to have been decimated by the slave trade.

This grotesque reign of terror that continues to this day in various forms strongly suggests that we have been motivated by a superiority complex, a diabolical arrogance. Perhaps our need to dominate all life masks an even deeper inferiority complex. Our behavior may be rooted in a pathology of fragmentation, of mind from feelings, of human beings from nature. Our obsessive insistence upon separation from nature separates us from our own nature, from our own selves. This alienation preempts spiritual understandings, and leads to physical, mental, and social breakdown. We are blinded by this disintegration which prevents wisdom; we are drunk with its greed-driven force. The advanced deterioration and despair in the United States and other western societies today are symptoms of this fragmented personal and world view.

"Manifest Destiny", a particular U.S. conceitedness rationalized by a region declaring providential instruction and enlightenment, continues to be part of our character as a people. It is deeply etched into our subconscious, accepted thoughtlessly as absolute truth. Since the "founding" of the Republic of the United States of America on stolen land over 200 years ago, our "Constitutional Democracy" has acquired by force and deceit 9 territorial additions, 15 islands, and the Panama Canal Zone, increasing its control of land area by more than 4 times. The U.S. has intervened with armed forces into the sovereignty of at least 100 countries on more than 400 documented occasions, murdering and maiming millions of human beings. The U.S. has used the atomic bomb on 2 occasions. The U.S. has engineered at least 6,000 covert operations destabilizing popular movements, overthrowing governments, and assassinating leaders in the vast majority of the world's countries.

The presence of this past within us is no light burden. A painful but liberating process of healing and transformation of consciousness, and therefore of life and work styles, begins to unfold as we learn our sordid history and the depth of our dysfunctionality. Through brutal honesty — a willingness to accept our dark side — awareness expands and we begin to free ourselves from the blinding power of our learned separateness. To pursue a nonviolent way of life, I belive, requires our awareness of this LIE of our superiority and our participation in a process of healing from its sickness of fragmentation. Embracing this process enables us to reconstruct reality based upon the sacred interconnectedness of all life. We begin to learn through wisdom and humility.

I belive this more honest understanding of our people's history leads us to the conclusion that nation state empires such as the United States are irredeemable. Leo Tolstoy and Peter Kroptkin (late 1800 and early 20th century), George Orwell and Albert Camus (first half of the 20th Century), among others, articulated this theme of the dangers and irredeemablity of nation and rationalized injustices. It is critical for the people living within the territory of the United States, as well as those living in other nation states, to understand to act from our integrity and dignity as human beings who are part of a sacred ecosystem. We are not indebted to nation state structures. We must transcend and abandon them. We cannot continue to erode as individualists. We must learn how to interact in creative collective and community efforts. As we learn to become interdependent in grass roots, social and economic empowerment activities, we will enable ourselves to disengage from our complicity with and dependency upon the economic, political, and psychological seductions of what empire claims to offer. We have the opportunity to rediscover mutual aid and cooperation, and redefine our intimate web of personal, social, global, and ecological responsibility. There can be no global or personal peace or security without emotional, psychological, social, economic, physical, spiritual, intellectual, and ecological health and justice for all life.

My comfortable paradigm as a white Euro-American male was abruptly interrupted during my duty as a U.S. Air Force combat security officer in Vietnam in 1969. The bliss that possessed me was shaken by a series of very visceral experiences. I honestly do not know if I would have recognized the LIES had I not had the "fortune" of being ordered to Vietnam. There came a point during my Vietnam experience when the vulgarities of the war were obvious to me and offensive to my mind and stomach. I felt compelled to speak out against further U.S. bombing and urged my superiors to advocate for an immediate withdrawal of all U.S. armed forces from Southeast Asia. This was the first time I had ever questioned seriously the authority of our government, and the foundations of our, and my personal, character and values.

As a result of my Vietnam experiences, I began searching for another understanding, another model in which to know myself and the world. This search was required, and continues to require, much study, experience, as well as periods of deep reflection. Nonviolence describes most closely a paradigm of a radical alternative that operates on the principles of mindfulness of our deep interconnectedness with all life forms — the unity of everything. When we feel interconnectedness and experience this passion, it becomes more difficult for us to categorize, separate, and dehumanize people in a way that allows us to feel superior enough to treat them unfairly or cruelly.

Nonviolence requires renunciation of any and all claims to disproportionate privileges and power acquired by personal or imperial attitudes and actions of violence. This includes structural violence, such as racism, classism, sexism, and maintaining oligarchic structures which are forcefully preserved at the expense of the integrity and sacredness of other life. Growing up in any of the western or "First" world nations, or in oligarchic families in "Third" world countries, it is difficult to grasp that virtually all our comforts and privileges have been acquired and are being sustained by incredible forms of exploitation and lies. The United States with less than 5% of the planet's human population consumes nearly 50% of the world's resources, ten times more equitable amount. The so called undeveloped or "Third" world comprises 75% of the earth's population but is restricted to 15% of the world's resources. This grotesque disparity in distribution of resources has been and continues to be maintained and rationalized by various schemes of enforced exploitation. Every U.S. political administration, executive as well as legislative branches, has been and will continue to be an imperial power in order to assure the disproportionately privileged American Way of Life (AWOL), i.e. U.S. "national security". It really is not complicated. There is no peace without justice. There is no justice without a conciousness rooted deeply in interconnectedness.

I belive my upbringing in the lower middle class represents the values and conditioning of the vast majority of all people growing up in or migrating to materialist, "developed" societies. The process of disengaging and withdrawing from the addictions of such continuing, comfort, and privilege is formidable and, for most, is gradual if it happens at all. Nonviolence is a powerful force for the poor and for people of obvious conciense. It is not a method for those who continue to protect their privileges even while rehtorically espousing a "correct" politics of nonviolence. Thus is the importance of renunciation. Liberation from obsession with our possessions and privileges which directly causes others to go without, and harm the planet, tends to occur in stages and by degrees. Because it usually is a process over time, there is often confusion about the integrity of one's espousal of a nonviolent philosophy. However, nonviolence is not an idea that can for long be verbally articulated without also living and experimenting with it.

Just when I began to think I have progressed to a new conscious level of awareness, an event, a conversation, or an image "out of the blue" provokes an old learned response which feels violent, hostile, or confusing. It is this dialectical process of becoming aware, while often feeling stuck or regressive, that motivates me to sort it out with trusted friends, perhaps with "radical" therapists, trial and error experiences, and periods of silent contemplation and quiet discernment.

Liberation from our various addictions is a lifelong, radical transformational process, learning that less is more. For the most part this kind of deep transformation is usually provoked and stimulated by very personal, visceral experiences of feeling pain, suffering, and adversity rather than from accumulation of facts and information. It is important to realize that we are freeing ourselves from a greed/selfish power paradigm that has been developing for centuries, really for millenniums. We know that this demonic paradigm of blind greed, the presence of the past inherent in our collective unconscious, is destructive to life. It is based on belief in the separation of homo sapiens from nature, and from one another, rationalized by such factors as race, sex, class, age, national or geographical origin, language, religion, and cultural mores. All human beings possess a common ancestry. Many of the most renowned anthropologists and scientists conclude that cooperation and mutual aid, rather than competition, among homo sapiens and with all of nature, dominated human evolution for well over the first 99.8% of our time to date. Peter Kropotkin, who pioneered the positive study of ecology with his momentous *Mutual Aid*, argues that there is an instinct deeply rooted in our evolution that he describes as the "conscience of human solidarity." He eloquently talks of the "unconscious recognition of the force that is borrowed by each man from the practice of mutual aid," in effect, the "close dependency of every one's happiness upon the happiness of all." There is an ancient positive presence of the past, i.e. mutual aid, that is buried in each of us under layers of conditioning. Tapping into this dimension of our essence provides us much hope that the consciousness necessary for imagination, vision, courage, and interconnectedness is waiting to be liberated. We need to restore and honor the principles of the Commons.

My personal frustrations are exacerbated because for the most part the peace and justice "movement" in the United States does not address the structural issues, injustices, and institutions that furnish the foundation and guiding principles for the U.S. empire. Although the "movement" responds to many domestic and foreign policy issues, often with solid organizing and wonderful commitment, analysis of and radical response to the basic political and economic structures, and the values that underlay them, remain off limits. It is my belief that to the degree we believe in and work with the "American system", we are incapable of responding with the kind of radical (to the root) and revolutionary (a nonviolent turning around) energy and movement necessary for striving for truth and profound transformation. Nonviolence is a term often referring to specific behavior to be adhered to, and even rehearsed, for particular public demonstrations. This exposure may be a first step in learning about nonviolence but the term rarely describes a process of radical changes in internal attitudes, life and workstyles, and emotional growth, as we begin to understand interconnectedness. Development of collective, long term disengagement strategies through creation of networks of decentralized, locally reliant communities, is even more rarely considered.

In essence, nonviolence is a way of life requiring a radical restructuring of personal values, attitudes, and behavior. Virtually no one I know was consciously exposed to this moral from parents, school, or government. It is inevitable that once this consciousness is felt internally, it will be variously expressed in a more collective and political manner. We need to give each other permission to walk our talk, and trust our feelings, as we embark upon this "radical" journey. I like to think of the personal pursuit of nonviolence as walking on a path. Tough and rocky at times, and often lonely, it is leading us to new places, new experiences of consciousness, and a deeper understanding of ourselves and our relationship to all. It feels right. It is mysterious, yet real at the same time. It is hopeful and empowering.

Liberation from our dependence upon market jobs versus creative engagement; high speed movement and transiency versus deliberativeness and the sense of place; dislocation and fragmentation versus continuity; national and international currency versus regional currency and barter; highly consumptive lifestyles versus simple, cooperative sharing, will be necessary for revolutionary nonviolence.

Without vital, interactive community, renunciation is virtually impossible. Interdependence, not independence, become the model. Those of us who have grown up having learned how to be progressive individualists, now need to learn the dynamic of preserving a sense of self autonomy within the context intimate, sharing community. A truly decentralized, grass roots, participatory biocracy (democracy is for humans separate from nature) enables us to withdraw from our dependency upon the dangerous, dehumanizing, and violent global and national economy, i.e. the "free" market of the "new world order". As we simplify into local, bioregional communities of economic and energy self sufficiency, we create substance for a new foundation for the necessary radical change. This is our mandate as we approach the 21st century.

Nonviolence is not only realistic, it is our only hope if we are to survive with dignity on this planet. As Martin Luther King said, *"The issue is no longer between violence or nonviolence, but between nonviolence or nonexistence"*.

S. Brian Wilson is a Vietnam veteran, trained lawyer, and ex farmer, who has been nonviolently advocating for peace through justice for many years. A long time public war tax refuser, he has participated in a number of public fasts teaching about and resisting U.S. imperialist and terrorist policies in Latin America. He was one of the 4 participants in the 47 day water only 1986 Veteran Fast For Life in Washington, D.C.

He has traveled to number of "Third" world countries studying revolutionary popular movements and the effects of U.S. economic, political, and covert/overt military policies on self determination efforts.

Worship : Surrender, Sacrifice, Freedom.

— *Patricia McCarthy*

Mohandas K. Gandhi was a practical man. He used his hands and his feet, his back and his mind to test and enflesh what was in his heart and soul. By spinning and weaving the homespun and by walking to the sea for salt, by tilling the soil of communal living on Tolstoy Farm and by using the intellectual skills of a barrister, Gandhi expressed his beliefs in the rights and dignity of each person and all humanity's journey toward truth, toward God.

All of Gandhi's body and soul was in each action — no matter how seemingly insignificant the action appeared. Gandhi did not separate himself into separate parts in response to separate needs or requests. All of life and God and Gandhi and his search for truth were part of every activity. Gandhi lived intensely in the present and embraced eternity in each moment.

For these reasons it is difficult to consider Gandhi's sense of worship of God apart from every other aspect of Gandhi's life and teachings. Gandhi did not separate it and neither can we, so we keep all other aspects of his life's work in mind as we focus on his lived concept of worship.

Worship, for Mohandas Gandhi, was not mere ceremonial obeisance to metaphysical symbols or rigid adherence to dogmatic creeds which had become socially comfortable and politically convenient. Worship was the surrender of one's entire being to God, a surrender which transcended all human limitations. Worship of God could not be restricted to one cult or one nation or one cast. God could not be limited by national cultural boundaries.

No more than nonviolence for Gandhi was a compilation of tactics and techniques to achieve a goal peacefully was worship a pattern of specific sacrifices and offerings to God for the sake of religious beliefs. Worship was the leap of faith into the truth of God. It required all of one's heart and mind and soul and body. It demands work and personal discipline and sacrifice, but it was beyond the greatest efforts of even the most sincere man or woman.

Gandhi spent a lifetime in pursuit of the control of his senses and passions, but this zeal for self-purification cannot be wrongly mistaken as his religion. The self-purification was not a God but only a means for Gandhi to ready himself to meet God face to face. Gandhi practiced many restrictions in diet and lifestyle, but he did not deny his passions merely for the sake of developing perfect control. Gandhi prepared his body and spirit for openness to the transformation of being that only God can cause. "God to be God must rule the heart and transform it."

To receive the fullness of God and the freedom of our being each of us must go to God "empty-handed" as a poor person with no possessions, we must "disengage ourselves from trivialities". Self-purification was the process Gandhi used to disengage himself from the inessential in his attempt to reach the essential. Gandhi knew that the quality of his worship could not be judged by his efforts, but he also knew that his response was fundamental to an act or life of worship.

Gandhi was deeply conscious of the fact that life with God was not the fruit of human efforts. Yet Gandhi also knew that there were criteria to measure the truthfulness of worship. For Gandhi, these criteria were service and morality.

He recognized service of others, especially the poor and marginalized, as the mark of a religious person. Gandhi worshipped the living God, not merely the God of history but the God present in every person encountered in a day. Gandhi taught that worship was a matter of the heart but that lived expression of a God-centered heart took immeasurable strength and fidelity to daily acts of mercy and love.

In addition to service, morality is a key determiner of the quality of worship. For all people, life with God cannot be separated from life with each other. The moral values of one's personal life reflect the nature of one's worship more than adherence to a creed or attendance at religious services. No abuse, oppression or unconcern for another can be reconciled with true worship. Service of others and high moral standards are both the fruit and the measure of the truth of One's spirituality.

Finally, the willingness to suffer in love is at the heart of Gandhi's sense of worship. Nothing is more difficult to understand and accept than the mystery of suffering. Nothing was more central to Gandhi's worship of God. The embrace of suffering and the offering of one's life to God converts the one offering into a "votary of truth". This is worship — it is not what one does but what one is — a being in praise of God.

Not every one can accept this call to worship. Some are willing to give God time and honor. Others are able to spend their lives in the service of their neighbor for the love of God. Few willingly accept suffering in love as the heart of their worship. Gandhi, no more than any mortal, could not explain this embrace of suffering. He taught it passionately, he lived it faithfully. Gandhi knew in the deepest recesses of his being that the suffering must be unto death and he embraced it. "I worship God as truth only. I have not yet found him, but I am seeking after him. I am prepared to sacrifice the things dearest to me in pursuit of this quest. Even if the sacrifice demanded be my very life. I hope I may be prepared to give it."

Without the ultimate sacrifice of one's life, worship is irrelevant and empty. God engulfs us in a torrent of love which frees us to respond with the total surrender of all of our being. Worship is the abandonment to God of all our desires, hopes and dreams. It is the surrender of ourselves to God to be used as living witnesses to truth. In the emptying is the fulfillment. We need nothing because we have all things in God's truth. "God demands nothing less than the complete self-surrender as the price for the only real freedom that is worth having."

No just law, no jail, no oppressor could take freedom of worship from Mohandas Gandhi. He lived and died a free man because he gave away everything else for this treasure in God. Gandhi's life was an act of worship for the praise of God, in the service of truth and for the benefit of all humanity.

Sister Patricia McCarthy is a member of the congregation of Notre Dame. For over twenty-five years she has worked with the poor in the field of education, in particular with abused children. She has studied the theology and spirituality of nonviolence and given courses and lectures on the topic to students, adult education classes, parish groups, and religious communities throughout Canada, the United States, Ireland, North Ireland, and Japan. She organizes the annual prayer vigil every year at Trinity Site in Socorro, New Mexico where the first atomic bomb was tested on July 16, 1945. She has a column in a Rhode Island newspaper every month and has published articles in numerous other journals on the topic of nonviolence as a way of healing today's society.

Peacemaking Through Nonviolence

— *Michael N. Nagler*

It is blasphemy to say that nonviolence can be practiced by individuals and never by nations which are composed of individuals.

— *M.K. Gandhi*

The philosophy and strategy of nonviolence (must) become immediately a subject for study and serious experimentation in every field of human conflict, by no means excluding relations between nations.

— *Martin Luther King, Jr.*

The events of Somalia and what was once Yugoslavia have revealed alarming tensions in our post-cold-war world. One response to these tensions has been quite understandably the increased calls for UN Peacekeeping operations. The use of this type of intervention has evolved dramatically — with more operations in the four years 1988-1992 than in the previous forty — but far from adequately. General Secretary Boutros-Ghali has called for expanding the UN's mandate from 'peacekeeping' to 'peacemaking' and called for a standing peacemaking force. On the first point there is widespread agreement; as a student in Sarajevo said recently, "They could stop this war if they would send peacemakers instead of peacekeepers." However, no one has a very clear idea what UN peacemaking would be like; and as for the second point there is understandable resistance from many quarters to the idea of a standing UN army, especially now that UN military operations have come under the cloud of superpower domination during the Gulf War. We are caught in the dilemma of ignoring desperate calls for help or responding with military force which is increasingly problematic whether under UN auspices or not. One way or the other, as NATO head John Shalikasahvili said early in 1992, "the days of pristine peacekeeping as we have understood it for years are probably over". His solution was a NATO-former Warsaw Pact global police force.

The solution I propose here is nonviolent peacekeeping, called preferably nonviolent peacemaking to distinguish it from classical, armed peacekeeping interventions. Classical peacekeeping, from the point of view of those who now advocate an alternative, have the goal of keeping the peace but use the means of ordinary conflict. Nonviolent peacekeeping — also known as peace witnessing, interpositionary peace bridges and so forth — uses means that are more congruent with such ends. And that makes all the difference. One of the cardinal principles of nonviolence is, in Gandhiji's words, that "means are everything". Classical peacekeeping can reduce a conflict (when it works) but it cannot lead to long-term peace. We do not call for the abandonment of armed peacekeeping (at least not before a viable alternative is in place), but the theory and the actual history of nonviolent peacemaking show it to be much more effective not only in the short term (surprisingly enough it seems to be not only more effective but safer than peacekeeping by force of arms), but in the long-term project of leading to an eventual regime of stable peace.

Briefly, nonviolent peacemaking is carried out by people committed to positive, constructive means of reconciliation without the use of weapons or — ideally at least — of coercion of any kind. They do many things armed peacekeepers find themselves doing today : giving aid and comfort to the afflicted, escorting the endangered, resettling the dislocated; feeding, teaching and reconciling; but they do it all without relying on the protection or the sanction of force. How this can possibly work was accounted for in a famous definition of 'power' by Mahatma Gandhi :

Of Power there are two kinds. One is obtained by threats of punishment. The other arises from acts of love.

'Love' is not meant here in the sentimental sense, of course, but has perfectly practical bearing on what we are pleased to call 'Realpolitik': When Quakers broke the food blocked on Germany and Austria after World War One, they were not motivated by emotional love towards particular Germans, but by a higher sense of what makes politics work. And in fact, they seem to have been correct. Thirty years later Quaker relief groups were given permission to operate among the Jews right inside Germany even as the war was raging. Because they did not use threats of punishment (which we might call 'Force One'), but what Gandhi referred to as 'acts of love' ('Force Two') they made an impression on the mind-set even of severely dehumanized people — an effect which, had it been somehow amplified enough, might just have made World War Two unnecessary.

Most formal, institutionalized conflict management mechanisms that we're relying on in the world today, especially on the international scale, are based on threat force. I won't dwell on this sobering point, but even those institutions mandated to make peace classically, attempt to achieve that end by inhibiting 'Force one', including their own resort to threat-force, rather than by implementing 'Force Two'. It is time that attempts at 'peacebuilding' concentrate not so much on the auspices of power, be it national, transnational or global, but on the kind of power deployed.

'Force One' and 'Force Two' are entirely different animals : To limit the force unleashed by fear is good, it is devoutly to be wished, but it is not to be confused with enabling the force that could be engaged by empathy. By nature, in long-term practical results, they are not the same thing at all, and this is one of the most important distinctions to recognize in peace research — and life in general.

As an example, we can take the Iraq conflict. As soon as Saddam Hussein invaded Kuwait a public debate sprang up about the merits of attack or sanctions. But from the point of view of this two-force theory, sanctions are a form of attack; a milder form, quite possibly in some situations a correct form, but one that is not different in kind from the force that sends plane over the air space of another state, for example if it has not been persuaded by the sanctions. We know now what hardship has befallen the ordinary citizens, and especially the innocent children of Iraq as a result of this 'alternative' to violence. Sanction and attack are different degrees of the power that arises from (threats of) punishment.

So 'shall we use force or sanctions?' was a false dichotomy in the Persian Gulf, as it is today with the situation we are faced with in the Balkans and will be faced with in many other regions. Pulled punches are not the same as outstretched hands.

Section VII of the UN charter, containing the original mandate for UN peacekeeping, mentions precisely these two options, sanctions or military interposition. This 'array' of choices, which seems exhaustive because the two seem like polar opposites, is in reality like Dorothy Parker's acid comment that Katherine Hepburn, in her first performance, 'went through the whole gamut of emotions from A to B.' It is time to explore options that do not recycle, reorganize or contain the same energies that cause conflict but engage other energies which are inherently more likely to build up to stable peace. If 'sanctions or force' are options A to B, nonviolent peacemaking begins at C; D-Z are many other ways the UN and many other agencies and national states and indeed individuals could implement 'Force Two' in a program of long-term stable peace. It makes sense now to begin with nonviolent interventions which could be applied in region after region and which now have experience and theory behind them, but the work will not end there. Nonviolence, as Gandhiji labored to show us, is an infinitely creative force.

Even as the discourse of the general public and, we assume, policy-makers was confined in this false polarity of attack or sanctions, a very small ad-hoc group of international volunteers tried to carry out a nonviolent interposition on the Iraq-Saudi border. They were evacuated to Baghdad by Iraqi civilians fifteen days into the bombing whence most of them were removed some days later to Amman.

This might be thought as a poor argument for the effectiveness of such interventions. Consider, however, that this group was almost totally untrained (their strategy, for example, was rather poorly suited to what was obviously going to be an aerial attack) and isolated, not to say ignored in terms of public support. By virtue of being what was most needed, a nonaligned peaceful presence, they remained outside the classical 'polarity' of degrees of force and more or less invisible to public strategic discourse (as a State Department official posted in the Middle East at the time later told me, they were "completely irrelevant".) Yet they organized relief work in Amman some members of the team remained there), helped counter media distortions back home, learned a lot themselves (in the words of one participant the experience "bolstered my belief in the potential impact of practitioners of non-violence, ... particularly [with] advance training and the support of established peace and justice groups".) And they were not entirely alone.

While spontaneous interpositions in conflicts have been used to stop conflicts since the dawn of civilization (the Buddha is said to have stopped a war this way in the sixth century BCE) the idea of institutionalizing such peacemaking, of preparing for it ahead of time, is very recent. Peace scholars go back once again to the great 'Founder', Mahatma Gandhi, who begins articulating the concept of an unarmed 'peace army' *(shanti sena)* almost as soon as he has seen the effectiveness of non-violence at first hand in South Africa around 1913. Then in the twenties, back in India, he came out with detailed ideas for regional or neighborhood peace armies and continued to develop the concept until the end of a his life. Nothing ever persuaded him that they would not work on a grand scale; in one of his boldest and most misunderstood proposals he advocated that India respond with nonviolent peace brigades to the anticipated Japanese invasion during WWII,. He was still promoting some version of this after independence for resolving the Kashmir dispute at the time of his death.

The Mahatma was not given a chance to test this method in largescale conflicts himself, being imprisoned by the British and unsupported by his own party members during most of this period and on this issue; but by far the most dramatic *shanti sena* the world has so far seen was organized in the thirties in what was then the Northwest Frontier Province of India by the *Mahatma's* close disciple Khan Abdul Ghaffar Khan among the notoriously warlike Pathans whose descendents later would frustrate the overwhelmingly superior forces of the Soviet Union, by more traditional methods. Fully 100,000 Pathan warriors — all devout Muslims, by the way — vowed to resist the British without weapons in their hands or violence in their hearts, and kept their vow under unbelievable provocation, adding immesurably to the freedom struggle by their unsung efforts.

After Gandhi the idea of nonviolent peacekeeping slowly spread in India, where *shanti senas* have continued to operate, and elsewhere. Similarly motivated ad hoc groups have operated domestically to stop riots in several parts of the United States, including Berkeley, where I watched them prevent an ugly battle between students and the ROTC on my campus, as well as throughout India and in many places in the world. They have attempted to contact General Sandino in the jungles of Nicaragua in 1926, resettled refugees on Cyprus, restored order among populations terrorized by impending attack and negotiated a settlement to a longstanding succession conflict in Northern India and stopped a civil war, namely in Algiers in 1962. So we have evidence of very small, private, under-funded efforts accomplishing remarkable successes in conflicts that are intercommunal, intranational, even international.

The 1980's were an important decade for the development of peace brigades. Three non-governmental organizations; one Indian *(Shanti Sena)*, one religious (Witness for Peace) and one secular-international (Peace Brigades International) saw action in Guatemala, Nicaragua, El Salvador, Sri Lanka and to a lesser degree other regions, such as Quebec. Other groups have arisen very recently, and the Stockholm based Global Peace Service has had a series of international consultations to bring about a global coordinating body to recruit, train and field nonviolent peace teams, as well as acquaint the general public of their accomplishments and significance.

To summarize what these groups have accomplished significant reductions in conflict with extremely dangerous areas and extremely minimal means while at the same time suffering very minimal personal casualties. Three PBI workers were slashed with knives in Guatemala last year and several received death threats. Three relief workers have been killed by sniper fire in Bosnia, but inetrestingly no one has been killed while attempting to carry out what might be thought the most dangerous type of peacekeeping operation, outright interposition.

Both in Sri Lanka and Guatemala workers with Peace Brigades International (PBI) provided a shield that not only protected individuals who would certainly have been killed but made it possible for forces of peace and justice to consolidate and expand — the first thing repressive regimes try to prevent. And they have done remarkably well at protecting local communities. When Ernesto Cardenal was Minister of Culture in the Sandinista government I had occasion to ask him during a visit to Berkeley whether he thought the faith-based groups operating in his country were helping. To my surprise (Cardenal is far from dedicated to nonviolence) he told me with considerable passion that "We need more of these groups and we need them quickly. Wherever they have been there has been no violence." Later his translator repeated that statement for the gathering, but unconsciously added his own modification (a very common kind of distortion that all nonviolent advocates experience) : 'There has been almost no violence.' Cardenal practically pounded the table; 'I said absolutely no violence.'

Nonviolent peacemaking is an idea whose time has come; but it is no longer just an idea. It is an idea with a track record.

Where does the UN come in in this history? Up to now, the world's premier peacemaking body has feared to tread into this area. In 1954, and on other occasions Vinoba Bhave, Gandhiji's famed follower, offered the UN a peace army of 50,000 volunteers for service in the Bangladesh war. The UN did not take him up to it. Since that time things have improved slightly. As mentioned, UN operations have been side by side with ad hoc peacemakers, e.g. in the Balkans, and PBI has been given NGO status. But my proposal goes much further : The UN should systematically organize and conduct unarmed, nonviolent peacemaking and peacekeeping operations based on the experience of nongovernmental agencies in this field, either by creating a new agency or within existing peacekeeping mandates, and should create and maintain standing contingents for this purpose as long as is necessary.

Two objections are often raised to the idea of nonviolent peacekeeping. The first is that it is dangerous. Here it is good to recall that the efforts just described have been carried on without exception by a handful of small, nongovernmental organizations operating on voluntarism and private-sector fund-raising and have remained for the most part virtually ignored by the mass media. Yet they have successfully inhibited conflict in highly violent areas like Central America and Sri Lanka, and with virtually no casualties. 'Force Two' is powerful and efficient both at inhibiting conflict and protecting the practitioner — think of Mother Teresa who brought the war in Beirut to a standstill just by going in to rescue some orphans, without so much as a pistol to protect her person. Furthermore, this is not the point. Classical, armed peacekeeping is also dangerous. So is war. That doesn't seem to have stopped either of these activities. Advocates of nonviolent peacekeeping do not claim that their brand of intervention, because it relies on another kind of force, confers some magical safety on its practitioners. We expect casualties. We claim that the historical record, and the theory developed by those who have studied non-violence, argue that it is less dangerous than reliance on threat-force.

The other objections runs, isn't the UN already doing this sort of thing? As we have explained, no. One of the peculiarities of nonviolence is that it is incredibly robust in the face of external resistance — it is amazing how much punishment and threat a person can face down when properly motivated — but it is very sensitive to internal contradiction. Armed peacekeeping, however desirable in comparison to know alternatives, is almost by definition such a contradiction, You cannot really mix 'Force Two' with 'Force One' e.g. hold arms in reserve if non-use of arms doesn't work. Sensing this, the December, 1992, international volunteer peacemaking mission to Sarajevo, which had up to then cooperated in various ways with the UN protection force (UNPROFOR), declined to go the last stretch through 'sniper's alley' in a column between tanks provided by that force. They went it alone (and suffered no casualties in the process), quite correctly. As senior peace brigadist George Willoughby writes, "armed military forces flying the UN flag is a makeshift approach to the task of peacekeeping"; what is needed now is a "properly trained force skilled in conflict resolution" and willing to operate outside the protection of weapons. The UN has not mounted nonviolent peacemaking brigades.

This is not to say that the soldiers who make up UN peacekeeping missions are not capable of participating in nonviolent peacemaking. Many are. The right situation can bring out extraordinary courage in anyone, and when it does nonviolence works for them, or perhaps we should say through them, whoever they may be. Military training does not attract the same people or bring out of them the same human potential they would have if they were going into a situation with empathy and courage as their only protection. So the two crucial differences between what we might call classical peacekeeping and nonviolent peacekeeping are, first that the nonviolent peacekeepers are unarmed and second that they want to be. This to paraphrase Gandhiji again, makes all the difference. It creates an entirely different climate of possibility.

It is important to realize that extremely brave and committed men and women (I keep starting to say, brave young men and women, but in fact Brad Lyttle who has just penetrated into Mostar is in his seventies) are going into intense conflict situations right now whether or not the UN or an independent global body comes forward to support them. Yet the UN should support them, for its own good and for theirs. If I were the secretary general of the UN (and had world opinion more or less behind me), I would actually scarp classical peacekeeping tomorrow, giving all UN soldiers the option of being retrained for nonviolent peacekeeping. In the real world, however, what I recommend is transarmament; to phase in some nonviolent peacemaking operations and phase out armed peacekeeping progressively as the former prove their effectiveness. There would be three steps to beginning this transition.

1. Identify resource people who know how peace armies work, experimentally or theoretically. They could be brought together for a conference, say at the UN University in Costa Rica or a suitable progressive peace institution like the University of HI, Manoa or Meiji Gakuin. The task of such a conference would be to identify the needs that must be met to develop and institutionalize nonviolent peacemaking.

2. Recruit, organize and train volunteers. As a professor with twenty years' experience teaching nonviolence at a major research university, I can give my absolute personal assurance that idealistic volunteers are available. The task will only be to identify them and get them together with those who have leadership skills, experience and understanding of this peculiarly challenging discipline. In nonviolent peacemaking

recruitment and training are the keys, where military peacemaking leans towards equipment and expenses. All recruitment must be individual and voluntaristic, unlike for armed peacekeeping where it is sometimes possible to enlist ready-made corps from national governments. The training of nonviolent peacemakers is a difficult subject that will unquestionably require further study : The priceless experience of nongovernmental agencies will again be helpful here.

As suggested already, not only are military peacekeeping operations in many respects a useful model, they could very often involve the same people. Courage is courage, you just have to learn to point it in a somewhat different direction. Ordinary combat veterans, too, are an already partly trained manpower pool.

3. Select an intervention. First a disaster or a human-assisted disaster like Somalia : than perhaps a subnational war like the former Yugoslavia, but there is no inherent reason nonviolent peacemaking could not eventually be used, as armed peacekeeping is increasingly being used, to prevent war. It could be well to have the new corps being modestly, drawing n what they already know how to do, e.g. protect threatened individuals by escorting them; but the UN difference is that the body would empower the groups to go beyond that kind of intervention as opportunities present themselves (as they certainly will). Its logistic support would include giving the corps full publicity both to protect them and to maximize their influence on the conflict (and indeed the entire 'conflict regime'), to keep communications open supply them with whatever medical, agricultural, educational material is required. In terms of long-term progress toward real peace, the UN's role would then be to give the groups major opportunities to debrief the public after successful missions.

An important corollary to peacemaking operations themselves is in fact educating the general public. UNESCO could take on the historical effort of documenting and explaining how nonviolence 'peacebuilding' has worked and how it should be further developed to suit modern conditions. It is the UNESCO Characters that says war begins in the 'minds of men'; UNESCO could directly undertake education that can give men another mind-set. In the same way, if with slightly less international prestige, a global peace service of some kind could multiply the effect of these volunteers. Peace research has taught us never to underestimate the effectiveness of right means coupled with right ends. When Alain Richard of PBI has referred to as the 'contagion' of peace that often allowed his team to win over intransigent opposition and prevail over seemingly impossible odds is confined to a small scale only because we have not mounted it on a larger one.

I would like to close by citing four major advantages of nonviolent peacekeeping an two objections that arise even within what Gandhiji called the science of nonviolence. First the advantages :

Cost — classical peacekeeping is cheaper than war, but nonviolent peacekeeping is cheaper still. You get much more non-bang for the buck. It requires even less equipment, it is done by idealistic volunteers who love their work, and it is remarkably efficient. The PBI Volunteers in Nicaragua in 1983, who apparently pacified Jalapa, a war zone on the Honduran border, for as long as they remained constituted a 'brigade' of ten people.

Political viability — UN peacekeeping has been hampered by its ad hoc status, yet the understandable fear of a standing army that would look like a world police force (not to mention an excuse for some Security Council nations' power plays) prevents the world from moving in the needed direction. Most people and states would have no such problem with a standing peace army. The prospects of being invaded by well-intensioned and highly skilled peacemakers, mostly young idealistic people, is terrifying only to tyrants, if they understand the power it entails.

UN effectiveness — as Marrack Goulding, recently called the world's peacekeeper-in-chief, has put it, "The United Nations can cajole, argue, bluster ... but it cannot compel." Nonviolent peacekeeping would turn this weakness of the UN into its greatest strength. Nonviolence is that form of power specifically designed to operate in situations where you cannot or do not wish to compel. 'Persuasion, not coercion' is the motto of nonviolence. This is again part of a very substantial issue; it is no too much too hope that by resolving one of its basic contradictions, namely the use of 'Force One' to produce what can only be produced by reconciliation, nonviolent peacemaking would unlock the potential of the UN. No single measure could more enhance the effectiveness of the UN at the present time than for it to support and adopt nonviolent peacekeeping.

Long-term peace development effectiveness — classical peacekeeping has been sputtering along. It has prevented or limited some conflicts, but it has not, and cannot change the direction of international relations. It cannot do this because it puts in play (or holds in readiness) the same force that peaceless interactions use, albeit for another purpose. But nonviolent peacemaking suffers from no such handicap. There would be some false starts, some errors and some casualties, but once it became clear that there is a way to make peace without the sanction of force (i.e. 'Force One') the world would have found a new direction towards enduring peace.

Now the objections :

Is interposition *swadeshi*? Those claiming the blessing of Gandhiji on an interventionary or interpositionery service of the type envisioned here must admit that in one potentially serious respect the *Mahatma's* vision, as far as he expressed himself on this subject, was different. In accordance with his cardinal principle of *swadeshi*, operating in one's own area and from one's own native resources, his conception of the *shanti sena* was, as we have seen, quite local. While he described what we would call today a kind of civilian based defense in all its fundamentals, particularly in connection with the anticipated Japanese invasion, and while he went a step further than contemporary conceptions of CBD in proposing that the local brigades consist of highly trained and disciplined volunteers on permanent duty (as opposed to an ad hoc mobilization of all willing citizens), he does not seem to have envisioned that they would go abroad and interpose themselves in others' conflicts as a third party. Rather, he seems to have felt that they would at most mobilize collectively for national defence against an external invader : "They would be constantly engaged in constructive activities that make riots impossible. Theirs will be the duty of seeking occasions for bringing warring communities together, carrying on peace propaganda, engaging in activities that would bring and keep them in touch with every single person, male and female, adult and child, in their parish or division. Such an army should be ready to cope with an emergency, and ... risk their lives in numbers sufficient for the purpose".

The step from self-defence to third-party interposition cannot be taken lightly; if it violates *swadeshi*, it is different in kind from what Gandhi purposed and what in fact came into existence in a limited way in India. Perhaps it would not be mere casuistry to appeal, however, that the world has shrunk continuously since Gandhiji passed from the scene and that when sudden catastrophic conflicts erupt anywhere, they affect all of us, even more immediately than in 1948. This is especially true when the conflicts — and ironically this is usually the case when closely related people become enemies — precipitate the kind of gross dehumanization we have seen in the Balkans and Somalia (and Ossetia and Burma and Tibet and elsewhere). In this negative sense the world is somewhat more of a village, the *swadesh* of everyone.

As Gandhiji himself declared, "It is my firm belief that when one person rises spiritually, the world rises with him (or her), and when one person falls the world falls with him (or her) to that extent." The official world defends its callous disregard of suffering in the Balkans because we 'Have no national interest' in a place which is not oil-rich or strategically placed. This is extremely offensive. Have we no human interest? Where people and organizations carrying out this idea, or others in the world at large, were ignoring conflicts in their home community. It seems to me that nonviolent interposition would be part of a sound peace strategy if 1) There were local as well as international teams and 2) the support groups and team members themselves take very seriously the need to communicate to the public what they had achieved and the principle on which it was based so that their achievement could be understood and made part of the great effort in which all must now be involved, to create a peace culture.

Another objection that sometimes comes up is that interposition, in addition to being a third-party mechanism, enters the picture very late. Wouldn't it be much less costly to intervene sooner? of course it would; but we live in a world where severe conflicts occur, or become public, suddenly and will continue to do so for some time. This is another reason nonviolent intervention should not be the only mechanism in a new struggle towards abiding peace; it is not a reason such intervention should not exist. Let us all hope for the day when nonviolent interventions are no longer necessary; but we can hasten that day by working to prepare such interventions now.

During a MacNeil-Lehrer News-hour just before Christmas an American Catholic nun, discussing our military/humanitarian intervention in Somalia said, "In a season when we long so for peace and to comfort the afflicted ...wouldn't it be wonderful if we had at the same time a force that provided agrarian help, economic help? Why not have grandmothers along to hold the abandoned, orphaned children? ... We don't plan for peace, and we don't have a program for peace. We only have a program for war."

Nonviolent intervention is part of a program for peace.

*Michael Nagler founded the Peace and Conflict Studies Program (PACS) at the University of California in Berkeley, where he regularly teaches the upper-division nonviolence course, and has spoken and written widely for campus, religious, public and special interest groups on the subject of peace and nonviolence for twenty-five years, in addition to his career in classics. He has consulted for the U.S. Institute for Peace and many other organizations. **Dr.Nagler** is collaborating on a new book on Gandhi by Eknath Easwaran, President of Blue Mountain Center of Meditation, and writing a second book on nonviolence, as well as articles for the Marin Experimental Teaching and Training Center (METTA) newsletter and other media.*

(Excerpted from "Peace Making through Nonviolence" by Dr. Michael Nagler, permission to reprint granted by Dr. Michael Nagler.)

Nonviolence Begins With Breakfast

— Ingrid Newkirk

On the side of every NASA space craft that lifts off the pad at Cape Kennedy is inscribed a set of symbols, placed there on behalf of the entire human race in the hope that alien intelligences will understand and respect their message. The message is, "We come in peace." Sadly, we don't. At least, not yet.

Picture our astronauts landing on a flat planet. The hatch swings open and our earth ambassadors clamber awkwardly down the ladder. Below, waiting for them, is a group of the first beings from another planet they have ever encountered. Now imagine what would happen if these "aliens" sound, move and look EXACTLY like frogs or mice or baboons. Would Ground Control advise the astronauts to remain true to the slogan emblazoned on the side of their craft? If so, it would certainly be another first for humankind. More likely, the "peaceful mission" would disintegrate on the spot, and the aliens would find themselves thrown into cages and shuttled back to Earth for a spot of intergalactic dissection.

On our own planet we have already encountered millions of alien intelligences : sea-going animals — like octopuses who decorate their caves with "trinkets" they collect from the sea floor, cuttlefish who communicate through motion and color waves, and whales whose well-developed social structure includes baby-sitting aunts; land animals — like fallow deer who practice birth control by reabsorbing their own fetuses when there is insufficient plant life to sustain a bigger herd, gentle beavers whose engineering feats have provided blueprints for some of our own underwater building endeavors, and our "best friend" the faithful dog who will risk his own life to save that of a human being; and animals of the air — who can construct homes for their families using only clay and twigs, dive on a dime, and circumnavigate the globe without benefit of a compass or map.

What have we done to these aliens? We have caged them for our entertainment, eaten them, made shoes and coats from their skins, put bits in their mouths, muzzles on their noses and chains about their necks. We've even used them to test nerve gases and other accessories of the wars we wage against each other. .

So, putting the "We come in peace" message on our spacecraft is an acknowledgment that, although acting as if "Might makes Right" can be deliriously advantageous for us, the Master Race here on Earth, such a policy could be our death warrant in space. Our message really means : "Helloo, out there. If you are bigger and stronger than we are, please don't hurt us." In other words, "Do what we say, not what we do."

Perhaps we can be excused for our unbridled aggression early on when we held a more realistic view of our place in life's orchestra, as one of many players rather than the self-appointed leader of the band. When we first began hunting animals we were simply trying to survive in the same way aboriginal peoples and, indeed, lions and eagles still do. But today, in the developed world, we have better options. We do not need to continue our undeclared war on the other animal nations. We can easily feed, clothe and entertain ourselves without robbing other beings of the very things that provide their own warmth, sustenance and fulfillment.

Being important or clever has never made it acceptable to be a bully. Rather, those with more should be magnanimous and protective to those with less or with none. Somehow we must remember this when we start feeling puffed up, about ourselves. Certainly we are members of a rather grand species. We can build everything from tape recorders to weather satellites and even install pipes to carry water into the Kalahari. But it helps to remember that the other animals have impressive, if different, abilities, too. They live simply and efficiently in ways we only respect; surviving steadfastly under stark conditions without any of the accoutrements of "civilization," such as grocery stores, motorized transportation, and irrigation systems. For example, the results of a six year study by behavioral scientist Dr. Theodore Barber reveals linnets can compose songs as intricate and dynamic as a Beethoven symphony and deliver them at such a speed that we NEED our recorders to catch notes hidden from the human ear; The New Scientist reports that the humble newt can "see" the lasting electro-magnetic field; studies of desert mice show that they obtain enough water to sustain themselves on arid planes by placing pebbles outside their burrows to catch the dew; and ethologists associated with Jane Goodall's Gombe Stream Research Center report that other-than-human primates treat illness and injuries by using naturally-occuring plant forms of emetics, antibiotics and healing salves.

Doubtless, it requires great effort for us to grasp the nature and needs of a being as physically different from us as a frog, a mouse, or a baboon. Yet, look at what we have done to life forms as similar to ours as the chimpanzee, a being whose blood plasma we can exchange for our own and who shares almost 90% of "our" DNA. As I write, there are hundreds of chimpanzees confined in laboratories in the United States, many on military bases. They rock back and forth inside barren steel cages no bigger than a kitchen refrigerator. Simply because we can get away with it, we irradiate them and infect them with AIDS, hepatitis, and other infectious diseases as if they are no more than test tubes with faces. Some of the chimpanzees have gone mad, the rest are slowly getting there as a result of their total isolation confinement. We know they are intelligent and social beings, yet we have not only seized them from their homelands and families and deprived them of the freedom to pursue their lives, but we have given them nothing to see, do or touch, and no contact with others of their own kind. It is only prejudice that allows us to disrespect them and treat them like objects instead of living beings.

I found myself dwelling on the destructive nature of prejudice in 1991 when the last American hostages were released from captivity in Lebanon. Like the massacre at Mai Lai, the Serbian prison camps and other wartime atrocities, what Joseph Ciccippio and his fellow prisoners suffered could be chalked up to the terrible consequences of their captors' lack of empathy toward those they viewed as "different." Ciccippio, who may suffer seizures for the rest of his life as a result of random and unprovoked beatings, also suffered exposure from being chained out on a balcony through two winters. Understandably, the men suffered psychological trauma as well as physical and often believed their deaths were imminent.

Hearing of Ciccippio's ordeal made me think back to the lack of compassion and empathy for others I witnessed as humane society law enforcement officer. I remember confiscating an abused puppy whose face had swollen to the size of a grapefruit from a blow from an iron bar that had crushed the bones in his nose; cutting the chains from the neck of a frozen; starving dog in the early hours of a bitter winter morning; watching the horrified expressions in the eyes of horses being beaten in the face as they were herded panic-stricken down the slaughterhouse ramp to their deaths; listening to the sound of rabbits trying to claw their way out of a laboratory testing chamber filling with noxious fumes.

To those who say, "How can you compare the suffering of these animals to that of human beings?" I answer, "How can you not?" What we need is not distance but closeness, not apathy and scorn but empathy and outreach. For suffering is suffering, victims are victims, and injustice is injustice, no matter where it occurs, to whom, or when. that was true when white Americans headed into the deep south to support the rights of blacks to vote and it is true now.

The message on our spacecraft can be seen as a goal to strive for. Attitudes are changing and, as a result, we look back in shame on our appalling treatment of human beings with disabilities, the disadvantaged, the elderly, institutionalized people, and all manner of "others" we have abused. Instead of trying to make amends, case by case, we can simplify things by applying our principles across the board, deciding to oppose any and all acts of aggression, oppression, exploitation and meanness, whether or not we and those we know or can easily relate to are the immediate victims. Such a decision will affirm that there is something more to our wish for peace than a personal desire to be spared pain, hardship, suffering and death.

Adopting the Golden Rule of "Do Unto Others..." without placing meaningless, narrow limits on who those "others" are, means facing the fact that even the smallest bird can feel the nuclear blast, the slaughterer's knife, the hunter's gun, and the trapper child's fingers about its throat. Such a realization, embraced without excuses or resistance, changes the way we behave towards the bird. Best of all, perhaps, it moves us ever closer to a time when we can say to all beings, "We come in peace." And mean it.

Ingrid Newkirk, a well-known animal rights advocate, is Chairperson of Peace for Ethical Treatment of Animals in Washington, D.C. PETA was incorporated to educate policy- makers and the public about issues involving the intense, prolonged and unjustifiable abuse of animals, and to promote an understanding of the inherent rights of sentient animals to be treated with respect and decency.

Satyagraha And Liberation
Of Russia In 1905

— Yelena Demidova

In 1917 Mohandas K. Gandhi, analysing the concept of *satyagraha*, wrote that people needed real historic evidence of the efficacy of *satyagraha* since written history is so overwhelmingly loaded with military achievements. Meanwhile there are a great number of undocumented instances of successful use of satyagraha in our lives. One example is the 1905 liberation movement in Russia also known as the first bourgeois-democratic revolution.

The fundamental principle of the movement was its adherence to the concept of Truth and Justice. Peasants, workers, the intelligentsia, the bourgeoisie and the landowners unitedly struggled for human dignity and the restoration of civil liberties. They thought it was possible to restore social justice by setting up a body that represented the people's voice and which could inform the government of the urgent needs of the people.

Those who opposed the Tsarist government did not wish to conquer or destroy the opponent. Violence that ensued was unleashed by the Tsarist State Government. The people strove to "open the eyes" of the Tsar by appealing to his sense of justice and love. The people's movement up to this point had no hostile intentions.

The nonviolent liberation movement of 1905 followed the Truth expressed by Leo Tolstoy who, around the same time as the liberation movement in Russia, influenced Mahatma Gandhi in South Africa. Tolstoy wrote about the close connection between power and violence. The more one yearns for power the more one is inclined to use violence to gain and preserve it. The people from all layers of Russian society who participated in the 1905 liberation movement to seek justice eschewed violence. They advocated a peaceful settlement of the problem. However, the forces who, as Tolstoy predicted, were more interested in capturing (revolutionaries) or keeping (conservatives) in power used violence to crush the movement. In this context Tolstoy's shocking conclusion that State power is useless merits closer scrutiny.

There was one more feature of *Satyagraha* that the participants of the Russian liberation movement adhered to firmly. They were persistent in their aim to attain their goal and were willing to make whatever sacrifice needed to achieve it. While the nonviolent movement was in progress every thirtieth adult man in Russia was held prisoner.

Mohandas K. Gandhi wrote : "*Satyagraha* is spreading over everyone like the sky; it is contagious and all people — adults and children, men and women become *satyagrahis.*"

The population of Russia, especially those from large cities, rallied to bring about nonviolent change. Even school children held meetings, submitted petitions and participated in demonstrations. Everyone thought the laws in force were unfair and unjust and refused to obey them. The people realized their power during the course of the agitation. They were able to remain firm in their belief in spite of the repression. When the government instituted criminal proceedings against some of the *satyagrahis* for their participation in the disobedience campaign, hundreds of their colleagues submitted their confessions in writing claiming to have done the same thing as those being charged and demanding the same punishment. This action was successful. The government had to abandon the persecution since they could not imprison the entire Russian Bar.

The general strike in October was the climax of the revolutionary movement and the government had to yield to the will of the liberation front by issuing the Manifesto of October 17 granting the people civil liberties. Though this did not meet all the demands of the *satyagrahis* it was a victory the liberation movement won through nonviolent action. To achieve their objective the workers paralyzed the whole country. The railways and telephones and telegraph services did not work and there were rumblings of a mutiny in the military. Since the apparatus of oppression was showing signs of crumbling the Tsar was forced into relenting.

Gandhi believed people can be oppressed only to the extent they allow themselves to be oppressed. When the people realize the oppression is stifling they can take action to correct the situation. The important aspect of a properly conducted nonviolent campaign is that there is room for compromise. In the Russian revolution the relationship between the Tsar and the subjects was like the relationship between father and son. The Tsar depended upon his subjects to remain in power and the subjects depended on the Tsar to provide them with stability, security and cohesive society. While a violent revolution would have destroyed everything that the society stood for and worked for a nonviolent revolution based on the spirit of love and compassion made it possible to reach an amicable compromise.

The principle of *satyagraha* is based on one's ability to judge a situation honestly and truthfully. If truth is on the side of the *satyagrahi* then victory is theirs but if truth is not on their side then the people would have to suffer the consequences of an evil action. Participants in the Russian liberation movement took that risk and found that truth was, indeed, on their side.

The events of 1905 were far from being ideal. Before success was achieved the Tsar's oppressive forces unleashed a great deal of violence to suppress the movement. The people who made up the basic active force of the liberation movement too were far from being ideal. Violence broke out in various places. However, for the most part the liberation movement adhered to the spirit of Gandhi's philosophy of *satyagraha*. Gandhi described *satyagraha* as a spiritual force and believed human beings are fundamentally nonviolent. History shows that anyone at any time or in any place who fights for truth becomes a *satyagrahi* whether the person realizes it or not. Nonviolence may be the characteristic of a single person or a whole group of people. In the liberation of Russia it was the characteristic of all Russian people who strove for truth and the dream of setting up God's Kingdom on earth. The combined forces of love and truth helped them conquer oppression and win the rights through nonviolent means.

There are two important lessons to learn from the historic reality of the Russian liberation experience of 1905. First, and most importantly, it is essential to emphasize repeatedly the need to adhere to nonviolence under all circumstances. In the Russian movement this was not done adequately. The result of this inadequate planning and preparation for nonviolence many of the participants resorted to violence when confronted with violence by the armed forces.

The second important element is to plan for positive action which was lacking in the Russian movement. The 1905 liberation struggle in Russia was led by the liberals whose program was full of negative ideas. The issue of the Manifesto of October 17th, though far short of the people's expectations, appeared to satisfy the liberals. The movement had generated tremendous energy throughout the country and the liberal leaders had no program to direct the energy into creative channel.

This situation was, understandably, exploited by representatives of extremist parties like the Bolsheviks and the Socialists. To win the allegiance of the people the Bolsheviks and Socialists projected themselves as champions of Truth and Justice. In reality their objective was to establish another ruthless dictatorship. They presented this idea to the people as the ultimate form of justice. This form of misrepresentation caused an outbreak of tremendous violence negating all the good that was achieved by the nonviolent actions of thousands of people around the country.

Yelena Demidova is a post graduate student at the Institute of Philosophy in Russia. Her thesis is devoted to Satyagraha's Prototypes in the Liberation Movement of Russia in 1905.

The Philippines : It's Time To Listen To Gandhi

— Fr. Niall O'Brien

The Philippines is a rich and beautiful land. The people are known for their gentleness and hospitality and those of us who have lived here a long time would add that the people are intelligent, industrious and compassionate. All the ingredients for peace and prosperity.

The island of Negros, where I have lived for thirty years, is like the rest of the Philippines archipelago in the above respect, but in another way it is entirely different. For more than twenty years we have had a war in progress. As I write, guerilla groups mass in secret mountain hide-outs, still holding their own after twenty-five years of war.

To bring you back. Most of the good land of Negros supports sugar cane and most of the three-and-a-quarter million population is involved and dependent on sugar — in one way or another. The sunny side of this industry is the plush hotels of the capital city of Bacolod, the excellent universities, the shopping malls. The dark side is the three-hundred-thousand field-workers who cultivate and cut the seven-hundred-thousand hectares of sugar cane and struggle to support one-and-a-half million hope starved dependents. It is here on the endless plantations that the trouble begins. Here lies the smoldering heart of the revolution.

Many sugar workers over the years have escaped from the plantations to yet undiscovered valleys in the mountains or uplands cleared of trees. There they have become frugal settlers. However some wealthy land owners in the lowlands, not content with what they have, followed them. These wealthy people have procured government land titles giving them ranches and various claims to the land which the settlers had cultivated without the benefit of legal title. Rich ranchers have pursued the settlers out of these often mean settlements. No wonder Negros presents, and has presented for a hundred years, the classic revolutionary situation.

Twenty-five years ago the standard of the peasants was taken up by young idealistic students. First there was a moment when they stood uncertain on what way to go, the way of Mao or the way of Gandhi? The students chose the way of Mao — armed struggle. Starting in the country side, they would take over outlying villages and gradually move inward until finally they would strangle the cities and sweep away the old institutions and impose a new order of justice and equality.

Looking back, it is easy to see why Mao should have been the model. In 1969 he was riding high with his cultural revolution, the hero of the youth. The Philippine press, or the world press for that matter, did not know the real 'goings on' inside China. I recall those glowing articles, shallow and deceptive. Yes, there was a hint at a darker side but few knew just how dark. Some did but their voices were to shrill and the students didn't listen.

Mao had one glorious success to his credit : China had stood up and as far as the outside world was concerned she was now feeding her people her self. Mao's formula, strategies, and tactics were put together in a handy catechism : The Little Red Book. His logic was simple and appealing : Power flows from the barrel of a gun, a philosophy which all the great nations of the world seem to subscribe to and which the mainstream churches and religions have never challenged adequately.

Well, that was twenty-five years ago. The insurgency prospered. They did invest in the countryside and they did gain credibility. In response, the dictator Marcos enhanced his power demanding larger military budgets to control the insurgency. He hypnotized the West : the problem, he implied, was Communism not the social conditions of the peasantry. As Marcos got worse, the revolution grew stronger; they grew together. The revolutionaries reached some 26,000 battle cadres. By 1985 they could almost have challenged Marcos' troops in the open.

Then Marcos called a 'snap' election. It was to be another of those masterpieces of magic by which he drew his own name out of the hat and won a new lease of approval from the United States. The revolutionaries ordered a massive boycott of the elections, (though secretly among their own ranks they were divided about the boycott strategy). But the ordinary people made their own decision. Against all odds and in spite of the memories of past fraud and the call to boycott the elections, the people went out and voted. They voted against Marcos and when he refused to grant their victory, they amassed in the streets and toppled his government. This event is called the EDSA event because that is the name of the wide road where the main confrontation took place. This is simplification of what happened, but the irony is inescapable that, in the final analysis, it was the unarmed people who threw Marcos out while the revolutionaries stood on the side lines and watched. It was Gandhi who triumphed against Marcos, not Mao.

President Cory Aquino had been the symbol of the people's resistance. She had borrowed the term nonviolence and promised to introduce real land reforms and clean up the administration.

Peace talks between the revolutionaries and the Cory Aquino government broke down and fighting resumed with the military deploying new strategies. They encouraged religious fanatics — bombing civilian populations out of the mountains so that insurgents had no civilian support. Massive human rights violations took place in places like Negros; and it all seemed to work. The lid, it seemed, was firmly placed on the cauldron of revolution.

Meanwhile, the revolutionaries had other problems. Marcos, who stoked the revolution, was gone and the American bases were shut down by the newly elected Senate. The revolutionaries were aghast by the success of nonviolence. This was not mentioned in their Red Book. The Soviate Union crumbled and when the people of the world looked inside the cracked shell, they found it almost empty. The Negros revolutionaries retreated into the remote mountains. The military and the government were in the ascendancy again. President Aquino had it in her power to undo the injustices which gave rise to the war with equitable land distribution in Negros. But, she chose not to fulfill this promise. True, she was hampered by the army's continuous attempts at *coup d'etat*. But, there were ways to overcome this obstacle. She could have used her great personal prestige and patronage to push for strong Agrarian Reforms, beginning with her own large plantation. In fact, the whole country waited to see what she would do with this plantation. Not even a token gesture was made. Why would other landlords follow?

While writing, a typical case was brought to my notice. The peasants, after a long bureaucratic struggle for land reform, finally got the papers from the Department of Agrarian Reform, then found themselves blocked by the armed guards of the landowner. A visiting human rights lawyer posed the question to me : "They have tried the legal means — what is left for them now?" I knew this question did not come just from her, but was the result of her conversations with the peasants. The question implies armed struggle is inevitable. Once again Negros stand on an historical threshold. We are back to the choice : Mao or Gandhi?

When I say the choice is between Mao or Gandhi, I am using a figure of speech. In truth, not many have heard of Gandhi. The choice is between the failed legal and democratic system and the new revolutionary doctrine apparently used so successfully just across the China Sea. Since religion offers no radical critique of violence as a means of solving conflicts, it is obvious to idealistic students that Mao's methods are the only alternatives.

Now, a quarter of a century later the shine has gone off Mao, and the extraordinary events at ESDA have raised the possibility of another way. Yes, the events were controversial, there were wheels within wheels. Nonetheless, even for the revolutionaries, it was obvious something 'new' had happened. A chance for the

Gandhian way was opening up. The people were not using Gandhi's name, but they were using the term 'nonviolence' which was Gandhi's special gift to the 20th century. They began to ask the unthinkable question : could nonviolence be as effective as violence? Used properly could it be more effective? Could active nonviolence, the longest way round, be the sure way home?

The immediate period after the fall of Marcos was a period of euphoria. It was soon followed by disillusionment when it became clear that the new government was either unable or unwilling to bring about the changes which would give peace a solid foundation. President Aquino rode across the Red Sea on the back of the people, but failed to lead them across the desert of reform to the promised land.

Since Mrs. Aquino had identified herself with the language of nonviolence and nonviolent change, the disillusionment with her also meant disillusionment with the power of nonviolence. Fortunately, only for those who had never really understood the power of nonviolence, nonviolence is not a magic wand which will banish injustice overnight.

It always leaves me with a feeling of deep sadness when people dismiss non-violence — and I know what they are dismissing is only a shallow image of nonviolence — not that wonderful theology, philosophy and spirituality which Gandhi taught and used so effectively against the British Empire. If blood was shed afterwards in the division of the subcontinent into Pakistan and India, it was not because they had listened to Gandhi, but because they had not listened to him.

So, what would Gandhi's program be at this juncture in the Philippines?

Gandhi's program would start with the ordinary people — a total respect for them, especially the poor. He also respected their culture. He realized of course that culture is ambivalent; there is a shadow side to all culture, so he opposed and personally dealt lethal blows to the age old caste system. He realized that the people are the wealth of a country. India was not the land of the subcontinent; it was the people of the subcontinent.

On Gandhian principles, the Philippine government would give up its fifty year old fascination with city-based development and industrialization and give first priority to the problems of the peasants who make up 70% of the population. Their self-reliance, and their independence should be developed through farm related small industries. Taxation should be progressive, rather than indirect, and migrant workers should not be fleeced by government exchange rates. There is need for a change of heart so that those on the top of the educational ladder do not use their education to consolidate their economic dominance, but rather to transform the whole society from below.

The revolutionaries too have something to learn from Gandhi : Gandhi respected the religion of the people, be it Muslim or Hindu and he used the values of religion to correct the unacceptable parts of the culture, such as the caste system, while working at the same time for the reform of Hinduism itself. In this spirit, faced with the Philippine situation, he would surely appeal to the power at the heart of the church for social change. The church is a sleeping giant. If ever it were to awake to its own true calling, it could truly transform the Philippine social scene.

Gandhi used to say that he believed in Christ but not in Christians. His understanding of the Gospel was that Christ taught that nonviolence is the only way to true social transformation. This Gospel teaching has been sidestepped by the churches for a long time and in its place we have the 'Just War Theory' which owes more to Cicero than to Christ.

Someone has said that the history of the Christian Church is the history of escaping from the teaching of the 'Sermon on the Mount'. Catholics are prone to explain it away by saying that the injunctions of Matthew 5-7 "are intended only for a special category of Christians, more particularly the clergy". The reform churches tended to say that it was impossible to fulfill these commands so they served the purpose of bringing us humbly to our knees, making us admit our sinfulness and rely totally on Christ. In the 19th century the interpretation was that the commands themselves were not as important as the attitude of mind and disposition of heart which they embodied. In all three interpretations, under certain circumstances, you could kill, but you must love the person you were killing.

Scholars across the religious divide are radically reevaluating the 'Sermon on the Mount' and the consequences of Jesus' teachings on loving enemies, as is clear from this extract from Bosch's Transforming Mission:

Today, however, most scholars agree that these and similar interpretations are inadequate, that there is no getting around the fact that, in Matthew's view, Jesus actually expected all his followeres to live according to these norms always and under all circumstances ....

If we recognize this we also, however, have to concede that, down through the centuries, precious few followers of Jesus have actually lived up to these expectations. There is a discrepancy between what Jesus taught and what actually happened to his teaching. This is particularly true of his injunction to love our enemies which, more than any other command, reflects the true nature of Jesus' boundry-breaking ministry ....

It forms the culmination of Jesus' ethic of the reign of God.

If Gandhi had a word for Christians in Philippines today, it would be for us to accept this teaching of Christ on nonviolence. It was Gandhi's constant effort to get people to be true to their own faith. If he were alive in the Philippines today, he would plead with us to accept that Magna Carta for Christian life which Jesus gave us in the 'Sermon on the Mount'.

It often bothers and perplexes me that Gandhi is so little known in the Philippines. As we stand now before a new age, disillusioned with so much of what has gone before, we in the Philippines must begin to learn from the greatest human being of the twentieth century. And when I feel downhearted at the chicanery, the deceit, the endless all engulfing mud-slides of corruption, the seemingly impregnable economic and social structures of fortress Negros, I am consoled with these wonderful words of Gandhi : *"Think of all the things that were thought impossible until they happened"*.

And I know someday Negros will be transformed : The lions will share their power with the lambs and the lambs their gentleness with the lions and a little child shall lead them both. And in every place that blood has been spilt, or bitter tears have fallen, a flower shall spring up and — through it all — I see the impish smile on the face of Bapu Gandhi and I imagine him saying : *"Nothing is, but dreaming makes it so"*.

Father Naill O'Brien, *is an active member of Pax Christi. For several years he has worked in Negros, Philippines, among the sugar workers, fighting for their rights nonviolently. He has traveled to many countries speaking about his experience in Philippines and his firm belief in Gandhi's TRUTH.*

Knowledge Without Character : Power, The University, And The Violence Of The Status Quo

— *Michael True*

Wisdom without love and courage is cowardice,
as with the ordinary intellectual.

— **Ammon Hennacy**

I saw the old god of war stand in a bog
between chasm and rockface.
He smelled of free beer and Carbolic and
showed his testicles to adolescents, for he had
been rejuvenated by several professors.

— **Berthold Brecht**

The task of "nonviolence" — meaning the effort to remove conflict to resist injustice, and to bring about social change without harming persons — is not so different now from what it was in Gandhi's time. For the university community -- students, teachers, scholars, and researchers — that task remains "revolutionary", not in the post-Marxian sense of violent upheaval, but in the 18th century sense of "returning to" or "turning towards" another way of being in the world.

Nonviolent movement involves "empowering" rather than "overpowering" others, particularly those voiceless ones victimized by economic and political exploitation. It is a movement emphasizing not "globalization from above" — the power of rich corporations or imperial nations — but "globalization from below" — the integrative, cooperative power of the natural world and the people who dwell therein.

This transformation of relationships, as Gandhi called it, begins with language itself. For as the poet, Denise Levertov has said, we will not have "language of Peace" until we "restructure the sentence our lives are making," until we reclaim a "grammar of justice," a "syntax of mutual aid."

For academics — or anyone trying to unite knowledge and character — learning a language of peace begins with waging a nonviolent campaign within that "imperial" university that has dominated American higher education since World War Two. For forty years, university language has been, like the foreign policy of the United States, the language of "threat power," rather than "integrative power," to use Kenneth Boulding's useful distinction.

As an institution, the university has been a breeding ground for what Gandhi regarded as one of the Seven Blunders of the World, "Knowledge without character," harboring forces within its walls that are antithetical to its proper vocation. Although impressive in its diversity, its learning, and its availability to large numbers of people, the American university is, at base, astonishingly anti-intellectual, provincial, and nationalistic. For forty years, the shadow of nuclear weapons and imperial policies associated with them have cast a long shadow across it. Its priorities are symbolized, most recently and clearly, by Harvard University's choosing as its 1993 graduation speaker a person famous not for scientific, artistic, or academic achievement, but for military achievement, the Head of the Joint Chiefs of Staff.

Since the U.S. emerged as the most powerful country in the world, economically and militarily, the university has served as a sounding board, a think tank, a farm club for threat power and the Pentagon. Michigan State University provided a cover for the C.I.A. in Vietnam; M.I.T. devised a pacification program against landless peasants; John Hopkins develops deadly chemical and biological weapons. Walking across the campus of any major university - Texas, Minnesota, Wisconsin, Stanford -- one inevitably comes upon a huge building resembling NORAD, harboring research facilities under the direction of the academic equivalent of Dr.Strangelove. In that environment, silencing or ignoring or harassing anyone who criticizes the political status quo is commonplace — Howard Zinn and others at Boston University, Noam Chomsky at M.I.T. Is it any wonder that educated discourse on major moral and political issues is rare in such settings, and in the public forum as well? Although writers — Gore Vidal, Levertov, and Allen Ginsberg — have underscored the moral consequence of this decline, the silence of literary historians and critics, and the humanities generally, has been deafening.

So learning a new language and way of being in the world will not be easy, if the university is to contribute to that revolution, that turning away from violence that Gandhi envisioned. In order for that vision to become a reality, we — students and teachers, kindergarten through graduate school — must foster a closer connection between knowledge and character, in an effort to eliminate the "blunder" that Gandhi indentified.

This transformation of power will be accomplished only as we build communities and structures around priorities of justice and nonviolence, beginning with the university. Among the victims of imperialism, it was probably the first to go, and "non-violence" or "integrative power" as a subject of study went with it. Even after twenty years of the important discipline/inter-discipline of peace studies and the publication of Gene Sharp's classic study, The Politics of Nonviolent Action (1973), we have only one college with a minor in nonviolence and no graduate programs in the history, philosophy, and strategy of nonviolence.

A good beginning might be to reclaim an intellectual tradition that unites knowledge and character, from the 17th century to present. This means attending to values and suggestions of several thinkers native to this ground, in building a "nonviolent" university. Learned and humane, they left the country--and the world--wiser, better integrated, more generous and hospitable than it was before them.

The first is the nonviolent activist, Ammon Hennacy, who — like Gandhi — was passionately and .intellectually devoted to justice and peace. A draft resister during World War I, Ammon Hennacy was arrested thirty two times for protests against nuclear weapons and capital punishment and spent much of his later life feeding the hungry and housing the homeless at Catholic Worker Houses in Salt Lake City, New York City and elsewhere. In his writings, particularly The Book of Ammon (1970), Ammon Hennacy recounts and reflects upon his "experiments with truth," including this saying, written after a day working in the field in 1945 :

Love without courage and wisdom is sentimentality, as with the ordinary church member. Courage without love and wisdom is foolhardiness, as with the ordinary soldier. Wisdom without love and courage is cowardice, as with the ordinary intellectual. Therefore, one with Love, Courage, and Wisdom is one in a million, who rules the world, as with Jesus, Buddha and Gandhi.

Any University — or person — wishing to unite knowledge and courage would have a difficult time finding a better mission statement.

Ammon Hennacy would agree, however, that he belonged to people who had endeavored to resist injustice and to build a civil society without harming persons: from William Penn and John Woolman, to Eugene Victor Debs and Dorothy Day and Martin Luther King. These models, seldom held up for imitation or serious study in the American University, were his guides.

Closely associated with them, in intellectual commitment and values, were three other Americans more directly involved in the University in their time. In each case, they worked to purge the institution of pretension and violence and to recall it to its proper vocation, a task that anyone committed to "the idea of a university" must take up once again.

The first is Ralph Waldo Emerson, whose remarkable essay, "The American Scholar", emphasized the necessity of a scholar's being "free and brave". Speaking at Harvard in 1837, Emerson cautioned his audience that "Thought and knowledge are natures in which apparatus and pretension avail nothing. Gowns and pecuniary foundations . . . can never countervail the least sentence or syllable of wit," he added. "Forget this, and our American colleges will recede in their public importance, while they grow richer every year." For man/woman thinking, Emerson said, "tranquility, amid dangerous times" arises from the presumption that the scholar is "protected class". The "divide" scholar — today's disengaged or deracinated academic — seeks "temporary peace by the diversion of his thoughts from politics or vexed questions, hiding his head like an ostrich in the flowering bushes, peeping into microscopes, and turning rhymes, as a boy whistles to keep his courage up."

More recently, two intellectuals in the nonviolent tradition — Randolph Bourne and Paul Goodman — have pointed out that Emerson's "divide" scholar shirks his/her responsibility not only by withdrawing from politics, but also by embracing the politics of status quo with a vengeance. As university scholars and researchers in all disciplines commute from Cambridge, New Haven, and Berkeley to Washington, D.C., the latter condition is worse than the first. Under such circumstances, being associated with "respectable" institutions that cooperate with the military/industrial complex can be disappointing, infuriating, depressing. To whom, after all, does the university owe its allegiance — to those dominating history or those victimized by it?

The complex task of dissociating the university from "threat power" — and the Pentagon flow charts that dominates its management style — will not be easily accomplished, for reasons suggested by Bourne during the First World War and Goodman during the Cold War. Having tolerated and embraced a policy of violence, academics generally follow a path marked out for them by those in power. "Their thought becomes little more than a description and justification of what is going on," Bourne accurately observed. "The conviction spreads that individual thought is helpless, that the only way one could count is as a cog in the great wheel,....[and] the ex-humanitarian, turned realist, sneers at the snobbish neutrality, colossal conceit, crooked thinking dazed sensibilities of those who are still unable to find any balm of consolation for this war." "As a result," Bourne added, "nothing is done to prevent a war : from passing into popular mythology as a holy crusade."

A similar disposition has characterized university faculty, with obvious exceptions, since World War Two, as knowledge without character became the order of the day. Little by little, as Goodman pointed out in "The Ineffectuality of Some Intelligent People" (1865), professors extricate themselves from the daily effort of building an intellectual community that matters. "They rationalize their avoidance of important life-choices by saying that only 'big' decision-making has public consequences." They verbalize experience and keep it verbalized, "rather than use it as an action upon others"; they become merely academic. "Scholarly detachment is necessary for intellectual consideration, but finally the flow of words must come home to oneself, in action or character change," Goodman added, "otherwise we have more conversation pieces and ping-pong, a speech-game designed for ceremony, or to show off, or at best to one-up and establish a pecking order."

So what has anyone representing such a reprehensible institution and constituency offer, one might ask, by way of encouraging knowledge with character in a university setting?

In responding to that question, I must rely on two examples from my own academic experience. Although I first learned about nonviolence on the streets of Durham, North Carolina, during the Civil Rights Movement, I first heard about the writings and life of Ammon Hennacy in Duke University library. The African American students whom I taught at nearby North Carolina Central University during the day took me to school in the evening on the streets of Durham, picketing the "crows nest" — the balcony where they had to sit, if they wanted to go to the movie. Admiring those brave, intelligent young people, I joined the demonstrations reluctantly, certain that some sniper on the top of the Jack Tarr Durham hotel was pointing a gun at me. I have been trying to put together my "street" experience of nonviolence and my "library" experience of language and literature ever since.

Three decades later, as a teacher at Nanjing University, I observed, at close range, another nonviolent campaign, initiated again by brave, intelligent young students resisting humiliation and repression on campuses and cities through China. In brief period, they brought about necessary reforms and helped to reclaim their country, in a way that anyone committed to knowledge with character might admire.

Building a coalition of nonviolent activists and academics is essential, I think, if we are going to have a university in the U.S. worth bothering about. Although their priorities differ, nonviolent activists and academics are neutral allies. As with all strategists and philosophers, practitioners and theorists, they need one another desperately. Until now, the center of the nonviolent tradition in the U.S. has been the work of the individuals or small groups : Quakers, War Resisters, Catholic Workers, United Farm Workers, Southern Christian Leadership Conference, Peace Brigades International — people who daily risk their lives to build a civil society without resort to killing. To them must be added an extended community of teachers and scholars, men/women thinking in all disciplines, at every level, and the university as an institution as well.

In libraries and classrooms, and perhaps on the street, young people might then experience the transforming power of nonviolence from teachers combining knowledge and character. Thus would Gandhi's vision inform and enrich what is best in America's intellectual tradition.

Michael True, Professor of English, Assumption College, is co-Chair of the Board, Consortium on Peace Research, Education and Development. His books include **To Construct Peace** *(1992),* **Ordinary People : Family Life and Global Values** *(1991), and* **Daniel Barrigan : Poetry, Drama, Prose** *(1988).*

The Power Of Suffering Love

— James McGinnis

The price of peacemaking is the same as the power of the peacemaker. It is the power of suffering love, as Gandhi put it :

Up to the year 1906 (in South Africa), I simply relied on appeal to reason . . . . Since then the conviction has been growing upon me that things of fundamental importance to the people are not secured by reason alone but have to be purchased with their suffering. Suffering is the law of human beings; war is the law of the jungle. But suffering is infinitely more powerful than the law of the jungle for converting the opponent and opening his ears, which are otherwise shut, to the voice of reason. Nobody has probably drawn up more petitions or espoused more forlorn cause than I and I have come to this fundamental conclusion that if you want some thing really important to be done, you must not merely satisfy the reason, you must move the heart also. The appeal of reason is more to the head but the penetration of the heart comes from suffering. It opens up the inner understanding in people. Suffering is the badge of the human race, not the sword.

This is the power of nonviolent love. We meet it throughout the Scriptures. In Isaiah, the Messiah is described as the "suffereing servant". *"He will bring true justice to the nations . . . (but) he does not break the bruised reed or snuff out the smoldering wick"* : (Isa. 42:1-4). *"I offered my back to those who struck me, my cheeks to those who tore at my beard,"* he says of himself (Isa. 50:4-11). *"On him lies a punishment that brings us peace, and through his wounds we are healed . . . Harshly dealt with, he bore it humbly; he never opened his mouth, like a lamb that is led to the slaughter-house . . . If he offers his life in atonement, he shall see his heirs, he shall have a long life and through him what Adonai wishes will be done"* (Isa. 52:13-53:12).

Jesus takes up the mantle of the suffering servant and becomes the *"lamb of God who takes away the sin of the world"* and reconciles us with God and with one another. Paul continues this reflection in his letters. *"Resist evil and conquer it with good"* (Rom. 12:21). The "good" that Paul describes in this section of Romans includes *"blessing those who persecute us,"* *"equal kindness,"* offering food to our enemies if they are hungry or drink if they are thirsty. In reaching out to our so-called enemies as persons, we distinguish the persons from the actions or policies needing resistance.

Paul is paralleled by Matthew 5:38-48, where love of enemies and resisting injustice are described in terms of turning the other cheek, walking the extra mile, and giving the undergarment as well as the coat. These "transforming initiatives," as some have called them, transform a situation of injustice and conflict by startling the oppressor and public opinion into a new way of seeing the victims and their victimization. This is Gandhi's path of suffering love as well as Jesus' way in embracing his cross. It is this kind of love that Martin Luther King preached and lived. Let's listen to his words :

There is another word for love. It is agape, Agape is more than romantic love. It is more than friendship. Agape is understanding, creative, redemptive good-will for all. Agape is an overflowing love, expecting nothing in return. Theologians describe it as the love of God operating in the human heart. And so when you rise to love at this level, you love all persons not because you like them, not because their way appeals to you, but you love every person because God loves them. This is what Jesus meant when he said, "love your enemies" because there are people I find it pretty difficult to like. Like is an affectionate emotion and I can't like anybody bombing my home. I can't like anybody who would exploit me. I can't like anybody who would trample over me with injustice. I can't like anybody who threatens to kill me day in and day out.

Jesus reminds us that love is greater than like. Love is understanding, creative, redemptive good-will for all persons. I've seen too much hate myself. Hate is too great a burden to bear. Somehow we must be able to stand up before our most embittered opponents and say we will match your capacity to endure suffering. We will meet your physical force with soul force. Do to us what you will and we will still love you. Throw us in jail and we will still love you. Send your hooded perpetrators of violence into our communities after the midnight hour and drag us out on some wayside road and leave us half-dead as you beat us and we will still love you. But be you assured that we will wear you down by our capacity to suffer. And we will so appeal to your heart and conscience that we will win you in the process. And our victory will be a double victory.

Such love would be unbelievable if we didn't have those images before us of Dr. King and his followers, children and adults, spat at, clubbed, attacked by police dogs, cannonaded with firehoses, thrown into paddy wagons and jailed, shot. We have the images of Jesus on a cross before us frequently, but how often have we really looked at that image and taken it in? That's the kind of Lord we are to follow? That much love? Be a "lamb"?

As the message and witness of Jesus, Gandhi, King, and so many others have shown the answer to "how far are we to go?" is "all the way". Daily and ultimately, figuratively and literally, we are asked to lay down our lives for others. The words and emotions of two Nicaraguan mothers who had recently lost their sons in the struggle against the Contras seared their way into my heart as I listened to them in the northern city of Jalpa right after Christmas in 1983 : "This is how we can live out the words of Jesus, to lay down our lives for others and then forgive those who killed our sons." My eyes were riveted on their faces and I could see the depth of love and forgiveness behind their words.

The dying to ourselves involved in such a life of reconciliation and nonviolence is a daily challenge. It can begin with the tiny struggles to love those with whom we are at odds in some way. For me, this is frequently our teenaged children. Sometimes I feel the desire to retaliate, to get even, when I feel wronged by them. "That's the last favor I'll do for you for a long time, buster!" has come to my lips more than once. This is my opportunity to learn the power of suffering or agapaic love.

Several years ago I was given a stick of salami during Holy Week while I was fasting, so I put it in the back of the refrigerator to save for Easter. To appreciate the import of this story, you need to know how much I love salami! But on Easter Monday I discovered that others had found the salami and only a tiny bit remained. I was furious and let it be known that the culprits would have to buy me another one, immediately. I stormed around the house shouting my anger at this inconsiderateness, blasting the kids verbally. This wasn't the first time something like this had happened. I had to put a stop to it now. But how? I had blasted the kids verbally before and it hadn't worked. Why not try a different tactic? So more for strategic than virtuous reasons, I tried one of "transforming initiatives" : like turning the other cheek. I went out and bought another salami myself and had a surprise "happy hour" before dinner in which the whole family could enjoy the salami. I'm not sure about the impact of that initiative on the kids, but it did transform my heart a little and has led me to look for similar approaches in other confrontational situations. The capacity to forgive is absolutely essential to love, especially to loving our enemies, as Dr. King points out so well : "Forgiveness is a catalyst creating the atmosphere necessary for a fresh start and a new beginning . . . The evil deed (of an enemy) is no longer a mental block impeding a new relationship."

Nonviolence involves confrontation, yes, but confrontation whose goal is reconciliation. Dr. King certainly did not avoid confrontation. His Letter from a Birmingham City Jail is a moving response to his critics who challenged his commitment to nonviolence because his tactics regularly provoked violence. In his reply, Dr. King distinguished a "positive peace", which he equated with keeping the lid on violent situations and pretending that this so-called order was the same as peace. The negative peace of injustice or "institutional violence" has to be brought to the light of day so that it can be transformed into a "positive peace", a peace that encompasses justice and love (Shalom). How we surface an issue, how we confront those who we think have wronged us is the key, whether they be family members, friends, co-workers, government officials.

Jesus provides guidance for us in his teaching on correcting our brothers or sisters (Matt. 18:15-18). The first step is not to call a press conference and denounce the person in public, but to try ways of converting the person in private. Gandhi gives us examples of how to do this at all levels. One of the keys to his approach was truthfulness. We must always recognize that our truth : is not "the truth" and that our opponents may well have a piece of the truth as well. We have to be committed to "the truth" above all, which means clinging to what we believe is our portion of the truth ("*Satyagraha*" means "clinging to the truth") while remaining open to our opponents' portion of the truth. This requires honest searching, a willing ness to acknowledge our brokenness and portion of the blame for the conflict, humility, courage, and a willingness to "die" to ourselves.

All this we can practice daily. I think of this practicing as a series of what Gandhi calls "experiments with truth". He became the person we know today by just such a life of experimenting with the truth. He was not always the great person we read about and admire. He became Gandhi, precisely by working at it daily. We can experiment with the truth of suffering love daily as well. Refusing to think the worst of my children when they make mistakes, continuing to love them through the messiness and pain of adolescence, continuing to do "favors" even when I have to confront them about their negative behavior — I am really having to work at this. In the midst of a family member's failures, we can choose to let our negative feelings dominate or we can refuse to think the worst and choose to think the best about the person. "Worst case scenarios" may be common to military planners, but they must not prevail for people who want to practice nonviolence or suffering love.

How many times could we take the first step toward reconciliation with someone with whom we are at odds, especially when we think they are a fault and should come to us? Swallowing our pride, as it were, and offering reconciling gestures does not have to mean allowing ourselves to be walked on. That's important especially for women. There's a difference between suffering love and taking abuse from someone whose behavior needs to be challenged. The "suffering servant" passages in Isaiah need to be read with this realization. Jesus was a "lamb" and so are we to become, but Jesus also says to us : "remember, I am sending you out like sheep among wolves; so be cunning as serpents and yet harmless as doves" (Matt. 10:16).

The "cunning" for me means primarily thinking through conflict situations carefully and identifying strategies that will have a chance of promoting reconciliation. One of the most helpful resources for me along this line has been a book by a friend named Dudley Weeks, entitled Conflict Partnership. Dudley's thought and practice have been greatly influenced by both Gandhi and King. His approach is similar — view our conflicts as something between our selves and our opponents that is keeping us apart, something both of us need to address as "partners" against this barrier between us, and work with our opponents in such a way that they begin to see the conflict in these terms. In my case, it might sound like — "Son, there's something going on between us that isn't good. I'd really like to figure out with you what it is, so that we can work to change it. I want us to enjoy each other more, rather always be fighting." Dudley offers a wealth of practical strategies for approaching conflicts this way and for bringing our opponents around to this same way of viewing conflicts.

Another area in which we can be conducting experiments with the truth of suffering love is our willingness to sacrifice for others. Jesus, Gandhi, King, and the two Nicaraguan mothers did not willingly sacrifice their own lifes or their sons' without many prior tiny sacrifices. There were countless ways Jesus learned to sacrefice himself as he was growing up in a poor home in a poor land. In his public ministry, he learned daily what "availability to others" meant. He learned in his desert retreats, in his fasting and other forms of self-denial, in his patient nurturing of his disciples, most of whom eventually deserted him. More and more courageously Jesus conformed his will to the demanding mission given him by God.

Gandhi's experiments with truth took him along a similar journey. He realized early on that the root of violence is a desire to put "me first". Humans violate or exploit one another and the earth because of a desire to enrich ourselves. Personal greed is the source of violence. I must preserve and enrich ourselves. Personal greed is the source of violence. I must preserve and enrich myself at all costs. Often this "self" gets extended to include famil;, tribe, clan, community, nation — with poverty and war as the results. The way to root out this internal source of human violence is to begin at the personal level and our "me-ism". It is in this context that we have to understand Gandhi's many experiments with food and fasting, with sexuality and his eventual commitment to celibacy, with cleaning toilets and other menial tasks, with community living, with prayer and silence. Each area offered him dozens of ways he could, in the words of Jim Douglass, who probably knows Gandhi better than any North American today, "reduce himself to zero" and become a pure instrument of God's power of love and truth in the world.

In Jim's prophetic book *Lightning East to West*, he quotes Gandhi's secretary Pyarelal on Gandhi's "$E=mc^2$," a power that could match, even surpass, the power of the atom in nuclear bombs: "The corresponding law governing the release of spiritual energy is to be found in the formula enunciated by Gandhi, viz. that even an infinitesimal of an individual, when he has realized the ideal *Ahimsa* (nonviolent love) in its fullness so that in thought, word and deed, he — in short, his whole being — becomes a function of *ahimsa* as it were, he becomes filled with its power, the power of love, soul force, truth force, or the god-head within us, to which there is no limit and before which all opposition and hatred must cease.....

James McGinnis, is the founder of The Peace and Justice Center in St. Louis, he has worked for justice and peace as an educator for twenty-five years. He has traveled to many countries speaking about the similarities existing in different religious beliefs through his personal faith. He believes strongly in the need for all humanbeings to share their faith journey with one another.

(Excerpted from "Journey into Compassion" by James McGinnis, permission to reprint granted by James McGinnis.)

A Mother's Anguish

— Dorothy Walpole

I wish I had some words of wisdom and insight to contribute to your wonderful publication but my pen would be full of wishful thinking.

I feel such sadness that our world has run so low on moral cooperation, loyalty, honesty and truth. The faster we go with all our hightech machinery, transport, labour saving devices, movies, videos, computerized special effects etc., the lower our human values seem to sink. Children no longer have security of the street, the choice to go visiting unsupervised or to the park with their mates, or the opportunity to do similar things that we did as children. These things led to independence, strength of character and developed their own imaginations and adventure not those of some 'special effects computerhead.' Children are surrounded by violent people and actions, and exposed on all fronts to violence on television, videos, movies, and by adults and other children.

There is an undercurrent of aggression in our world. A lot of people are just waiting for that bump in the supermarket, queue jumper or flat tyre — to prick the surface, giving them an excuse to errupt. As a teacher of young children, I give those in my care a fairly healthy diet of self-esteem, lots of fun, plenty of music, high challenge — low stress tasks and more opportunity to try to empower them to be able to have choices and be 'their own selves' (as children would say).

If only we could harness the energy, strength and passion it must take to create violence or violent acts and redirect it for the good of mankind 'what a wonderful world it would be'.

Short of moving to the country, selling the 'tele', building a high fence or going underground, I have no solution as to how we protect our young from the violence that seeps in through the cracks.

Dorothy Walpole is a first grade teacher in Mayfield, New South Wales, Australia. Like teachers anywhere she is extremely agitated by the violent culture and its effect on children.

Knowledge With Character

— *John McAleer*

When the next century arrives, computer analysts, sifting through their data, may notice that one specific date, January 30th, had particular relevance in the lives of four men prominent in the affairs of the century just ending. On that date Franklin Roosevelt was born, Adolf Hitler came to power, Winston Churchill was buried, and Mohandas Gandhi was assassinated.

Shortly before his death, Gandhi wrote : "If it costs my life, I should most willingly give it in order to secure the performance of a sacred and solemn promise." This statement betokens a commitment to ideals so rarely evinced by men caught up in public life that, were it ascribed to Roosevelt, Churchill, or Hitler, few could be found to credit the validity of the attribution. That Gandhi said it, however, non could doubt. Not only did he hold fast, throughout life, to his principles. He died for them.

Today the aspirations of Hitler, Churchill, and Roosevelt must be sought for in history books. Their claims to be called to mind on January 30th are largely forgotten. But the importance of that date in Gandhi's life gains, with each passing year, fresh significance. The convictions he lived by and died for are not only a living force in the modern world, the number of those who espouse them grows steadily.

The present writer, perhaps by chance, or perhaps by cosmic appointment, cherishes the distinction of having observed, for two years prior to Gandhi's death, January 30th as Gandhi's special day of remembrance. On that date, in 1946, at Poona, when I asked him to "set a phrase for me to live by," Gandhi, recalling to me Emerson's dictum. "Speak the rude truth in all ways," gave me a signed photograph of himself on which he then wrote, in Gujarati, "Truth at all costs," to open the way for me to a fuller perception of what my role in life ought to be? My inquiries were not long under way before I found myself confronting a subject which already had become indissolubly linked with Gandhi's name — his gospel of nonviolence. That commitment, hitherto, I had contemplated with respect but wariness. I was then in military uniform, a sergeant called up from the reserve to service in the U.S. Army Medical Department. True enough, as a medic I had never held a gun in my hands but, technically, I was, nonetheless, a warrior. What now was I to do if my search for enlightenment directed me to speak out for non-violence? Even then, though, the question was academic. The war had ended and I would soon return to civilian life. Yet consistency demanded that, in this probationary phase of my noviceship, I pursue the issue to its resolution. Otherwise, pledged in the service of truth, my discipleship would be a sham.

Here Gandhi himself, as he had done for me before, cleared the brambles from my path. Concerning his own role in the military, in the Boer War, the Zulu "rebellion", and WWI, he had written, "All I can claim for my conduct is that it was actuated in the interests of nonviolence." That said, he had gone on to say: "There is no escape for any of us save through truth and nonviolence. War is wrong, an unmitigated evil. It has got to go. Not violence, not untruth but nonviolence, truth is the law of our being." In Gandhi's judgement, then, nonviolence and truth were inseparable. The term he used to identify the commitment to nonviolence, *Satyagraha*, brought further enlightenment. *"Satya"* meant "truth" and *"Satyagraha"* meant recourse to truth-force. It is, he said, "a relentless search for truth and a determination to reach truth." He clarified further : "A *Satyagrahi* must believe in truth and nonviolence as his creed and therefore have faith in the inherent goodness of human nature which he expects to evoke by his truth and love expressed through his suffering." Now I not only knew the scope of the commitment Gandhi had given me. I knew that I, too, was a *Satyagrahi*.

"Love," I then saw, contributed an essential element to the equation I was striving to encompass. At times Gandhi characterized nonviolence. or *Ahimsa*, as "truth-force", as "soul force", or "love-force". How this could be ceased to perplex me when I came upon this illuminating phrase : "Love is the reverse of which the obverse is truth .... we can conquer the whole world by truth and love." Here, then, in nonviolence, Gandhi, paradoxically using a metaphor of conquest, offered men the moral equivalent of war. My quest was not done, though, till I found an encompassing phrase which brought me back full circle to an awareness of the tremendous value Gandhi, in that simple maxim, "Truth at all costs," assigned to the word "cost" : "I endeavor to represent love in every fiber of my being. I am impatient to realize the presence of my Maker, who to me embodies truth, and in the early part of my career I discovered that if I was to realize truth, I must obey, even at the cost of my life, the law of love."

In my own subsequent career I have sought to hold firm to the maxim Gandhi asked me to live by. My novel on the Korean War *(Unit Pride)*, according to critics the definitive novel on that war, has been described by them as a book that shows a moral courage that guarantees it a place alongside *"The Red Badge of Courage"* and *"Alls Quiet on the Eastern Front"*, as more than a turning point in war literature but the book that brings to a halt the glorification of war. My book on Emerson and Thoreau have brought to countless readers new awareness of Thoreau's commitment to nonviolent noncooperation with evil. My biography of Rex Stout has spread a knowledge of those organizations he led with zeal, The Society to Prevent WW3, The Writers Board for World Government, and Freedom House. And, with humble appreciation, I take satisfaction in having provided Indira Gandhi the occasion to pay tribute to those ideas that link Thoreau and Gandhi in the verse foreword she wrote for my volume of Thoreau studies, *Artist and Citizen Thoreau*. There she wrote :

> *"Whoever reads Thoreau*
> *is struck*
> *By the ethical force*
> *Of his ideas*
> *And the clarity*
> *Of his writing.*
> *Thoreau's great influence*
> *On Mahatma Gandhi*
> *Is well known.*
> *His words ring long*
> *In the mind.*
> *Those who live*
> *In the storm of politics*
> *Need the quiet pool within*
> *for sustenance.*
> *Thoreau lived by such a pool."*

Because of Gandhi's kindness to me nearly half a century ago, I, too, have lived by such a pool.

*Dr. John McAleer teaches at Boston College, Massachussetts. During his sojourn in India during WWII **Dr. McAleer** came in touch with Mahatma Gandhi. Gandhi's philosophy and life is deeply etched on his thoughts, he has never ceased to teach those ideals to his students.*

A New World ?

— Sister Falaka Fattah

*For our future world Without violence cooperation
replaces competition and, love replaces oppression.
For our future world without violence all
religions disappear into one religion and all nations
melt into one nation.
As inhabitants of this brave new world I am you
and you are me and we are one together.
And in the final analysis perhaps the activity
of the research for this non-violent world embodies
our essential worship of God...*

Sister Falaka Fattah *was born* **Frances Ellen Brown** *in Philadelphia, U.S.A.
She took the name* **Fattah** *in the late sixties. She worked as a writer and editor
for the Philadelphia Tribune, the Philadelphia Independent, the Philadelphia Afro-
American Bulletin Newspaper and National Magazine, and was editor of Open Mike.
A national Disc-jockey magazine.*

Sister Fattah *founded the House of Umoja as a publishing company and welcomed
delinquent youths into her family. Today the House of Umoja consists of twenty-three
homes in Philadelphia. When the work is completed it will be the first Urban Boystown
in the U.S.A. Umoja also runs a job training center and a Security Institute for
black youths. She has received several awards for community service and journalism
and her work has been praised by President Jimmy Carter and President Ronald
Reagan.*

Out Of Ashes Peace Will Rise

— *Marilou Awiakta*

Selu : Seeking the Corn Mother's Wisdom

Our courage
is our memory.

Out of ashes
peace will rise,
if the people
are resolute.
If we are not
resolute.
we will vanish.
And out of ashes
peace will rise.

In the Four Directions.....
Out of ashes peace will rise.
Out of ashes peace will rise.
Out of ashes peace will rise.
Out of ashes peace will rise.

Our courage
is our memory.

When Earth Becomes An " It "

— *Marilou Awiakta*

Selu : Seeking the Corn Mother's Wisdom

When the people call the Earth "Mother",
      they take with love
  and with love give back
    so that all may live.

  When the people call earth "It",
        they use her
    consume her strength.
    Then the people die.

  Already the sun is hot
      out of season.
    Our Mother's breast
      is going dry.

  She is taking all green
        into her heart
  and will not turn back
      until we call her
        by her name.

Dying Back

— *Marilou Awiakta*

Selu : Seeking the Corn Mother's Wisdom

On the mountain
the standing people are dying back-
hemlock, spruce and pine
turn brown in the head.
The hardwood shrivels in new leaf.
Unnatural death
from acid greed
that takes the form of rain
and fog and cloud.

In the valley
the walking people are blank-eyed.
Elders mouth vacant thought.
Youth grow spindly, wan
from sap too drugged to rise.
Pushers drain it off-
sap is gold to them.
The walking people are dying back
as all species do
that kill their own seed.

Marilou Awiakta is a poet and author who grew up on a reservation for atoms, not Native Americans — Oak Ridge, Tennessee, which during her childhood was part of the secret Manhattan Project. *Awiakta's* unique perspective fuses her three heritages : Cherokee Indian, Celtic and scientific. She has written several books including **Selu : Seeking the Corn Mother's Wisdom**, (Fulcrum, 1993); **Abiding Appalachia : Where Mountain and Atom Meet** and **Raising Fawn and the Fire Mystery**. She was honoured with the Distinguished Tennessee Writer Award in 1989 and is profiled in the 1994 Oxford Companion to Women's Writing in the United States.

Permission to print granted by the Poet and the Publishers

Jewel Of The Universe

— Don Mullan

How I love you Mother Earth
JEWEL OF THE UNIVERSE
Perfectly positioned
You encourage life and sustain it.

Upon you, humankind rushes to and fro
seldom stopping to acknowledge
Your beauty or dignity.

We take the mystery of day and night
and year to year
for granted.
We seldom marvel at the speed with which you spin
and the vast solar orbit you travel,
resulting in the rich splendour of your seasons.

More and more
as our knowledge expands
we learn that you alone
are the only known life giver.
Our nearest neighbours
Venus and Mars
are either too hot or too cold.

Teach us Mother to love and respect you
as an infant reverses its own.
As a child is nurtured by its mother,
so too, all Earth's children are nurtured by you.

You provide for our every need . . .
physically you build us
mentally you enrich us
emotionally you heal us

and spiritually you are part of our essence.

As your children
teach us to share in the greatness of your generosity.
It was never your intention to care for some
while neglecting others.

You provide enough for everyone's need
but not for everyone's greed.
This is your most basic law of nature.

As members of your family,
teach us to love one another
as you love us,
by sharing your resources
fairly and with justice.
Your surface and your seas
are the breadbaskets of all humanity.

Teach us O Mother Earth
that hunger and oppression
insult your self less generosity.
And teach us O Mother
that no man or nation has the right
to possess your destruction.

In loving you,
may present and future generations acknowledge
we do not inherit you from our parents . . .
we borrow you,
from our children.

Gandhi Of Porbundar

— Don Mullan

*Perhaps if I were
a renowned theologian
or someone of importance,
the Church would cross-examine me,
for my belief.
But
I would defend it. . .*

*For
I belive that
Mahatma Gandhi
is no less a saint
than St. Francis of Assisi
was a mahatma.*

*I am a Christian disciple of Gandhi
and speak with both he and Francis
through the same Spirit which called
all
into being*

*Give me courage
O God
to at least try to follow
the ways of
Jesus of Nazreth,
Francis of Assisi
and
Gandhi of Porbundar.*

Don Mullan *was born in Derby, Ireland, in 1956. He grew up in the Creggan Estate, one of Northern Ireland's most troubled areas. As a boy at 15 he witnessed the British paratrooper's Bloody Sunday massacre and personally saw three unarmed civilians shot dead just five yards from where he stood. He offers his poem as tribute to all those who work for a "World Without Violence".*

A Lofty Diadem

— John Jeffs

Who lives in the troubled Northern Ireland, wrote this poem moments after the news of Gandhi's assassination.

On The Death Of Mahatma Gandhi

Dead. *All thy counsel, love and care*
Have brought thee but to this,
To where thy poignant, life-long prayer
Halts, at the bullet's kiss.

Quenched. All the light from thee that flowed
As from the rising sun,
when darkness flies his golden goad,
Quenched by a trapped man's gun.

Gone. All the horror now returns
From whence it fled from thee--
But lo! high in the darkness burns,
Bright as eternity

The blazing star thy soul became,
To a great people wronged,
Who never more will bow in shame,
For to them you belonged.

(Permission to reprint given by the poet).

Hank The Drummer

— Maggi Kerr Peirce

Written in 1989 when her son Hank strode off to play war games.

My son Hank is a broth of a lad
And many years ago
He joined a Re-enactment troop
Of the Revolutionary War.

They'd march in ranks and dress like Turks
And joyfully fire their gun
They'd charge up hills and roar through woods
To Hank — twas glorious fun.

He was a drumer, straight and tall
With waistcoat sewen by my hands.
His helmet gleamed in the military ranks
As he led the marching bands.

My Husband and I, We'd always attend
The skirmishes here and there
And when we'd see our drummer boy
We were the proudest pair.

One fine May morning he ran upstairs
While the wee birds they were singing-o
And a boy he went up, and a man he returned
In his shinning red ragal-i-o.

"Bye Mom, I'm off," he laughingly cried,
And me there, scrubbing so busily,
"Have a good time son," I barely replied,
Intent on working steadily.

The door slammed shut — and I looked up
I ran to the window quickly-o

He was striding out the garden gate,
His lithesome form, with the drum slung low.

And I thought of the mothers down the ages
Thought of the sweethearts in times of yore
Knowing their dear ones ne'er would return
Except as tattered shreds of war.

So I stood and howled in my cosy house
Not for the "game" that Hank was in
But for all the women who'd lost their loves
For every war, that was always a sin.

For the old men send the young to their death
And the poppies still grow on Flanders' fears
And the crows circle o'er the land of Culloden
And Vietnam is written in blood and tears

And I swear that morning I saw the hosts
Of Mothers and sisters and sweethearts gay
Who stood on the dusty roads of the world
Watching their soldiers marching away.

And relief flowed through my veins that morn
That my young Hank with his eyes so bright
Would safely march through his sportive fray
Beating his drum Rat-a-tat-a-tat — to our arms that
night.

Enough

Maggi Kerr Peirce

Written in 1992 this poem reveales the high state of anger at the bombings in Ulster, one Catholic, one Protestant, killing innocent people.

Hell roast you IRA
God damn you UVF
Where the Hell are you leading us?
With all the rest?

The blood has flowed the country round
It's hit both young and old
We sit on the fences everywhere
Fearing the stories told.

For whether we live in America
Or whether we live in Ulster
We are aware that nothing's changed
Mid religious political bluster.

You still scream vengeance to the skies
And the biblical "tooth for a tooth"
Still holds sway o'er our native land
Do you not want to face the truth?

For whatever group is bearing arms
Whatever hand throws the stone
In Derry, Belfast, or sweet Armagh
'Tis the people who must atone.

For our children are being bred in hate
And where will this nightmare end?
In the dusty page of history book
Not anywhere else my friend.

Blood looks the same — Papish or Prod
Spilled from soldier, wee wean or Mother
Black, or rusty or guttering red

from old granny or hooded brother.

You must agree, all you good people
These massacres must cease
Do you want poor Ulster in smithereens?
Or a truly lasting peace?

Maggi Pearce - *born* **Margaret Kerr**, *Belfast, Northern Ireland, has lived in the United States since 1964. She has taught many classes on the Art of Storytelling, Stretching the Imagination, Journals and Dairy Writing, etc. She is a renowned storyteller. Presently her programmes are made up of not only song and ballad, but recitations, both dialectic and drawing room, and her well known storytelling. She wrote these two poems at different times in a high state of anger after there had been two bombings in 1992 in Ulster, one Catholic, one Protestant. Innocent people were killed each time.*

The story behind ...

A New World Prayer

— Lou Torok

In 1971 millions of Americans watched in horror as television reported the bloody prison uprising at the Attica (NY) State Prison.

From my own prison cell in the Ohio prison I watched the mindless anger and bloodshed on television and wondered if there wasn't a better way to solve these painful problems of anger, frustration, betrayal and fear.

If I could just speak to the prisoners and the guards ... what language could I use that would not betray them . . . but would help both sides see their actions in new light?

I sat down at my typewriter and wrote A New World Prayer. It was published in newspapers all over the world. Chaplains at the Attica Prison used it in their services of reconciliation. Hundreds of thousands of free copies were mailed by volunteers to anyone who wrote for a copy.

Twenty years later we are still searching for answers to recurring destructive confrontations.

It is my hope that a **New World Prayer** can show the way to a safer more mature society.

I recognize that I belong to the family
of man
Made up of all human beings
Of every race, color, creed, and ideology
Now living on this Planet Earth.

I understand that there can be no
common good
Without an individual good.

I am responsible for myself

And for all human beings
Who share this earth with me.

I Know that our enemies
Are those among us
Who will not
Join in sharing the responsibility
For our common good.

I accept my own personal responsibility
To replace darkness with light
To replace hatred with love
To replace suspicion with trust
To replace lies and hypocrisy with
Honesty.

To replace abuse with fairness
To replace frustration with patience
To replace fear with understanding
To replace bias, prejudice, and
discrimination with tolerance
To replace ignorance with knowledge
To replace indifference with concern
And to replace apathy with action.

I believe that all men are entitled
To equal opportunities
To live, to grow, and to flourish
As human beings
With dignity and with self-respect.

I acknowledge that
It is better
To live and work for peace
Than to die for peace.

As a member of the family of man
Now living on this Planet Earth
I thus commit myself
And challenge my children
And their children
To do as well.

Permission granted to reprint by Lou Torok on 11/15/1993.

Lou Torok, born in 1927 in Toledo, Ohio, was raised in orphanages and foster homes and served in the U.S.Navy in World War II in the South Pacific.

Lou Torok served prison sentences in San Quentin, California; Maine State Prison and the Ohio Penitentiary for charges ranging from grand theft to burglary and assault.

He is the founder of Prison Pen Pals which has matched over 2 million citizens and prisoners by mail over the past 18 years. He is the founder of the Child Abuse Institute of Research (C.A.I.R.), a public education program.

Lou Torok has worked for 20 years as an advocate for prisoners serving as national Officer of the 7th Step Foundation and as a consultant to the Playboy Foundation and many other organizations.

He served as a founding member of the Cincinnati Free Store and has been active as a youth counselor and advocate. He served as Youth Chairman for the Kiwanis Club of Campbell County, Kentucky.

Lou Torok returned to prison in August 1991 and began writing again as The Convict Writer. He has written several books, plays, and newspaper articles.

Beyond Violence

— *L. W. T. Wolcott*

The ultimate human experience is the need, the possibility,
the vitality for creative relationship.
Violence destroys relation.
Violence isolates violated and violator...
Isolation is the final evil.

Non-violence:
Its root word, ahimsa, is non-harming, non hurting,
non-interference with any creature's right to life
or way of being.
Refusal, at whatever cost, to violate the thing that lives.

The Mahatma, Gandhi, probed its deeper essence :
Non-violence expects an inner cleansing.
It is an inner motion wiping out the violence of a self
rivalry with other selves.
It is the claim that comes when anxiety's storm has passed,
When the flamed emotion dies.
It is released from personal animosities.

For M. K. Gandhi "non-violence"
took an added significance which he extended
from negative to positive,
to purpose, to action, to affirming a common humanity,
transforming, enabling, empowering.

A warm appreciation it can be
at the wonder of each fellow creature
in the marvel environment of earth and universe.

From appreciation to reconciliation.
Reconciliation is adversaries coming together to change
places in an atmosphere of readiness to listen,

in an ambience of openness to learn.

The word Satyagraha,
Gandhi - coined, can now define non- violence.
I see in that word persistence that never submits to wrong
and never permits violence to the wrongdoer.
Long suffering loyalty to all that is right and noble.
Enduring distress for the sake of those who bear it,
and for those who cause it.

I see in that word a discernment too few have had
of the meaning of Christ's cross.
Here is an attitude of will that perseveres in truth,
ready even to suffer for the suffering,
returning good for evil.
Piercing the walls of distrust with a new awareness.
Burning down the walls of hatred with unequenchable love.

Love is more than human liking.
It comes to us and through our minds
and hearts spreads outwards.
The Ramayana says devotion - bhakti - to God
leads us to kindness ...
The gospel says that love - agape - from God
leads us to love's self-giving...
to the rest who share the earth.

Such love, with kindness, is fearless.
It charges the lines of abuse with a challenge to change.
It dares to smile at the glowering frown
to give to those who hurt,
to love all those who hate,
to care for all those who curse,
to sacrifice on behalf of those who despise.

Such love is bold.
It confronts our injustice and judgement
and condemns our oppression with mercy.
it exposes our foes and ourselves.
It leaves us and them without defense
and no excuse to justify our passions.

And so we begin to understand

to understand ourselves and each the other.

Such love is wise.
It rejects, out right, untruth in human relations,
but presents the furious no antagonism
to fortify their rage.
It condones no violence, yet mirrors to the violent
their capacity for right.
And offers them uncompromising friendship.
disclosing the delight of harmony.

We exchange places.
So now we see through the others' eyes.
We walk in their shoes.
We cross the bridge to sit beside them.
We welcome them to see,
to walk in our shoes,
to cross the bridge to sit beside us.

Non-violence now becomes a way of life.
We may not attract
quite everyone
to avoid Gandhi's "Seven Blunders".
nor bring about a perfect world of peace, goodwill.
Yet as we live with integrity, by reconciling love,
we will cause it to ripple from neighbor to neighbor,
to stranger and to enemy,
and it will influence the cooperative resolution
of social crises,
and we will leaven the world with the rising peace,
shanti, salaam, shalom,
We will renew the joy of living
in our global village home.

Dr. L. W. T. Wolcott *is a Methodist Missionary, Gandhi scholar and theologian. He has travelled and worked in different parts of the world, spreading the message of nonviolence and compassion.* **Dr. Wolcott** *also is on the national advisory Board of the M. K. Gandhi Institute.*

A Sleep of Prisoners

— *Christopher Fry*

Behind us lie
The thousand and the thousand
and the thousand years
Vexed and terrible. And still we use
The cures which never cure . . . .
Hold and wait for ever. We see, admire
But never suffer them : suffer instead
A stubborn aberration.
O God, the fabulous wings unused,
Folded in the heart . . . . . .

(Reprinted with permission of author and publisher)

Christopher Fry (Harris) is playwright, dramatist, actor, teacher and translator from England, well-known in the world of performing arts. He has received several awards and honors for his work. Queen's Gold Medal for Poetry, 1962; New York Drama Critic Circle Award, 1951; Heinemann Award for Literature, 1962 are just a few of them.

The Peace Flag — *Maxine Hong Kingston*

Maxine Hong Kingston is a teacher at the University of California, Berkeley.
This is a photograph of her with one of the flags she sewed during the Persian
Gulf War. She flew them from her home and office amidst her neighbour's yellow
ribbons. Her house and one of the flags burned down in the Oakland/Berkeley fire
of 1991 along with the manuscript of **A Book of Peace**. She has written another
Book of Peace. This photograph was taken by the poet, Garrett Hongo.